GAS PUMP GLOBES

Collector's Guide to Over 3,000 American Gas Globes

Scott Benjamin and Wayne Henderson

Motorbooks International
Publishers & Wholesalers ®

First published in 1993 by Motorbooks International Publishers & Wholesalers, PO Box 2, 729 Prospect Avenue, Osceola, WI 54020 USA

© Scott Benjamin and Wayne Henderson, 1993

Motorbooks International is a certified trademark, registered with the United States Patent Office

The information in this book is true and complete to the best of our knowledge. All recommendations are made without any guarantee on the part of the author or Publisher, who also disclaim any liability incurred in connection with the use of this data or specific details

We recognize that some words, model names and designations, for example, mentioned herein are the property of the trademark holder. We use them for identification purposes only. This is not an official publication

Motorbooks International books are also available at discounts in bulk quantity for industrial or sales-promotional use. For details write to Special Sales Manager at the Publisher's address

Printed and bound in the United States of America

Library of Congress Cataloging-in-Publication Data

Benjamin, Scott.
    Gas pump globes / Scott Benjamin, Wayne Henderson.
      p.   cm.
      Includes index.
      ISBN 0-87938-797-1
      1. Gasoline pumps—Equipment and supplies—Collectors and collecting—United States. 2. Gasoline pumps—United States—Catalogs. 3. Petroleum industry and trade—United States—History. I. Henderson, Wayne. II. Title.
TL153.B39   1993
629.28'6—dc20   93-8834

On the front cover: A rare Pure Quill globe (15in metal) is featured along with a Bristolville Oil & Gas Company Eureka Gas one-piece etched globe and a Sinclair High Compression one-piece fired-on globe. A.Daniel Messaros/Messaros Photography

On the title page: Globes sit atop the pumps at this Pure Oil Company cottage station on north Main Street in Anderson, South Carolina, back in 1941. Wayne Henderson

On the index page: An extremely rare collectible is an internally lit domed glass sign such as the one hanging in front of this Pure Oil cottage station on Main Street in Waynesville, North Carolina. The gas pumps were all topped with globes in this 1941 photo. Wayne Henderson

Contents

Foreword

It is mid-December 1917, and my 1914 Ford Runabout ventures through three inches of moonlit snow toward a familiar light one mile head.

The light ahead holds a twofold mission for me, and the cold, biting air on my face hastens my eagerness to arrive.

As I approach the once-familiar light, it now seems to project a different image. I immediately observe a crimson hue filtering over what was once a bland setting. The attendant, recognizing my motorcar, smiles as I roll to a stop. "Good evening, Bob," he says to me. "Thanks for stopping by."

His grin clearly expresses his excitement to show his best friend the first newly decorated Texaco filling station in Chicago.

With a quick glance around, I can easily comprehend his pride. The two very tall gasoline dispensers tower over us, unaffected by the cold Chicago wind.

"Fill'er up, Jerry," I said. "What a fillin' station!"

Watching the motor fuel disappear from the pump, I discover the source of the crimson hue: two bright red "Texaco Gasoline" globes perched proudly atop the pumps. Jerry pointed out a few other items, but he didn't have to. Everything beckoned my attention.

Driving away, I couldn't help but wonder what the future would hold for such a placid setting. Could it ever again change that much?

The Chicago wind has carried me several decades forward, but the picture of that filling station remains fresh in my mind.

I often felt compelled to return to that site, until one day I found myself there, staring at an empty building.

Motorists were encouraged to "Drive In, Save Money" at the "Big Tire Sale" at this Sinclair station on West Queen Street in Hampton, Virginia, back in 1934.
Wayne Henderson

The crimson hue had disappeared, as had Jerry, and the site once again returned to its original blandness. Overcome with a feeling of nostalgia, I visualized in my mind the Texaco globes atop those pumps. "I've got to find one of those tops!" I said to myself. "Oh, I'll find one! If it's the last thing I do, I'll find one!"

Welcome to the fascinating world of collecting gasoline globes. We all have our stories, and here is ours: Gasoline globes decorated our landscape from about 1912 to the 1950s. Most were phased out in the fifties, but some companies kept globes until the early eighties. The number of different globes made during that time is staggering. This book documents more than 4,000 different globes, yet we estimate that the total number actually made is higher still.

New and previously unknown globes show up in various places nearly every week. Perhaps this is why collecting globes is so interesting. In 1975, after an unsuccessful trip looking for globes in Pennsylvania, I determined that it was too late for me to fare well in the hobby. Every bulk oil plant or antique store I stopped at had no globes. I was even laughed at. "Those things, well, we haven't seen those in years!" It was very discouraging. But on the next trip I did better. Even today, the number of globes still found on gas pumps is amazing. Though they seemed to be picked over, globes regularly turn up at places like bulk plants and gasoline stations. You just have to keep looking. Don't quit—the globes are out there somewhere.

We have tried in this book to accumulate as much data about gasoline globes as most collectors would need to know. Many areas of discussion are covered, as well as the history, prices, and descriptions of more than 4,000 globes.

The prices in this book range from wholesale to retail. With our more than forty years of collective experience involving globe pricing, globe trends, shows, and auctions, we believe these prices are as close to true market values as possible.

Needless to say, a lot of time went into collecting the material for this book. We sincerely hope this book accurately reflects the many facets of gasoline pump globe collecting.

We thank the following people for their help in putting the book together: Preston Aust, Barry Baker, Ken Black, Dale Brown, Peter Capell, Gary Hildman, Lonnie Hop, Tom Licouris, Jim Masson, Chris McKee, Bruce Miller, Glen Miller, Kyle Moore, John Phippen, Larry Starkweather, Jim Welty, Walt Wimer, and R. V. Witherspoon.

And a special thanks to our wives, Jeannette Benjamin and Debbie Henderson, for all their help, organization, typing, photo compilation, and coordinating efforts scattered across time zones, and for just putting up with our intense involvement in this hobby. Thanks!

Chapter 1
Collecting Gasoline Globes

There are thousands of different types of globes out there to collect. Perhaps this is why the hobby is so fascinating to so many people. Basically, you need to decide which globes to collect. Some enthusiasts pick one company—such as Gulf, Texaco, or Sinclair—and go after every globe they manufactured. Interestingly, no collector possesses every globe the bigger companies made. You can come close, but there is always one more globe that eludes you. This keeps it interesting. Some people collect only metal-frame globes, or only pretty globes, and so on. You may want to select a state and collect only globes used in that state. Several unique collections have been created in this way.

It's always wise for new collectors to decide which types of globes they want to collect, then upgrade to better globes as soon as they can.

If you really want to succeed in the hobby, you must "network." That is, talk with other collectors, go to shows, run ads, and keep handy the names of other collectors. In general, follow all leads and be helpful and cooperative in your associations with other collectors.

Some people wonder what types of globes go with what types of pumps. Visible pumps were around from the early teens until the very early 1930s. This era was dominated by the one-piece or metal-frame globes. These globes best suit the visible pump. Glass globes with inserts were made as early as the late 1920s, but were rare. Clockface pumps were common in the 1930s, so metal-frame globes or glass-body/glass-insert globes worked best here. The 1940s pumps had glass-body globes, and 1950s pumps have plastic-body types.

Here is a general guideline for globe types. Find the year of the pump you are restoring, and match it up:

Globe type	Year(s) manufactured
One-piece	About 1912 to 1931
Metal-body	About 1914 to mid-1930s
Glass-body/glass-insert	1928 through 1940s
Plastic-body	1932 to present (but generally 1950s)

Note: One company still uses globes to this day, the Dixie Oil Company (see the listing for TENNECO in the Major Oil Company Globes section).

Globes *are* out there, believe it or not. You just have to know where to look. If you hit only the smaller shows, you won't find much. A combination of the ideas already mentioned will get you many of the globes you want. And keep in touch with the dealers, often referred to as "pickers," who buy globes just to resell. They will look for the most sought-after items. Get to know who is a collector and who is a dealer. Some collectors won't sell anything at all, even extras. By meeting as many people as you can, you will discover your best resources.

The dream of every collector is to find a globe still lying around at a bulk plant or service station. This may seem an unlikely occurrence, but it happens nearly every week. So hit all the old service stations, the oil bulk distributors, and the antique stores, and you'll occasionally turn up some globes. Good luck!

Chapter 2
Glossary of Terms

Term	Definition
4in base	Some early one-piece globes had smaller 4inch bases.
6in base	Ninety-eight percent of all globes come with a standard 6inch diameter base.
7in base	Some companies used larger bases on globes, including Standard Oil Company and Eldred Oil.
13.5in	Diameter of inserts that typically fit plastic or glass bodies.
15in	A metal-frame globe—its size, or its inserts—that measures 15inch.
16.5in	A metal-frame globe—its size, or its measures 16.5inch.
Air globe	Globe that sat on an air pump, usually saying "Air." This is not a gas globe.
Aircraft	A 1920s super premium grade. Later, a fuel for airplanes.
All-glass	Can mean glass body and glass inserts. Sometimes used interchangeably with the term "one-piece."
Aviation	See "Aircraft."
Balcrank	Any glass-body globe that uses three screws, positioned at twelve o'clock, four o'clock, and eight o'clock, to hold the insert in place. Manufactured by Balcrank.
Band	Globe body, as in "metal band," or a retaining ring designed to hold a glass insert to a body.
Banded glass	Glass-body globe that uses an internal ring to hold the insert in place.
Blunt-nose Eagle	White Eagle gasoline globe with a large, rounded beak.
Body	Glass or metal holder that holds inserts and lenses.
Branded	Any item with the oil company logo or brand name on it.
CAPCOLITE/CAPCO	Plastic body for 13.5in inserts made by the Cincinnati Advertising Products Company (CAPCO) in Cincinnati, Ohio.
Cast face	An insert, usually 15in, for a metal-frame body. It has its letters or design cast deep into the

	insert, similar to an etched one-piece globe.
Chimney top	One-piece etched globe that has a smaller opening at the top which looks similar to a base. This opening should then have a metal cap that covers it—hence the term "chimney cap."
Clam	See "Shell."
Clover body	Clover-shaped body usually holding clover-shaped inserts; used by Cities Service Oil Company.
Co-op/farm co-op	Gasoline marketer owned by an association of farmers to supply their farm needs. Most market to the general public as well, but profits are distributed on a cooperative basis.
Crown	Crown-shaped globe used by the Standard Oil Company of Indiana.
Cut-throat Eagle	White Eagle gasoline globe with a slit under its throat. The beak is similar to the blunt-nose Eagle.
Diesel	Kerosene-type fuel used primarily in trucks and farm equipment. This was a specialty fuel prior to the mid-1930s.
Discounter/tracksider	Independent or chain-operated service stations often located along a rail line. They received products by rail car, and sold gasoline at prices noticeably lower than surrounding major brand stations.
Etched letters	Letters etched into an insert, which is very rare, or more typically etched into a one-piece globe.
Ethyl	Premium-grade gasoline named for the chemical additive tetraethyl lead. This chemical was distributed on an exclusive basis by the Ethyl Gasoline Corporation.
Flame	One-piece flame that went on Standard Oil Company signs only. Sought after by most globe collectors, although it was never actually used on gas pumps.
Fuel oil	Heating oil used for oil-burning heating equipment.
Gargoyle	Oval one-piece Mobil Oil globe used only on oil cabinets.
Generic globes	Describes the early globes before company logos were used. These globes said "Gasoline," "Filtered Gasoline," and so on.
Gill body	A hollow glass body similar in design to the hull body, but the 13.5in inserts are held in with a narrow metal band. Original manufacturer was Gill Glass Company, Pennsylvania.
Gill lenses	The 13.5in inserts or other similar sizes that have no notches at nine o'clock or three o'clock. Must go on a Gill body.
Glass	Glass-body globe with glass inserts which could be a Gill body, Hull body, regular glass body, or other style. Also refers to the body itself.
High profile	Metal body that holds 15 or 16.5in inserts. It has one seam only in the middle. The metal above the insert is raised up and has a "high profile" when viewed from the front.
Holder	See "Body."
Hull body	Glass body made by the Hull Glass Company of Swissvale, Pennsylvania. It holds 13.5in glass inserts and the body center is hollowed out, unlike the typical solid-glass bodies.
Independent	Single station or chain operation that is a regional marketer without production. May or may not be involved in refining.
Inserts	Any glass advertisements with an oil company name or generic logo that attach to a body.
Jewel body	Metal body with twenty-four colored, glass jewels around body.
Jobber	Petroleum wholesaler operating in a limited geographic area.
Jobber association	Group of petroleum wholesalers operating under a common cooperative brand.
Jobber brand	Regional brand used by a petroleum wholesaler.
Kerosene	Fuel grade used for heating or light or as a tractor fuel.
Leaded glass	Assembled multi-piece Texaco stained-glass globe or window insert.
Lenses	See "Inserts."
Logotype	Distinctive lettering as it appeared in a logo, without the use of the entire logo design.
Lollipop-shaped	Typical round globe, distinguishing this style from an odd-shaped or globe sphere-shaped one.
Low profile	Metal body that holds 15 or 16.5in inserts and has several ridges across the top. Overall it is very flat and when viewed from the front, the inserts are what is mostly seen.
Major	Integrated oil company; operates exploration and production, refining, transportation, and marketing over a regional or national area.
Metal	Metal-frame globe with glass inserts, or just the metal body itself.
Metal rim	Metal body.
Metal ring	Any metal ring that holds the inserts into a metal-frame globe.
Milk glass inserts	Inserts, usually for 15in metal-frame bodies, made of milk glass. The company logo was then etched into these or fired onto the surface of the insert.
Milk glass	Certain globes that were made with actual milk-colored glass, sometimes giving off a pearlescent color effect. Term is also used by collectors to mean any glass globe, which is not always correct.
Motor	A 1930s economy grade of gasoline with limited tetraethyl lead content.
Narrow body	Glass body that typically is only 5in wide.
Notched inserts	The 13.5in inserts with notches usually at nine o'clock and three o'clock.
Oil globes	Globes typically used on oil cabinets or such places. Some globes were used on both oil cabinets and gasoline pumps.
One-piece	Globe that has no inserts and is a single piece of glass.
One-piece plastic	Formed or assembled one-piece plastic globe. Does not have removable inserts.
Picker	Person who picks up collectibles to resell them.
Plastic	Usually meaning a plastic body with glass inserts, or the body itself.
Premium	Top grade of gasoline—high tetraethyl lead content.
Raised-letter Crown	Red Crown, Red Crown Ethyl, Solite, or Crown are the raised-letter crowns used by Standard Oil. These names are on both sides of the globe.
Raised letters	One-piece cast globe; where the letters are raised up off the surface.
Regular	Primary grade of gasoline—minimal tetraethyl lead content.
Repro	Reproduction globe.
Rim	See "Metal."
Ring	See "Metal ring" or "Gill body."
Ripple	Gill body globe, often colored, with a ripple texture to it.
Round globe	A few companies used globes shaped like a ball or sphere. Examples include many sphere-shaped, early generic "gasoline" globes.
Screw-on base	Any globe with a copper, aluminum, or metal base that screws onto the bottom of the globe.
Shell	Shell-shaped globe used by the Shell Oil Company.
Sphere globe	See "Round Globe."
Standard flame	See "Flame."
Three-piece globe	Any globe with two inserts and a body. More often used to reference a glass-body globe with two inserts.
Torch	See "Flame."
Two-piece	A few companies used a globe bodystyle that had two glass halves which attached in the middle by a piece of metal with screws.
White glass	White-colored glass. Unlike milk glass, it has a somewhat duller off-white appearance.
Wide body	Glass body that is wide—usually 7-8in.
Window insert	Globe insert intended for use as a lighted insert in a building or other structure. Not used as a pump-top globe.

Chapter 3
Types of Globes

There are four basic globe types or categories. To succeed in the hobby, you must understand their differences and the significance of each.

Plastic-body, glass-insert): These have 13.5in glass inserts and were produced from circa 1932 to the present. They were most common in the 1950s.

Glass-body, glass-insert: These have 13.5in glass inserts, were produced from the late 1920s through the early 1960s and were most common in the mid-1930s and 1940s.

Metal-body, glass-insert: The usual size for their inserts is 15 or 16.5in. They were produced from the mid-teens through mid-1930s, though some were made as late as 1960. They were typically used in the 1920s and early 1930s.

One-piece, no-insert: Produced and used primarily between 1912-1931, they include etched, raised-letter, baked-on, fired-on, and chimney-cap globes.

There are several variations of each of the four main categories. Most globes have a standard 6in diameter base, but some are found with 7in or 4in bases.

Plastic-Body, glass-insert Globes

Typically, a glass insert fits on each side of a two-piece plastic body. The insert diameter is 13.5in, with notches at nine o'clock and three o'clock. These notches are not as deep as the 13.5in inserts for glass-body globes, and the inserts themselves are thinner than most for glass.

If you took a circle and cut it in half, this is about what the notches look like for plastic-body globes.

The notches on inserts for glass bodies are elongated half-circles. They are much deeper or longer. Lenses for plastic globes are usually thinner, and those for glass bodies are generally thicker. However, we have seen thin lenses with deep notches. Collectors say, "These go on plastic, right?" Not really. Deep-notched inserts were made for glass bodies, whether they are thin or thick glass. The reason for this was basically to allow for a better fit on the glass body. The inserts we have seen that are thin glass with deep notches were too old to be on a plastic globe for that particular company. By the way, any 13.5in insert without notches must go on a Gill or banded-glass body.

Plastic bodies are usually white, but yellow, red, green, orange, tan/cream, and blue originals exist. "CAPCO" or "Capcolite" is often inscribed on the underside of one of the two pieces. As mentioned, CAPCO stood for Cincinnati Advertising Products Company, from Cincinnati, Ohio. They manufactured many types of globes. These bodies were patented in about 1932. So some, particularly Phillips and Conoco, can be quite old.

One screw on the top and two through the base hold the globe together. To assemble or disassemble the globe, point the base at three o'clock, loosen the screws completely, and the upper half-body comes off. Then, carefully remove each insert separately.

Some older plastic bodies are wider, and some have a ridge only on one half where they come together at the top. These date from the early to mid-1930s. Inserts for glass bodies don't fit well into a plastic body. They are too thick, and don't line up correctly. We've seen some fit adequately, but you risk chipping the edges of any lens that fits too tight.

Oval plastic globes with glass inserts are a lot less common. Other than the shape, the body fit and other factors are basically the same. The oval lenses are not notched, though.

A couple dozen companies used oval-shaped plastic globes, and several used unusual-shaped all-plastic globes, including Mileage and Co-op. Vickers Oil Company used different-sized rectangular all-plastic globes, while Phillips 66 used two different shield-shaped all-plastic versions. These are all very interesting to the collector.

Glass-Body, glass-insert Globes

This category has many exceptions and variations. Insert diameter is typically 13.5in, as previously mentioned, and notches are deeper at both three and nine o'clock. The inserts are also normally a bit thicker than those for plastic bodies. Lenses with no notches are for Gill bodies, which will be explained shortly.

The Gulf Oil Company and several others used 12.5in glass inserts that fit only on smaller, wide-glass bodies. Other than Gulf globes, not many of these ever turn up.

Some companies used inserts with diameters of 13 3/8, 13 5/8, 14, 14 1/4, 14 7/8, and 15in. There probably were other sizes as well. Bodies for these inserts are difficult to find. Most of these odd sizes go on various Gill-type bodies. A Gill globe is basically a narrow-glass body that is hollow in the center. The notchless inserts are held on by a narrow metal ring that attaches to the body, with one screw at the bottom of the ring. These bodies were made by the Gill Glass Company of Pennsylvania, hence the name.

Gill also manufactured ripple-textured globes, so named for their ripple-type surface on the outside of the glass. The inside glass was often painted and then baked on so that when the globe lights up, it looks quite beautiful. Red is the most common color found today. Other colors include clear, white, orange, yellow, blue, green, and brown. The latter three are the rarest. There are also different shades of the green, red, and yellow. The older versions of these globes have a screw-on base that is usually made of copper. Some were made of steel and aluminum as well. In fact, any screw-on base on any type of glass body signifies an older glass body, from around the early 1930s.

The 14 7/8 and 15in inserts were used by only a couple of companies and attach to a large, solid (in the center) glass body. A ring similar to a Gill body holds the inserts onto the body—talk about a large and heavy globe! These globes are extremely rare. The inserts will fit a metal-frame 15in globe and when one can't find one of these unusual glass bodies, metal will have to do. Kanotex, Pennzoil, and a couple other companies used these large bodies.

Hull bodies, made by Hull Glass Company, are hollow like the Gills, except they hold notched-type inserts. Some Hull bodies have unusually shaped bases and some are inscribed "Hull" toward the bottom of the globe. There are many other versions of glass bodies that hold inserts, too many to mention them all. The two most common types are the narrow-glass and the wide-glass bodies. Both are solid pieces, the narrow one approximately 5in wide (front to back) and the wide version around 7 to 8in wide. These bodies hold most insert types. Again, many variations exist with different widths, different bases, styles, and so on. Many companies were making globes in those days, thus the reason for so many different types. It is not so important to be familiar with all these versions. However, it is important to be able to differentiate between a Gill, Hull, ripple, and regular glass globe.

On rare occasion, some inserts will have notches at twelve, four, and eight o'clock. These types went on the more unusual bodies with holes that lined up in the same respective positions. Marland Oil among others, sometimes used these globe types; Cincinnati Balcrank was the manufacturer.

Another unusual style of globe body was used by D-X, Empire Refining, and a few other companies, and is asked about by many collectors. We call this a banded-glass body or globe. The globe body is hollow like the Hull body, but with a recessed metal rim that holds each insert on with four screws from the inside. It's also like a Gill, whereas the inserts are not notched. Some lenses are interchangeable with Gills. The globe manufacturer is unknown.

Gill bodies, including ripples, are sought after more because of their rarity and, in the case of ripples, for their beauty. Some prefer the Hull body to the regular glass globe while others opt for the narrow-glass over the wide-glass, and vice versa.

Inserts are much more common than bodies, so collectors will commonly come across inserts without bodies. If you have inserts without notches, you will need to find a Gill body. Notched lenses give you more options. Certain gasoline companies used only wide-glass bodies or only narrow-glass bodies. Although it would be impossible to list them all here, we'll mention a few. Oil companies that usually used the narrow-body glass globes included Sinclair, Texaco, Marathon, Fleet-Wing, Pennzoil, and Cities Service. Companies that normally chose the wide-bodies included Sohio, Phillips, Skelly, Wolf's Head, Coreco, Ashland, and White Rose. Some companies used both. Amoco, Atlantic, Crown, Kanotex, Dixie, and Derby used a number of Gill bodies, with Kanotex, Bay, and Dixie globes more often found on ripple bodies.

Colored-glass globes are very rare, much rarer than ripples. Fleet-Wing used red glass on occasion, and Freedom Oil used yellow glass.

There were a few other oddball glass globes manufactured. Waverly Oil Company used a two-piece glass globe that fastened in the center. Cities Service used clover-shaped globe bodies with clover-shaped inserts that fit like regular notched inserts. The most unusual one we've seen is a *clover-shaped* Cities Service Hull body that held *round* inserts.

Oval glass bodies exist today, but are rare. Only a few companies used them, such as Cavalier, Hicksatomic, and Pugh Peerless.

As mentioned, lenses made for glass bodies don't fit well into plastic bodies. The reverse is also true. Lenses made for plastic bodies are thinner glass and not deeply notched, so they don't fit well into glass bodies. However, certain narrow-glass bodies will hold inserts for plastic. Also, most notched 13.5in inserts will fit in a Gill body as well. The Gill band simply covers these notches. Some people take a pretty insert for plastic and put it in a pretty Gill ripple body. This greatly increases the globe's value, but it is not original. For display purposes it is probably okay, but a potential buyer should be informed that this is not the way it originally came. It's like fitting your Model A with air conditioning—convenient, but not original.

Metal-Body, glass-insert Globes

Metal-frame globes typically hold 15 or 16.5in glass inserts with a snap ring that holds the insert onto the body by pressure. The ring is split in one spot. These inserts are not notched, but sometimes have a small inverted cone-shaped filing on the inside bottom. The indentation fits over a seam on the inside of the metal globe body. But this is not all that important. If you line up the globe and look at it closely, the inserts often appear crooked.

There are many exceptions in this category, more for the type of inserts than the bodystyles.

There are two basic bodystyles that fit both the 15 or 16.5in inserts, the high-profile and the low-profile bodies. It is important to distinguish between the two types. A picture of each is included in this book. The advantages of high-profile bodies are twofold. One, they will hold all inserts except oddball types. Two, when looking at a high-profile body, you see the body around the lenses, which adds to the color and contrast of the globe. The low-profile bodies do hold most inserts, but some fit tighter and some don't fit at all. When looking directly at a low-profile mounted globe you mainly see just the inserts. Again, as in the glass types, some companies used only the high-profile, some only the low-profile, and some used both.

Texaco, for their leaded-glass globes, used an unusual metal body that is unique to the company. It is flat on the top and very wide. They also had a metal body for 20in leaded-glass inserts. As far as we know, Texaco is the only company that used leaded-glass inserts.

The most interesting body type ever made was a rare 15in metal body, with about twenty-four 1 1/4in "jewels" attached around the whole globe. Usually these jewels are red, blue/indigo, and white. Dixie Distributors and Sterling used these on rare occasions, perhaps other companies used them as well. These globes are phenomenal when lit up!

Several of the Standard Oil brands used a fancy high-profile body with several "tiers" of metal ridges, sometimes with a 7in base. These are very attractive bodies, but the 7in base sometimes poses a problem mounting on the typical 6in base pumps.

Wadhams Oil Company and others used metal inserts that were painted on the surface. Some generic "Gasoline," "Filtered Gasoline," and a few very early companies used metal inserts with punched-out perforations. When lit, these inserts projected the light out from the inside of the globe and were quite attractive. Their surface feels like sandpaper.

Texaco, White Star, Atlantic, and Socony used milk glass inserts. Socony and Texaco fired their logo onto the surface, and White Star and Atlantic etched the surface, then painted on their logo. There are probably other companies that used milk glass inserts. However, except for Socony, these are all extremely rare.

Cast inserts are more common than milk glass overall, but are still very rare. Tydol, Socony, Atlantic, Cities Service, Hearn, Venus Oil Company, Pennzoil, and Valvoline, to name a few, used cast-face inserts. These inserts are very thick, heavy glass with deep letters or logos molded into them. The letters were then painted or fired on, or sometimes both techniques were used on the same insert.

Socony used porcelain inserts that fit into a smaller (about 14in) metal body. These inserts are very rare. Even rarer are odd-sized, smaller metal-body globes with inserts.

Now, for a few removal and installation details. To remove a snap ring on a metal body, you must get a sharp object under the ring without touching the insert. Then lift or pry up slowly and carefully. Keep your hands on the snap ring so it doesn't fly off. You really need three hands, so use a knee to hold back one side of the ring, then one hand on the other side, and one hand to pry or lift. Or, once you get one side of the snap ring up about 1/4in, put your hand under it and hold it tight. Move the ring inward so it becomes smaller and lift it around and out of the metal body. The ring then expands as the pressure is relieved, so don't let it fly! I had one ring fly several feet and hit another globe directly. Luckily that globe didn't break, but it could have been costly.

To install an insert, set it inside the globe body, put one side of the snap ring down, and bend the other side of the ring around and toward the center, carefully and slowly. It will snap, but won't break the insert.

One-Piece, no-insert Globes

Our last category consists of one-piece, no-insert globes. There are a few subcategories that you need to be aware of.

First, there are the etched globes. These are most likely the earliest globes a company may have used. The company name or logo was etched into the glass, then painted in—circa 1912–1926.

Another version of this subtype is the chimney-cap globe. A small metal cap fit on a 4in (usually) collar or opening on the top of the globe. These globes are very early and only a few companies used them. Texaco, Gulf, Standard Oil, Atlantic, Mills Oil, and a few other makes can sometimes be found. A chimney-cap globe is always earlier than a regular one-piece etched globe

from that same company. The chimney cap probably served as a vent for possible "dangerous fumes" that could accumulate in the globe in the mid to late teens.

Very early one-piece etched globes sometimes have a smaller 4in base to fit some early pumps. Indian Gas, Barnsdall, and some of the generic gasoline globes have these smaller bases. The globes are smaller too, often only 8 to 14in tall.

Fired-on or baked-on one-piece globes came later, usually around 1927–1930. The company logo was baked on to the surface of the glass body. Some companies used these as their first globes.

Raised-letter or cast one-piece globes were not used as frequently (circa mid-1920s to 1931). This type of one-piece was a favorite with Texaco, Gulf, Tydol, and Cities Service. The globes were cast from a mold, and paint was fired on to the surface, or the letters. Several smaller companies used these types, but rarely, and often with the same image as an etched or baked globe, indicating they were from the same era.

A few companies like Pennzoil and Penn Drake used some different techniques. The rare Penn Drake one-piece etched and the rare Pennzoil with bell, etched (not the Safe Lubrication style) were first etched, then the background was painted, and then the lettering and the design were painted over or around the background paint. What a nightmare to restore!

The background and lettering on Musgo globes was fired on and the Indian in the center was hand painted. so each Musgo globe was unique.

Some companies used odd-shaped one-piece globes, which can be an interesting collector item. Cities Service used a clover-shaped, raised-letter one-piece. White Eagle used tall, one-piece glass eagles—in four different styles. Standard Indiana and Standard Kentucky used the common crown-shaped globes, and Shell used the familiar shell-shaped types.

There are many odd-shaped, one-piece, no-insert globes on the collector market today. Webb Oil Company and Ford Benzol used globes shaped like an old keyhole. Barnsdall had a one-piece etched globe shaped like the Washington Monument with a curved top.

A few companies used oval one-piece etched globes such as Vahey Oil Company, Pure Oil Company, and Interstate Oil Company.

Here is a chronological listing of the four globe type categories, with the earliest versions listed first:

Chimney-cap etched one-piece
Etched one-piece
Raised-letter one-piece or fired-on one-piece
Metal-frame
Glass-frame
Plastic-frame

Many companies never used chimney-cap, one-piece etched globes, so you will start with the one-piece etched as a company's earliest globe and go from there. Later companies never used one-piece or even metal-frame globes. Some only used plastic. The point is that if you have a one-piece etched chimney-cap Texaco, a regular one-piece etched Texaco, a raised-letter one-piece, and so on, this simple chart tells you which is older.

Chapter 4
Theory Behind Pricing Gasoline Globes

So, you've got this neat old gasoline globe you just picked up, and the $64,000 question suddenly hits you: "I wonder what this is really worth? Did I pay too much, or is it a steal?"

These are typical questions many collectors ask before or after buying a globe. How about the globe sitting at the antique store for $800? It looks expensive—but is it really worth it?

Each globe has a value and, like a house for sale, each can be expected to bring a certain price. For example, a 1,500 square foot house in a certain area should bring a certain price (we said *should* here). A globe, then, even if this particular brand has never sold before, should command a certain price or approximate value. Prices do vary by region, but not by much overall. So, how can one price a globe? Start with the basic facts.

Fact Number One: The type of globe—plastic body with glass inserts, glass body with glass inserts, metal frame with glass inserts, or one-piece—greatly affects the value. Why? Generally speaking, most plastic-body globes are worth $90–$175 these days. Many glass-body types are commanding from $225–$400. Metal-frame globes go for $300–$700, unless rare. And many one-piece globes are valued between $450–$1,500. Be aware that these prices are generalized, however; a rare or pretty globe in any of these categories can go far above the mentioned guidelines. But this gives you a base with which to start.

Fact Number Two: Rarity of a globe can increase its value, and in most cases, it does. In some cases, though, it doesn't. As you read on, you'll see the distinctions.

Fact Number Three: The beauty of a globe greatly affects its value, *always*. The prettier a globe, the more money it is likely to bring. Globes with pictures on them tend to demand the highest prices. Pictures may include everything from airplanes, animals, scenery, people, buildings, and so on. These days, picture-type plastic-body globes bring $250–$550. Glass-body picture types bring $450–$1,000 and up. Metal-frame picture globes go for as much as $800–$2,500. One-piece versions easily sell for anywhere between $1,400 and $2,500. Again, these are general guidelines, but they cover many or most globes on the collector market today. Some can go even higher.

Non-picture globes that are still colorful and have nice graphics or designs do very well. They don't bring as high a price as do the picture globes, but they run a close second.

When determining the market value of a globe, you need to weigh these three factors to arrive at a realistic price. Experience will help to fill in the gaps.

The globes that don't demand much money are the plain globes or one-word globes (for example, a globe that only says "Lion"). These globes just aren't that popular, no matter how rare. The reason is there were hundreds of small, unknown, independent companies manufacturing globes. Considering their obscure origins, unless those globes are pretty, they don't mean a lot to the majority of collectors since they probably have never heard of the manufacturer. Almost every medium-size collection has such unique or rare globes. There are exceptions here; certain companies—even small ones—are so popular that anything with their name on it would be sought after. But this is the exception rather than the rule.

Let's use an example of a nonexistent globe. Say you find a one-of-a-kind globe that says "Cherry Gasoline" but just has black letters on white and is on a metal frame. It's not worth $1,500; it's worth about $300–$400, retail.

If that same globe said "Cherry Tree Antiknock Gasoline" and was on that same metal frame, but with fancy red, script-style letters and a colored background, it would be worth between $500 and $850.

If that same globe had a cherry tree pictured on it with cherries and four colors, whether it was one-of-a-kind or twenty examples were known, it would demand well over $1,500, maybe more.

Note that in this case, rarity didn't count, but beauty did.

Rarity does help, but more so in certain brands. A rare or unique Texaco, Sinclair, or other popular company would sell no matter what. If plain, it wouldn't bring as much as a beautiful globe from that same company, but it'll do well anyway, which is exactly the point. Only experience can help you price this sort of globe.

Another interesting consideration is what a reproduction body will do to the value of a globe with original inserts. Five or ten years ago that repro body did a lot to the value, but today it does much less. Most collectors still prefer original bodies on their globes, but original bodies are getting harder to find. Repro bodies are more widely accepted among collectors, as long as they know they are buying one. Today, repro bodies sell for about 75 percent of what an original body brings. We're talking about a $25 to $50 price difference here. In our opinion, if an all-original Mobilgas on glass sells for $350, then one on a repro body with original lenses would be worth about $300 to $325—a little less difference for plastics. Good metal reproduction bodies vary little in price with originals, but aluminum ones vary a bit more.

Some collectors are looking for any rare globe from any company. Here, rarity counts a lot. After a certain type of globe sells a few times, it establishes a certain price. Again, only experience will tell you who will pay what for which globe. Attending auctions will help you learn a great deal about pricing globes.

(You will note in the pricing section that some globes are marked "No Listing." These globes could have a value attached to them, but are so rare or unique that we left out the price. So few of these globes sell, that a true value is hard to pinpoint.)

Chapter 5
Gasoline Globes as Investments

A few years ago, hardly anyone was asking which globe was a good investment. It was more like, "If I chose a Gargoyle or a White Eagle, could I get my money back in six months or one to two years?" Now, people are asking which specific globes are good investments and which appreciate in value the fastest.

Any globe is a good investment as long as you don't pay too much above retail for it. Obviously, the less you pay for a globe, the better the investment return can be when you decide to sell.

All globes increase in value over time, and many increase faster than others. But which ones appreciate the fastest? Some get hyped up and appreciate in value too quickly, such as Gargoyles did in 1991. Prices easily approached the $1,500 range. We advised collectors that this was too much for such an available globe. Repro Gargoyles then hit the market, and the price for originals dropped by about $300–$500. Currently, Gargoyles bring $1,000–$1,300 retail.

Most globes, though, will never drop in value, even a little. Some just creep up slowly. In 1974, Dino globes sold for about $25 to $35, top retail—if you had to pay for one. Many globes were free in those days! Good one-piece globes brought $65–$125. But look what happened. Today, many years later, Sinclair Dino globes retail for $75–$125, and those one-piece globes have gone up to ten to twenty times their original value.

From 1975 to 1979, Musgo globes brought about $200 retail and now their price has gone up ten to fifteen times that, and more. "One-piece globes are the ticket," you say? Nope. "Better globes, then?" Yes. It's the same in any hobby. The better and rarer items always appreciate faster than the more common or plainer-looking items.

Standard Crowns have gone up little in twenty years, unless you're talking about the rarer raised-letter ones or the odd-colored ones. In fact, most common glass, plastic, and metal globes have gone up only a couple hundred dollars in the last ten to fifteen years. The the same story can be told about plain-Jane one-piece globes.

But one day you'll find that plastic globe with a pretty design or picture. You'll find a glass globe with five colors from a rare company, or a metal from a well-known company with only two such globes known. Now you have a globe that will appreciate faster than the others.

So, it's that globe with a little something extra—one from a rare company, or with a pretty or unique design on it—that typically will appreciate faster. Why? Because most collectors have good taste and know a special globe when they find one. The smart collector asks a lot of questions, and it doesn't take long to figure out what constitutes an extra-special example.

What are the hottest collector items today? In our opinion, they include the ripple globes of any color, and the colored, original plastic-body globes. Texaco Ethyl glass or the pretty or colorful major brand name globes are moving up fast in price as well, along with picture-type glass globes. Basically, the rarer globe—if pretty—goes up the fastest.

Some rare and expensive globes peak in price, so as an investment consider the rare and better-quality globes, but check lesser priced examples too. What we're saying is that if you had $3,500 to spend right now for *investment purposes only,* you shouldn't buy a Musgo for $3,500. The reason is that they have gone up very fast and that trend probably will not continue, at least for a while. But there are several $500 and $1,000 globes currently available that will double in value in the next year or two.

If you have $1,000 to invest, you should buy one or two good globes as opposed to ten more common ones. We've always told collectors that quality globes sell faster, appreciate faster, and trade more easily.

Most collectors don't buy globes for investment purposes, though. They buy a particular globe because they like the globe itself—its history, its appearance, and so on. Most collectors don't care what it's going to be worth in ten years. So, we aren't knocking the cheaper globes. But the economics do hold true if you are collecting for investment.

If you have several more common globes and want that expensive goodie but can't afford it, it's best to sell the common ones and get the good ones. You can always go back and replace the common ones later, but don't wait too long. We always encourage upgrading a collection, but do it carefully—it takes time. Don't sell ten miscellaneous common (plastic and glass) globes for $2,500 and then buy four globes for the same amount that are either priced too high, or are just four more common globes. For example, let's say you buy a Mobil 15in metal for $650, a mint Gold Crown for $500, a Gulf one-piece for $800 (not Good Gulf or No-Nox), and a Tydol on metal for $550. You did upgrade, but you get a grade of C– overall. All four globes are priced above retail by about $100 each, and all four are common globes. None will increase much in the next few years. Instead, spend $600–$1,000 for a raised-letter Crown, or $800–$1,200 for a Gulf No-Nox one-piece, or buy two nice ripple globes. These globes are much rarer and will appreciate faster.

Again, we're talking to collectors interested in investment return. It takes experience to make these decisions. Talking to people, going to shows, and getting involved will help.

Chapter 6
Reproduction Gasoline Globes

Reproduction globes have been a big concern for the last several years in the minds of many collectors. Repro globes first appeared around 1974 or earlier. They caused confusion for collectors, but luckily back then nearly all were dated at the bottom.

The first repros were the car globes, such as "Cadillac Sales and Service," "Ford Sales and Service," and so on. About the same time came the generic "Gasoline" globe on a plastic body. Then, other brands and dealers got involved.

So the old story that "the guy had the globe for fifteen years, so I know it's original" doesn't mean a lot these days. It's either real or a phony. Remember, a repro can be twenty years old.

About four years ago, we realized the danger of these repros getting mixed in with the originals. Like a virus, they would spread and eventually taint the whole hobby and in the years to come, who would remember or who could tell a repro from an original if it wasn't dated?

To combat this problem, a list was created of every known repro globe and in the last four years that list has grown substantially. But at least for the hobby, this list serves as a reference guide and history, if you will, for future collectors. There are now well over 200 known types of repro globes, and they are listed at the end of this chapter.

How does one spot a repro? Let's discuss the easiest way, first. About 65–70 percent of the globes are dated at the bottom. These globes typically are 13.5in diameter glass inserts made for plastic bodies. So, look at the bottom of a suspect insert. Some may fit into a glass body, Gill body, or the smaller metal bodies (repros themselves) that hold the 13.5in inserts.

Next, study the list. Many repros imitate bodystyles or categories that never even existed. The first category, for instance, includes the 13.5in inserts for plastic or glass bodies. A number of companies never made globes in this category. Signal globes came only in 15in metal frames, so any Signal on a glass or plastic body is a repro. Musgos are one-piece globes only, so any Musgo on glass or plastic is a repro. Reading and studying the list will help sort out any questions you might have.

One item in particular makes it difficult for all collectors: the 13.5in repro metal body. Most metal globes with glass inserts are original and have 15 or 16.5in inserts. So, when you find one of these 13.5in repro inserts in a repro body and someone says, "It's in a metal frame... so it's original," it's not. This is where it gets confusing. Ninety-nine percent of all original metal-frame globes have either 15 or 16.5in inserts, not 13.5in. There are several metal-frame 15in inserts being reproduced and none are dated, except a few Canadian types. Reference this list and know who you are dealing with. Use the notes to help determine whether it is likely that the globe is original or not.

Most of the 15in undated metal-frame inserts are coming from Canada and being sold here in the US. We don't know why they don't date these inserts. Some of the repros pretend to be globes that, if original, are incredibly rare and well-documented; if you found such an insert on the market, it would likely be a phony. Again, reference the list, read it and understand it. In our example, look at the quantity available. Rare original lenses for 15in frames are seldom found in quantities of more than two or four at a time.

There has been a recent breakthrough for the hobby, however. A friend of ours has located a person who can test the inserts for originality. He dates the paint by whether it is the older, leaded paint or a newer paint. This is, of course, a last resort, but if no one can help you and you just paid a lot of money for a globe, at least there is a way to check the date. (Contact the authors if you need this information.)

Most original inserts have a rougher texture on the back side. But there are exceptions; we've seen rough inside-surface repros and smooth originals too.

Watch out for great deals when purchasing several inserts of the same brand. We've heard many stories lately that sounded too good to be true, and in fact they were just that. Many repro globes have a smooth surface on the back or inside of the insert. Most collectors know something about repros, and who sells originals and who sells repros. So again, start asking questions.

Get to know authentic globe colors. This can't be stressed enough. Repro colors are usually off a bit. Once you start seeing more and more originals, repros will stand out as phonies by their color alone.

We've seen a few repros where the paint on the back of the insert is not fired on or silk screened. A fingernail or edge of a coin will easily scrape the paint off the back of the insert. This has occurred on some 15in inserts for metal-frame globes only.

Concerning the reproduced plastic, glass, or metal bodies, we feel that as long as the seller tells you what you are buying, those bodies are not a big deal. There are never enough bodies to mount all the inserts around, so these repro bodies *are* needed. Yet, some collectors still prefer the original bodies.

The best advice we can offer is to use the provided list, remember the points made here, ask a lot of questions and you should do well in obtaining original globes.

List of Known Reproduction Gasoline Globes

The following reproductions are separated into the four major categories of gasoline globes: plastic-body, glass-body, metal-body, and one-piece (as well as some subcategories).

Plastic- or Glass-Frame Gasoline Globes with 13.5in Glass Inserts

Although most of the repros in this first category are dated, not all are, so beware. See the list of known globes elsewhere in this book for descriptions, if not given here.

Company name	Details
American Gas	All 13.5in notched lenses are repros; repros should be dated at bottom.
Amoco	All 13.5in notched lenses are repros; should be dated at bottom.
Ashland A Plus	Large "A" logo; twenty-five made by Ashland Oil; repros are not dated.
Ashland Flying Octanes	Blue "Flying Octanes"; twenty-five made by Ashland Oil; not dated.
Associated Gasoline	Oil can with "More Miles to the Gallon"; all 13.5in inserts are repros; should be dated at bottom; existed as 15in inserts for metal-frame only.
Atlantic	Rectangle logo; should be dated at bottom.
Atlantic Hi-ARC	All 13.5in notched lenses are repros; should be dated at bottom.
Atlantic White Flash	All 13.5in notched lenses are repros; should be dated at bottom.
Bay	Shield shown; should be dated at bottom.
Beacon	Lighthouse shown; should be dated at bottom; originals very rare and of a different design.
Buffalo Gasoline	Picture of buffalo; should be dated at bottom.
Chevron	Dated 1991.
Chevron	Originals rare; not dated (circa 1989).
Cities Service Green	Green letters with black outline; dated 1992.
Cities Service Red	Red letters w/ black outline; dated 1992.
Cities Service Yellow	Yellow letters w/black outline; dated 1992. No original Cities Service globes have lettering outlined in black.
Cities Service Koolmotor	Black, white, and yellow; should be dated at bottom.
Clark	Note that Clark used globes into the 1980s and many late originals are of poor quality; should be dated at bottom.
Conoco	Triangle; should be dated at bottom.
Conoco Gasoline	Minuteman; all 13.5in inserts are repros; existed as 15in inserts for metal-frame only.
Diamond D-X Lubricating Gas	Dated 1991; D-X Lubricating Gas; should be dated at bottom.
Dixie	Shield; currently in use; Dixie Oil Company, Tifton, Georgia.
Dixie	With crossed flags; originals of this design say "Rebel"; all with "Dixie" are repros.
Doggone Gas	With dog; all are repros; not dated.
Esso	Should be dated at bottom.
Esso Extra	Block letters; should be dated at bottom.
Ethyl	With Ethyl Corporation logo; should be dated at bottom.
Farmers Union Coop	Plow and shield; should be dated at bottom; originals are rare.
Fleet-Wing	Bird; should be dated at bottom.
Flying A Gasoline	Letter "A" with wings; should be dated at bottom.
Frontier Rarin' to Go	Black rearing horse; some not dated; early one with red band design; originals deeply notched for glass only; repros made to fit plastic body only.
Gasoline	All 13.5in inserts are repros; red, orange or green backgrounds; originals only one-piece or metal-frame.
General Petroleum	All 13.5in inserts are repros; circa 1989; not dated; originals 15in inserts for metal-frame only.
Gilmore Blue Green	Lion shown; all 13.5in inserts are repros; some dated 1991; some have earlier date; existed as 15in inserts for metal-frame only.
Gilmore, Roar with	Lion across top and checked flag at bottom; all 13.5in inserts are repros; existed as 15in inserts for metal-frame only.
Golden West Oil Co.	Picture of sunset over water, mountains; originals very rare; should be dated at bottom.
Grizzly Dubbs Cracked Gasoline	Picture of standing bear; originals extremely rare; should be dated at bottom.
Gulf	Should be dated 1982 at bottom.
Gulf	12.5in inserts; not dated.
Gulf No Nox Ethyl	All originals are 12.5in.
That Good Gulf Gasoline	All 13.5in inserts are repros; should be dated at bottom.
Humble Gasoline	"Humble Oils" in center; should be dated at bottom.
Husky	Picture of husky dog; should be dated at bottom.
Imperial Refineries	Shield; should be dated at bottom. *Note:* Imperial used globes into the 1980s, and many still exist today.
Indian Gas	With teepee; all are repros; should be dated at bottom; never existed as originals.
Indian Gasoline	With designs; all are repros; never existed as originals.
Liberty Gasoline	Picture of Statue of Liberty; should be dated at bottom; originals extremely rare and of a different design.
Lion Knix Knox	Picture of lion in center; most are dated at bottom.
Magnolia Gasoline	Flower in center; all 13.5in inserts are repros; should be dated at bottom; existed as 16.5in inserts for metal-frame only. So all 15in inserts are repros, too!
Magnolia Maximum Mileage	All are repros; should be dated 1991 at bottom; existed as 16.5in inserts for metal-frame only.
Marathon Mile-maker	Running man in center; should be dated at bottom.
Mobilgas	Pegasus; should be dated at bottom.
Mobilgas	With blue outline ring; all are repros.
Mobilgas Aircraft	Should be dated at bottom.
Mobilgas Special	Pegasus; should be dated at bottom.
Mobil Regular	Flat shield logo, dated at bottom
Mobil Premium	Flat shield logo, dated at bottom
Mohawk Gasoline	Large Indian head profile in center; all 13.5in inserts are repros; should be dated at bottom; existed as 15in inserts for metal-frame only.
Mojave Gas	Indian; several colors; all are repros; not dated; never existed as originals.
Musgo Gasoline	Indian in headdress; all 13.5in inserts are
Michigan's Mile Maker	repros; originals were one-piece globes only.
Mustang Gasolene	Horse pictured; all are repros; not dated.
Olympic Quality Gasoline	Greyhound dog in center; should be dated at bottom.
Pennzoil	Liberty bell; should be dated at bottom.
Phillips 77 Aviation	Should be dated at bottom.
Phillips 66	Ethyl on shield; should be dated at bottom.
Phillips 66	Shield; should be dated at bottom.
Phillips Unique	Should be dated at bottom.
Polly Gas	Shows bird; all 13.5in inserts are repros; should be dated at bottom; existed as 15in inserts for metal-frame only.
Pure Products of the Pure Oil Company	Zigzag border; should be dated at bottom.
Purol Gasoline, The Pure Oil Company	Arrow through center; should be dated at bottom; originals existed as 15in inserts only.

Rainbow Gasoline	Rainbow, pump, car shown; all 13.5in inserts are repros; should be dated at bottom; existed as 15in inserts for metal-frame only.
Red Crown Ethyl	Should be dated at bottom; no originals known.
Red Crown Gasoline	Small red crown in center; should be dated at bottom; original 13.5in inserts *extremely rare*.
Red Crown Gasoline	Smaller red crown in center; should be dated at bottom.
Richfield Ethyl	Shield with small ethyl symbol; should be dated at bottom; existed as 15in inserts for metal-frame only.
Richfield Gasoline of Power	Should be dated; originals existed as 15in only.
Richfield Hi Octane	Should be dated at bottom.
Road Runner Gasoline	Road runner pictured as on the original globe; should be dated at bottom; originals very rare.
Road Runner Gasoline	Road runner pictured as on the oil can; circa 1991; all are repros; should be dated at bottom; originals very rare.
Salyer's Gasoline	Woman riding goose; not dated; originals very rare.
Seaco Aviation	Airplane; not dated (circa 1989).
Shell	Yellow shell pictured (all are repros); should be dated at bottom; originals one-piece clam shaped, one-piece round shaped or 15in metal only.
Super Shell	All are repros; should be dated at bottom; originals one-piece clam shaped or one-piece round shaped only.
Signal	Stop light with "Go" sign pictured; all 13.5in inserts are repros; should be dated at bottom; existed as 15in inserts for metal-frame only.
Sinclair Aircraft	Airplane; should be dated at bottom; originals on glass extremely rare.
Sinclair Dino Gasoline	Dinosaur; larger than original; if dinosaur is larger than 2in, it is a repro; some current repros now being made with smaller dinosaur like original; should be dated at bottom.
Sinclair H-C Gasoline	"H-C" in center; should be dated at bottom.
Skelly	Design like the one-piece; red, white, and blue; should be dated at bottom.
Skelly	Should be dated at bottom.
Smitholene Aviation Gasoline	With plane; should be dated at bottom; originals are rarer.
Sunray	With sun; 1991; should be dated at bottom; originals on orange plastic bodies with no dates.
Blue Sunoco	Yellow diamond in center; all are repros; should be dated at bottom; existed as 15in inserts for metal-frame only or 12-1/2in glass.
Texaco	Large red star with green "T"; should be dated at bottom.
Texaco Diesel Chief	Should be dated at bottom; originals rare.
Texaco Ethyl	Should be dated at bottom.
Texaco Fire-Chief Gasoline	Fire hat and Texaco emblem; should be dated at bottom; originals very rare.
Texaco Sky Chief	Should be dated at bottom.
Texas Rose	Rose and small ethyl symbol; should be dated at bottom.
T.P. Products	With teepee; all 13.5in inserts are repros; should be dated at bottom; existed as 15in inserts for metal-frame only.
Tri-Star Red Hat Gasoline	Red top hat in center; all are repros; should be dated at bottom; no original 13.5in inserts known to exist.
Tulsa Hi-Test	Cattle skull; should be dated at bottom.
Tydol	Should be dated at bottom.
Union Gasoline	Shield; all 13.5in inserts are repros; should be dated at bottom; existed as 15in inserts for metal-frame only.

Union 76 Ethyl	Should be dated at bottom; existed as 15in inserts for metal-frame only.
Union 76 Gasoline	All 13.5in inserts are repros; should be dated at bottom; existed as 15in inserts for metal-frame only.
Wake Up 99	Shows rooster; not dated (circa 1989); originals extremely rare.
White Eagle Gasoline	Large white eagle in center (all are repros); originals one-piece round or eagle shaped only.
White Rose Gasoline	Boy holding sign; should be dated at bottom.
White Rose No Knock	Boy holding sign; should be dated at bottom.

Note: There is a new company producing a series of globes such as those used by Mobil, Shell, Texaco, and others. These are 14in tall with a 4in base. They are all-plastic (two pieces put together). Such globes never existed as originals, thus it should be noted that all are reproductions.

Also, some repro companies now offer half-size glass globes, such as Shell globes, and all of these are repros. Originals are 16-17in tall.

Canadian Plastic- or Glass-Frame Gasoline Globes with 13.5in Glass Inserts
B-A Service Products

Nevr-nox	Should be dated at bottom.
Bengal Gasoline	Shows tiger; all 13.5in inserts are repros; should be dated at bottom; existed as 15in inserts for metal-frame only; originals very rare.
High Compression	
H-C Supertest	Should be dated at bottom.
Maple Leaf	Shows leaf; dated at bottom.
Red Indian	Indian head in headdress; not dated.
Red Rose Gasoline	Rose pictured; circa 1990; should be dated at bottom.
Silent Chief	Norseman pictured; circa 1990; not dated; originals *extremely* rare.
White Rose	Rose pictured; should be dated at bottom.

Oval-Shaped Plastic-Body Globes with Glass Inserts

Amoco	Never existed as an original oval globe.
Ford Sales and Service	No original ovals known; not a gas globe.
Gargoyle	Originals one-piece raised-letters.
Pennzoil	No originals known.

13 1/2in Plastic-Frame Automotive Globes
(These were probably the first reproduction globes, from about 1973 or before. The globes are not dated.)

Buick Sales and Service	Valve-in-head motor cars.
Cadillac Authorized Service	Cadillac shield.
Chevrolet Corvette	Crossed flags.
Chevrolet Sales and Service	Chevy emblem.
Chrysler Sales and Service	Chrysler emblem.
Dodge Brothers Sales and Service	Six-sided star with "DB."
Ford Benzol	Originals extremely rare.
Ford Mustang	With horse.
Ford Sales and Service	Ford script logo.
Lincoln	Black background.
Lincoln	Blue background.
Mercedes-Benz	With emblem.
Nash	With emblem.
Oldsmobile Sales and Service	With emblem.
Plymouth	With flagship.
Pontiac Service	With Indian head.
Studebaker	Studebaker old tire emblem.
Stutz The Car that Made Good in a Day	Stutz logo.
Whizzer Authorized Sales and Service	Whizzer logo.

Note: Some collectors have found original automotive globes. Though very rare, these usually appear in one-piece or metal-frame styles. On rarer occasions, glass 13.5in original inserts are found.

Metal-Frame Globes with 15in Glass Inserts

(None of the repros are dated, unless noted.)

American	With shield; originals *very* rare.
Ascot	With car; originals extremely rare; if found, probably a repro.
Associated Gas	With oil can trimmed in blue; originals rare and most known originals trimmed in green.
Associated White Gold Gas	Green, black, white; originals rare.
Beacon Gasoline	Lighthouse, yellow background; originals rare.
Central Michigan	
Bay Petroleum	Leaping lion; all 15in are repros.
Conoco	Fully detailed minuteman; never existed; original has *solid black* minuteman with no detail shown.
El Camino	Bell/mission pictured; only *one* original known, extremely rare.
Ford Sales and Service	Dark blue and white.
Gasoline	Metal perforated inserts; circa 1989; originals have a sandpaper-like surface over the metal inserts.
General Antiknock Gas	Originals are rare.
Gilmore Blue Green	Should be dated at bottom.
Gilmore Fleet	Flag shown.
Gilmore Gasoline	
Monarch of All	Lion pictured; never existed to our knowledge.
Grizzly Gasoline	With bear; originals extremely rare.
Hancock "Cock O' the Walk"	Shows rooster; originals rare.
Husky Gas	Husky dog pictured; originals rare.
Imperial	Three stars across center; originals rare.
Koolmotor High Test	
Anti Knock Gasolene	Green background.
Liberty Gasoline	Shows Statue of Liberty; originals rare.
Magnolia Gasoline	Flower in center; all 15in are repros; early 1980s; originals are 16.5in only.
Mobile Gasoline	With race car; never existed; all are repros.
Mobilgas	Pegasus.
Mohawk Ethyl	"Ethyl" written across bottom; originals *extremely* rare.
Mohawk Gasoline	Indian head shown.
Phillips Benzo Gas	Originals extremely rare.
Polly Gas	Yellow border; dated at bottom; originals very rare.
Purol Gasoline	Cast faces with arrow (circa 1981); heavy glass recessed letters; no known originals found yet, but did exist at one time.
Red Crown Gasoline	Crown shown.
Red Parrot Gas	Parrot pictured; no originals found as of this writing.
Richlube Motor Oil	Shows car; never existed; all are repros.
Sareco	Indian; all are repros; company made up.
Seaside Gasoline	Six-sided star with seagulls.
Shell Gasoline	Shell pictured in red back ground; originals extremely rare; no mint originals known to exist that say "Gasoline"; check condition.
Signal	Black background with stop light.
Sunoco, Blue	Yellow diamond in center.
Texaco	Leaded glass; reproductions usually appear on a regular metal body; originals always appear on a *very* wide (about 10–12in) and unique-looking metal body which should be painted white or green.

Texaco	Red star with green "T" in center; originals rare.
Texaco Ethyl	Smaller red star with green "T" in center; originals *extremely* rare in 15in metal.
Time Ethyl	With clock, never existed—all are repros.
Union Gasoline	Shield with red and white stripes; originals very rare.
Union 76	Red and black; no shield; never existed.
Union 76 + Ethyl	Red and black; no shield; never existed.
White Rose Gasoline	Boy holding sign; originals rare; check condition.
White Rose No Knock	Boy holding sign; originals rare; check condition.

Canadian 15in Metal-Frame Globes

B-A Service Products Nevr-nox	Dated.
B-A Service Products	
Peerless Ethyl	Dated.
Esso	With Ethyl logo.
Esso Extra	Dated.
Imperial	With three stars; not dated.
Maple Leaf Co-op Gasoline	Dated.
North Star	Dated.
Red Head Gasoline	Boy pictured; not dated.

One-Piece Gasoline Globes

(*Note:* All repros are the fired-on type.)

Airliner Gasoline	Airplane (all are repros); never existed as an original one-piece globe.
Aviation Gasoline	Airplane pictured; three repros known; circa late 1980s.
Black Hawk Gasoline	Indian (all are repros); never existed as an original globe.
Cities Service	Round; originals etched only.
Conoco	Triangle; all are repros; never existed as an original one-piece globe.
Conoco Minuteman	Man pictured; all are repros; never existed as an original one-piece globe.
Deep-Rock	Deep Rock bow-tie logo.
Diamond D-X Lubricating	
Motor Fuel	All are repros; never existed as an original one-piece globe.
Dog-On Good Gas	All are repros; never existed as an original one-piece globe.
Flying A	All are repros; never existed as an original one-piece globe.
Gilmore	All are repros; never existed as an original one-piece globe with lion on it.
Gulf No-Nox	Originals usually etched or raised letters.
Magnolia	With flower; all are repros; never existed as an original one-piece globe with a flower.
Mobilgas	Originals are etched; never existed as an original one-piece globe with horse.
Phillips 77 Aviation	All are repros; never existed as an original one-piece globe.
Phillips 66	All are repros; never existed as an original one-piece globe.
Pure or Purol	Shows arrow; originals very rare.
Richfield Ethyl	All are repros; never existed as an original one-piece globe.
Shell	Clam-shaped; do not exist yet as repros, but will very soon. Super Shell and Super Shell Ethyl are coming also.
Shell	Round-shaped, red or yellow, originals are *etched only*; never existed like this.

Shell Gasoline	Never existed with the word "Gasoline" in a one-piece globe; round shape.
Sinclair Aircraft	With plane.
Skelly	Has large "S" logo.
Socony	Originals etched only.
Socony Motor Gasoline	Name written on globe.
Standard Crown	Clear glass or smoky green tinted.
Standard Crowns	*Most* that are repros have regular flange-type glass bases. Originals usually have threaded bases with screw-on metal bottoms. However, please note that early lettered original Crowns only have regular flange bases.
Standard Red Crown	Raised letters; smaller than original (usually not painted, circa 1981). Please note that this globe, as of March 1991, is being reproduced again from the original mold. Distinct feature is the slight ridge which outlines the four crosses. Raised letters are smaller than original. Unfortunately, originals exist and look the same.
Standard White Crown	With or without hole in top; see "Standard Crowns" for details.
Sunoco	All are repros; never existed as one-piece globe.
Texaco	Originals etched or raised letters only.
Texaco Fire Chief	All round ones are repros.
Tioga	All are repros; never existed as an original one-piece globe; originals were on a glass body, glass inserts only.

Tokheim (gas pump)	No originals known of when this book was published.
White Eagle	Originals are etched only.
White Rose	Boy and slate.

Note: All small one-piece globes with a "coin slot" on top are reproductions.

One-Piece Automotive Globes
(All repros are the fired-on type.)
Buick
Chevrolet Service
Corvette
Ferrari
Ford Truck Service
International Trucks
Rolls-Royce
Note: There may be other "car or service" globes, but originals are extremely rare and usually etched glass.

Repro Gasoline Globe Bodies and Holders
•12-1/2in glass bodies are being reproduced, though not many are around.
•13-1/2in plastic bodies in several colors such as red, green, blue, yellow, black, clear, and so on, are being reproduced. Also, oval bodies are being reproduced in white, clear, and colors.
•13-1/2in glass bodies, narrow as well as the wide "lollipop" styles, are being reproduced.
•13-1/2in metal-frame bodies—99 percent of all known to exist would be reproductions.
•15in metal-frame bodies have been reproduced in metal, and also in aluminum.
•16.5in metal bodies are soon to be reproduced.

Chapter 7
Restoring Gasoline Globes

In this chapter, we will cover the restoration of gasoline pump globes. But before we get into that, we will answer a recently asked question: If you have found an etched one-piece globe, is it okay to restore it and, if so, what does that do to its value?

It is an accepted practice among collectors that an old globe—especially an etched, one-piece globe—is similar to an old Model A. It's basically all there, but it may just need a new paint job. Just as a new paint job on a Model A is definitely going to *help* its value, not take away from it, the same goes for a one-piece, etched globe.

We are speaking mainly of one-piece globes here because we don't feel there are a lot of globes that can be restored. We'll get into that later. If you have an etched one-piece that has no paint or a bad paint job, it would behoove you to increase its value by putting a good coat of paint on it. We do not feel that this takes away from its value, and that there is little difference in value in a one-piece globe with its original paint and one that has been nicely restored—if any difference at all. The value is in the etching, not in the age of the paint.

Now, which globes can actually be restored? The most obvious type that can be restored successfully is the metal-frame body. This can be done by simply taking the old body and either sandblasting or hand sanding the paint off, whichever method is required for the job. Then, apply a coat of good primer and a fast-drying enamel paint. Try to stick with the original color as closely as possible. If you don't know the original color and no one else has any idea, go by the color of the lenses. That is, choose the color that would work best with the lenses.

Some hobbyists have asked about restoring lenses. For the most part, these should not be restored. If there is just a small damaged area that calls for minor repairs, it might be worth the effort. But, generally, once a lens is worn there is little or no value to the piece. You could buy clear glass lenses and make up any beautiful globe you wanted and say that it had been restored—but the piece would then be a reproduction. This theory also applies to fired-on one-piece globes. Again, once a fired-on one-piece has lost its original paint, there is nothing left to show what was on the globe. Sometimes it is possible to identify faint markings on the globe, and try to restore it by adding new paint. Or, for that matter, you could take a blank lens or even a one-piece body and claim that it is something it is not. Simply said, once a fired-on

On the left is a one-piece etched Marland globe after general painting and before scraping with razor. At

right is the finished Marland globe (after scraping with razor).

globe has lost its paint, it is basically worthless.

So what it comes down to is that the only globes that could be restored are etched one-piece globes, raised-letter globes, and metal-body globes. The raised-letter one-piece globes include the Standard Crowns, even though they don't all have letters, and the Shells, which have recessed letters. These can—and should—be restored.

Etched one-piece globes are fun and fairly easy to restore. Collectors have restored many of these types over the years. To prepare the globe, try to get as much or all of the old paint off as possible. Use paint remover and a light metal brush. Sometimes it takes several coats of paint remover to get all the old paint off. Then take a steel wool pad and lightly wipe off the globe. Rinse the globe with water and let it dry.

Next, you need to illuminate the globe. Hook up an old wooden base with a light bulb on it to an electrical socket. When you spray on the paint, make sure it goes on evenly. Etched globes *must* be sprayed, as brushing leaves uneven marks on the globe. Work with only a small area at a time, taping off and masking the other areas. Newspaper and masking tape work best. Use a fast-drying enamel. If you are painting the globe several different colors, follow the same procedure.

If the word "gasoline" or another designation is painted around the bottom of the globe, tape off a rectangle around the word and cover with newspaper the areas you don't want painted. Once each word or design is sprayed to its appropriate color, remove all the tape and newspaper. Using a sharp razor blade, scrape off the excess paint. As you are doing this, periodically keep wet the globe with water. This prevents the loose paint flakes from sticking to the freshly painted surfaces.

Now, your globe should look as if it were new-old-stock (NOS).

Raised-letter one-piece globes are harder to restore. The old paint is often difficult to remove since it was originally fired on. A professional airbrusher may have more success. If you do attempt it yourself, it may be better to tape off the exact areas that need to be done, unlike for an etched one-piece globe as already described.

As far as broken bases, B-B or pellet gun holes, and the like are concerned, if someone can fix them with glass, they should be repaired. A professional glass repair person may be the key here. Globes with broken inserts can be made to look much better too.

By the way, ripple-glass globes have fired-on paint on the inside of the glass. If you find one that is worn, minimal touchup is okay, but don't go too far. Again, you could take a clear ripple and paint it purple and say, "Guess what I found!"

As far as Crowns are concerned (non-raised-letter types), we'll leave that up to you. For what it's worth, most collectors won't buy a rarer blue or green Crown that has been repainted. Most collectors wait until an original with good paint comes along. The problem here, though, is originality. Gold, red, and white Crowns are very common. Green, blue, silver-grey, or purple Crowns are much rarer and more valuable. A white Crown or faded red one could be made into any other colored globe easily. For instance, you could have a white Crown that is painted green. Much worse is that a later buyer of that globe actually believes he or she has an original green Crown. Repainting a Crown is acceptable in terms of restoring the globe, but keep to its original color. If you sell the globe, honesty dictates that you inform the buyer that it has been repainted.

Chapter 8
Packing Gasoline Globes for Shipment

Here are some tips on packing gasoline globes. It's a loss to the hobby to have even a single globe broken.

First of all, plan to double box the globe. This is a must! The outer box should be large, at least a 20 cubic inches. Allow at least 5–6in around all sides, top, and bottom of the globe for the first box. Styrofoam peanuts are great because they do the job and are light in weight. Once the globe is boxed, place the box in a second larger box. Allow at least 4–6in or more between the smaller box and the larger box, and again use Styrofoam peanuts or other packing material. Newspaper works well when other packing material is not available, but it gets heavy. Make sure to line the bottom of each box with at least 4in of soft padding. Place a few loose sheets of cardboard across the top of the inner box for extra protection.

When packing a glass-body globe with glass inserts, remove the inserts! Otherwise, you run the risk of damaging the inserts due to vibrations in transport, which can cause them to break. (If you've never removed inserts before, refer to the chapter titled "Types of Globes," which describes the procedure.) Place thin bubble pack, or, if not available, several sheets of newspaper (six to ten) between the two inserts and pack accordingly. Pack the glass body separately or in another area of the box. That way, during shipping it won't bump and break the inserts. By the way, never stack more than six to eight inserts on top of each other, when shipping and even when simply storing. The weight alone could break or crack the bottom insert.

When packing plastic-body globes with glass inserts, either ship them assembled or take them apart before packing. We've done it both ways with no problem. But when shipping a fully assembled globe, make sure that the three screws on the plastic body are screwed tight.

Metal-frame globes with glass inserts should be taken apart. Again, loose inserts and a metal body make a bad combination. If the inserts are very tight or hard to remove, pack them well but make sure the inserts are snug. Place the metal-frame globe inserts in a small box placed inside of a bigger box, with the metal body on top. This adds protection to the upper portion of the box in case it is hit from above or something heavy rests on it. Metal bodies are nearly indestructible.

One-piece globes are simple to pack. Just double box them and that's it; there is nothing to take apart. Remember to place two or three sheets of cardboard on top before you close up the bigger box.

On rare or expensive globes, it is best to use overnight delivery services such as Federal Express. It's not worth taking chances on breakage and although it's more costly, you'd rather not see your globe arrive in "kit" form. Avoid shipping a globe during extremely cold weather. Globes are more brittle then and break more easily, even plastic globes.

Be sure to mark the box "fragile" on all sides, insure it, and pray.

Chapter 9
Future of Gasoline Globe Collecting

Imagine how rare gasoline globes will be in thirty years, fifty years, 100 years! What will they be worth? Even the reproductions dated 1981 or 1991 will become valuable in fifty or 100 years. Imagine that!

For any types of collectibles, the most important way to preserve their history is to document as much data about them as possible. Then, as new information is uncovered, the original data can be added to and stored with the new data. This book, with all the thousands of globes listed, will be updated with more information on more globes in a second book already in progress. This way, future-generation collectors will have a resource to turn to.

But what does the future hold for the collector of gasoline globes? It is certain that more globes will continue to turn up. There are many hundreds of globes still sitting forgotten in boxes, closets, attics, or base-

ments. As these globes surface, more and more will emerge as rare and unusual types—along with the common ones as well.

The number of globes currently found in collections, both known and unknown, is staggering. As these "turn over," new globes will become available. So there will always be globes turning up. It is true, globes are getting harder to find, but they are out there.

Reproduction globes will become more prevalent as the originals get harder to find. Some will be dated, some won't—like the present situation. But, if we keep expanding the current list of known reproduction globes, we will at least have a base from which to work. The average collector who simply wants a globe to display on his or her restored gas pump will turn to reproductions due to the fact that the price (or availability) of a globe to match the selected pump color scheme may simply be out of reason.

As for the collector of the future who insists on originality, single globes or entire collections will no doubt become available as the present generation of collectors age and the collections are eventually sold off. And like today, globes will continue to be traded among collectors or otherwise moved from collection to collection.

Some globes will continue to surface from bulk plants and service stations, and many will be found in the hands of oil industry employees or retirees. As these "non-collectors" realize the value of their holdings, more and more globes will find their way to the collector market.

To enhance your own globe collecting future, it is important to travel, meet people, and ask questions. Attend the shows, subscribe to all the publications, keep in touch with other collectors by phone and by mail. Photograph your collection, and carry and show your photos so others may learn more and so you can spot the minor variations of your favorite globes and add to your collection. Good globes will be available to true collectors at reasonable prices for many years to come. Cooperate with and help others, and most will help you in return. Most of all, don't forget to appreciate the globes, as well as all forms of gas and oil advertising, as history and art, not just for the dollars and cents they represent, and you will enjoy collecting for many years to come.

Examples of various globe types include these (l-r): Hull body for 13.5in inserts, showing back insert; Gill body, showing black band to hold 13.5in inserts; Gill wide body for rare 14in inserts; and two metal bodies, low-profile (left) and high-profile.

Globe types include (l-r): glass body (wide) for 13.5in inserts; glass body (narrow) for 13.5in inserts; Coreco Gas one-piece fired-on, which shows the typical wear of a globe that was left outside for a long period (Dave Anderton); and a Standard Red Crown globe showing the usual wear at the top, with most of the paint still intact at the bottom.

Directory
Globe Listings:
List of Known Globes, Prices, Descriptions, Company Histories, Gasoline Grades

How to Use the Globe Listings

The globe listings on the following pages are arranged in three groups: major oil companies and their affiliates; independent oil companies; and generic globes and globe bodystyles.

In order to find a particular globe listing, you must first determine which classification it will appear in. A table of contents follows, as well as an alphabetical cross-reference index of brand names. If the brand name as it appears on the globe does not appear in this index, then proceed to the listings of independent oil company globes, prices, and histories. Globes are listed alphabetically by brand name in the independent section, not by company name. In some instances, however, globes are listed out of alphabetical sequence in order to be categorized with other globes from the same company. In that case, the globes from that particular company appear under the company's primary brand name. An example is Midwest Oil Company's Ace High brand. The company's primary brand name was Midwest, but for a twenty-year period the Ace High name alone was used. In that case all globes from Midwest, including those that say only "Ace High," as well as those from an affiliate that say "Trophy," appear under "Midwest." Both Ace High and Trophy are listed in their respective sections, with a note to see "Midwest."

If your globe does not appear in either the major or independent oil company sections, it could be one of the few globes that are unknown to us at this writing. Our list was continually updated before this book went into production, but with a project of this scale, we expect to discover new globes for years to come. If your globe simply is not listed, please contact us at the following addresses and we will see that your globe is listed in all future editions of this book:

Scott Benjamin
P.O. Box 611
Elyria, OH 44036
(216) 365-9534

Wayne Henderson
20 Worley Road
Marshall, NC 28753
(704) 649-3399

Major Oil Company Sections

The major oil company section is broken down into forty-seven headings. Within each of those classifications globes are listed in something of a chronological order in conjunction with the order in which affiliates were purchased by the major company listed. It is organized in a manner that is practical for collectors.

For example, all brands related to, say, the Pure Oil Company are listed under PURE: Hi-Speed, Woco-Pep, and so on, while Union 76 globes are listed under UNION. Although Union Oil purchased Pure in 1965 and the Union 76 brand name replaced Pure in 1970, collectors tend to look at Pure items as separate from Union items. The same principle applies to Amoco-Standard globes. Amoco and Pan-Am globes are listed in the AMOCO section while Standard, Utoco, and related brands are listed under STANDARD. The reason for this is, again, collectors who specialize in Amoco might have only a passing interest in Standard, and likewise most Standard (Indiana) collectors have little interest in Amoco. The table of contents breaks down the company headings and the brands that appear therein.

Globe Information

Once you locate the listing for a particular globe, you will also find a great deal of information about that globe. A typical listing starts with the COMPANY NAME and LOCATION followed by a brief history and an explanation as to why it appears with this particular major heading.

Then comes the GLOBE NAME followed by its RARITY GUIDE NUMBER, YEARS USED, SIZES, and PRICING. Descriptive text follows the listing.

Globe Names

The globe name is either the actual wording that appears on the globe, as in "SINCLAIR HC GASOLINE," or it is the term by which collectors refer to the globe, as in "SINCLAIR DINO POWER-X" (Sinclair Power-X globe with the dino logo at the top).

Rarity Guide

The rarity guide is a series of numbers, one through five, that specifies a level of rarity. It is interpreted as follows:

(1) A very common globe—readily available in collector circles.

(2) A common globe—fairly available among most collectors.

(3) Available—these globes, though available, are more scarce and thus harder to find.

(4) Rare or very rare—very few known to exist; seldom offered for sale.

(5) Extremely rare or unique—less than ten known; many are unique and a few globes listed as such are known only in old photographs.

Years Used

The "years used" indicates the time period during which the particular globe could have appeared in official use. Many logos introduced in the 1930s and first used on metal-band globes were carried over into the 1950s and later, and the same logo appeared on glass-body or even plastic-body globes. In these instances, older locations that had metal-band globes in place were not updated, while newer locations were imaged with newer style globes. Let's look at Richfield (New York) as an example:

When the Richfield shield logo was introduced in 1937, globes were designed with the logo and the brand names Richfield Hi-Octane (regular) and Richfield Ethyl (premium). These globes remained in use until at least 1956, when Richfield Ethyl was replaced by Richfield Premium. Although glass- and plastic-body globes, with the same identical design, may have been intended for use after World War II, locations with the metal-band globes in place were not necessarily reimaged until there was a brand name change and therefore a reason to update.

When Richfield Premium replaced Richfield Ethyl in 1956, the new Richfield Premium globe was made only in a 13.5in size for glass or plastic bodies. No doubt the metal-band Richfield Ethyl globe that had been on a pump since 1937 would be replaced, and in order to maintain the image, the Hi-Octane globe on an adjacent pump would be replaced with a glass or plastic globe to match. On those locations where only one product—regular-grade Richfield Hi-Octane—was offered, it is reasonable to assume that a metal-band globe, installed on that pump in 1937, would not have been replaced until 1964 when the entire Richfield brand was replaced by Sinclair.

Of the several companies that maintained the same brand or image from the 1930s until the 1950s, older style globes were often left in use for years. There are also several exceptions to the rule that metal-band globes were not introduced after World War II. Several companies—Citizens 77, Speed/Super Speed, and Mutual—regularly specified the use of metal-band globes until the manufacturers discontinued them in the late 1950s. So, you see there *are* exceptions to every rule in gas and oil collectibles.

Globe Size and Type

Lens size and body type are identified in the sizes and types category. The following descriptions are used:

1. ONE-PIECE ETCHED, BAKED, CAST, PAINTED: Solid one-piece body that the design is applied directly to either by etching and paint, baked-on paint, or a painted cast (raised) design.

2. 12, 14, 15, or 16.5in METAL: Metal globe body, of any style, designed to hold a lens of the size listed. Any special metal bodies are described in the text, so the general listing refers to either a "high profile" or a "low profile" of that size.

3. 12.5, 13.5, or 15in GLASS: Glass globe body, solid or hull type, designed to hold a lens of the size listed, with two mounting screws positioned at three and nine o'clock. Many varieties and wide or narrow widths exist. The 15in inserts, however, have no notches at three and nine o'clock.

4. 13.5in CAPCO: Any plastic-body globe designed to hold a 13.5in lens with notches at three and nine o'clock.

5. GILL, RIPPLE GILL, 14in GILL: Glass-body globe, hollow in the center, designed to hold a lens, with an external ring closed at the bottom with a bolt and nut. Ripple Gill bodies are cast in clear glass, with a textured finish and a clear or baked-on color finish designed to diffuse light. Lenses for Gill bodies have no notches.

6. OVAL GLASS: Oval glass body designed to hold an oval glass lens, with screws positioned at three and nine o'clock.

7. OVAL CAPCO: Oval plastic body with removable lenses.

8. HULL: A hollowed-out glass body. Specified as different from a GLASS BODY only when necessary, as in a Fleet-Wing red Hull glass body.

9. Any specialty bodies/shapes, such as two-piece glass or plastic. Anything unusual is described in the globe text.

Note that some one-piece and metal-frame globes had 7in bases. Typically Standard Oil used 7in base globes, but occasionally other companies did too. In our opinion, pricing these and desirability is the same.

Pricing

In the pricing specifications, the amounts listed are flat wholesale and flat retail. For instance, a globe priced to the lower side of the range would be considered a "good deal" or "wholesale" while that same globe priced to the higher side would still be a "good deal," only at retail. Market factors have determined a much wider range between wholesale and retail on the higher priced globes than on globes of lesser value. Pricing is relative to the design and desirability of a globe, but not necessarily to its rarity. The numbers are current as of fall 1993, and the *relative* values should remain the same for years to come. The pricing statistics come as a result of our many years of experience in collecting gas pump globes, and are realistic.

Descriptions

The descriptive text is exactly that: a simple description of each globe listed. Special marks within the text include the following:

• Quotation marks: They indicate the exact wording on the globe: "Flite Fuel" for example.

• All-upper-case or lower-case lettering in quote marks: This shows how letters appeared in the actual design: "regular GASOLINE" for example.

• Slash mark with quote marks: This indicates when one word was superimposed over the other in the design: "REGULAR/GASOLINE" for example.

• Ring or outline ring: Any circular color markings on the globe face.

• Band or line: Any horizontal color markings on the globe face.

• Ethyl (EGC) and (EC) logo: (EGC) refers to an Ethyl logo with the words "ETHYL GASOLINE CORPORATION" in the banner at the bottom. Used from 1926 on, although officially replaced in April 1942 by Ethyl Corporation, listed (EC) in the text. While a globe with the (EGC) logo could have been used anytime after 1926, a globe with the (EC) logo would have to date from 1942 and later.

Order of Globe Listings by Major Oil Companies

AMOCO: Amoco, Pan-Am
ASHLAND: Pepper, Ashland, Tri-State, National/White Rose, Aetna, Frontier, Freedom, Valvoline, IQS, Payless and Dance, Super-America, Oskey Brothers, North Star, Red Head, Rotary, Hoods, Tresler, Comet, Pyroil

ATLANTIC: Atlantic

CHAMPLIN: Champlin, Harbor, Eason

CHEVRON: Standard (CAL), Chevron, Calso

CITIES SERVICE: Cities Service, Lincoln Oils, Red Parrot, Loreco, Crew-Levick, Warner-Quinlan, Shoemaker, Jenney

CLARK: Clark, Target, Owens

COLONIAL: Colonial, American

CONOCO: Conoco, Marland, Western (Husky, Mileage, DS), Malco (Valley, Numex), Douglas, Kriegler, Kayo

CO-OP: Farmland (Co-op, Falcon), Cenex, Midland, MFA, Missouri Farm Bureau, Southern States, Tennessee Co-op, Growmark (Aladdin, FS), Fargo, Central Co-op, Statex, GLF, Landmark, Farmoil, Iowa Farm Service

CROWN: Crown, Thrift, Peoples

DERBY: Derby, Sovereign

DIXIE DISTRIBUTORS: Dixie

D-X: D-X, Diamond, Sunray, Premier, Barnsdall, Monamotor, Hawkeye, Iowa Gas

EXXON: Standard (NJ), Esso, Exxon, Stanocola, Humble, TP, Colonial-Beacon, Powerine, Grizzly, Litening, Oval-E, Carter, Enco, Pate, Oklahoma, Gaseteria-Bonded, Johnson, Hoosier-Pete, Ryans, Senco, Deem, Sun-Flash, Alert

FINA: Fina, Panhandle, Amlico, Elreco, Pemco, Golden Rule, Cosden, Col-Tex, Onyx, Wides

FLYING A: Tydol, Flying A, Associated, Seaside

GULF: Gulf, Wilshire, Superior 400, Coryell 70, Bulko, Traffic

HESS: Hess, Olixir, Southern, Delhi-Taylor/Billups Eastern

HUDSON: Hudson, Silver King, Hornet, Major's, Highway, Fisca

HUSKY: Husky, Hecco, Husky Hi-Power, Frontier, Beeline

IOMA: Independent Oils, Red Hat, High Hat, Royal 400

KERR McGEE: Deep Rock, Kerr McGee, Kermac, Triangle, Mileage Mart, Trackside, Peoples, Mutual, Sparky

KENDALL: Kendall

LION: Lion

MARATHON: Linco, Marathon, Tower, Speedway 79, Old Dutch, Republic, Hi-Way, Bonded, Consolidated, Cheker, Sun-Glo, Imperial, Imperial of Michigan, Rock Island, Tulsa, Colonial-Progressive, Duro, United, Zephyr (Naph-Sol), Osceola

MARTIN: Martin, Zephyr (J. D. Street), Martin Oil Service

MOBIL: Socony, Magnolia, General Petroleum, White Eagle, Vacuum-Mobilgas, Wadhams, Bartles-McGuire, White Star, Independent of PA, Metro, Gilmore, Mobilgas, Mobil

PENNZOIL: Pennzoil, Pennzip, Wolf's Head, Keystone, United, Fleet-Wing, Penn-Drake

PHILLIPS: Phillips 66, Benzo-Gas, Unique, Independent (Tulsa), Manhattan, Paraland, Wasatch, Red X

PURE: Pure, Woco-Pep, Hi-Speed, W. H. Barber (Fyre Drop, Meteor), Save More, Super Par, Pacer, Dickey

QUAKER STATE: Quaker State, Sterling

RICHFIELD: Richfield, Richfield of New York, Richfield of California, Walburn, Betholine, Lamson, Rio Grande, Rocket

SHAMROCK: Shamrock, Cliff Brice

SHELL: Shell

SIGNAL: Signal, Hancock, Watson, Regal, Billups, Spar, Rose, Supertest, SOC, Dixie Vim-Charter

SINCLAIR: Sinclair, Pierce-Pennant, Parco, Larco, Covey, Simpson, Stoll, Okaw

SKELLY: Skelly, Surfco

SOHIO: Sohio, Boron, Caldwell &Taylor, Fleet-Wing, Refiners, Canfield

SPUR: River States, RS Royal, Webb, Spur, Wood River, Ingram, Hosco

STANDARD: Standard (IN), Red Crown, Standard of Nebraska, Pep 88, Utoco, Arro, Stanavo, Rainbow

STANDARD OIL: Kyso, Standard Oil

SUNOCO: Sunoco

TENNECO: Bay, Citizens, Speed, Gulf Coast, Tenneco, Direct, Red Diamond, Dixie, Sunset

TEXACO: Texaco, Indian

TOTAL: McClanahan, Leonard, Total, Roosevelt, Michigan Maid, Mid-West, Mid-West/White Rose, Cavalier, Col-Tex, Anderson-Prichard, Apco, Kanotex, Lesh, Vickers, Bell, Knight, Ben Franklin

UNION: Union, Union 76

Brand Name Cross-Reference Index

To Find:	See:
ACTO	EXXON
AETNA	ASHLAND
ALADDIN	CO-OP/FS
AMERICAN LIBERTY	FINA
AMOCO	AMOCO
ANDERSON-PRICHARD	TOTAL
APCO	TOTAL
ARRO	STANDARD
ASHLAND	ASHLAND
ASSOCIATED	FLYING A
ATLANTIC	ATLANTIC
BARECO	D-X/Barnsdall
BARNSDALL	D-X
BAY	TENNECO
BEELINE	HUSKY/Frontier
BELL	TOTAL/Vickers
BEN FRANKLIN	TOTAL/Vickers
BENZO-GAS	PHILLIPS
BETHOLINE	RICHFIELD (NY)
BILLUPS	SIGNAL
BONDED	EXXON/Gaseteria
BONDED	MARATHON
BUFFALO	INDEPENDENT/Westland
BULK	GULF
CALDWELL & TAYLOR	SOHIO
CALSO	CHEVRON
CANFIELD	SOHIO
CARTER	EXXON
CAVALIER	TOTAL/Leonard
CENEX	CENEX
CHAMPLIN	CHAMPLIN
CHEKER	MARATHON
CHEVRON	CHEVRON
CHIEF	PHILLIPS
CITIES SERVICE	CITIES SERVICE
CITIZENS 77	TENNECO/Bay
CLARK	CLARK
CLIFF BRICE	SHAMROCK
CLOVERLEAF	KERR MCGEE
COMET	ASHLAND/Tresler
COLONIAL (GA)	COLONIAL
COLONIAL/PROGRESSIVE	MARATHON/Rock Island
COLONIAL BEACON	EXXON
COL-TEX (APCO)	TOTAL
COL-TEX (COSDEN)	FINA
CONOCO	CONOCO
CONSOLIDATED	MARATHON
CO-OP (DBL CIRCLE)	CO-OP
CORYELL	GULF
COSDEN	FINA
COVEY	SINCLAIR
CREW-LEVICK	CITIES SERVICE
CROWN CENTRAL	CROWN
DANCE	ASHLAND/Payless
DEEM	EXXON
DEEP ROCK	KERR MCGEE
DERBY	DERBY
DIAMOND	D-X
DICKEY	PURE
DIRECT	TENNECO
DIXIE (GA)	TENNECO
DIXIE DISTRIBUTORS	DIXIE
DIXIE VIM	SIGNAL
DOUGLAS	CONOCO
DS	CONOCO
DURO	MARATHON/Rock Island
D-X	D-X
EASON	CHAMPLIN
ELRECO	FINA
EMPIRE	PENNZOIL/Wolf's Head
ESSO	EXXON
EXXON	EXXON
FALCON	CO-OP
FARM BUREAU	CO-OP
FARMERS UNION	CO-OP
FELCO	CO-OP/Statex
FLEET-WING	SOHIO
FLYING A	FLYING A
FORT PITT	ASHLAND/Freedom
FREEDOM	ASHLAND
FRONTIER (NY)	ASHLAND
FRONTIER (COLO)	HUSKY

To Find:	See:	To Find:	See:
FYRE DROP	PURE	NUNBETTER	RICHFIELD/Lamson
FYR-ZON	CO-OP	OLD DUTCH	MARATHON/Speedway
GARGOYLE MOBILOIL	MOBIL	OLIXIR	HESS
GASETERIA	EXXON	ONYX	FINA/Cosden
GENERAL	MOBIL	OSCEOLA	MARATHON/Rock Island
GILMORE	MOBIL	OVAL-E	EXXON/Carter
GLF	CO-OP	OWENS	CLARK
GOLDEN RULE	FINA	PACER	PURE
GRIZZLY	EXXON	PAN-AM	AMOCO
GULF	GULF	PANHANDLE	FINA
GULF COAST	TENNECO	PARALAND	PHILLIPS 66
HANCOCK	SIGNAL	PARCO	SINCLAIR
HARBOR	CHAMPLIN	PARCO	D-X
HAWKEYE	D-X	PAYLESS	ASHLAND
HESS	HESS	PEMCO	FINA
HI-SPEED	PURE	PENN DRAKE	PENNZOIL
HI-WAY	MARATHON/Republic	PENNRECO	PENNZOIL
HIGH HAT	IOMA	PENNZIP	PENNZOIL
HIOTANE	KERR MCGEE	PENNZOIL	PENNZOIL
HORNET	HUDSON	PEOPLES	KERR MCGEE
HOODS	ASHLAND	PEOPLES	CROWN
HOOSIER PETE	EXXON/Gaseteria	PEPPER	ASHLAND
HOSCO	SPUR	PHILLIPS	PHILLIPS 66
HUDSON	HUDSON	PHILLIPS 66	PHILLIPS 66
HUMBLE	EXXON	PIERCE	SINCLAIR
HUSKY	CONOCO	POLLY-GAS (WILSHIRE)	GULF
HUSKY	HUSKY	POWERINE	EXXON
ILLINOIS FS	CO-OP	PREMIER	D-X
IMPERIAL REFINING	MARATHON/Cheker	PURE	PURE
IMPERIAL (MI)	MARATHON/Cheker	PUROL	PURE
INDEPENDENT	MOBIL	PYROIL	ASHLAND
INDEPENDENT "I"	PHILLIPS	QUAKER STATE	QUAKER STATE
INDEPENDENT OILS	IOMA	R&C	TOTAL/Leonard
INDIAN	TEXACO	RAINBOW	STANDARD
INGRAM	SPUR	RED HAT	IOMA
IOMA	IOMA	RED HEAD	ASHLAND
IQS	ASHLAND	RED PARROT	CITIES SERVICE
JENNEY	CITIES SERVICE	RED FOX	MARATHON
JOHNSON/BRIL BRONZ	EXXON/Gaseteria	REFINERS	SOHIO
KANOTEX	TOTAL	REGAL	SIGNAL
KAYO	CONOCO	REPUBLIC	MARATHON
KENDALL	KENDALL	RICHFIELD (CAL)	RICHFIELD (CAL)
KERMAC	KERR MCGEE	RICHFIELD (NY)	RICHFIELD (NY)
KERR MCGEE	KERR MCGEE	RIO GRANDE	RICHFIELD (CAL)
KEYSTONE	PENNZOIL	ROCK ISLAND	MARATHON
KNIGHT	TOTAL	ROCKET	RICHFIELD
KRIEGER	CONOCO/Douglas	ROCOR	RICHFIELD
KYSO	STANDARD OIL	ROOSEVELT	TOTAL/Leonard
LAMSON	RICHFIELD	ROSE	SIGNAL
LARCO	SINCLAIR	ROTARY	ASHLAND
LEONARD	TOTAL	ROYAL	ASHLAND/White Rose
LINCO	MARATHON	RS-ROYAL	SPUR
LION	LION	RYANS	EXXON
LINCOLN OILS	CITIES SERVICE	SA	ASHLAND
LITENING	EXXON	SAVE-MORE	PURE
LORECO	CITIES SERVICE	SEASIDE	FLYING A
MFA	CO-OP	SENCO	EXXON
MAGNOLIA	MOBIL	SHAMROCK	SHAMROCK
MAJOR'S	HUDSON	SHELL	SHELL
MALCO	CONOCO	SHOEMAKER COAL	CITIES SERVICE
MANHATTAN	PHILLIPS	SIGNAL	SIGNAL
MARATHON	MARATHON	SILVER KING	HUDSON
MARLAND	CONOCO	SIMPSONS	SINCLAIR
MARTIN	MARTIN	SINCLAIR	SINCLAIR
McCLANNAHAN	TOTAL/Leonard	SKELLY	SKELLY
METEEOR	PURE	SOC	SIGNAL
METRO	MOBIL	SOCONY	MOBIL
MIDLAND	CO-OP	SOUTHERN	HESS
MID-WEST	TOTAL/Leonard	SOUTHERN STATES	CO-OP
MILEAGE	CONOCO	SOHIO	SOHIO
MILEAGE	CS/Warner-Quinlan	SOVEREIGN SERVICE	DERBY
MILEAGE MART	KERR MCGEE	SPARKY	KERR MCGEE
MISSOURI FARM BUREAU	CO-OP	SPEED	TENNECO/Bay
MOBILGAS (VACUUM)	MOBIL	SPEEDWAY 79	MARATHON
MOBILGAS (SV)	MOBIL	SPAR	SIGNAL/Billups
MOBIL	MOBIL	SPUR	SPUR
MONAMOTOR	D-X/Barnsdall	STANDARD (CAL)	CHEVRON
MUTUAL	KERR McGEE	STANDARD (IN)	STANDARD
NORTH STAR	ASHLAND	STANDARD (NJ)	EXXON
NUMEX	CONOCO/Malco	STANDARD OIL (KY)	STANDARD OIL

To Find:	See:
STANOCOLA	EXXON
STATEX	CO-OP
STERLING	QUAKER STATE
STOLL	SINCLAIR
SUN-FLASH	EXXON/Humble
SUNOCO	SUNOCO
SUNRAY	D-X
SUNSET	TENNECO/Dixie
SUPERAMERICA	ASHLAND
SUPERIOR 400	GULF
SUPER PAR	PURE
SUPER SPEED	TENNECO/Bay
TARGET	CLARK
TENNECO	TENNECO
TENNESSEE CO-OP	CO-OP
TEXACO	TEXACO
THRIFT	CROWN
TOWER	MARATHON
TP	EXXON
TRACKSIDE	KERR MCGEE
TRAFFIC	GULF
TRANSPORT	PENNZOIL
TRESLER COMET	ASHLAND
TRIANGLE	KERR MCGEE
TRI-STATE	ASHLAND
TULSA	MARATHON/Rock Island
TYDOL	FLYING A
UNION 76	UNION
UNIQUE	PHILLIPS
UNITED	MARATHON/Rock Island
UNITED (PA)	PENNZOIL
UTOCO	STANDARD (IN)
VALLEY	CONOCO/Malco
VALVOLINE	ASHLAND
VICO/PEP88	STANDARD (IN)
VICKERS	TOTAL
WADHAMS	MOBIL
WARNER-QUINLAN	CITIES SERVICE
WASATCH	PHILLIPS 66
WATSON	SIGNAL/Hancock
WEBB	SPUR
WESTERN	CONOCO
WHITE EAGLE	MOBIL
WHITE ROSE	ASHLAND
WHITE ROSE (MIDWEST)	TOTAL/Leonard
WHITE STAR	MOBIL
WIDES	FINA
WILSHIRE	GULF
WOCO-PEP	PURE
WOLF'S HEAD	PENNZOIL
WOOD RIVER	SPUR
ZEPHYR (NAPH-SOL)	MARATHON/Rock Island
ZEPHYR (J D STREET)	MARTIN

Gasoline Grades

For your convenience, the following listing of gasoline trade names and their respective grades and time spans are included along with the globe listings and historical material in this book. All dates are approximate, and some products were offered regionally or were experimented with in certain areas of the country outside of the time spans listed.

Gasoline marketing was in a constant state of change from the time the first premium grades were introduced in the early 1920s until most marketers settled on a three-unleaded-grade system in the late 1980s. Of particular interest to collectors are the depression-era sub-regular grades. These products, of minimal quality offered at minimal price, were used for relatively short periods in the 1930s and were not available at all stations, making collectibles related to these products much rarer than items from the regular and premium grades offered by that brand at that time.

AMOCO AND PAN-AM
AMOCO-GAS: single grade 1915-1922; unleaded premium grade 1922-1932
AMOCO: unleaded premium grade 1932-1961
AMERICAN STRATE: regular grade 1922-1926; sub-regular grade 1926-1937
AMERICAN GAS: regular grade 1926-1961

ARTEX: sub-regular grade 1934-1947
AMERICAN ETHYL : experimental premium grade 1933-1935
PAN-AM: single grade 1923-1925; regular grade 1925-1939
PAN-AM PURPLE: premium grade 1925-1929
PAN-AM ETHYL: premium grade 1929-1932
PAN-AM ORANGE: premium grade 1932-1939
PAN-AM BLUE: sub-regular grade 1929-1932
PAN-AM QUALITY: regular grade 1939-1956
PAN-AM PREMIUM: premium grade 1939-1956
PAN-AM ECONOMY: sub-regular grade 1939-1947
AMERICAN: regular grade 1956-1961
AMOCO: premium grade 1956-1961

ASHLAND
WHITE PEPPER: regular grade 1924-1935
RED PEPPER ANTI-KNOCK: benzol premium grade 1926-1946
GREEN PEPPER ANTI-KNOCK: ethyl premium grade 1928-1935
SUPER PEPPER: regular grade 1935-1946
ASHLAND FLYING OCTANES: regular grade 1946-1968
ASHLAND FLYING OCTANES ETHYL: premium grade 1946-1960
ASHLAND A-PLUS: premium grade 1960-1968

ATLANTIC
ATLANTIC GASOLINE: single grade 1915-1927; regular grade 1927-1932
ATLANTIC 68-70: premium grade 1925-1928
ATLANTIC ETHYL: premium grade 1927-1936
ATLANTIC CAPITOL: sub-regular grade 1928-1935
ATLANTIC WHITE FLASH: regular grade 1932-1953
ATLANTIC HI-ARC: premium grade 1936-1953
ATLANTIC: regular grade 1953-1970
ATLANTIC PREMIUM: premium grade 1953-1957
ATLANTIC IMPERIAL: premium grade 1957-1970

CHAMPLIN
CHAMPLIN GASOLINE single grade 1920-1927; regular grade 1927-1962
CHAMPLIN PRESTO premium grade 1927-1930; middle grade 1930-1956
CHAMPLIN ETHYL premium grade 1930-1956
CHAMPLIN REGULAR regular grade 1962-1970
CHAMPLIN DE LUXE premium grade 1962-1970

CHEVRON
West Coast Marketing Area:
RED CROWN GASOLINE single grade 1910-1926; regular grade 1926-1930
RED CROWN ETHYL premium grade 1926-1936
STANDARD GASOLINE regular grade 1930-1946
STANDARD ETHYL premium grade 1936-1940
STANDARD SUPREME W/ETHYL premium grade 1940-1946
STANDARD FLIGHT sub-regular grade 1938-1946
CHEVRON GASOLINE regular grade 1946-c1970
CHEVRON SUPREME premium grade 1946-c1970
Rocky Mountain Marketing Area:
CALSO GASOLINE regular grade 1938-1946
CALSO SUPREME W/ETHYL premium grade 1938-1946
CALSO FLIGHT sub-regular grade 1938-1946
CHEVRON GASOLINE regular grade 1946-c1970
CHEVRON SUPREME premium grade 1946-c1970
Northeastern Marketing Area:
CALSO GASOLINE regular grade 1946-1957
CALSO SUPREME premium grade 1946-1957
CHEVRON GASOLINE regular grade 1957-c1970
CHEVRON SUPREME premium grade 1957-c1970

CITIES SERVICE
CITIES SERVICE regular grade 1914-1947
KOOLMOTOR benzol grade 1914-1947
CITIES SERVICE ETHYL premium grade 1927-1947
CITIES SERVICE REGULAR regular grade 1946-1954
CITIES SERVICE PREMIUM premium grade 1946-1954
CITIES SERVICE regular grade 1954-1956
CITIES SERVICE 5-D PREMIUM premium grade 1954-1956
CITIES SERVICE MILEMASTER regular grade 1956-1965
CITIES SERVICE SUPER 5-D premium grade 1956-1965

CLARK
CLARK SUPER 100 premium grade 1932-1971

COLONIAL
COLONIAL EAGLE regular grade 1956-c1970
COLONIAL ROYAL EAGLE premium grade 1956-c1970
COLONIAL GOLDEN EAGLE super-premium grade 1956-1962

CONOCO
CONOCO GASOLINE single grade 1913-1926; regular grade

1926-1935
CONOCO ETHYL premium grade 1926-1950
CONOCO BRONZE regular grade 1936-1950
CONOCO regular grade 1950-c1965
CONOCO SUPER premium grade 1950-1954
CONOCO ROYAL premium grade 1954-c1965

CROWN
CROWN regular grade 1931-1956
CROWNZOL benzol premium grade 1931-1956
CROWN SILVER regular grade 1956-1973
CROWN GOLD premium grade 1956-1973

DERBY
DERBY GASOLINE single grade 1920-1930
DERBY GASOLINE regular grade 1930-1946
DERBY FLEXGAS ETHYL premium grade 1930-1962
DERBY FLEXGAS regular grade 1946-1962
DERBY regular grade 1962-c1970
DERBY PREMIUM ETHYL premium grade 1962-c1970

DIXIE DISTRIBUTORS
DIXIE OILS GASOLINE regular grade 1926-1928
DIXIE HI-TEST premium grade 1926-1928
DIXIE POWER-TO-PASS regular grade 1931-c1960
DIXIE ETHYL premium grade 1931-1949
DIXIE PREMIUM premium grade 1949-c1960
DIXIE BLUE sub-regular grade 1930-1932
DIXOLINE sub-regular grade 1932-1940
Note: From 1928 until 1931, Dixie marketed at least six grades of gasoline. The grade relationships of these products cannot be determined.

D-X
DIAMOND regular grade 1920-1933
NEVR NOX premium grade 1920-1933
DIAMOND D-X LUB MOTOR FUEL regular grade 1933-1936
NEVR NOX ETHYL premium grade 1933-1936
D-X LUBRICATING MOTOR FUEL regular grade 1936-1946
D-X ETHYL premium grade 1936-1946
POWER sub-regular grade 1933-1946
D-X LUBRICATING GASOLINE regular grade 1946-1968
D-X ETHYL premium grade 1946-1955
D-X BORON premium grade 1955-1968

ESSO
STANDARD MOTOR GASOLINE single grade 1911-1924
STANDARD GASOLINE regular grade 1924-1933
STANDARD ETHYL GASOLINE premium grade 1924-1926
ESSO premium grade 1926-1939
ESSOLENE regular grade 1933-1939
ACTO sub-regular grade 1933-1939
ESSO regular grade 1939-1972
ESSO EXTRA premium grade 1939-1972
GOLDEN ESSO EXTRA super-premium grade 1956-1961
ESSO PLUS sub-regular grade 1961-1972
Note: As a general rule, for Esso affiliate brands (except Humble) substitute the brand name for Esso in the grade; for instance, "Carter Extra," "Enco Plus," and so on. Humble grade names are unique and thus listed below.
HUMBLE FLASH-LIGHT single grade 1922-1928
HUMBLE FLASHLIKE regular grade 1928-1932
HUMBLE FLASHLIKE W/ETHYL premium grade 1929-1932
HUMBLE MOTOR FUEL regular grade 1932-1939
ESSO premium grade 1932-1939
ACTO sub-regular grade 1932-1939
HUMBLE regular grade 1939-1961
ESSO EXTRA premium grade 1939-1961
THRIFTANE sub-regular grade 1939-1947
GOLDEN ESSO EXTRA super-premium grade 1958-1961

FLYING A
Eastern Tydol Region:
TYDOL GASOLINE single grade 1910-1926; regular grade 1926-1942
TYDOL ETHYL premium grade 1926-1942
TIDEX sub-regular grade 1935-1946
TYDOL FLYING A GASOLINE regular grade 1942-1956
TYDOL ETHYL premium grade 1942-1950
TYDOL FLYING A ETHYL premium grade 1950-1956
FLYING A GASOLINE regular grade 1956-1960
FLYING A SUPER EXTRA premium grade 1956-1960
Western Associated Region
ASSOCIATED GASOLINE single grade 1915-1926; regular grade 1926-1932
ASSOCIATED ETHYL premium grade 1926-1932
ASSOCIATED FLYING A regular grade 1932-1940

ASSOCIATED AVIATION ETHYL premium grade 1930-1940
FLYING A GASOLINE regular grade 1940-1956
FLYING A ETHYL premium grade 1940-1956

GULF
GOOD GULF GASOLINE single grade 1913-1926; regular grade 1926-1985
GULF NO NOX premium grade 1926-1982
GULF TRAFFIC sub-regular grade 1935-1942
GULF CREST super-premium grade 1956-1962
GULFTANE sub-regular grade 1962-1975

HUDSON
HUDSON GASOLINE regular grade 1933-1946
HUDSON TRANSPORT sub-regular grade 1933-1946
HUDSON REGULAR regular grade 1946-c1970
HUDSON AAA-1 ETHYL premium grade 1938-1950
HUDSON ETHYL premium grade 1950-1962

KERR McGEE
DEEP ROCK GASOLINE regular grade 1920-1932
KANT NOCK GASOLINE premium grade 1920-1928
KANT NOCK W/ETHYL premium grade 1928-1932
SUPER KANT NOCK GASOLINE premium grade 1932-1936
DEEP ROCK REGULAR GASOLINE regular grade 1932-1936
DEEP ROCK SUPER GASOLINE regular grade 1936-1950
DEEP ROCK ETHYL GASOLINE premium grade 1936-1950
DEEP ROCK GREEN sub-regular grade 1936-1940
DEEP ROCK REGULAR regular grade 1950-1980
DEEP ROCK PREMIUM premium grade 1950-1980
KERR McGEE REGULAR regular grade 1965-c1980
KERR McGEE PREMIUM premium grade 1965-c1980

KENDALL
KENDALL GASOLINE single grade 1922-1926; regular grade 1926-1946
KENDALL ETHYL premium grade 1926-1946
KENDALL POLLY POWER regular grade 1946-1976
KENDALL DeLUXE premium grade 1946-1970
KENDALL SUPER DeLUXE premium grade 1970-1976

LION
LION GASOLINE single grade 1924-1930; regular grade 1930-1956
LION ETHYL premium grade 1930-1946
LION KNIX KNOX premium grade 1946-1956

MARATHON
MARATHON GASOLINE single grade 1920-1926; regular grade 1926-1954
MARATHON ETHYL premium grade 1926-1946
MARATHON MILE MAKER premium grade 1946-1954; regular grade 1954-present
MARATHON SUPER-M premium grade 1954-present

MOBILGAS
SOCONY MOTOR GASOLINE single grade 1915-1922; regular grade 1922-1926
SOCONY SPECIAL premium grade 1922-1926
SOCONY regular grade 1926-1934
SOCONY ETHYL premium grade 1926-1934
MOBILGAS regular grade 1934-1962
MOBILGAS ETHYL premium grade 1932-1936
MOBILGAS SPECIAL premium grade 1936-1962
METRO sub-regular grade 1934-1955
Note: Various Mobilgas affiliates adopted these trademarks at various times during the 1930s. The listing above represents only the northeastern "Socony" marketing-area grade progression.

PENNZOIL
PENNZOIL single grade 1921-1926; regular grade 1926-1936
PENNZOIL ETHYL premium grade 1926-1936
PENNZIP regular grade 1936-1958
PENNZIP ETHYL premium grade 1936-1958
TRANSPORT GASOLINE sub-regular grade 1946-1958

PHILLIPS 66
PHILLIPS 66 regular grade 1928-1959
PHILLIPS 66 ETHYL leaded premium grade 1929-1953
FLITE FUEL premium grade 1953-c1980
SIXTY SIX regular grade 1959-c1980
PHILBLUE sub-regular grade 1928-1930
PHILLIPS UNIQUE sub-regular grade 1930-1940
PHILLIPS BENZO-GAS benzol premium grade 1928-1934
PHILLIPS 77 unleaded premium grade 1929-1935
PHILLIPS 77 AVIATION unleaded premium grade 1933-1935
Note: Phillips 77 and 77 Aviation were high-octane gasolines made without tetraethyl lead. The high-octane properties came from blending refined gasoline with natural gasoline.

PURE

Northeastern Primary Marketing Area
PUROL GASOLINE regular grade 1914-1933
DETONOX premium grade 1926-1929
ENERGEE DETONOX premium grade 1929-1930
PUROL PEP benzol premium grade 1927-1932; regular grade 1932-1939
PUROL ETHYL premium grade 1932-1939
XCEL sub-regular grade 1934-1937
PURE PEP regular grade 1939-1961
PURE ETHYL premium grade 1929-1947
PURE PREMIUM premium grade 1947-1961
PURE FIREBIRD REGULAR regular grade 1961-1970
PURE FIREBIRD SUPER premium grade 1961-1970
Southern Wofford Marketing Area
WOCO-PEP benzol premium grade 1926-1942
WOCO-ETHYL premium grade 1926-1932
PUROL PEP regular grade 1927-1939
PUROL ETHYL premium grade 1932-1939
XCEL sub-regular grade 1934-1937
PURE PEP regular grade 1935-1961
PURE ETHYL premium grade 1939-1947
PURE PREMIUM premium grade 1947-1961
PURE FIREBIRD REGULAR regular grade 1961-1970
PURE FIREBIRD SUPER premium grade 1961-1970

QUAKER STATE

STERLING GASOLINE regular grade 1926-c1970
STERLING ETHYL premium grade 1926-1960
STERLING SUPER BLEND premium grade 1960-c1970
EMOLENE BLUE sub-regular grade 1932-1935
EMOLENE GASOLINE sub-regular grade 1935-1940

RICHFIELD

West Coast Marketing Area (prior to breakup):
RICHFIELD GASOLINE OF POWER regular grade 1920-1937
RICHFIELD AVIATION premium grade 1924-1928
RICHFIELD ETHYL premium grade 1928-1937
East Coast Marketing Area (prior to breakup):
RICHFIELD GASOLINE OF POWER regular grade 1926-1937
RICHFIELD ETHYL premium grade 1928-1937
BLUE STREAK GASOLINE sub-regular grade 1926-1928
ROCOR sub-regular grade 1928-1937
Richfield Oil Company of New York 1937-1964:
RICHFIELD HI-OCTANE regular grade 1937-1964
RICHFIELD ETHYL premium grade 1937-1956
RICHFIELD PREMIUM premium grade 1956-1964
ROCOR sub-regular grade 1937-1946
Richfield Oil Company of California 1937-1970:
RICHFIELD HI-OCTANE regular grade 1937-1970
RICHFIELD ETHYL premium grade 1937-1954
RICHFIELD BORON premium grade 1954-1970

SHAMROCK

SHAMROCK TRAIL MASTER regular grade c1946-c1980
SHAMROCK CLOUD MASTER premium grade c1946-c1980

SHELL

SHELL GASOLINE single grade 1912-1926; regular grade 1926-c1980
SHELL 40 AVIATION unleaded premium grade 1928-1932
SUPER SHELL ETHYL premium grade 1926-1934
SUPER SHELL premium grade 1934-1940
SHELL PREMIUM premium grade 1940-1957
SUPER SHELL premium grade 1957-c1980
SILVER SHELL (East) sub-regular grade 1934-1939
SHELL GREEN STREAK (West) sub-regular grade 1934-1939

SINCLAIR

SINCLAIR GASOLINE single grade 1916-1922; regular grade 1922-1937
SINCLAIR BENZOL benzol premium grade 1922-1926
SINCLAIR AIRCRAFT benzol premium grade 1925-1931
SINCLAIR HC premium grade 1926-1937; regular grade 1937-1961
SINCLAIR ETHYL premium grade 1937-1953
SINCLAIR POWER-X premium grade 1953-1961
SINCLAIR GREEN sub-regular grade 1932-1933
SINCLAIR US MOTOR SPEC. sub-regular grade 1930-1938
SINCLAIR PENNANT sub-regular grade 1930-1934
SINCLAIR DINO GASOLINE regular grade 1961-c1980
SINCLAIR DINO SUPREME premium grade 1961-c1980
Note: Sinclair sub-regular grades were regional.

SKELLY

SKELLY AROMAX regular grade 1928-1940
SKELLY AROMAX ETHYL premium grade 1928-1936
SKELLY POWERMAX premium grade 1936-1940
SKELLY FORTIFIED regular grade 1940-1950
SKELLY FORTIFIED PREMIUM premium grade 1940-1950
SKELLY GASOLINE regular grade 1950-1956
SKELLY PREMIUM premium grade 1950-1954
SKELLY SUPREME premium grade 1954-1956
SKELLY REGULAR regular grade 1956-1972
SKELLY KEOTANE regular grade 1956-1972

SOHIO

RED CROWN GASOLINE single grade 1912-1926; regular grade 1926-1930
RED CROWN ETHYL premium grade 1926-1928
SOHIO ETHYL GASOLINE premium grade 1928-1939
SOHIO X-70 regular grade 1930-1950
REKNOWN GREEN sub-regular grade 1932-1934
REKNOWN sub-regular grade 1934-1942
SOHIO SUPREME premium grade 1939-1954
SOHIO X-TANE regular grade 1950-1958
BORON SUPREME premium grade 1954-c1980
EXTRON regular grade 1958-c1980

SPUR

SPUR GASOLINE single grade 1928-1946; regular grade 1946-1962
SPUR ETHYL premium grade 1946-1962
SPUR REGULAR regular grade 1962-1965
SPUR PREMIUM premium grade 1962-1965
Note: In 1965, Spur introduced a five-grade blending system. Some locations continued to market only Spur Regular and Spur Premium, while most locations offered GO-1 through GO-5 blended grades.

STANDARD

RED CROWN POLARINE GASOLINE single grade 1912-1916
RED CROWN GASOLINE single grade 1916-1922; regular grade 1922-1941
SOLITE A PERFECT GASOLINE premium grade 1922-1926
RED CROWN ETHYL premium grade 1924-1936
SOLITE WITH ETHYL premium grade 1936-1941
STANOLIND BLUE sub-regular grade 1931-1941
STANOLIND GREEN naptha grade 1938-1941
RED CROWN regular grade 1941-1961
WHITE CROWN premium grade 1941-1956
GOLD CROWN premium grade 1956-1961
BLUE CROWN sub-regular grade 1941-1948
AMERICAN REGULAR regular grade 1961-1971
AMERICAN SUPER PREMIUM premium grade 1961-1971

STANDARD OIL

CROWN GASOLINE single grade 1912-1926; regular grade 1926-1961
CROWN ETHYL premium grade 1926-1940
CROWN EXTRA premium grade 1940-1961
KYSO GREEN sub-regular grade 1930-1933
SUPER CROWN EXTRA super-premium grade 1956-1961

SUNOCO

SUNOCO single grade 1920-1931
BLUE SUNOCO single grade 1931-1946; regular grade 1946-1950; single grade 1950-1956
SUNOCO DYNAFUEL premium grade 1946-1950
Note: In 1956, Sunoco introduced the first gasoline blending pump. Initially six grades, Blue Sunoco 200 through Blue Sunoco 250, were offered. Sub-regular grades 180 and 190 were added in the 1960s, as well as Super Premium 260. The following grades were offered independent of the blending pump in select markets.
BLUE SUNOCO 200 regular grade 1956-c1970
BLUE SUNOCO 190 sub-regular grade 1961-c1970

TEXACO

TEXACO GASOLINE single grade 1910-1926
TEXACO ETHYL premium grade 1926-1932
TEXACO FIRE CHIEF regular grade 1932-c1985
TEXACO FIRE CHIEF ETHYL premium grade 1932-1938
TEXACO SKY CHIEF premium grade 1938-c1985
INDIAN GASOLINE sub-regular grade 1933-1942

UNION

UNION GASOLINE single grade 1913-1926; regular grade 1926-1932
UNION ETHYL premium grade 1926-1946
UNION 76 GASOLINE regular grade 1932-1955
UNION 7600 GASOLINE premium grade 1946-1955
REGULAR 7600 GASOLINE regular grade 1955-1965
ROYAL 76 GASOLINE premium grade 1955-1965

Major Oil Companies and Their Affiliates

AMOCO and PAN AM
Standard Oil Company of Indiana, Chicago, Illinois

The American Oil Company was founded in Baltimore in 1910, refining and marketing kerosene. In 1915, they introduced a gasoline-benzol blend they called Amoco-Gas. Without crude oil production of their own and forced to buy on the open market, they operated with the possibility of shortage at any time. This was remedied in 1923 when a supply agreement was signed with Pan American Petroleum, based in New Orleans, giving 50 percent interest in American Oil to Pan-Am in return for the assurance of crude oil supply.

Pan American, primarily a production company with trace marketing in several southern states, had begun its operations in 1916 and by the time of the 1923 merger, was already an international company. In 1925 Standard Oil of Indiana purchased a controlling interest in Pan-Am, in the wake of Pan-Am's involvement in the Teapot Dome scandal. In 1933 Pan-Am, now a subsidiary of Standard of Indiana, purchased the remaining 50 percent of American Oil and converted the Pan-Am marketing facilities in Georgia and Florida to the Amoco brand, retaining the Pan-Am name in Alabama, Louisiana, Mississippi, and Tennessee. Arkansas and Kentucky were added at a later date, while the Amoco brand name was used in all states from Maine to Florida as well as West Virginia and Ohio. Standard bought the remaining interest in Pan-Am in 1954, and in 1956 the Pan-Am name was replaced by Amoco in the six southern states.

About the same time, the Amoco brand had been introduced in Texas. While the eastern seaboard states and Texas retained the old red and black Amoco oval, marketing in the former Pan-Am states was under an Amoco torch and oval logo similar to the ones used by Standard and affiliates since 1946. In 1961, the entire Amoco marketing area was converted to the American brand name and pumps were reimaged. At this time, all globes were discontinued. Thus, see the STANDARD listing for Standard and Utoco globes.

American Oil Company, Baltimore, Maryland
AMOCO GAS
(4) 1915-1932 15in Metal $275-$450
AMOCO GAS
(4) 1915-1932 16.5in Metal $275-$500
Deep red upper and lower sections, with horizontal black band across the middle. White lines top and bottom, and white "AMOCO-GAS" on black band.
AMOCO
(2) 1932-1961 15in Metal $250-$400
AMOCO
(2) 1940-1961 Gill $250-$350
Same as above, with "AMOCO" replacing "AMOCO-GAS" on black band.
AMERICAN GAS
(1) 1926-1961 15in Metal $250-$400
AMERICAN GAS
(1) 1940-1961 Gill $250-$350
Bright blue outer ring with large red dot in the center. White "AMERICAN" around top of blue ring, "GAS" around bottom.
AMERICAN STRATE
(5) 1922-1938 15in $300-$550
White globe face with red "AMERICAN" arched around top and red "STRATE" arched around bottom. Small red and blue shield in center, with blue "GASOLINE" in outlined box across shield.
AMERICAN ETHYL
(5) 1933-1934 15in Metal No Listing
Experimental. White globe face with thick red outline ring. Red-outlined yellow band arched across upper globe face. Black "AMERICAN" arched in yellow band. Ethyl (EGC) logo on lower globe face, below band.
AMERICAN ETHYL
(5) 1934-1935 15in Metal No Listing
Experimental. This globe appears in a photo taken at an Amoco station in West Virginia in 1934.
Colors cannot be determined, but globe has dark-colored outer ring around light-colored center.
Ethyl (EGC) shield in center. "AMERICAN" in upper half of ring, "GASOLINE" in lower half.
Ring is split by light-colored line at center on either side.
ARTEX
(3) 1934-1947 15in Metal $250-$400

ARTEX
(4) 1940-1961 Gill $225-$325
White globe face with large red script "Artex" at angle across face. Lettering has bright blue dropshade.
(AMOCO) DIESEL FUEL
(4) 1946-1961 15in Metal $200-$300
Very plain blue "DIESEL" over "FUEL" on white face.

Pan-Am Southern Corporation, New Orleans, Louisiana
See Amoco introduction for Pan-Am history.
PAN-AM GASOLINE
(5) 1923-1925 One-Piece Cast Square $1,200-$1,800
Earliest known Pan-Am globe is a rounded diamond shaped one-piece globe. No other details are known.
PAN-AM GASOLINE/MOTOR OIL
(5) 1925-1929 15in Metal $350-$600
Cream-colored face with green band across center and red-ringed sunburst in center. Cream-colored "PAN-AM" on band, green "GASOLINE" around top of globe face, and green "MOTOROILS" around bottom.
PAN-AM
(4) 1925-1929 15in Metal $325-$450
Similar to above, except no lettering above and below sunburst.
PAN-AM PURPLE
(5) 1925-1929 15in Metal No Listing
Similar to red, white, and blue PAN-AM below, with "PURPLE" above sunburst and "GASOLINE" below burst.
(PAN-AM) BLUE
(5) 1929-1930 15in Capco No Listing
White globe face with blue outline ring. Blue outline ring around center circle with blue sunburst design in center circle. Blue lines across center form white band across center of globe. Blue "BLUE" in center band. Small "P.A.P.CO." (for Pan American Petroleum Company) at bottom of face.
PAN-AM
(4) 1929-1939 15in Metal $325-$550
Similar to PAN-AM GASOLINE/MOTOR OIL above, except blue band across center and sunburst are outlined by heavy red line. White background. No lettering top and bottom.
PAN-AM
(5) 1929-1935 13.5in Glass No Listing
Same as 15in metal.
PAN-AM ETHYL
(5) 1929-1932 15in Metal $325-$550
White globe face with blue outline around edge and center circle. Large Ethyl (EGC) logo in center. Red "PAN-AM" around top, "GASOLINE" around bottom.
PAN-AM ORANGE
(4) 1932-1939 15in Metal $300-$550
White globe face with black band across center. White "PAN-AM" on band. Orange sunburst with outline in center, orange-colored "ORANGE" arched across top, and orange-colored "GASOLINE" arched around bottom.
PAN-AM QUALITY
(3) 1939-1947 15in Metal $300-$525
White face with blue band across center. Red sunburst in center. White "PAN-AM" on band, red "QUALITY" arched above sunburst, "GASOLINE" below sunburst.
PAN-AM PREMIUM
(4) 1939-1947 15in Metal $300-$525
Same as above, except "PREMIUM" replaces "QUALITY" at top of globe face.
PAN-AM ECONOMY
(4) 1939-1947 15in Metal $300-$525
Same as above, but "ECONOMY" replaces "QUALITY" at top of globe face.
PAN-AM TORCH and oval
(4) 1947-1956 12.5in Glass $225-$375
Pan-Am "Torch and Oval" logo on solid white face.
AMOCO
(3) 1956-1961 12.5in Glass $200-$350
Red upper face and blue lower face, with white band across center. White band has red line at top, blue line at bottom, and "AMOCO" in blue.

American Strate Gasoline 15in inserts on metal body.

American Gas 13.5in inserts on Gill bodies.

Artex 15in inserts on metal body and Cities Service Oils Shoemaker Coal Corporation 15in inserts on metal body. John Phippen

Pan-Am Orange 15in inserts on metal body.

Pan-Am Economy Gasoline 15in inserts on metal body.

Tri-State Super Motor 13.5in inserts on glass body.

Royal Gasoline 15in inserts on metal body. Dave Walthers

White Rose Enarco Gasoline 15in inserts on metal body.

Valvoline one-piece etched.

Freedom Motor one-piece etched globe.

Champlin Presto Antiknock Gasoline one-piece etched globe.

Champlin Gasoline 15in inserts on metal body. Dave Walthers

Red Crown Gasoline one-piece etched globe.

Red Crown Polarine Gasoline one piece etched globe.

Red Crown 15in inserts on metal body.

AMERICAN
(3)   1956-1961   12.5in Glass $200-$350
Same as above, except "AMERICAN" replaces "AMOCO."
(AMOCO) DIESEL W/LINES
(4)   1956-1961   12.5in Glass $175-$250
White face with blue lines above and below center. Blue "DIESEL"
across center inside lines.

American Oil Company of Texas

Formed in 1955 as a separate marketing division, operating
Amoco brand stations in Texas.
AMOCO
(4)   1955-1961   12.5in Glass $200-$350
Deep red upper and lower sections, with horizontal black band across
middle. White line top and bottom, and white "AMOCO" on band.
AMERICAN GAS
(3)   1955-1961   12.5in Glass $200-$350
Bright blue outer ring with large red dot in the center. White "AMER-
ICAN" around top of ring, "GAS" around bottom.

ASHLAND AND AFFILIATES
ASHLAND OIL AND REFINING, Ashland, Kentucky

Ashland Oil was founded in 1924 as a refining division of the
Swiss Oil Company of Lexington, Kentucky, which had numerous ties
to the National Refining Company. Ashland began marketing gasoline
under the brand name Pepper. The gasolines were dyed red and
green, and remained clear as well, to market their famous Red Pepper, Green Pepper, and White Pepper products. Stations under the
Pepper brand name were operated in an area of about 250 miles
around the Ashland, Kentucky, headquarters. Branded gasoline marketing was all but discontinued during World War II, and after the
war when retail gasoline sales resumed, the brand name Ashland was
chosen, Ashland Oil having replaced the corporate name Swiss Oil in
about 1935.

Ashland has grown through the many mergers listed below, with
branded Ashland outlets found within about a 200 mile radius of Ashland, Kentucky, and with company owned and operated stations,
mostly under the SuperAmerica brand, throughout the central and
eastern United States.

Pepper
RED PEPPER
(5)   1924-1928   One-Piece Etched   No Listing
Description not available.
RED PEPPER ETHYL
(5)   1926-1928   One-Piece Etched   No Listing
Description not available.
WHITE PEPPER
(5)   1924-1928   One-Piece Etched   No Listing
White globe with black outline ring around yellow globe face. White-
outlined black expanding and contracting lettering, with
"WHITE/PEPPER" on yellow face.
RED PEPPER BETTER ETHYL
(5)   1928-1935   15in Metal $300-$600
White globe face with red "RED PEPPER" arched around top, and red
"BETTER ETHYL'" (in quotes) arched around bottom. Black-outlined
Ethyl (EGC) logo in center, with blue rays extending out from logo.
RED PEPPER ETHYL (EGC)
(4)   1935-1946   15in Metal $300-$575
White globe face with black-outlined red-colored "RED/PEPPER" on
upper face, large Ethyl (EGC) logo on lower face.
WHITE PEPPER
(5)   1928-1946   15in Metal $250-$450
Upper half black, lower white. Black outline in lower half, "White" in
white above. Black-outlined red letters on lower half "Pepper."
GREEN PEPPER ANTIKNOCK
(5)   1928-1946   15in Metal $400-$700
White globe face with thin red outline. Orange-outlined green-colored
"GREEN" over green-outlined orange-colored "PEPPER" on upper
globe face. Orange line under "PEPPER," with orange-outlined green
"ANTI-KNOCK" below line on lower globe face.
SUPER PEPPER
(5)   1935-1946   15in Metal $300-$500
SUPER PEPPER
(4)   1935-1946   13.5in Glass $225-$400
White globe face with green-outlined italic "SUPER," with speed lines
over block "PEPPER." Glass globe has green outline.

TRUCK PEPPER
(5)   1935-1946   13.5in Glass $225-$375
Red outline ring around globe face and separating upper white half of
face from lower black half. Black-outlined red "TRUCK" in upper
white area, above solid white "PEPPER" in lower black area.

Ashland

In 1946, the Pepper brand name at service stations was replaced
by the corporate Ashland brand name. The Ashland logotype "Ashland" in stylized lettering arched with descending letter height from
left to right, was introduced at this time.
ASHLAND FLYING OCTANES green
(3)   1946-1960   13.5in Glass $200-$350
ASHLAND FLYING OCTANES green
(2)   1946-1960   13.5in Capco $100-$175
White globe face with red Ashland logotype over most of globe face,
with pale green "FLYING/OCTANES" lettering in lower right corner.
ASHLAND FLYING OCTANES green/clear
(5)   1950s   13.5in Capco $100-$175
Same as above, on clear lens. Possible error globe.
ASHLAND FLYING OCTANES blue
(2)   1960-1968   13.5in Capco $100-$175
Same as above, with light blue "FLYING/OCTANES."
ASHLAND ETHYL (EC)
(4)   1946-1960   13.5in Glass $200-$375
ASHLAND ETHYL (EC)
(3)   1946-1960   13.5in Capco $100-$185
Same as above, with small Ethyl (EC) logo to the right of "FLYING
OCTANES."
ASHLAND A-PLUS
(1)   1960-1968   13.5in Capco $90-$150
White globe face, with large red "A" covering face. White "ASHLAND"
across upper part of "A," large italic white "PLUS" on crossbar of "A."
ASHLAND–No Flying Octanes
(5)   1946-1950   13.5in Glass $200-$350
Same as above with "Ashland" logotype only. Does not have "FLYING
OCTANES."
ASHLAND DIESEL
(4)   1946-1960   13.5in Capco $90-$150
Same as above, but green "DIESEL" replaces "FLYING OCTANES."
ASHLAND DIESEL
(4)   1960-1968   13.5in Capco $90-$150
Same as above, except for blue "DIESEL" lettering.
ASHLAND FUEL OIL
(5)   1946-1960   13.5in Capco $90-$150
Same as above, but with green "FUEL OIL."
ASHLAND FUEL OIL
(5)   1960-1968   13.5in Capco $90-$150
Same as above, but with blue "FUEL OIL."
ASHLAND KEROSENE
(4)   1946-1960   13.5in Capco $90-$150
Same as above, but with green "KEROSENE."
ASHLAND KEROSENE
(4)   1960s   13.5in Capco $90-$150
Same as above, but with blue "KEROSENE."

Tri-State, Kenova, West Virginia

Tri-State, an independent refiner serving much the same territory as Ashland did in its earliest days, merged with Ashland in 1930.
The Tri-State gasoline brands were retained until the early 1960s as
an Ashland secondary brand.
TRI-STATE SUPER MOTOR
(4)   1930s   13.5in Glass $200-$400
White globe face with green outline ring. Black-outlined bold red lettering "TRI-/STATE" over bold green italic "SUPER/MOTOR," with
speed lines. Lettering "TRI-" is rounded on top.
TRI-STATE ETHYL (EGC)
(4)   1930s   13.5in Glass $200-$350
White globe face with red outline. Black-outlined bold red lettering
"TRI-/STATE" at top of globe face, with large Ethyl (EGC) logo on
lower face. Lettering "TRI-" is rounded on top.
TRI-STATE
(3)   1946-1960   13.5in Glass $225-$325
White globe face with green outline. Black-outlined thin red lettering
"TRI-/STATE" on center of globe face.
TRI-STATE ETHYL (EC)
(3)   1946-1960   13.5in Glass $225-$350
White globe face with green outline. Black-outlined thin red lettering
"TRI-STATE" on upper globe face, with small outlined Ethyl (EC) logo
below.

National Refining, Cleveland, Ohio

The National Refining Company was a large refiner and marketer based in Cleveland, Ohio, and founded in 1882. Marketing was concentrated throughout the eastern and central states, with a subsidiary in Canada that was spun off as a separate company in the 1930s and survived until its 1964 merger with Shell. National marketed the famous White Rose Gasoline and for many years, their boy and slate logo being one of the best recognized trademarks in the country. After World War II, however, National was greatly weakened in the marketplace, and the major portion of the company merged with Ashland in about 1957. National White Rose stations were rebranded Ashland in 1950. Unique in the gasoline business, the White Rose brand name was franchised to Mid-West Refineries of Muskegon, Michigan, in about 1946, and although Mid-West merged with Leonard in 1955, the White Rose name remained in use in Michigan through the early 1970s.

WHITE ROSE ENARCO GAS
(5)   1915-1918   One-Piece Baked $700-$1,100
White globe with orange outline ring and orange ring around white center circle. Orange "WHITE ROSE" arched at top between inner and outer rings, "GASOLINE" at bottom, orange script "Enarco" above "MOTOR OIL" in center circle.
WHITE ROSE ENARCO GAS
(5)   1915-1918   15in Metal $300-$500
White globe face with orange outline ring and orange ring around white center circle. Orange "WHITE ROSE" arched at top between inner and outer rings, "GASOLINE" at bottom, orange script "En-ar-co" above "MOTOR OIL" in center circle.
WHITE ROSE GASOLINE boy/slate
(4)   1920-1930   15in Metal $1,200-$1,800
White globe face with multicolored boy holding red-and-yellow bordered black slate. White lettering on slate "WHITE ROSE/GASO-LINE," small lettering around slate border.
WHITE ROSE GASOLINE Milk Glass
(5)   1920-1925   15in Metal   No Listing
Same as above, except with milk glass faces.
WHITE ROSE NO KNOCK boy/slate
(5)   1922-1930   15in Metal $1,200-$1,800
Same as above, with "WHITE ROSE/NO KNOCK" on slate.
ROYAL GASOLINE
(3)   1925-1928   15in Metal $250-$350
White globe face with purple outline ring and purple 1/3 width band across center. White "ROYAL/GASOLINE" on center purple band, small "THE NATIONAL REFINING/COMPANY" just below purple band.
WHITE ROSE GASOLINE boy/slate
(4)   1926-1930   One-Piece Baked $1,200-$2,000
White globe with multicolored boy holding red-and-yellow bordered black slate. White lettering on slate "WHITE ROSE/GASOLINE," small lettering around slate border.
WHITE ROSE NO KNOCK boy/slate
(5)   1926-1930   One-Piece Baked $1,400-$2,000
Same as above, with "WHITE ROSE/NO KNOCK" on slate.
WHITE ROSE ETHYL
(5)   1926-1930   One-Piece Baked $1,400-$2,000
Same as above, with "WHITE ROSE/ETHYL" on slate.
WHITE ROSE GASOLINE boy/slate
(4)   1928-1935   13.5in Glass $450-$750
White globe face with multicolored boy holding red-and-yellow bordered black slate. White lettering on slate "WHITE ROSE/GASO-LINE," small lettering around slate border.
WHITE ROSE ETHYL GASOLINE
(5)   1928-1935   13.5in Glass $450-$750
Description not available.
ROYAL GASOLINE, THE NATIONAL REFINING CO.
(5)   1928-1935   14in Gill $300-$500
ROYAL GASOLINE, THE NATIONAL REFINING CO.
(3)   1928-1935   14in WIDE Gill $250-$400
ROYAL /GASOLINE, THE NATIONAL REFINING CO.
(3)   1928-1935   13.5in Glass $225-$325
White globe face with purple outline ring and purple 1/3 width band across center. White "ROYAL/GASOLINE" on center purple band, small "THE NATIONAL REFINING/COMPANY" just below purple band.
WHITE/boy and slate/ROSE
(3)   1936-1940   13.5in Glass $275-$400
Green globe face with 1/3 width cream-colored band across center. Cream-colored "WHITE" in upper green area, "ROSE" in lower green area, with boy and slate logo in center. "EN-AR-CO" on slate.

WHITE/ETHYL/ROSE
(4)   1936-1940   13.5in Glass $225-$350
Same as above, with outlined circle in center with small Ethyl logo inside circle.
ROYAL/GASOLINE, THE NATIONAL REFINING CO.
(4)   1936-1940   13.5in Glass $200-$325
White globe face with green outline ring and 1/3 width band across center of globe face. White "ROYAL/GASOLINE" on center band, small green "THE NATIONAL REFINING/COMPANY" just below green band.
SUPER ROYAL
(3)   1936-1940   13.5in Glass $200-$325
Green globe face with 1/3 width cream-colored band across center of globe face. Large green "SUPER/ROYAL" on band.
NATIONAL/WHITE ROSE/***
(3)   1940-1955   13.5" Glass $200-$325
Green globe face with cream-colored box with rounded sides in center. Cream-colored "NATIONAL" in upper green area, red "WHITE/ROSE" in center box, and three white stars on lower green area.
NATIONAL/WHITE ROSE/ETHYL
(4)   1940-1955   13.5in Glass $200-$350
Same as above, with "ETHYL" replacing stars in lower green area.
NATIONAL/ROYAL/***
(4)   1940-1955   13.5in Glass $200-$325
Same as above, with large green "ROYAL" replacing "WHITE/ROSE" in center box.
NATIONAL/SUPER ROYAL/***
(3)   1946-1950   13.5" Glass $200-$325
Same as above, with large green "SUPER/ROYAL" replacing "WHITE/ROSE" in center box.

White Rose/Mid-West Refining, Grand Rapids, Michigan

The White Rose brand name was licensed to Mid-West Refineries in 1946, and although Mid-West merged with Leonard Refineries in 1955, the White Rose name continued in use in Michigan until 1970.
WHITE ROSE
(3)   1946-1970   13.5in Capco $125-$175
Green globe face, with cream-colored box with rounded sides in center. Red "WHITE/ROSE" in center box.
NEW/WHITE ROSE/ETHYL
(4)   1946-1955   13.5in Capco $125-$175
Same as above, with cream-colored "NEW" in upper green area and "ETHYL" in lower green area.
ETHYL/WHITE ROSE/ETHYL
(4)   1955-1970   13.5in Capco $125-$200
Same as above, with "ETHYL" replacing "NEW" in upper green area, as well as remaining in the lower green area.

Aetna Oil, Louisville, Kentucky

Aetna Oil, dating from the 1910s, marketed through service stations in central and western Kentucky and southern Indiana. Aetna merged with Ashland in 1950. The Aetna brand was replaced by Ashland in the early 1960s.
AETNA (gold background w/mountain)
(5)   1930s   15in Metal   No Listing
Description not available.
AETNA MOTOR GAS (w/mountain)
(5)   1930s   13.5in Capco   No Listing
Red globe face with thick red and thin gold outline. Red "mountain" on lower face, with gold lettering "MOTOR/GASOLINE." Gold upper area (background), with red "AETNA" across top of globe face.
AETNA MOTOR GAS (w/mountain)
(5)   1930s   13.5in Glass $250-$425
Same as above, except white background behind mountain.
AETNA BENZOL GAS
(5)   1930s   13.5in Glass $250-$450
White globe face, with red outline ring and double red outline around red mountain in center circle. Red "AETNA" above mountain, white "PETROLEUM PRODUCTS" below. Black "THE BETTER" arched around top, "MOTOR FUEL" around bottom, with red "BENZOL-GAS" with black dropshade diagonally across globe face.
AETNA TOP QUALITY MOTOR OILS
(5)   1930s   13.5in Glass $225-$400
Similar layout as above, with black "TOP QUALITY" arched around top, "PARAFFIN BASE" around bottom, and red and black "MOTOR OILS" diagonally across globe face.
AETNA XL LUBRICATED ANTI-KNOCK
(5)   1930s   13.5in Glass $225-$400
White globe face with black outline ring. Grey, black, and white circle

design in center, with large "XL" in center of circle. Red "AETNA" arched around top, "LUBRICATED-ANTI-KNOCK" arched around bottom.

AETNA ETHYL (EGC)
(4)   1930s   13.5in Glass $200-$350
White globe face with thick red outline ring. Red "AETNA" arched around top, with large Ethyl (EGC) logo below.

AETNA LAB FUEL
(5)   1930s   13.5in Glass   No Listing
Description not available.

AETNA on white
(2)   1940s   13.5in Glass $200-$300

AETNA on white
(3)   1940s   13.5in Capco $90-$125
White globe face with green outline ring. Red "AETNA" logotype lettering, with green dropshade across globe face.

AETNA on green
(3)   1950s   13.5in Glass $225-$350
Medium green globe face with black-and-white-outlined yellow oval across center. Red "AETNA" logotype lettering, with green dropshade across oval.

AETNA on lime green
(3)   1950s   13.5in Capco $100-$175
Same as above, with much brighter lime green background.

AETNA A-PLUS
(5)   1960-1961   13.5in Capco $150-$300
White face with large red "A" covering face, same as an Ashland A-Plus globe. White script "Aetna" across upper part of "A," large italic "PLUS" on crossbar of "A."

(AETNA) MOTO-ZIP
(4)   1940s   13.5in Glass $200-$350

(AETNA) MOTO-ZIP
(4)   1950s   13.5in Capco $100-$150
Same as above, with dark green "MOTO-ZIP" lettering replacing "AETNA" on oval.

Frontier Refining, Buffalo, New York

Founded in Buffalo in 1931, Frontier Refining marketed gasoline in western New York and Pennsylvania. Frontier merged with Ashland in April 1950, and Frontier stations were rebranded Ashland in about 1960.

FRONTIER DOUBLE REFINED (BOWTIE)
(4)   1935-1950   13.5in Glass $225-$375
White globe face with large, blue-outlined red "FRONTIER" in bowtie lettering across face. Blue "DOUBLE/REFINED" below "FRONTIER."

FRONTIER DOUBLE REFINED
(2)   1950-1955   13.5in Glass $200-$325
Same as above, with blue "FRONTIER" above red "DOUBLE/REFINED."

FRONTIER ETHYL
(2)   1950-1955   13.5in Glass $200-$325
Same as above, with red "ETHYL" replacing "DOUBLE/REFINED."

FRONTIER DOUBLE REFINED (BURST)
(3)   1955-1960   13.5in Glass $200-$350
Blue globe face with large white burst covering most of face. Red "FRONTIER" across center of burst, with blue "DOUBLE" above and "REFINED" below.

Freedom-Valvoline, Freedom, Pennsylvania

Valvoline, founded as the Continuous Oil Refining Company in Binghamton, New York, in 1866, introduced the famous trademark "Valvoline" in 1873. So well known were the company's Valvoline lubricants that the company name changed to Valvoline Oil Company in 1902.

In the early 1920s, Valvoline began marketing gasoline in New York and Pennsylvania, and continued to do so until the 1944 merger with Freedom Oil Company of Freedom, Pennsylvania. Freedom had also marketed gasoline since the 1920s, and the few remaining Valvoline stations were rebranded Freedom after World War II. Freedom was in the process of discontinuing gasoline marketing, selling its stations to Esso, when the company merged with Ashland Oil in early 1950. Since that time, the primary product has been Valvoline Oils, marketed by the Ashland retail network throughout the world.

VALVOLINE GASOLINE & MOTOR OILS
(4)   1920s   One-Piece Etched $1,000-$1,700
White globe with no outline ring around face. Green and white "Corliss valve" logo in center. Green "VALVOLINE" in bowtie lettering across valve. Red "GASOLINE" arched around top, "MOTOR OIL" around bottom.

VALVOLINE GASOLINE
(5)   1920s   One-Piece Etched $1,200-$2,000

White globe with green globe face. White outline "Corliss valve" logo in center, with white "VALVOLINE" in bowtie lettering across valve. White "GASOLINE" below "VALVOLINE."

VALVOLINE PENNSYLVANIA MOTOR OILS
(5)   1920s   One-piece baked   No listing
White globe with green/white "Corliss valve" logo in center. Green "VALVOLINE" in bowtie lettering across valve. Red "PENNSYLVANIA" arched around top, "MOTOR OILS" around bottom.

VALVOLINE 100% PURE PENNA MOTOR OILS
(5)   1920s   One-Piece Baked $700-$1,200
White globe with green and white "Corliss valve" logo in center of face. Green "VALVOLINE" in bowtie lettering across center. Green "100% PURE PENNA" arched around top, "MOTOR OILS" around bottom.

VALVOLINE GASOLINE (Cast Face)
(5)   1920s   15in Metal $700-$1,100
White globe face with green and white "Corliss valve" logo in center. Green "VALVOLINE" in bowtie lettering across valve. Red "GASOLINE" arched around top, "MOTOR OIL" around bottom.

VALVOLINE GASOLINE
(5)   1930s   15in Metal $350-$750
Green globe face with white outline around green and white "Corliss valve" logo. Large white bowtie "VALVOLINE" across logo on center of globe, above white "GASOLINE."

VALVOLINE RED STAR
(5)   1920s-1930s   15in Metal $350-$750
White globe face with orange outline ring. Orange outline around white and green "Corliss valve" logo. Green bowtie "VALVOLINE" across valve on center of globe, green "RED STAR" arched around top, "GASOLINE" around bottom.

VALVOLINE
(5)   1930s   13.5in Glass $250-$450

VALVOLINE
(5)   1930s   13.5in Capco $200-$350
White globe face with green outline ring. Green-outlined white "Corliss valve" logo, with orange-outlined green bowtie lettering "VALVOLINE" across "valve" on center of globe face.

VALVOLINE ETHYL
(5)   1930s   13.5in Capco $200-$350
Description not available.

VALVOLINE MOTOR OILS
(5)   1930s   13.5in Glass $250-$450
Same as VALVOLINE above, with green "100% PURE PENNA" arched around top, "MOTOR OILS" around bottom.

VALVOLINE GO MIX
(3)   1960s   13.5in Capco $200-$325
Pale blue globe face with white band across center. White bowtie "VALVOLINE" in upper blue area, red "GO-MIX" with black speedboat and line in center white area, and white "OUTBOARD/FUEL" in lower blue area.

FREEDOM MOTOR
(5)   1920s   One-Piece Etched   No Listing
White globe with blue outline ring around white face. Blue "FREEDOM" in elongated typestyle above "MOTOR" in normal block lettering.

FREEDOM GASOLINE
(4)   1920s   15in Metal $350-$550
Yellow globe face with blue "FREEDOM" arched around top, "GASOLINE" around bottom, with four dark blue keystones joined at the bottom to a center square to form a cross. Yellow "W" in center square, with yellow "FOWCO" running horizontally and vertically on cross.

FREEDOM
(4)   1930s   15in Metal $350-$500
White globe face with four light blue keystones joined at the bottom to a center square to form a cross. White "E" in center square, with white "FREEDOM" running vertically and horizontally on cross.

FREEDOM ETHYL (EGC)
(5)   1930s   15in Metal $325-$475
White globe face with outline ring. Large Ethyl (EGC) logo in center, with dark-colored "FREEDOM" arched around top, and "GASOLINE" around bottom.

FREEDOM
(5)   1930s   13.5in Yellow Glass $750-$1,000
White globe face similar to above, with much darker blue "FREEDOM" cross on special yellow glass body.

FORT PITT GASOLINE
(5)   1920s-1930s   15in Metal $600-$900
Description not available.

Independent Quality Service

An Ashland secondary brand that operated for independent, unbranded dealers from the mid-1940s through the 1960s.

IQS
(3)   1940s   13.5in Glass $225-$375
White globe face with blue outer ring. White "INDEPENDENT" arched around top, "*QUALITY SERVICE*" arched around bottom, with red reverse-bowtie "I.Q.S." in center.
IQS ETHYL
(4)   1940s   13.5in Glass $250-$400
White globe face with blue outer ring. White "INDEPENDENT" arched around top, "*QUALITY SERVICE*" arched around bottom, with red "I.Q.S./ETHYL" in center.

Payless, New Albany, Indiana

Payless was the postwar creation of James Thornton, operating discount service stations "from Canada to the Gulf Coast," as their slogan claimed. In the mid-1950s, Payless acquired the marketing of Louisville's Dance Oil Company, Thornton having married the owner's daughter Bonnie Dance. Ashland Oil, long a supplier to both Dance and Payless, bought the operation in about 1970. A few Payless outlets remain today, although most have been converted to SuperAmerica. James Thornton formed the Louisville-based Thornton Oil Corporation after selling Payless, and continues to operate Thornton stations in six states.
PAYLESS "WHALE OF A BUY"
(5)   1946-1950   13.5in Glass   No listing
White globe face with black jumping whale in blue waves across center. Blue outlined red caption above whale "WHALE OF A BUY." Red "PAYLESS" formed lettering across lower face.
PAYLESS ROAD TESTED REGULAR
(4)   1950-1965   Oval Capco $150-$250
White globe face with deep blue outline. Red, white, and black textured "PAYLESS" across top of face, with yellow-outlined blue "REGULAR" across lower globe face and blue freeform "ROAD TESTED" across center.
PAYLESS EXTRA SPECIAL
(3)   1950-1965   Oval Capco $150-$250
White globe face with deep blue outline. Red, white, and black textured "PAYLESS" across top of globe face, with yellow-outlined blue "EXTRA/SPECIAL" in freeform lettering below.
PAYLESS GOLDEN THUNDERBIRD SUPER ETHYL
(5)   1960s   Oval Capco $200-$300
No description available.
PAYLESS NO. 2 DIESEL CLEAN FILTERED
(5)   1950-1965   Oval Capco $175-$300
White globe face with green, black, and white textured "PAYLESS" over black-outlined green "No 2 DIESEL" over much smaller green "CLEAN/FILTERED."
PAYLESS KEROSENE HEATER OIL
(5)   1950-1965   Oval Capco $175-$300
White globe face with green, black, and white textured "PAYLESS" over green "KEROSENE," over black-outlined green "HEATER OIL."
DANCE "92" A WHALE OF A BUY
(5)   1940s   13.5in Glass $350-$550
White globe face with red "DANCE" arched around top, "A WHALE OF A BUY" around bottom, and large yellow "92" in center.
DANCE "100" ETHYL
(5)   1940s   13.5in Glass $350-$550
Same as DANCE "92" above, with yellow "100" and small Ethyl (EC) logo in center replacing "92."
DANCE PINK GOLDEN POWER PACK
(4)   1950s   13.5in Glass $400-$700
DANCE PINK GOLDEN POWER PACK
(4)   1950s   13.5in Plastic $400-$700
Pink globe face with large white "D," with red dropshade covering most of face. Black and white halftone figure of ballerina superimposed over "D," with white band across lower globe face. Gold "GOLDEN POWER PACK" on band.
DANCE GENUINE ETHYL blue
(4)   1950s   13.5in Glass $400-$700
DANCE GENUINE ETHYL blue
(4)   1950s   13.5in Plastic $400-$700
Light blue globe face, with same design as above. Red "GENUINE ETHYL" on lower band.
DANCE SUPER HI-TEST green
(5)   1950s   13.5in Glass $400-$700
Green globe face, with same design as above. "SUPER Hi-TEST" on lower band.

SuperAmerica, Minneapolis, Minnesota

Northwestern Refining Company, the St. Paul Park refining unit of the Erickson family, began operating the SuperAmerica gasoline-convenience store units about 1962. In 1970 SuperAmerica, a marginal convenience-store operation, was sold to Ashland Oil and by the mid-1970s began to expand out of its north central base. Many of the Ashland affiliate brand locations, closed during the gasoline shortages of 1973 and 1978, were rebuilt as SuperAmerica convenience stores. Today, the operation is considered the model of efficiency and customer service-oriented gasoline station/convenience store chains.
SA
(5)   1962-1965   One-Piece Plastic   No Listing
White lettering "SA" on red plastic trapezoidal formed globe.

Oskey Brothers Petroleum, St. Paul, Minnesota

Oskey Brothers has operated the North Star brand stations in the north central states since the 1920s. Ashland acquired the chain in about 1980, and has since closed many locations or converted them to SuperAmerica. The company has no connection with Canada's North Star Oil Company.
NORTH STAR GASOLINE
(5)   1920s   One-Piece Baked $700-$1,000
White globe face with blue outline ring and blue ring around center circle. Large blue star in center. Red "NORTH STAR" arched around top, "GASOLINE" around bottom.
NORTH STAR ETHYL
(5)   1920s   One-piece baked   No listing
White globe with blue outline ring around globe face and around white center circle. Blue outlined red "NORTH STAR" arched around top, "GASOLINE" around bottom with Ethyl (EGC) logo in center circle.
NORTH STAR GASOLINE
(4)   1930s   15in Metal $350-$650
White globe face with large blue star in center. Blue "burst" lines out from star on each side. Red "NORTH STAR" arched at top, "GASOLINE" at bottom.
NORTH STAR GASOLINE
(4)   1946-1965   13.5in Glass $225-$350
White globe face with large blue star in center. Red "NORTH STAR" arched at top, "GASOLINE" at bottom.
NORTH STAR E-TANE
(5)   1955-1965   13.5in Glass $250-$400
Same as above, with "E-TANE" replacing "GASOLINE."
NORTH STAR R-TANE
(5)   1955-1965   13.5in Glass $250-$400
Same as above, with "R-TANE" replacing "GASOLINE."
NORTH STAR DIESEL FUEL
(5)   1946-1965   13.5in Glass $200-$350
Same as above, with "DIESEL" replacing "GASOLINE."
NORTH STAR MARINE
(5)   1946-1965   13.5in Glass $325-$550
Same as above, with "MARINE" replacing "GASOLINE."
NORTH STAR oval
(3)   1965-1980   One-Piece Plastic Oval $175-$250
Oval formed plastic faces glued to plastic band forming body. Blue ring around white area at left extending to blue area at right, split diagonally. Large red "N" on white area, large white star on blue area
NORTH STAR oval
(4)   1965-1980   One-Piece Plastic Oval $175-$250
Oval deep-formed plastic faces glued back-to-back, with same logo design as above.

Red Head Oil Co., Wooster, Ohio

Red Head, operating discount gasoline stations with service bays, unique in the industry, was founded in Wooster, Ohio, in the mid-1930s and operated stations in Ohio, Pennsylvania, and West Virginia when they were bought out by Ashland in about 1970. Many have since been converted to SuperAmerica, but some Red Head stations remain today.
RED HEAD
(4)   1945-1965   13.5in Glass $250-$375
White globe face with red and black lines forming band across center. "HI-OCTANE" arched around top, "GASOLINE" around bottom, and red-colored "RED HEAD" across center band.
RED HEAD ETHYL
(4)   1945-1965   13.5in Glass $250-$375
White globe face with black outline ring and black outline around center white circle. Red-colored "RED HEAD" logotype lettering arched around top, "GASOLINE" around bottom, with Ethyl (EC) logo in center.

Southern Oil of New York, Horseheads, New York

Operated the Rotary brand stations in New York and Pennsylvania from the mid-1920s until the 1970s, when the operation was acquired by Ashland Oil.
ROTARY
(3)   1930s   15in Metal $250-$425

Top row (l-r): Ford Benzol, one-piece baked, Ford Motor Co.; Wasatch Ethyl, 13.5in on plastic; Buffalo Gasoline, 13.5in on glass; and American Strate, 15in metal, American Oil Co. Second row: Sterling Gasoline, 13.5in glass inserts on glass body with attached Quaker sign, Peter Capell; Johnson Winged 70, 13.5in inserts on Gill orange ripple body; Hy Gold Supreme 13.5in glass inserts on glass body; and Spur, 13.5in inserts on glass body. Third row: Royal Gasoline one-piece etched globe; Texaco Ethyl red-background one-piece raised globe; Prairie Cities, 15in inserts on metal body; and Silver Gas, 13.5in glass inserts on plastic body. Bottom row: Morco, 15in inserts on metal body, Dave and Doug Geiger; Red Crown Gasoline, one-piece etched globe; Musgo, one-piece fired-on; and Badger 60–62, 13.5in glass inserts on glass body, Janice Prasher.

Top row (l-r): United Fuel Oil, 13.5in glass inserts on glass body; Guyler Anti-Knock, 13.5in glass inserts on Gill body; Pan-Am, 15in inserts on metal body; and Sinclair Gasoline with Ethyl, 13.5in glass inserts on glass body. Second row: Coreco Gas, 13.5in glass inserts on glass body; Trophy Power-flash, 13.5in glass inserts on Gill body; Canfield, 13.5in glass inserts on glass body; and Richfield West Coast, 15in inserts on metal body. Third row: Rainbow Gasoline, 15in inserts on metal body, True's Oil Company; Phillips 66 brand, 15in inserts on metal body; Metro Gas Gargoyle, 15in inserts on metal body, Peter Capell; and Purple Flash, 15in inserts on metal body, John Phippen. Fourth row: Atlantic Pacific Service Company, 15in metal, George and Donna Champ; an East Coast Shell globe with 15in inserts on a metal body, Bruce Miller; a Shell Aviation globe, 15in inserts on a metal body, Bruce Miller; and a Texaco Gasoline one-piece etched chimney-cap globe.

Top row (l-r): Globe Ethyl Gas 13.5in glass inserts on red Gill ripple body; Royaline Gasoline one-piece etched globe; Pennzoil Ethyl one-piece etched globe; and Pennzoil one-piece fired-on globe. Second row: Superior Gasoline 15in inserts on metal body; Red/Gold Crown crown-shaped globe, Standard Oil Company of Indiana; Gold Crown crown-shaped globe, Standard Oil Company of Indiana; and Green Crown crown-shaped globe, Standard Oil Company of Indiana. Third row: Oil Creek Elim-A-Nox, 15in inserts on metal body; Oil Creek Ethyl, 15in inserts on metal body; Fleet-Wing Golden 13.5in glass inserts on glass body; and Lighthouse Gasoline one-piece fired-on globe. Bottom row: Dixie Vim Regular Southern Oil Stores, Inc., 13.5in glass inserts on yellow Gill ripple body; Knight Oil Company Regular, 13.5in glass inserts on red plastic body; Red Crown Gasoline, 16.5in inserts on metal body, Standard Oil Company of Indiana; and Coastal Anti-Knock, 13.5in glass inserts on glass body.

Top row (l-r): Sunray Gasoline 13.5in glass inserts on orange plastic body; Phillips Unique 13.5in glass inserts on glass body; Indian Gasoline 15in inserts on metal body; and Hoosier Pete Heater Oil 13.5in glass inserts on glass body. Second row: Hudson Ethyl 13.5in inserts on Gill red ripple body; Purol Gasoline one-piece etched globe; Penn-Drake one-piece etched globe; and Crown Gold Gasoline 13.5in inserts on Gill body, Crown Central, Baltimore, Maryland. Third row: Sinclair Aircraft one-piece fired-on globe; MonaMotor one-piece etched globe; Signal 15in inserts on metal body; and Pennolene 15in inserts on metal body. Fourth row: Marathon Best in the Long Run 13.5in glass inserts on glass body; Marathon Super-M, 13.5in glass inserts on glass body; White Rose Gasoline one-piece fired-on globe; and White Rose No Knock one-piece fired-on globe.

Top row, left-right (l-r): Tiwoser High Test Gasoline 15in inserts on metal body; Super Shell Ethyl one-piece etched shell-shaped globe; Pure Woco-Pep 15in inserts on metal body (white porcelain); and Gulf one-piece fired-on globe. Second row, l-r: Anthony White Mule Gas one-piece etched globe; Dance Oil Company Genuine Ethyl 13.5in glass inserts on blue Gill ripple body; Phillips 66 Flite-Fuel plastic shield-shaped globe; and Rocor 15in inserts on metal body. Third row, l-r: Pierce Pennant Gasoline one-piece fired-on globe; Red Hat Gasoline 15in inserts on metal body; Independent Ethyl 13.5in inserts on glass body; and Mobilgas 16.5in inserts on metal body. Fourth row, l-r: Texaco Ethyl 15in inserts on metal body; Rebel 13.5in inserts on glass body; Fyre Drop 15in inserts on metal body; and Citizens 77 brand 15in inserts on metal body.

Top row, left-right (l-r): Arrow Ethyl Gasoline one-piece etched globe; Sterling Gasoline 15in inserts on metal body; Purol Ethyl 15in inserts on porcelain metal body; and Blake Oil Company Gasoline one-piece etched globe. Second row, l-r: Zip Rose High Compression 15in inserts on metal body; Standard Red Crown crown-shaped, raised-letters, Standard Oil of Indiana; Flying A Super Extra 13.5in inserts on Gill body; and Frontier Gas 13.5in inserts on glass body. Third row, l-r: Sinclair H-C Gasoline one-piece etched globe; The Motor Inn Gasoline one-piece etched globe; Eldred Betty Blue one-piece etched; and Indian Gasoline one-piece etched globe. Fourth row, l-r: Bristolville Oil & Gas Company Eureka Gas one-piece etched globe; Richfield The Gasoline of Power 15in inserts on metal body; Red Pepper Ethyl 15in inserts on metal body; and Ride with Rose 13.5in glass inserts on glass body.

Top Row (l-r): Signal Products 15in inserts on metal body; Beacon Security Gasoline 15in inserts on metal body; and two Marathon 15in inserts on metal body. Note the color variation on the Marathon globe faces. Second row: Shell Roxanna Petroleum 15in inserts on metal body; Shell Motor Oil 15in inserts on metal body; Shell 12.5in globe; and a West Coast Shell globe with 15in inserts on a metal body. Bruce Miller Bottom row: Eldred Betty Blue 13.5in glass inserts on glass body; Texaco one-piece etched chimney-cap globe (John Phippen photo); Pennzoil Safe Lubrication one-piece etched globe; and Hy-Speed Gyro Gas one-piece fired-on globe.

Top row (l-r): Bruin Products 15in inserts on metal body; Red Crown Polarine one-piece etched globe, Standard Oil Company of Indiana; and Bell Regular 13.5in glass inserts on orange Gill ripple body. Bottom row: Sinclair Pennant 13.5in glass inserts on glass body; Tower Gasoline 13.5in glass inserts on glass body; and White Plume one-piece etched globe.

Standard Oil of Kentucky Crown Gasoline, 13.5in glass; Texaco Diesel Chief, 13.5in capco; and American Gas, Gill body.

Top row (l-r): Tioga Gasoline 13.5in glass inserts on yellow glass body, Kyle Moore; and Columbus Gasoline 15in metal, Bruce Hastedt. Bottom row: Rainbow Gasoline 15in inserts on metal body, True's Oil Company; and Bruin Oil 15in insert for metal body.

White globe face with red and blue outline rings. Red one-line "spiral" on center of globe face, broken by large blue "ROTARY" across center.
ROTARY BENZOL GASOLINE
(5)   1930s   15in Metal $450-$800
Yellow outer ring with black outline around edge and center. Red center, with yellow triangle on top of black triangle. Black lettering on yellow triangle "BENZOL/BLEND/ANTI-KNOCK/MOTOR/FUEL/?" Red "ROTARY" arched at top in yellow ring, "GASOLINE" below.
ROTARY ETHYL (EGC)
(4)   1930s   15in Metal $300-$550
Yellow outer ring, with black outline around edge and center. White center with large Ethyl (EGC) logo and blue rays. Black "ROTARY" arched at top in yellow ring, "GASOLINE" below.
ROTA-ZOL BLEND "?"
(4)   1940s   15in Metal $300-$550
White globe face with white border area, then blue and red outline rings. Large blue question mark (?) at top center of globe face, above red "ROTA-ZOL." Small blue triangle with blue-outlined white triangle on top of it at bottom of face. Red "BLEND" in white triangle.
ROTARY
(3)   1946-1960   Gill $225-$350
White globe face with red and blue outline rings. Red one-line "spiral" on center of face, broken by large blue "ROTARY" across center
ROTALINE
(3)   1946-1960   Gill $225-$325
White globe face with blue and red outline rings. Blue one-line "spiral" on center of globe face, broken by large red "Rotaline" across center.
ROTA-ZOL BLEND "?"
(4)   1946-1960   Gill $250-$425
White globe face with blue and red outline rings. Large blue question mark (?) at top center of face, above red "ROTA-ZOL." Small blue triangle with blue-outlined white triangle on top of it at bottom of face. Red "BLEND" in white triangle.
ROTA-ZOL BLEND
(4)   1946-1960   Gill $275-$450
Same as above, without question mark.
ROTARY KEROSENE
(5)   1946-1960   Gill $225-$350
White globe face with green outline ring. Small green "ROTARY" at top of globe, above "KEROSENE" in green half-bowtie lettering. Two short green lines below.

Hood Oil Company, Norcross, Georgia
A postwar southern operation, rebranded Fleet in about 1960 and acquired by Ashland about seven years later. In the 1980s, Fleet was sold to the son of the founder and continues in operation today.
HOOD'S FLO-POWER REGULAR
(4)   1950s   13.5in Red Capco $200-$350
Light blue globe face with red and white rocket diagonally across globe face. Black "HOOD'S" arched across top, "REGULAR" across bottom, with italic red "FLO-POWER" across center with black speed lines.
HOOD'S FLO-POWER SUPER
(4)   1950s   13.5in Red Capco $200-$350
Same as above, with "SUPER" replacing "REGULAR."
HOOD'S FLO-POWER ETHYL
(4)   1950s   13.5in Red Capco $200-$350
Same as above, with "ETHYL" replacing "REGULAR."

Tresler Oil, Cincinnati, Ohio
Tresler was founded in Cincinnati in 1926 and operated retail service stations in Ohio, Indiana, and Kentucky until 1985, when they were purchased by Ashland Oil. All have since been converted to SuperAmerica.
TRESLER GENUINE BENZOL GAS
(5)   1926-1930   One-piece etched   No listing
White globe with black "TRESLER" arched around top above red "GENUINE". Large black "BENZOL" across center of globe face with black "GAS" arched around bottom.
TRESLER BENZOL GAS
(5)   1930s   13.5in Glass $300-$550
White globe face with red outline ring and large red center circle. Blue "TRESLER" arched around top, "BENZOL GAS" around bottom.
COMET
(5)   1946-1955   13.5in Glass $225-$325
Colors not available. Solid-color globe face with white oval in center. Lettering "COMET" across center of face.
COMET ETHYL
(5)   1946-1955   13.5in Glass $225-$325
White globe face with outlined white oval in center. Lettering "COMET/ETHYL" on oval.

COMET DIESEL
(5)   1946-1955   13.5in Glass $200-$325
Blue globe with red outlined white oval in center. Red "COMET/DIESEL" in center.
REGULAR TRESLER COMET
(4)   1955-1964   13.5in Capco $125-$175
White globe face with blue-outlined white oval on lower globe face. Red "COMET" with speed lines in oval. Blue trapezoid on top of oval with white "TRESLER," red "REGULAR" at top of globe face.
SILVER COMET
(4)   1955-1964   13.5in Capco $225-$350
White globe face, with blue bird with upstretched wings covering most of face. Black-outlined white "SILVER" at top of globe face, red "COMET" arched with speed lines across center of face.
TC REGULAR
(5)   1964-1970   13.5in Capco $150-$225
White globe face with large red/white/blue "TC" Tresler logo covering most of globe face. White "REGULAR" in blue band below logo.
SUPREMIUM
(4)   1964-1970   13.5in Capco $100-$150
White globe face with red outline. Thick blue outlines around, with band across center. Red italic "SUPREMIUM" on band.

Pyroil Chemical Company, LaCrosse, Wisconsin
Pyroil marketed a chemical additive for gasoline and stations adding this lubricant to their products, and sold it under the Pyroil Lubrication Gasoline trademark. Pyroil was bought out by Ashland in 1988, and continues to market automotive chemicals today.
PYROIL LUBRICATING GASOLINE
(5)   1930s   15in Metal $350-$600
PYROIL LUBRICATING GASOLINE
(3)   1930   13.5in Glass $300-$450
White globe face with red outline and horizontal red lines forming a circle in center of face. Red-outlined black "PYROIL" across center of face, with black "LUBRICATING" arched around top, and "GASOLINE" around bottom.

ATLANTIC REFINING COMPANY,
Philadelphia, Pennsylvania
The Atlantic Refining Company was founded in Philadelphia in 1866 from earlier interests of the various founders, and brought together as a production and refining company. In 1874, Atlantic sold out to Standard Oil and until the breakup of Standard in 1911, functioned as a refining division. Atlantic began marketing in 1915, after the breakup of Standard, and throughout most of its history was in constant search for crude oil to keep its refineries and service stations operating. In 1965 Atlantic, then operating service stations all along the eastern seaboard, began merger talks with Richfield Oil Corporation of California, a West Coast refiner and marketer that traces its roots back to the turn of the century. Atlantic merged with Richfield in 1966, and from 1966 until 1970 marketed under the Atlantic name in the East and Richfield in the West.
With the 1969 merger with Sinclair, a new identity was needed, resulting in the introduction of the Arco brand name. Arco replaced both the Atlantic and Richfield brands, as well as some of the Sinclair brand. By the 1980s Sinclair had been sold off and was operating as a successful independent, and Arco had abandoned marketing in the East, where the Atlantic name was reintroduced by the independent marketing company that had purchased the former Arco marketing. In 1988 the new Atlantic was sold to Sunoco, and today stations operate under the Atlantic name in the northeast. See separate Richfield and Sinclair listings for more information on these affiliated companies.
ATLANTIC POLARINE GASOLINE
(5)   1915-1920   One-piece Etched $1,200-$2,000
ATLANTIC POLARINE GASOLINE
(5)   1915-1920   One-piece Chimney Top $1,500-$2,400
White globe with red-edged red, white, and black Atlantic "crossed arrows" logo in center. Blue "ATLANTIC" arched around top, "GASOLINE" around bottom, with small black "POLARINE" between logo and "GASOLINE." Only chimney cap says "POLARINE."
ATLANTIC GASOLINE (milk glass etched faces)
(5)   1918-1920   15in Metal $700-$1,500
White globe face with red-edged red, white, and black Atlantic "crossed arrows" logo in center. Blue "ATLANTIC" arched around top, "GASOLINE" around bottom, with small blue "POLARINE" between logo and "GASOLINE."
ATLANTIC GASOLINE blue lettering
(3)   1918-1933   16.5in Metal $300-$575

ATLANTIC GASOLINE blue lettering
(3)   1918-1933   15in Metal $300-$550
White globe face with red, white, and black Atlantic "crossed arrows" logo in center on irregular red field. Blue "ATLANTIC" arched around top, "GASOLINE" around bottom.
ATLANTIC GASOLINE cast faces
(5)   1918-1920   15in Metal $700-$1,500
Cast face painted as detailed above.
ATLANTIC GASOLINE black lettering
(5)   1918-1933   16.5in Metal $300-$575
ATLANTIC GASOLINE black lettering
(5)   1918-1933   15in Metal $300-$550
Same as above, with black lettering.
ATLANTIC MOTOR OIL
(5)   1920s   16.5in Metal $350-$650
Same as above, with "MOTOR OIL" replacing "GASOLINE" on lower globe face.
ATLANTIC ETHYL (EGC) blue burst
(3)   1927-1936   16.5in Metal $275-$500
ATLANTIC ETHYL (EGC) blue burst
(3)   1927-1936   15in Metal $250-$475
White globe face with blue outlines around edge and center. Blue "ATLANTIC" arched around top, "GASOLINE" around bottom, with large Ethyl logo in center with blue rays extending out to blue outline.
ATLANTIC ETHYL (EGC) yellow burst
(3)   1927-1936   16.5in Metal $275-$500
ATLANTIC ETHYL (EGC) yellow burst
(3)   1927-1936   15in Metal $250-$475
Same as above, with yellow rays extending out from Ethyl logo.
ATLANTIC 68-70
(5)   1925-1928   16.5in Metal $275-$500
ATLANTIC 68-70
(4)   1925-1928   15in Metal $275-$450
White globe face with blue outlines around edge and center. Red "ATLANTIC" arched around top, "GASOLINE" around bottom, with blue "68-70" in center.
ATLANTIC CAPITOL
(3)   1928-1935   16.5in Metal $275-$500
ATLANTIC CAPITOL
(3)   1928-1935   15in Metal $250-$450
White globe face with red and blue squares positioned above center, and blue and red squares below center in checkerboard style. White "ATLANTIC" on upper squares, "GASOLINE" on lower squares, with black "CAPITOL" across center of globe face.
ATLANTIC RAYOLITE KEROSENE
(4)   1935-1940   16.5in Metal $375-$650
ATLANTIC RAYOLITE KEROSENE
(5)   1935-1940   15in Metal $375-$650
Green-outlined white outer ring around globe face, with green "ATLANTIC" arched in ring at top, "KEROSENE" at bottom. Bright yellow circle in center of face. Green band across center, with yellow distinctive lettering "Rayolight" on band. "Rayolight" underlined, connecting lower portions of "y" and "g."
ATLANTIC WHITE FLASH
(3)   1932-1953   16.5in Metal $250-$500
ATLANTIC WHITE FLASH
(3)   1932-1953   15in Metal   AL $250-$450
Narrow white outer ring around globe face. Center of face is divided into quarters, with upper left-lower right red, and upper right-lower left blue. White-colored "ATLANTIC" arched around edge of upper left red quarter. White-colored "WHITE" with large "dot" above "I," above centerline of face, and white "FLASH" below centerline. Very distinctive lettering.
ATLANTIC HI-ARC
(3)   1936-1953   16.5in Metal $250-$500
ATLANTIC HI-ARC
(3)   1936-1953   15in Metal $250-$450
White globe face with blue band arched across center. Double red bars arched upper left and lower right of band. Blue lettering "ATLANTIC" across top of face, white "HI-ARC" on band.
(ATLANTIC) DIESEL FUEL
(4)   1935-1953   16.5in Metal $200-$300
(ATLANTIC) DIESEL FUEL
(4)   1935-1953   15in Metal $200-$300
White globe face with bright blue lettering "DIESEL/FUEL" in center of face. No company identification.
ATLANTIC WHITE FLASH
(2)   1932-1953   Gill $250-$350
Narrow white outer ring around globe face. Center of face is divided into quarters, with upper left-lower right red, and upper right-lower left blue. White "ATLANTIC" arched around edge of upper left red

quarter. White-colored "WHITE" with large "dot" above "I," above centerline of face, white-colored "FLASH" below centerline. Very distinctive lettering.
ATLANTIC HI-ARC
(2)   936-1953   Gill $275-$375
White globe face with blue band arched across center. Double red bars arched upper left and lower right of band. Blue lettering "ATLANTIC" across top of face, white "HI-ARC" on band.
ATLANTIC (crossed arrows)
(5)   1925-1935   Gill $300-$500
ATLANTIC (crossed arrows)
(5)   1925-1935   18in Metal   No Listing
White globe face with red, white, and black Atlantic "crossed arrows" logo in center on irregularly shaped red field. This lens fits Gill bodies, but was originally used as a light-up portion of a porcelain identification sign.
ATLANTIC
(2)   1953-1966   Gill $200-$300
White globe face with Atlantic red rectangle logo in center.
ATLANTIC PREMIUM
(3)   1953-1957   Gill $250-$350
White globe face with Atlantic red rectangle logo and blue mast-arm-style pole tilted on center of face, with blue "PREMIUM" below sign.
ATLANTIC IMPERIAL
(3)   1957-1966   Gill $250-$375
ATLANTIC IMPERIAL
(4)   1964-1966   13.5in Capco $150-$275
White globe face with large red, gold, and blue Imperial shield on face. Imperial shield has gold mirrored outline.
ATLANTIC IMPERIAL w/o mirror
(5)   1964-1966   13.5in Capco   No Listing
Same as above, with plain yellow-gold outline around shield.
ATLANTIC (new logo)
(4)   1966-1970   Gill $200-$300
White globe face with red, white, and blue Atlantic hexagon logo on face.
(ATLANTIC) DIESEL FUEL
(4)   1936-1970   Gill $200-$275
White globe face with bright blue lettering "DIESEL/FUEL" in center of face. No company identification.
(ATLANTIC) KEROSENE
(5)   1940-1970   Gill $200-$275
White globe face with blue "KEROSENE" across center. Double red bars at upper left and lower right of "KEROSENE." No company identification.

CHAMPLIN OIL AND REFINING, Enid, Oklahoma

Champlin Oil and Refining was an Enid, Oklahoma, based refiner and marketer founded in 1920. Marketing was concentrated throughout the midcontinent, eventually expanding to fifteen states from Tennessee to Colorado. Champlin had long been involved in unbranded marketing and with the purchase of Champlin by the government-owned oil company from Venezuela, the decision was made to withdraw from branded marketing. Retail marketing was sold off to American Petrofina, and the Fina brand replaced Champlin in 1984. The production and refining divisions survive as an Irving, Texas, based subsidiary of Citgo Petroleum, which is also owned by the Venezuelan government.
CHAMPLIN GASOLINE
(3)   1920-1930   One-piece etched $800-$1,300
White globe with blue "CHAMPLIN" arched around top and "GASOLINE" around bottom, and red "Iron Cross" logo in center with lettering "USE/CHAMPLIN/OILS."
CHAMPLIN GASOLINE INVERTED
(5)   1920-1930   One-piece etched $500-$750
Same as above, with entire design inverted. Used as a light fixture globe.
CHAMPLIN PRESTO
(5)   1927-1935   One-piece etched   No Listing
White globe with blue "CHAMPLIN" arched around top and "GASOLINE" around bottom, with red "PREST-O-/ANTI-KNOCK" in center.
CHAMPLIN GASOLINE
(5)   1925-1935   15in Metal $400-$750
CHAMPLIN GASOLINE
(3)   1930-1956   13.5in Glass $225-$350
CHAMPLIN GASOLINE
(4)   1930-1956   Banded Glass $250-$400
White globe face with blue outer ring and blue "CHAMPLIN" arched at top, "GASOLINE" at bottom, and red Champlin "Iron Cross" logo

with notched ends on blue center crossbar. White "CHAMPLIN" on center crossbar, with white "USE" above and "OILS" below.

CHAMPLIN ETHYL (EGC)
(3)   1930-1956   13.5in Glass $225-$350
White globe face with blue "CHAMPLIN" arched at top and "GASO-LINE" at bottom, with Ethyl (EGC) logo in center.

CHAMPLIN PRESTO
(4)   1934-1956   13.5in Glass $250-$375

CHAMPLIN PRESTO
(4)   1934-1956   Banded Glass $250-$400
White globe face with blue outer ring and blue-outlined white bowtie-shaped center band. Blue "CHAMPLIN" arched at top, "GASOLINE" at bottom, with red "PRESTO" in bowtie lettering in center band.

CHAMPLIN
(1)   1956-1962   13.5in Capco $100-$150
White globe face with large Champlin "Iron Cross" logo. Blue crossbar on cross has rounded instead of notched ends. White lettering "CHAMPLIN" on crossbar, no "USE" or "OILS" on cross, as on earlier version of this logo.

CHAMPLIN oblong logo
(3)   1962-1970   13.5in Capco $75-$125

CHAMPLIN oblong logo plastic lens
(5)   1962-1970   13.5in Capco $100-$150
White globe face with 1960s oblong logo in red, white, and blue.

Harbor, Tulsa, Oklahoma

A Tulsa-based Champlin secondary brand from the 1960s.

HARBOR
(4)   1960s   13.5in Capco $200-$300
White globe face with nautical flag covering most of face. Flag has three horizontal red, white, and black stripes, with black "HARBOR" on center white stripe.

Eason Oil Company, Enid, Oklahoma

An Oklahoma-based refiner and marketer that was one of the early participants in the Sovereign Service marketing program. By the early 1950s they were based in Enid, Oklahoma, and eventually merged with Champlin in the mid-1950s.

EASON GASOLINE
(5)   1930s   15in Metal   No Listing
Description not available.

EASON ETHYL
(4)   1930s   15in Metal $275-$425
Red outer ring around globe face. White center with large Ethyl (EGC) logo. Black-outlined white "EASON" arched in red ring at top, "GASO-LINE" at bottom.

CHEVRON and Affiliates: STANDARD OIL COMPANY OF CALIFORNIA, San Francisco, California

Standard Oil Company of California, known in the industry as "Socal," is the West Coast's largest gasoline marketer, tracing its origins to the 1879 founding of the Pacific Coast Oil Company. Standard Oil, which had maintained a San Francisco marketing office since 1879, purchased Pacific Coast Oil in 1900 and reorganized it as Standard Oil Company of California.

Standard of California is credited with one of the first retail gasoline stations, opened at the company's bulk plant in Seattle, Washington, in 1907. Always an innovator, Standard was soon operating hundreds of retail stations throughout the West. By the mid-1930s company stations were under the brand of Standard Stations Incorporated, and dealer-operated locations were called Standard Oil Dealers. In 1945 the Chevron name was introduced for Standard gasolines, and independent dealers in the Standard western territory, Standard Texas southern territory, and Calso territory became Chevron Gas Stations, while company owned and operated stations remained Standard stations, selling Chevron and Chevron Supreme gasolines. In 1961 Standard of California bought Standard of Kentucky, and from that year on Chevron gasolines were sold at Standard Oil stations in the Southeast. About 1977, the Standard name came down from all but a few service stations and was replaced by the Chevron name. Standard of Kentucky globes can be found under STANDARD OIL in this book.

Standard Stations, Incorporated, and Standard Oil-Chevron Dealers

RED CROWN GASOLINE
(5)   1910s   One-piece etched $1,800-$2,500
White globe with no outline around face. Red California-style crown in center with red-colored "RED CROWN" arched around top and "GASOLINE" around bottom.

RED CROWN GASOLINE pat.   1915
(4)   1925-1930   15in Metal $450-$850
White globe face with blue outline ring. Blue center circle with white burst covering most of circle. Red California-style crown on burst in center. Blue-outlined red lettering "RED CROWN" arched around top, "GASOLINE" around bottom.

RED CROWN ETHYL on "chevron"
(5)   1926-1936   15in Metal   No Listing
Red globe face with blue-white-and-red-outlined chevron-shaped shield covering most of face. Small blue "RED CROWN" at top in shield above larger "ETHYL," above smaller "GASOLINE." Small Ethyl (EGC) logo in circle at bottom.

STANDARD GASOLINE (w/crown)
(3)   1930-1946   15in Metal $450-$800
Blue globe face with red outline ring. Red outline around center white circle. Small red California-style crown on center circle. White "STANDARD" arched around top, "GASOLINE" around bottom.

STANDARD ETHYL (EGC)
(4)   1936-1940   15in Metal $350-$600
Same as RED CROWN ETHYL above, except "STANDARD" replaces "RED CROWN" at top of shield.

STANDARD FLIGHT (w/red arrow)
(3)   1938-1946   15in Metal $500-$850
Blue outline ring around white outer ring around dark blue center circle. White lettering "Flight" at angle across upper area of center circle, with red "arrow" with speed lines passing left-to-right across face. White "GASOLINE" arched around bottom of center circle.

STANDARD FLIGHT (w/blue arrow)
(3)   1938-1946   15in Metal $400-$750
Same as above, with white-outlined light blue arrow.

STANDARD'S SUPREME WITH ETHYL
(4)   1940-1946   15in Metal $450-$800
White globe face with geartooth edge and red outline area. Blue "STANDARD'S" arched around top over small Ethyl (EGC) logo in circle. Blue-outlined red italic "SUPREME" just under Ethyl logo, with small blue "(WITH ETHYL)" below "SUPREME." Blue "GASOLINE" arched around bottom.

CHEVRON GASOLINE
(4)   1946-1957   15in Metal $400-$650
Red ring around blue globe face. White band across blue area above center. Red "CHEVRON" with blue dropshade and winged "V" on band, red "GASOLINE" on blue area just below band.

CHEVRON SUPREME
(3)   1946-1957   15in Metal $350-$600
Red ring around white globe face. Red "CHEVRON" with blue drop-shade and winged "V" just above center, above blue "SUPREME." Small red italic "GASOLINE" below "SUPREME."

CHEVRON GASOLINE
(4)   1950-1957   15in Metal $300-$550
Same as CHEVRON GASOLINE above, except no dropshade on lettering and "CHEVRON" does not extend into outer ring.

CHEVRON SUPREME
(4)   1950-1957   15in Metal $300-$550
Same as above, except no dropshade on lettering and "CHEVRON" does not extend into outer ring.

The California Company, Rocky Mountain Marketing Area

In the late 1930s, Standard Oil of California expanded its marketing into the Rocky Mountain area. Not being able to use the Standard name in this area due to its use by Standard of Indiana, gasoline was marketed under the Calso (CALifornia Standard Oil) name. In 1946 the Calso stations, all dealer and jobber operated, were rebranded with the new "Chevron Gas Station" logo. Chevron globes, listed above, were used at all Standard stations in the West and Chevron stations in the Rocky Mountain area.

CALSO w/green and blue lines
(3)   1938-1946   15in Metal $300-$550
White globe face with blue outline ring. Blue "CALSO" across top of face, above smaller blue "GASOLINE." Pale green, white, and blue horizontal lines below lettering.

CALSO "UNSURPASSED"
(4)   1938-1946   15in Metal $300-$550
Same as Calso, above, with "UNSURPASSED" below horizontal lines.

CALSO'S SUPREME WITH ETHYL (EGC)
(4)   1938-1946   15in Metal $450-$800
Same as STANDARD'S SUPREME above, with green border and "SUPREME" and blue "CALSO'S" replacing "STANDARD'S" on upper globe face.

(CALSO) FLIGHT (w/green arrow)
(4)   1938-1946   15in Metal $550-$850
Same as STANDARD FLIGHT above, with green arrow.

California Oil Company, Northeast Marketing Area

In 1945–46, Standard Oil of California purchased Monogram Oil Company and set up the California Oil Company in Perth Amboy, New Jersey, as an East Coast marketing subsidiary. Stations were branded Calso, same as in the Rockies, and were found from Maine to Virginia. In 1957, Calso stations were rebranded Chevron.

CALSO GASOLINE
(4)   1946-1950   13.5in Glass $225-$350
Green globe face with white horizontal band above center. Blue "CALSO" on band, with "L" extending into upper green area. Blue lettering "GASOLINE/PRODUCT OF/THE CALIFORNIA OIL COMPANY" on lower green area.

CALSO SUPREME
(4)   1946-1950   13.5in Glass $225-$350
Green globe face with white horizontal band below center. Blue "CALSO" in upper green area, with red "SUPREME" with blue dropshade on band. Blue "A CALIFORNIA/GASOLINE" on lower green area.

CALSO red/white
(3)   1949-1957   Gill $225-$375
CALSO red/white
(3)   1950-1957   13.5in Capco $125-$175
Red globe face with white outer ring. Large white "CALSO" with extended "L" covering most of face. White "GASOLINE" below "CALSO." Small black "THE CALIFORNIA OIL COMPANY" below "GASOLINE."

CALSO SUPREME
(3)   1949-1957   Gill $225-$375
CALSO SUPREME
(3)   1950-1957   13.5in Capco $125-$175
Same as above, with white "SUPREME" above black "GASOLINE" on lower globe face.

CALSO red/black
(3)   1950-1957   13.5in Capco $125-$175
Same as CALSO above, with "GASOLINE" in black.

CHEVRON GASOLINE
(4)   1957-1969   13.5in Capco $100-$175
White globe face with large "CHEVRON," with winged "V" above center. Italic blue "GASOLINE" above very small "CALIFORNIA OIL COMPANY" below "CHEVRON." Chevron "hallmark" logo at bottom of globe face.

CHEVRON SUPREME
(5)   1957-1969   13.5in Capco $100-$175
Same as above, with "SUPREME GASOLINE" replacing "GASOLINE."

CITIES SERVICE & AFFILIATES
CITIES SERVICE OIL COMPANY, Tulsa, Oklahoma

Cities Service was founded in 1910 as a public utility, operating municipal natural gas, lighting, ice, and other utility-type services, hence the name Cities Service. Venturing into petroleum marketing about 1914, Cities Service was a scattered collection of refining and marketing companies operating gas stations throughout the East and Midwest. By the mid-1930s the various concerns were all marketing under the Cities Service brand name, and black and white colors which gave way to green and white stations in 1946. In the 1950s many elaborate service stations were built, but Cities Service continued to have an image problem. In 1965 the time-tested Cities Service brand name was replaced by Citgo, and the entire marketing program was revitalized.

Many new stations were added at that time, only to close in record numbers during the 1970s gas shortages. In 1981 Southland Corporation, operator of the 7-Eleven convenience stores, and the government-owned oil company in Venezuela purchased the marketing division, Citgo Petroleum, while Occidental Petroleum purchased the remaining divisions of Cities Service Oil Company. In the late 1980s, Southland, in bankruptcy, sold their share of Citgo to Venezuela and the company, with the ensured supply of a government-owned oil company, again began marketing aggressively. Citgo now supplies thousands of stations in forty-six states, and new locations are added every day.

Note: No "CITGO" globes are known to exist.

CITIES SERVICE OILS ONCE ALWAYS
(5)   1914-1926   One-piece round etched   No Listing
Small white globe with black "CITIES SERVICE OILS" arched

around top. Black and white "CS" clover and triangle logo in center. Black-outlined pointed rectangular box below logo, with black "ONCE-ALWAYS" inside box.

HIGH TEST/KOOLMOTOR/ANTI-KNOCK
(5)   1914-1926   One-piece round etched   No Listing
Green globe face with white outline ring. Green-and-white-outlined white bar-and-circle band across center. Black "KOOLMOTOR" on band. Black "HIGH TEST ANTI-KNOCK" arched around top, "GASOLENE" around bottom.

CITIES SERVICE OILS ONCE ALWAYS
(3)   1920-1936   16.5in Metal $275-$450
CITIES SERVICE OILS ONCE ALWAYS
(3)   1920-1936   15in Metal $275-$400
CITIES SERVICE OILS ONCE ALWAYS
(5)   1920-1936   11.25in Metal   No Listing
White globe face with black "CITIES SERVICE OILS" arched around top. Black and white "CS" clover and triangle logo in center. Black-outlined pointed rectangular box below logo, with black "ONCE-ALWAYS" inside box.

CITIES SERVICE OILS AVIATION
(5)   1930s   15in Metal   No Listing
Globe face as described above, with red "AVIATION" painted on outside across lower face.

CITIES SERVICE "SHOEMAKER COAL CO."
(5)   1935-1936   15in Metal   No Listing
Same as CITIES SERVICE OILS above, with black "SHOEMAKER COAL CORP" arched around bottom.

CITIES SERVICE "CREW-LEVICK" cast face
(4)   1920s   15in Metal $700-$1,100
Cast face same as CITIES SERVICE OILS above, with "CREW-LEVICK" in box.

CITIES SERVICE "CREW-LEVICK"
(5)   1932-1936   15in Metal $250-$600
Same as CITIES SERVICE OILS above, with black "CREW-LEVICK" around bottom.

(CITIES SERVICE) EMPIRE GAS
(5)   1920s   15in Metal   No listing
White globe face with black clover and triangle logo in center. Red "EMPIRE" arched around top, "GAS" around bottom.

CITIES SERVICE OIL CO. KOOLMOTOR
(4)   1920s   15in Metal $275-$500
White globe face with black "CITIES SERVICE OIL CO." arched around top, "GASOLINE" around bottom, and red "KOOLMOTOR" across center.

HITEST ANTI KNOCK/KOOLMOTOR/GASOLENE
(4)   1920-1925   15in Metal $300-$550
Green globe face with white outline ring. Green-and-white-outlined white bar-and-circle band across center. Black "KOOLMOTOR" on band. Black "HIGH TEST ANTI-KNOCK" arched around top, "GASOLENE" around bottom.

HIGH TEST/KOOLMOTOR/ANTI-KNOCK
(3)   1925-1934   15in Metal $275-$525
Green globe face with black outline ring. Green-and-white-outlined white bar-and-circle band across center. Black "KOOLMOTOR" on band. White "HIGH-TEST" arched around top, "ANTI-KNOCK" around bottom.

HIGH TEST/KOOLMOTOR/ANTI-KNOCK
(4)   1926-1934   One-piece clover $900-$1,600
White globe with black-outlined green globe face. Green-and-white-outlined white bar-and-circle band across center. Black "KOOLMOTOR" on band. White "HIGH-TEST" arched around top, "ANTI-KNOCK" around bottom.

CITIES SERVICE OILS ONCE ALWAYS
(5)   1926-1934   One-piece clover $900-$1,700
White globe with black clover outline ring. Black "CITIES SERVICE OILS" arched around top, black and white clover and triangle in center, and black-outlined pointed rectangular box below logo. Black "ONCE ALWAYS" inside box.

CITIES SERVICE OILS (Ethyl decal)
(5)   1927-1934   One-piece clover $900-$1,700
Same as above, with large Ethyl (EGC) logo on decal covering clover logo in center.

CITIES SERVICE OILS ONCE ALWAYS
(4)   1934-1936   13.5in Glass $250-$350
White globe face with black clover outline ring. Black "CITIES SERVICE OILS" arched around top, black and white clover and triangle logo in center, and black-outlined pointed rectangular box below logo. Black "ONCE-ALWAYS" inside box.

CITIES SERVICE OILS KOOLMOTOR
(4)   1934-1936   13.5in Glass $275-$375

Same as above, with black-outlined green "KOOLMOTOR" replacing "ONCE-ALWAYS" box below logo.
CITIES SERVICE OILS ETHYL
(5)   1934-1936   13.5in Glass $275-$400
Same as above, with black-outlined orange "ETHYL" replacing "ONCE-ALWAYS" box below logo.
HIGH TEST/KOOLMOTOR/ANTI-KNOCK
(3)   1932-1934   Three-piece glass clover $350-$650
Green globe face with black clover outline ring. Green-and-white-outlined white bar-and-circle band across center of face. Black "KOOL-MOTOR" across band. White "HIGH-TEST" arched around top, "ANTI-KNOCK" around bottom.
CITIES SERVICE OILS ONCE ALWAYS
(3)   1932-1936   Three-piece glass clover $350-$600
White globe face with black clover outline ring. Black "CITIES SER-VICE OILS" arched around top, black and white clover and triangle logo in center, and black-outlined pointed rectangular box below logo. Black "ONCE-ALWAYS" inside box.
CITIES SERVICE (OILS) [logo] KOOLMOTOR
(3)   1934-1936   Three-piece glass clover $350-$650
White globe face with black clover outline ring. Black and white clover and triangle logo in center. Black "CITIES SERVICE" arched around top, black-outlined yellow "KOOLMOTOR" arched around bottom.
CITIES SERVICE (OILS) [logo] ETHYL
(5)   1932-1936   Three-piece glass clover $350-$700
Same as above, with black-outlined red "ETHYL" replacing "KOOL-MOTOR."
CITIES SERVICE
(3)   1936-1947   Three-piece glass clover $300-$550
CITIES SERVICE
(5)   1932-1934   14in Round inserts/ $450-$750
                    hull clover body
White globe face with black clover outline ring. Small black "CS" clover and triangle at top, above black "CITIES/SERVICE."
CITIES SERVICE KOOLMOTOR
(3)   1936-1947   Three-piece glass clover $350-$625
CITIES SERVICE KOOLMOTOR
(5)   1932-1934   14in Round inserts/ $450-$750
                    hull, clover body
Same as CITIES SERVICE above, with black-outlined yellow "KOOL-MOTOR" below "CITIES SERVICE."
CITIES SERVICE ETHYL (EGC)
(5)   1936-1947   Three-piece glass clover $350-$650
CITIES SERVICE ETHYL (EGC)
(5)   1932-1934   14in Round inserts/ $450-$850
                    hull, clover body
Same as CITIES SERVICE above, with small Ethyl (EGC) logo below "CITIES SERVICE." Black-outlined red "ETHYL" superimposed across logo.
CITIES SERVICE REGULAR
(5)   1947-1954   15in Metal $275-$450
White globe face with green clover outline around edge. Green "CITIES SERVICE" over smaller "REGULAR" inside clover outline.
CITIES SERVICE PREMIUM
(5)   1947-1954   15in Metal $275-$450
White globe face with orange clover outline around edge. Orange "CITIES/SERVICE" over smaller "PREMIUM" inside clover outline.
CITIES SERVICE (green)
(2)   1947-1957   13.5in Capco $75-$135
White globe face with green clover outline around edge. Large green "CITIES/SERVICE" in center.
CITIES SERVICE (red)
(2)   1947-1957   13.5in Capco $75-$135
Same as above, with red replacing green.
CITIES SERVICE (yellow)
(4)   1954-1957   13.5in Capco $75-$150
Same as above, with yellow replacing green.
CITIES SERVICE (orange)
(4)   1954-1957   13.5in Capco $75-$135
Same as above, with orange replacing green.
CITIES SERVICE clover and triangle
(4)   1932-1934   Pair lens, $175-$300
                    15in Metal (window)
White globe face with thick green clover outline with triangle in center. This was used as a light-up sign. A metal globe band was framed into a service station building to form a window, and these lenses were installed in the frame.

Lincoln Oil Company, Flint, Michigan
A southern Michigan marketer, operating more than fifty stations when they were merged into Cities Service in 1930.

LINCOLN OILS
(5)   1920-1930   15in Metal $300-$500
Globe face is divided into three even bands, red on top, white in the middle, and blue on the bottom. Large blue LOCO logo on center band, with diagonal red arrow through logo. White "LINCOLN" on red band, "OILS" on blue.

Elwood Oil Company, Elwood, Indiana
An Indiana jobber brand converted to Cities Service in 1931.
RED PARROT GASOLINE w/red parrot
(5)   1923-1931   15in Metal   No Listing
White globe face with "RED PARROT" arched around top, "GASO-LINE" around bottom, and detailed red parrot in center.

Louisiana Oil Refining Company, Shreveport, Louisiana
Originally a Gulf Coast refiner and marketer, Louisiana Oil Refining Company, or Loreco, became a part of Cities Service in 1932.
LORECO GASOLINE/MOTOR OIL
(5)   pre-1932   15in Metal $325-$500
White globe face with white and red outline rings. Black "GASOLINE" arched around top, "MOTOR OIL" around bottom, and red-and-white-outlined red diamond in center with white "LORECO" on diamond.
LORECO ETHYL
(3)   pre-1932   15in Metal $275-$425
White globe face with black and white outline rings. Black outline around white center circle. Red "LORECO" arched around top, "GAS" around bottom, with large Ethyl (EGC) logo in center with blue rays.
LOREX MOTOR FUEL
(4)   pre-1932   15in Metal $250-$425
White globe face with dark blue "LOREX," with light blue dropshade in decreasing height across face. Red italic "Motor Fuel" below "LOREX."

Crew-Levick Company, Philadelphia, Pennsylvania
An early Philadelphia lubricants marketer that merged with Cities Service about 1925. See CITIES SERVICE CREW-LEVICK globes above for details.

Warner-Quinlan Company, New York, New York
Founded in New York City before 1900, Warner-Quinlan was marketing throughout New England when purchased by Cities Service in 1933.
WARNOCO
(5)   1920-1925   One-piece etched   No Listing
White globe with red "WARNOCO" arched around top of face. Small red "W" on lower globe face, with blue detailed wings to either side.
SUPER X MOTOR FUEL
(5)   1925-1930   One-piece baked $500-$900
White globe face with red outline ring. Large black-and-white-outlined red "X" on black diamond in center. Black-and-white-outlined red "SUPER" arched around top, "MOTOR FUEL" around bottom, with black "REG. U.S." and "PAT. OFF." to either side of "X."
SUPER X HIGHTEST
(4)   1932-1933   13.5in Glass $225-$350
Yellow globe face with red outline ring. Large red "X" in center, with smaller "HIGH" and "TEST" to either side. Red "SUPER" arched around top, "GASOLINE" around bottom.
MILEAGE w/owl
(4)   1930-1933   15in Metal $800-$1,400
White globe face with blue outline rings. Blue outline around white center circle. Red and blue perched owl and blue triangle design in center circle, with banner across owl. "FOR WISE DRIVERS" on banner. Blue "MILEAGE" arched around top, "GASOLINE" around bottom.
MILEAGE NOT A NOX
(4)   1930-1933   15in Metal $275-$450
White globe face with band across center. Script "Mileage" and design at top. White "NOT-A-NOX" on band, "GASOLINE" arched below.
MILEAGE PLUS GASOLINE
(4)   1927-1930   15in Metal $250-$400
White globe face with outlined white center circle. "MILEAGE" arched around top, "GASOLINE" around bottom, with large "PLUS" in center.

Shoemaker Oil Company, Auburn, New York
Purchased by Cities Service about 1935. Little is known about this company.
BLUE GRASS GASOLINE "SHOEMAKER COAL" cast face
(5)   1920s   15in Metal   No Listing
White globe face with cast lettering. Blue-colored "BLUEGRASS"

Calso 15in inserts on metal body.

Cities Service Oils one-piece etched small 12in globe.

Cities Service Koolmotor one-piece etched small 12in globe.

Koolmotor one-piece raised-letter clover-shaped globe.

Koolmotor one-piece etched globe, and Sinclair Aircraft one-piece etched globe.

Cities Service Oils 16.5in inserts on metal body.

Cities Service globes 15in inserts on metal bodies. John Phippen

Cities Service 15in inserts for window display only. Kent Blaine

Cities Service/Crew Levick 15in cast-face inserts on metal body.

Koolmotor Gasoline 15in inserts on metal body.

Cities Service Koolmotor clover-shaped lenses on clover-shaped glass body.

Cities Service Ethyl clover-shaped lenses on clover-shaped body.

Koolmotor clover-shaped glass inserts on clover-shaped glass body.

Cities Service Ethyl 13.5in clover-shaped glass inserts on clover-shaped glass body.

Farmers Union Gasoline 13.5in glass inserts on glass body.

arched around top, "GASOLINE" around bottom, with reverse-bowtie "SHOEMAKER/COALCORP" in center. Small blue "AUBURN, N.Y." at bottom.

Jenny Manufacturing Company, Boston, Massachusetts

Originally a mid-nineteenth century dealer in whale oils, coal, kerosene, and related products, Jenney Manufacturing entered the New England gasoline market in the early years of this century. By 1920, Jenney had a network of elaborate service stations in Boston and the surrounding area. With close ties to Cities Service for many years, Jenney was merged into Cities Service about 1965, and the Citgo brand replaced Jenney.

SOLVENIZED JENNEY HY POWER
(5)   1920s   15in Metal   No Listing
White globe face with black-outlined orange circle in center. Orange and black industrial scene in center circle, with "BOSTON" near bottom of scene. White band diagonally across upper area of center circle. Black-outlined orange "SOLVENIZED" arched around top, "HY-POWER" around bottom, with script black "Jenney" on diagonal band. White "MANUFACTURING CO." on "Jenney" underline.

JENNEY AERO GASOLINE
(5)   1920s   15in Metal   No Listing
Orange outline around globe face. Blue band across center, covering most of face. Narrow black areas above and below. Black and orange airplane on blue center area, with white "AERO" across airplane. Orange "JENNEY" in upper black area, "GASOLINE" below.

JENNEY ETHYL GASOLINE
(5)   1920s   15in Metal   No listing
Black globe face with yellow outline ring and yellow ring around white center circle. Yellow "JENNEY" arched around top, "GASOLINE" around bottom with large Ethyl (EGC) logo in center.

SOLVENIZED JENNEY HY POWER
(5)   1930s   Gill $800-$1,200
White globe face with black-outlined orange circle in center. Orange and black industrial scene in center circle, with "BOSTON" near bottom of scene. White band diagonally across upper area of center circle. Black-outlined orange "SOLVENIZED" arched around top, "HY-POWER" around bottom, with script black "Jenney" on diagonal band. White "MANUFACTURING CO." on "Jenney" underline.

JENNEY AERO SOLVENIZED
(4)   1930s   Gill $800-$1,200
White globe face with wide orange and narrow black outline rings. Black lines offset white center band. Orange and black airplane in center, with black-outlined blue "AERO" across airplane. Black-outlined orange "JENNEY" at top, "SOLVENIZED" at bottom.

JENNEY AERO
(3)   1946-1960   Gill $250-$375
White globe face with thick blue and thin red outline rings. Large red "AERO" across center. Blue "JENNEY" at top, "GASOLINE" at bottom.

JENNEY SUPER AERO
(4)   1946-1960   Gill $275-$400
White globe face with thick blue and thin red outline rings. Large blue "SUPER-AERO" across center. Red "JENNEY" across top, "GASOLINE" across bottom.

CLARK OIL AND REFINING CORPORATION, St. Louis, Missouri

Clark Oil Company began as a one-station operation by Emory Clark in 1932 in Milwaukee, Wisconsin. By the early 1930s, Clark had evolved into a chain operation, selling "discount" gas through company-operated stations in a number of Wisconsin towns. Significant growth came after World War II, when the operation expanded to include stations from Pennsylvania to Kansas, totaling more than 1,350 at the peak, including 122 stations acquired when Clark bought out the Owens Oil Company of Bloomington, Illinois, in 1968. In 1981 Clark Oil was purchased by the St. Louis-based Apex Oil, and sold again in 1988, this time to the Canadian conglomerate Horsham Corporation, which continues to operate the more than 900 Clark stations in twelve states.

CLARK HIGH GRADE GASOLINE
(5)   Early 1930s   15in Lens in odd   No Listing
                          metal band
White globe face with red "CLARK OIL CO." arched around top, "GASOLINE" around bottom, with red "HIGH/GRADE" diagonally across center. Globe frame is flat metal as opposed to formed high- or low-profile band.

CLARK SUPER 100
(4)   1936-1956   13.5in Glass $225-$350
CLARK SUPER 100
(4)   1936-1956   13.5in Orange $200-$300
                          Capco
Orange globe face with black-outlined white "CLARK" at the top of the face, italic black "SUPER" across center, and a stylized black and white "100" on the lower globe face.

CLARK
(3)   1956-1982   13.5in Glass $125-200
CLARK
(1)   1956-1982   13.5in Capco $ 50-$125
Orange globe face with black outline. White band across center of face, with black "CLARK" lettering.

Target

A 1960s Clark secondary brand.
TARGET
(4)   1960s   13.5in Glass $200-$300
White globe face with three red rings circling so as to simulate a target. Red-outlined white band across center, with black italic "Target" lettering.

Owens Oil Company, Bloomington, Illinois

A Bloomington, Illinois, based discount gasoline chain that operated 122 stations in ten states when purchased by Clark in 1968. By the early 1970s, the Clark brand name had replaced the Owens Oco-Pep brand.

OCO PEP REGULAR GAS
(4)   13.5in Capco $125-$175
White globe face with red outline ring. Red, white, and black arched red band across upper globe face. White "OCO PEP" on band. Red script "Regular" below band, above black "GASOLINE."
Note: You can assume that other OCO PEP globes do exist.

COLONIAL OIL INDUSTRIES, Savannah, Georgia

Colonial Oil Industries was founded in Savannah, Georgia, in 1921 as the American Oil Company. From 1921 until 1928 gasoline was sold under the American brand, but with the expansion of the Pure Oil Company into Georgia, American became a branded Pure Oil jobber. In 1933, when Pan American Petroleum merged with the American Oil Company (Amoco), and replaced the Pan-Am brand in Georgia with the Amoco name, Colonial sold the rights to the American name and became Colonial. In 1950 Colonial sold the Pure branded operation to Pure, and concentrated on a growing wholesale-terminal business. The Colonial gasoline brand was introduced in the mid-1950s in an effort to give their dealers a unified brand, and in about 1964 they began operating a discount service station chain, branded Interstate and selling Colonial gasoline. By the early 1980s they had replaced many Interstate stations with Enmark convenience stores, which they continue to operate today.

AMERICAN
(5)   1921-1928   15in Metal $375-$650
White globe face with large red-and-white-striped shield, with blue field and stars at the top and blue crossbar across center, with white "AMERICAN."

COLONIAL EAGLE
(3)   1956-1970   13.5in Glass $250-$400
COLONIAL EAGLE
(3)   1956-1970   13.5in Capco $150-$300
White globe face with red ring around outer edge. Large red, white, and blue Colonial shield with eagle covers most of face. Blue "EAGLE" arched around top, "GASOLINE" arched around bottom.

COLONIAL ROYAL EAGLE
(3)   1956-1970   13.5in Glass $250-$425
COLONIAL ROYAL EAGLE
(3)   1956-1970   13.5in Capco $150-$300
Same as COLONIAL EAGLE, with "ROYAL/EAGLE" at top.

COLONIAL GOLDEN EAGLE
(4)   1956-1962   13.5in Glass $250-$450
COLONIAL GOLDEN EAGLE
(4)   1956-1962   13.5in Capco $150-$325
Similar to COLONIAL EAGLE, except has gold ring around outer edge and blue-outlined gold "GOLDEN/EAGLE" at top, "GASOLINE" at bottom, and eagle in logo has blue and gold tones as opposed to blue and white in the other globes.

COLONIAL KEROSENE
(4)   1956-1970   13.5in Capco $100-$150

Same as COLONIAL EAGLE, except with blue "KEROSENE" top and bottom.

CONOCO and Affiliates
CONTINENTAL OIL COMPANY, Ponca City, Oklahoma

Continental Oil Company, founded in 1875 in Denver, Colorado, became an operating unit of the Standard Oil Trust, having been purchased by Standard in 1885. After the 1911 breakup of Standard, Continental was spun off as an independent company and by 1913 was involved in production, refining, and marketing. The Continental name survived a 1929 takeover by Marland Oil, and over the course of time the Conoco brand name has appeared in nearly all states of the Southeast, Midwest, and Mountain and Pacific Coast areas. Conoco expanded its scope worldwide during the 1950s, including the purchase of several marketing companies, such as Western Oil, Kayo, and Douglas, greatly expanding the company's marketing presence throughout the United States. Conoco has been a part of the giant chemical company Dupont since 1982, and markets in thirty-seven states today.

CONOCO MINUTEMAN GASOLINE
(4)   1913-1929   15in Metal $1,500-$2,500
Yellow globe face with blue "CONOCO" arched around top, red "GASOLINE" arched around bottom, with black silhouette of Continental soldier in center of face.

CONOCO MINUTEMAN ETHYL (EGC)
(5)   1927-1929   15in Metal $800-$1,400
Yellow outer ring around globe face with blue "CONOCO" arched around top, red "GASOLINE" arched around bottom around white circle in center, with large Ethyl (EGC) logo in center.

CONOCO TRIANGLE w/ green outline
(4)   1929-1950   15in Metal $300-$650
CONOCO TRIANGLE w/ green outline
(5)   1929-1950   18in Metal band neon   No listing
White globe face with green-outlined red Conoco triangle logo in center.

CONOCO ETHYL (EGC)
(4)   1929-1941   15in Metal $300-$650
White globe face with green outline. Red "CONOCO" arched around top, "GASOLINE" around bottom, with large Ethyl (EGC) logo in center.

CONOCO TRIANGLE w/green outline
(3)   1929-1950   13.5in Glass $225-$375
CONOCO TRIANGLE w/green outline
(3)   1933-1950   13.5in Green Capco $175-$300
White globe face with green outline. Green-outlined red Conoco triangle logo in center.

CONOCO ETHYL (EGC)
(4)   1929-1941   13.5in Glass $250-$400
White globe face with green outline. Red "CONOCO" arched around top, "GASOLINE" around bottom, with large Ethyl (EGC) logo in center.

CONOCO ETHYL (EC)
(4)   1941-1950   13.5in Glass $250-$375
CONOCO ETHYL (EC)
(4)   1941-1950   13.5in Capco $150-$275
Same as above, with Ethyl (EC) logo.

CONOCO red triangle
(2)   1950-1969   13.5in Capco $100-$175
CONOCO red triangle
(2)   1950-1969   13.5in Green Capco $150-$250
CONOCO red triangle
(2)   1950-1969   13.5in Red Capco $150-$225
White globe face with red and white Conoco triangle logo in center–no green.

Marland Oil Company, Ponca City, Oklahoma

Marland traces its early history to the Oklahoma oil fields of the early 1910s. By 1920 marketing had began under the famous Red Triangle logo, and by 1922 there were Marland service stations in eleven states. In 1929 Marland purchased Continental, but chose to retain the Continental Oil Co. name for the new corporation. The new Conoco logo was to be the famous Marland triangle rebranded with the name Conoco.

MARLAND GASOLINE
(4)   1920s   One-piece etched $1,200-$1,800
White globe with black outline around globe face and black-outlined red "MARLAND OILS" triangle in center, with black "MARLAND" arched around top and "GASOLINE" around bottom.

MARLAND GASOLINE
(5)   1920s   One-piece etched $1,400-$2,000
Similar to MARLAND GASOLINE above, except without outline ring.

MARLAND HI-TEST
(5)   1920s   One-piece etched   No Listing
Same as above, with black "HI-TEST" replacing "GASOLINE."

MARLAND GASOLINE
(5)   1920-1929   15in Metal $700-$1,000
White globe face with black outline and black-outlined red "MARLAND OILS" triangle, with black "MARLAND" arched around top and "GASOLINE" arched around bottom.

MARLAND GASOLINE
(4)   1927-1929   Gill $275-$450
MARLAND GASOLINE
(4)   1927-1929   Balcrank $275-$475
MARLAND GASOLINE
(4)   1927-1929   13.5in Glass $250-$425
Mint green globe face with dark blue outline. Blue-outlined red "MARLAND OILS" triangle in center, with blue "MARLAND" arched around top and "GASOLINE" arched around bottom.

MARLAND HI-TEST
(4)   1927-1929   Gill $300-$500
MARLAND HI-TEST
(4)   1927-1929   13.5in Glass $275-$450
Same as above, with "HI-TEST" replacing "GASOLINE" at bottom of globe.

(MARLAND) AVIATION GASOLINE
(5)   1927-1929   13.5in Glass   No Listing
White globe face with black outline ring. Black-outlined dark green "AVIATION" arched around top, "GASOLINE" around bottom, with red, white, and black detailed airplane and cloud scene in center.

Western Oil and Fuel, Minneapolis, Minnesota

Western Oil and Fuel was a Minneapolis-based marketing operation, founded in 1926, that introduced the famous Husky brand in the mid-1930s and operated the Husky stations into the late 1950s. The Husky brand name eventually went to H. Earl Clack, Incorporated of Cody, Wyoming, and Western continued to market under the Mileage brand. Conoco bought out Western in 1958, and about that time introduced "Western" as another gasoline trademark. By 1970 Conoco had converted all the Mileage and DS locations to the Conoco brand, but the Western stations, modeled after the competing Holiday and SuperAmerica convenience stores, remained Western up through the late 1970s when they were rebranded Jet.

HUSKY "QUALITY PETROLEUM PRODUCTS"
(5)   1935-1940   13.5in Glass   No Listing
Same as below, except dog is black, white, and red, with a red horizontal line separating northern lights from lower blue area. Black "QUALITY PETROLEUM PRODUCTS" arched above dog. Much more detail in dog.

HUSKY (w/northern lights)
(4)   1940-1960   13.5in Glass $500-$800
Globe face has blue outline ring around upper white area. Lower 1/3 is dark blue. Blue, grey, white, and red husky dog head with good detail, with orange and yellow "northern lights" design on upper globe face. Yellow "HUSKY" in lower blue area.
Note: These Husky globes, as well as later Husky Oil globes, appear in this section under "HUSKY."

MILEAGE
(3)   1940-1960   Gill $200-$325
Bright blue globe face with white band across center. Red "Mileage" on band.

SUPER MILEAGE
(3)   1940-1960   Gill $200-$325
Same as above, with italic "SUPER" added above "age" in "Mileage."

MILEAGE
(4)   1960-1969   Three-piece square plastic $150-$225
Red and white plastic trapazoidal globe in shape of 1960s Mileage logo.

WESTERN
(4)   1960-1969   Three-piece square plastic $150-$225
Red and white plastic trapazoidal globe in shape of 1960s Western logo.

Direct Service Oil Company, Minneapolis, Minnesota

A Minneapolis marketer purchased by Western Oil and Fuel in 1956.

DS
(3)   1935-1960   13.5in Glass $225-$325
White globe face with large red-outlined black circle in center. Red "DS" superimposed over circle.

MAJOR
(5)   1940s   13.5in Glass $200-$350
White globe face with blue outline ring. Red banner folded across center, with 15in white "MAJOR" on banner.

DS
(4)   1960-1969   Three-piece square plastic $150-$225
Red and white plastic trapazoidal globe in shape of 1960s DS logo.
Note: At least two other DS globes exist.

Malco Refining, Roswell, New Mexico
Malco Refining was a Roswell, New Mexico, refiner and marketer operating stations in New Mexico under the Malco and Numex brands, and under the Valley brand in Arizona. Conoco purchased Malco in 1959, but was forced to sell on antitrust grounds in 1964. Malco operated as an independent into the 1970s.
MALCO (w/NM logo)
(4)   1940s   13.5in Glass $275-$400
Yellow globe face with blue-outlined white circle in center. Four blue lines radiating out from circle on each side. Blue-outlined red "MALCO" on center white circle.
MALCO w/bird
(4)   1950s   13.5in Glass $250-$425
MALCO w/bird
(4)   1950s   13.5in Capco $200 $300
White globe face with red-outlined black "MALCO" across lower face and large stylized bird at top.

Valley
A Malco secondary brand from the 1950s.
VALLEY
(4)   1950s   13.5in Capco $100-$175
White globe face with blue mountain and valley scene, with blue and white lines above and below. Yellow-outlined black "VALLEY" across center of globe face.

Numex
A Malco secondary brand from the 1950s.
NUMEX
(5)   1950s   13.5in Capco   No Listing
Description not available.
NUMEX ETHYL
(5)   1950s   13.5in Glass   No Listing
Description not available.

Douglas Oil Company, Los Angeles, California
Founded in about 1927, and merged with Krieger in 1946. In 1961 Conoco bought Douglas and operated the nearly 300 Douglas stations until 1971, when they were sold off and rebranded, mostly Texaco.
Note: No Douglas brand globes are known to exist.

Krieger
A California independent that merged with Douglas in 1946.
KRIEGER "KRIEG-O-LENE"
(5)   1930s   16.5in Metal $550-$900
White globe face with large yellow-outlined black diamond covering most of face. Yellow band across center of diamond, with black "KRIEG-O-LENE" on band. Orange "KRIEGER" at top, with yellow underline and lettering "FIRST GRADE." Orange "GASOLINE" over "QUALITY/at a/PRICE" on bottom of diamond.

F.P. Kendall and Company, Chattanooga, Tennessee
F. P. Kendall and Company opened their first Kayo station in Chattanooga, Tennessee, in 1940. The chain expanded throughout the South and had approximately 170 stations in seven states when purchased by Conoco in 1959. Kayo was operated as a separate brand throughout the 1960s and 1970s, and in about 1980 the nearly 900 Kayo stations were rebranded Jet. Conoco began replacing the Jet brand in 1990.
Note: No Kayo-brand globes are known to exist.

CO-OPs–Various farm co-operatives
Farmland Industries, Kansas City, Missouri
Founded in 1928 as Consumers Co-operative Association, Farmland, which is commonly referred to as "Double Circle" in reference to their logo, supplies products to farm co-ops throughout the Midwest. They continue to market through co-ops under the Co-op brand name, and at retail under the Ampride brand.
USE/CO-OP/PRODUCTS (on shield)
(3)   1930s   Gill $200-$350
White globe face with red sixteen-point border around Co-op logo. White ring around edge of logo, with red center. Black "USE" on upper ring, "PRODUCTS" on lower ring, and large black "CO-OP" on diagonal band across center.

FARMCO (across shield)
(3)   1930s   Gill $200-$350
White globe face with red sixteen-point border around Co-op logo. White ring around edge of logo, with red center. Black "FARMCO" on horizontal band across center.
CO-OP (white on red)
(2)   1940s   13.5in Glass $200-$350
Red globe face with black and white outline and white "CO-OP" with black dropshade.
CO-OP (red on white)
(3)   1940s   13.5in Glass $200-$325
White globe face with red outline and red "CO-OP" across center.
CO-OP (green on white)
(4)   1940s   Gill $225-$350
White globe face with green outline and green "CO-OP" across center.
CO-OP (blue on red)
(4)   1940s   Gill $225-$350
Red globe face with blue outline and blue "CO-OP" across center.
CO-OP COMPETITIVE GASOLINE
(4)   1930s   13.5in Glass   No Listing
Description not available.
CO-OP (double circle)
(3)   1962-1985   One-piece plastic $150-$275
White plastic-formed faces assembled back-to-back with aluminum ring. Formed face of globe is in shape of interlocking circles, with red outline on left circle and blue on right circle, and black "CO-OP" across center.

Falcon
A postwar attempt at retail markets by Consumers Co-operative Association (CCA).
FALCON GASOLINE
(5)   1946-1955   Gill   No Listing
White globe face with detailed multicolored falcon at center of face. Red "FALCON" logotype lettering arched aound top, "GASOLINE" around bottom.
FALCON
(4)   1955-1970   13.5in Green Capco $275-$450
White globe face with detailed brown and yellow falcon in flight covering most of face. Green band across center of face, with white "FALCON."
FALCON ETHYL
(5)   1955-1970   13.5in Red Capco $275-$475
Same as FALCON, with red band across center with white "FALCON," and red "ETHYL" at bottom.

Co-op Shields
Used by various farm cooperatives.
QUALITY/CO-OP/PRODUCTS (on shield)
(4)   1930s   15in Metal $375-550
QUALITY/CO-OP/PRODUCTS (on shield)
(3)   1930s   13.5in Glass $250-$350
White globe face with red, white, and blue Co-op shield logo on face. "QUALITY" arched in top of shield, "PRODUCTS" around bottom, with "CO-OP" in diagonal band across shield.
QUALITY/PREMIUM/PRODUCTS (on shield)
(4)   1930s   15in Metal $375-$550
Same as above, with "PREMIUM" replacing "CO-OP" in band.

Farmers Union Central Exchange, St. Paul, Minnesota
A combination of several farm cooperative organizations that operate across the North Central states. The CENEX brand name was introduced about 1974 to establish a common identity for the various companies. In 1988 Farmers Union Central Exchange merged with Land O'Lakes, and all petroleum products are marketed under the CENEX brand name today.
FARMERS UNION (shield w/plow)
(5)   1920s   15in Metal   No Listing
Red globe face with yellow-and-red-outlined yellow shield in center with black "FARMERS/UNION" over plow. Interlocked "F/U" in red circle at top of shield.
FARMERS UNION GASOLINE (w/plow, shield)
(4)   1930-1946   13.5in Glass $325-$600
Yellow outer ring around white center of globe face. Dark green "FARMERS UNION" arched around top of globe face, "GASOLINE" at bottom, with red, yellow, and black Farmers Union shield with plow in center. Black "CO-OPERATIVE STRENGTH" arched under shield.
FARMERS UNION GASOLINE (w/Co-op seal)
(3)   1946-1952   13.5in Glass $250-$350
Same as above, with brighter green lettering on outer ring and red and green "outline" co-op seven-point shield in center, with green "NA-

TIONAL" at top, "CO-OPERATIVES" at bottom, and black "CO-OP" across center.

FARMERS UNION ETHYL
(4)   1946-1952   13.5in Glass $200-$350
White globe face with wide green-outlined yellow band arched across upper face. Red-outlined green "FARMERS/UNION" on yellow band. Ethyl (EC) logo on lower globe face below band.

FARMERS UNION FULL POWER GASOLINE
(5)   1946-1952   Gill   No Listing
White face with red outline ring. Red bowtie-shaped band across center with black outlined white "FULL/POWER" in bowtie lettering across band. Yellow outlined line green "FARMERS" across upper globe face. "UNION" across lower globe facs.

(CENEX) CO-OP (shield)
(4)   1952-1972   One-piece plastic shield $150-$250
Formed plastic shield halves riveted back-to-back. Black border area around yellow shield area of globe face, with red V-shaped section at top. Black "CO-OP" diagonally across center.

(CENEX) SUPER CO-OP (shield)
(5)   1952-1972   One-piece plastic shield $150-$250
Same as above, with red border area and yellow "SUPER" on upper red "V" area.

Midland Cooperatives, St. Paul, Minnesota

Midland Cooperatives, founded in 1926, sold out to Land O'Lakes in 1985. Land O'Lakes merged with Farmers Union Central Exchange (Cenex) in 1988. All gasoline has been sold under the Cenex brand since that time.

MIDLAND GASOLINE
(5)   1920s   15in Metal   No Listing
Yellow globe face wtih black "MIDLAND" arched around top, "GASOLINE" around bottom, with red interlocking letter design in center. It has not been determined for certain whether this globe is from Midland Cooperatives, or from another company named Midland.

MIDLAND/CO-OP/WHOLESALE
(4)   1930s   Gill $350-$600
Green-outlined orange ring around outer globe face. White circle in center. White-outlined green "MIDLAND" arched around top, "WHOLESALE" around bottom, with white-outlined green "CO-OP" across center and green-outlined "shaking hands" extending from both "O's" in CO-OP into center circle.

CO-OP SUPER OCTANE GASOLINE
(3)   1930s   Gill $275-$425
Green-outlined orange ring around outer globe face. White circle in center. White-outlined green "CO-OP" arched around top, "GASO-LINE" around bottom, with green script "Super/Octane" diagonally in center.

HI TEST/CO-OP/ANTI KNOCK
(5)   1930s   13.5in Glass $375-$650
Red-outlined orange ring around outer globe face. White circle in center. Black-outllined red "HI-TEST" arched around top, "ANTI-NOK" around bottom, with black-outlined red "CO-OP" across center and green-outlined "shaking hands" extending from both "O's" in CO-OP into center circle.

MIDLAND "M"
(3)   1946-1960   13.5in Glass $200-$275
White globe face with black-outlined Midland "M" logo, with dots and red rectangle below "M" and white "MIDLAND" lettering.

MIDLAND "M" (no box)
(3)   1960-1987   13.5in Capco $750-$150
White globe face with large black "M," with red triangle and dots only. No border or lettering.

Missouri Farm Bureau, Jefferson City, Missouri

MISSOURI GREEN DIAMOND
(5)   1940s   Gill $350-$650
White globe face with yellow-outlined vertical green diamond in center. Yellow area in shape of Missouri, in center of diamond, with green "FARM/BUREAU" and yellow "GREEN DIAMOND" below yellow area.

Southern States, Richmond, Virginia

Founded as Virginia Seed Service in 1923, Southern States began marketing petroleum products in the 1930s and continues today.

SOUTHERN STATES COOPERATIVES
(5)   1934-1962   15in Metal $400-$750
White outer ring around globe face with orange "MOTOR OIL" arched at top, "GASOLINE" at bottom. Blue center circle area with blue and orange Southern States logo in center, and white "SOUTHERN/STATES/COOPERATIVE/SCS" on logo. Script "Quality" on blue area below logo.

Tennessee Cooperatives, La Vergne, Tennessee

CO-OP REGULAR
(4)   1946-1970   13.5in Glass $250-$375
White globe face with large Tennessee Co-op logo (perspective view of Tennessee map in red on green background, with progressive green "CO-OP" lettering) offset to upper left of face. Green speed lines arched around from top, ending at red "REGULAR" offset to lower right of globe face.

Growmark Industries, Bloomington, Illinois

Founded as Illinois Farm Supply in the 1920s, Growmark Industries gasoline was marketed under the Magic Aladdin brand until after WWII. The FS brand was introduced about 1960 and continues in use today.

ALADDIN GAS
(5)   1930s   15in Metal   No Listing
White globe face with black Illinois Farm Supply logo in center. Black "ALADDIN" arched around top, "GAS" horizontally across bottom.

ALADDIN GASOLINE
(5)   1940s   13.5in Red Glass $450-$825
White globe face with Illinois Farm Supply logo in center. "ALADDIN" arched around top, "GASOLINE" around bottom.

ILLINOIS FARM SERVICE
(4)   1950-1960   13.5in Capco $225-$350
White globe face with red outline. Blue ring around logo in center with white "ILLINOIS FARM SUPPLY COMPANY" around blue ring. Blue-outlined white "S" in center, with diagonal box across center, red "SERVICE" inside box, and "PETROLEUM/PRODUCTS" on "S." Three red triangles around circle.

FS
(2)   1960-1970   13.5in Capco $75-$125
White globe face with red-outlined black "f," and red "s" logo in center.

Missouri Farmers Association, Columbia, Missouri

Missouri Farmers Association, or MFA, has marketed petroleum products since the 1930s, and continues to market through farm cooperatives and some retail locations in Missouri and western Tennessee.

MFA GASOLINE MOTOR OILS GREASES
(4)   1946-1960   13.5in Glass $250-$375
White globe face with small "MFA" shield in center. Red outline around edge, blue "GASOLINE" arched around top, "MOTOR OILS GREASES" around bottom.

MFA
(3)   1960-1970   13.5in Capco $125-$200
White globe face with red, white, and blue "MFA" shield in center.

Farmers Gas and Oil Company of Michigan, Ithaca, Michigan

FARMERS/CO-OP/PETROLEUM
(4)   1930s   15in Metal $300-$500
White globe face with blue outline around edge. Red seven-point co-op shield, with white ring around center red circle. Blue "FARMERS" arched around top of white ring, "PETROLEUM" around bottom, with red-outlined white band across center with blue "CO-OP."

FARMERS/HI OCTANE/CO-OP
(4)   1940s   Gill $250-$350
Blue-outlined white outer ring around red center of globe face. Blue-outlined red "FARMERS" arched around top, "CO-OP" around bottom with blue lettering "HIGH OCTANE" on white band across center red circle.

Central Co-operative Wholesale, Superior, Wisconsin

CO-OP "AFFIL W/NATL CO-OP INC." (white/red)
(5)   1930s   15in Metal $275-$425
CO-OP "AFFIL W/NATL CO-OP, INC." (white/red)
(5)   1930s   15in Metal $250-$375
Red globe face with reverse-bowtie "CO-OP" across center. Small white lettering arched around top "AFFILIATED WITH NATIONAL CO-OP INC.," and white lettering arched around bottom "DISTRIBU-TORS/CENTRAL CO-OPERATIVE WHOLESALE/SUPERIOR WIS."

CO-OP "AFFIL W/NATL CO-OP, INC." (white/ blue)
(5)   1930s   15in Metal $375-$550
CO-OP AFFIL W/NATL CO-OP, INC. (white/blue)
(5)   1930s   Gill $250-$375
Same as above, except with blue globe face.

Farmers Educational and Co-operative State Union, Omaha, Nebraska

FARMERS UNION (w/plow scene)
(5)   1920s-1930s   15in Metal $1,200-$2,200

White globe face with red and white co-op logo in center. Red lettering arched at top of logo "FARMERS EDUCATIONAL AND COOPERATIVE STATE UNION," at bottom "OF NEBRASKA, and farm field scene with plow in center. Blue "FARMERS" arched around top of face, "UNION" around bottom.

FARMERS UNION HIGH OCTANE
(4)   1930s   15in Metal $275-$450
White globe face with blue "FARMERS" lettering arched at top, "UNION" at bottom (identical to FARMERS UNION w/plow scene), with red outline around center white circle and red "HIGH/OCTANE" on circle.

STATEX HI OCTANE
(3)   pre-1958   13.5in Glass $200-$350
Light green globe face with irregular green logo at top, with white "STATEX" on logo. Dark green "GASOLINE" below logo and dark green band across bottom, with white "HI-OCTANE."

STATEX PREMIUM
(3)   pre-1958   13.5in Glass $200-$350
Same as above, with white "PREMIUM" replacing "HI-OCTANE."

FELCO
(2)   1958-1965   13.5in Capco $75-$125
White globe face with green diamond logo, with rounded corners in center of face. White "f" on logo and black "felco" below logo.

Co-operative GLF (Grange League Farm), Ithaca, New York

Founded in the 1920s, GLF served farmers in New York and Pennsylvania as well as parts of New England. In 1964, the company merged with Eastern States Farm Supply to form Agway, and continues to market petroleum products under that name throughout the Northeast.

GLF QUALITY w/painted steel faces
(5)   1930s   15in Metal   No Listing
Painted white steel face with red omega logo, with line across bottom. Large red "GLF" painted at top, script red "Quality" at bottom.

GLF QUALITY
(5)   1930s   15in Metal $250-$425
GLF QUALITY
(3)   1930s   13.5in Glass $225-$350
White globe face with large red omega sign covering most of face. Large red "GLF" arched above red script "Quality."

GLF QUALITY
(5)   1930s   15in Metal $275-$400
GLF QUALITY
(3)   1946-1964   13.5in Glass $225-$350
GLF QUALITY
(4)   1946-1964   13.5in Capco $125-$175
White globe face with large red omega sign covering most of face. Large red "GLF" above red script "Quality."

GLF QUALITY
(5)   1946-1964   13.5in Glass $225-$375
Red globe face with white lettering and logo. Exact opposite of above.

Landmark Co-operatives, Columbus, Ohio

QUALITY/FARM BUREAU/PRODUCTS (on shield)
(4)   1940s   13.5in Glass $275-$400
QUALITY/FARM BUREAU/PRODUCTS (on shield)
(4)   1940s   Gill $275-$400
White globe face with blue outline and red "8 point" border around co-op logo in center. White-outlined blue outer ring and center band with white "QUALITY" on top ring, "PRODUCTS" on bottom ring, with white "FARM/BUREAU" on diagonal band across center.

FYR-ZON GASOLINE
(4)   1950s   13.5in Capco $100-$175
White globe face with red over blue oval in center. White "Fyr-Zon" on upper red area, "GASOLINE" on lower blue area.

Farmers Union Co-operative Organization of Iowa

FARMOIL w/plow scene
(5)   1920s   15in Metal $1,200-$2,200
White globe face with smaller red-outlined white circle on lower globe face. Blue lettering arched around edge of small circle ":FARMERS UNION CO-OPERATIVE ORGANIZATION:" at top, "OF IOWA" at bottom, with red and gray farm field scene with plow in center of smaller circle. Red-outlined blue "FARMOIL" formed around top of circle.

Iowa Farm Service Company, Des Moines, Iowa

FARM BUREAU SPECIAL
(5)   1940s   13.5in Capco $150-$225
Red outer ring with geartooth edge. Red and white outlines around blue center circle. White "FARM BUREAU" arched top in red area, "SERVICE" around bottom, with white script "Special" diagonally across blue center.

FARM BUREAU HI-COMPRESSION
(5)   1940s   13.5in Capco $150-$250
Same as above, with script white "Hi/Compression" replacing "Special."

CROWN CENTRAL PETROLEUM, Baltimore, Maryland

Crown Central Petroleum traces its earliest history to the east Texas oil fields where in oil exploration got under way in 1917. By 1920, a Houston refinery was in operation providing high-quality lubricants. In 1930, Crown's headquarters shifted to Baltimore, Maryland, under new ownership and in 1933 retail marketing in the East was added to a chain of service stations already operated in Houston.

Throughout the 1930s and 1940s, jobbers were actively sought in markets from Pennsylvania to Alabama. In the mid-1960s Crown became involved in direct retail marketing, with the addition of the "Peoples" stations of Energy Oil Company. So successful was direct retailing that by the early 1970s, jobber accounts were abandoned in favor of all company-operated stations. Crown also entered the convenience store market in the early 1980s with the purchase of Sunoco's "Fast Fare" chain in the Southeast. Crown products are currently available at over 600 locations in the southeastern United States.

CROWN
(5)   1930-1933   15in Metal   No Listing
Orange face with white outlined black band arched across center of face. White lettering "CROWN" on black band with monogram style interlocked "C.C.P.CO." on lower globe face.

CROWNZOL
(5)   1930-1933   15in Metal   No listing
White face with orange outlined dark yellow band arched across center of globe face. Black "CROWNZOL" on yellow band. Monogram style interlocked "C.C.P.CO." on lower globe face.

CROWN GAS-OIL
(3)   1933-1956   Gill $225-$350
Orange globe face with white-outlined black band arched across center of globe. White lettering "CROWN" on black band, with white "OIL (star) GAS" on lower orange field.

CROWNZOL
(3)   1933-1956   Gill $225-$350
White globe face with orange-outlined dark yellow band arched across center of face. Black "CROWNZOL" on band, and small orange star on lower white field.

CROWNZOL (w/"HI-OCTANE USA" decal)
(4)   1950s   13.5in Capco   No Listing
Same as above, with decal over star.

CROWNZOL (w/ribbon decal)
(4)   1950s   Gill   No Listing
Same as above, with gold ribbon decal over star.

CROWN GOLD
(3)   1956-1973   Gill $275-$400
CROWN GOLD
(5)   1956-1973   13.5in Capco $150-$250
Mirrored gold globe face with orange and white Crown wing logo above center of face, and blue-outlined white lettering "GOLD" below logo.

CROWN SILVER
(3)   1956-1973   Gill $275-$400
CROWN SILVER
(5)   1956-1973   13.5in Capco $150-$250
Mirrored silver globe face, with word "SILVER" replacing "GOLD" as described for CROWN GOLD.

CROWN DIESEL
(4)   1956-1973   Gill $225-$300
White globe face with small orange Crown wing logo at top over blue "DIESEL/FUEL."

Thrift

A 1950s Crown secondary brand.

THRIFT REGULAR
(5)   1950s affiliate   Gill $225-$350
Similar to CROWN GAS-OIL above, except "THRIFT" replaces "CROWN" in band and white "REGULAR/GAS" replaces "OIL/GAS."

THRIFT PREMIUM
(5)   1950s affiliate   Gill $225-$350
Same as above, except "PREMIUM" replaces "REGULAR."

Various Cities Service clover-shaped inserts on clover-shaped bodies.
John Phippen

Various Cities Service clover-shaped inserts on clover-shaped bodies.
John Phippen

Super X Motor Fuel one-piece fired-on globe. Ron Prichard

Blue Grass 15in cast inserts on metal body. John Phippen

Marland Gasoline one-piece etched globe. Glen Blackmore

Marland High Test 13.5in inserts on plastic body. R. V. Witherspoon

Various Crown 13.5in inserts on Gill bodies. R. V. Witherspoon

Valley 13.5in inserts on plastic body.

Co-op Regular 13.5in inserts on glass body. Roger Brown

Farmers Union 13.5in inserts on Gill body.

DOC/Derby Super Ratio 15in inserts on metal body. Dave Walthers

Energy Oil Company, Annandale, Virginia

Founded as Peoples Self-Service Gas Stations, Incorporated, in Annandale, Virginia, in the late 1940s, Peoples operated a chain of retail gasoline stations in Virginia, Maryland, and Washington, DC. By the mid-1960s, the corporate name had become Energy Oil Company and over twenty stations were being operated. In 1967 Crown, which had supplied Peoples for years, purchased the chain and rebranded the stations Crown. Peoples then became a Crown secondary brand, appearing on a few remaining jobber-operated stations in North Carolina. The name was reintroduced for use on some company-operated stations that Crown purchased from Ashland in 1985, but these were rebranded Crown in 1987 and the Peoples brand is no longer in use.

Note: No Peoples globes are known to exist .

DERBY OIL COMPANY, Wichita, Kansas

Derby Oil Company was a midcontinent refiner and marketer founded in Wichita, Kansas, in 1920. In the late 1930s, Derby was instrumental in the creation of Sovereign Service, a marketing organization for independent dealers supported by a number of midcontinent refiners. After World War II, Derby concentrated on an expanding chain of retail service stations as well as numerous dealer-operated units and a large jobber-marketer arrangement with Piester. In 1955 Colorado Interstate Gas Company purchased Derby, and with its large oil production system allowed for greater expansion of the Derby refinery and marketing network. In the early 1970s Colorado Interstate Gas became a part of the Coastal Corporation, and in 1988 Derby stations, along with others in the Coastal organization, were rebranded Coastal.

DERBY (red background white star)
(5)   1920s   One-piece etched $900-$1,600
DERBY (red background white star)
(4)   1920s   One-piece baked $750-$1,100
White globe with red face. Large white star covers most of face. Interlocking "D/O/Co." in blue in center of star.
DERBY SUPER RATIO MOTOR FUEL
(5)   1920s   15in Metal $600-$900
White globe face with blue-outlined red circle in center. White star on red center circle, with blue interlocking "D/O/Co." in center of star. Blue "SUPER-RATIO" arched around top, "MOTOR FUEL" arched around bottom.
DERBY GASOLINE
(3)   1930-1935   13.5in Capco $125-$175
White outer ring around red center of globe face. Large white star in center, with interlocking "D/O/Co." on star. Blue "DERBY" arched around top, "GASOLINE" around bottom.
DERBY GASOLINE
(3)   1935-1946   Gill $250-$350
White globe face with red-outlined blue circle in center. Small white "textured" star in center blue circle, with blue "D/O/Co." interlocking on center of star. Blue "DERBY" arched around top, "GASOLINE" around bottom.
DERBY GASOLINE
(3)   1935-1946   Gill $250-$350
White globe face with blue-outlined red circle in center. Small white "textured" star in center red circle, with blue "D/O/Co." interlocking on center of star. Blue "DERBY" arched around top, "GASOLINE" around bottom.
DERBY'S FLEXGAS
(3)   1946-1950   13.5in Capco $125-$175
White globe face with blue-outlined red circle in center. Small white "textured" star in center red circle, with blue "D/O/Co." interlocking on center of star. Blue "DERBY'S" arched around top, "GASOLINE" around bottom, with dot in white ring at center on either side.
DERBY'S FLEXGAS ETHYL small (EGC)
(3)   1930-1941   Gill $275-$375
Red globe face with black-outlined white circle in center. Small Ethyl (EGC) logo in center with yellow rays. White "DERBY'S" arched around top, "FLEXGAS" around bottom.
DERBY'S FLEXGAS ETHYL large (EC)
(3)   1941-1962   Gill $275-$375
Red globe face with black-outlined white circle in center. Large Ethyl (EC) logo in center circle. White "DERBY'S" arched around top, "FLEXGAS" around bottom.
DERBY
(3)   1950-1970   Gill $200-$375
DERBY
(2)   1950-1970   13.5in Capco $100-$150
Blue and white outline rings around red globe face. Large white "textured" star on red face, with blue horizontal band across star below center. White "DERBY" on band.
DERBY PREMIUM ETHYL
(4)   1962-1970   13.5in Capco $100-$150
Red globe face with black-outlined white circle in center. Large Ethyl (EC) logo in center circle. White "DERBY" arched around top, "PREMIUM" around bottom.
DERBY DIESEL
(4)   1950-1970   Gill $200-$325
DERBY DIESEL
(4)   1950-1970   13.5in Capco $125-$175
White globe face with blue outline ring. Large red "DIESEL" with blue underline across center of face. Small red circle with white star "DERBY" logo at bottom.

Sovereign Service

Sovereign Service was a franchise program allowing independent dealers supplied by the various midcontinent refiners that participated in the program to be branded Sovereign Service. Dealers were held to high standards of operation, supported by cooperative advertising of the programs' features (independent dealers only, clean rest rooms, twenty-four-hour service, and so on). Derby was a leading participant in the program, along with Kanotex/Apco, Vickers, Rock Island, Eason, Elreco, Yale, Shallow Water, and perhaps others. The program was initiated in the late 1930s (about 1937) and survived as late as 1959. Globes from the individual brands are listed under that company in the book.

SOVEREIGN "SS"
(3)   1937-1959   Gill $200-$325
Brown globe face with large white-outlined yellow shield covering most of face. Brown "SOVEREIGN" diagonally across shield, with small brown shield at top of larger shield. Yellow interlocking "SS" on small brown shield.
SOVEREIGN ETHYL
(3)   1937-1959   Gill $200-$350
Red globe face with large white-and-red-outlined white shield covering most of face. Red "SOVEREIGN" diagonally across shield, with small Ethyl (EC) logo in black-outlined circle at top of shield.
SOVEREIGN QUALITY
(3)   1937-1959   Gill $225-$350
Same as "SOVEREIGN" above, with brown "QUALITY" added below "SOVEREIGN" on shield.
KANOTEX SOVEREIGN QUALITY
(3)   1937-1952   Gill $250-$400
Same as "SOVEREIGN QUALITY" above, with small black-outlined oval replacing "SS" shield at top of globe face. Multicolored Kanotex logo with red "KANOTEX" in small white oval.

DIXIE DISTRIBUTORS, INCORPORATED, Ann Arbor, Michigan

Dixie Distributors, Incorporated, was a distributor association put together by a group of Michigan-based oil jobbers in Ann Arbor, Michigan, in 1926. Almost immediately, independent jobbers from all around the country applied for a Dixie franchise and joined the association in order to be able to market their products under the Dixie name. The organization expanded greatly until World War II, when gasoline shortages forced many independents, including many of the Dixie affiliates, out of business. Marketing efforts by the majors after WW II were so much greater than an independent organization could hope to compete wit, and many former Dixie jobbers eventually were branded by the majors. Nevertheless, Dixie stations survived until the 1960s or later in some areas, and the organization survives today.

DIXIE OILS GASOLINE
(4)   1926-1928   One-piece etched $800-$1,200
White globe with dark blue ring around yellow center. White diamond on yellow center, with blue "OILS" on diamond. White "DIXIE" arched around top, "GASOLINE" around bottom.
DIXIE HIGH-TEST
(5)   1926-1928   One-piece etched   No Listing
White globe with dark blue ring around yellow center. White diamond on yellow center, with blue "OILS" on diamond. White "DIXIE" arched around top, "HIGH TEST" around bottom.
DIXIE POWER TO PASS
(5)   1928-1931   Blue Glass Oval $1,000-$1,600
Blue glass body for oval lenses that has rounded area between lens area and base. White "POWER-TO-PASS" lettering on lower area. Globe face is blue with white oval in center. Blue-outlined yellow diamond on center white oval. Blue "OILS" in diamond, white "DIXIE" arched around top, "GASOLINE" around bottom.

DIXIE POWER TO PASS
(5)   1928-1931   White Glass Oval $1,000-$1,600
White glass body same as above, with blue "POWER-TO-PASS."
DIXIE GASOLINE BLUE STREAK
(5)   1928-1931   Blue Glass Oval $1,000-$1,600
Blue glass body same as above, with white "BLUE STREAK" lettering.
DIXIE GASOLINE BENZOL
(5)   1928-1931   Green Glass Oval $1,000-$1,800
Green glass body same as above, with white "BENZOL" lettering.
DIXIE KNOCK OUT
(5)   1928-1931   White Glass Oval $1,000-$1,600
White glass body same as above, with blue "KNOCK OUT" lettering.
DIXIE LIBERTY
(5)   1928-1931   Yellow Glass Oval $1,000-$1,700
Yellow glass body same as above, with white "LIBERTY" lettering.
DIXIE NEVERNOX
(5)   1928-1931   Red Glass Oval $1,000-$1,600
Red glass body same as above, with white "NEVER-NOX" lettering.
DIXIE GASOLINE
(4)   1920s-1930s   15in Metal $350-$600
White globe face with blue oval covering most of face. White oval in center of oval, with yellow diamond on white oval. Red "OILS" on diamond, white "DIXIE" arched around top on oval, "GASOLINE" around bottom.
DIXIE GASOLINE POWER TO PASS
(4)   1931-1940   15in Metal $325-$550
DIXIE GASOLINE POWER TO PASS
(5)   1931-1940   15in Jeweled Metal $800-$1,400
DIXIE GASOLINE POWER TO PASS
(2)   1931-1960   Gill $275-$425
DIXIE GASOLINE POWER TO PASS
(4)   1931-1960   Yellow Ripple Gill $700-$1,200
DIXIE GASOLINE POWER TO PASS
(2)   1941-1960   13.5in Glass $225-$325
DIXIE GASOLINE POWER TO PASS
(2)   1941-1960   13.5in Capco $125-$175
DIXIE GASOLINE POWER TO PASS
(4)   1941-1960   Yellow Capco $150-$250
Yellow globe face with blue oval on center of face. White oval on center of blue oval, with yellow diamond on white oval. Red "OILS" on diamond, white "DIXIE" arched around top on blue oval, "GASOLINE" around bottom. Blue "POWER TO PASS" arched around bottom of globe face under oval.
DIXIE ETHYL (EGC)
(5)   1931-1940   15in Metal   No Listing
DIXIE ETHYL (EGC)
(5)   1931-1940   15in Jeweled Metal $800-$1,400
DIXIE ETHYL (EGC)
(3)   1931-1949   Gill $250-$375
DIXIE ETHYL (EGC)
(4)   1931-1949   Yellow Ripple Gill $700-$1,200
DIXIE ETHYL (EGC)
(3)   1931-1949   13.5in Glass $225-$350
Yellow outline ring around inner and outer edge of blue outer ring. Black ring around white center circle. White "DIXIE" in arched around top in blue ring, "GASOLINE" around bottom with large Ethyl (EGC) logo in center white circle. Yellow rays extending out from Ethyl logo.
DIXIE ETHYL (EC)
(4)   1941-1949   13.5in Glass $225-$350
DIXIE ETHYL (EC)
(4)   1941-1949   13.5in Yellow Capco $150-$275
Same as DIXIE ETHYL (EGC) above, except with newer Ethyl (EC) logo.
DIXIE PREMIUM
(3)   1949-1960   13.5in Yellow Capco $150-$275
Same as DIXIE GASOLINE POWER TO PASS, except red "PREMIUM" on center yellow diamond and no "POWER TO PASS" on lower globe face.
DIXIE BLUE
(5)   1930-1932   13.5in Glass $275-$425
White globe face with large blue "DIXIE" arched over "BLUE."
DIXOLINE w/lines
(4)   1932-1935   13.5in Glass $200-$300
White globe face with dark blue "DIXOLINE" diagonally from upper left to lower right on face. Light blue dropshading around each letter, and light blue line above and below lettering.
DIXOLINE
(3)   1935-1940   13.5in Glass $200-$300

DIXOLINE
(2)   1935-1940   Gill $250-$350
White globe face with blue outline ring. Blue "DIXOLINE" diagonally from lower left to upper right, with "D" and "E" extending through outline ring.

D-X and Affiliates
MID-CONTINENT PETROLEUM, Tulsa, Oklahoma
Mid-Continent was organized in 1916 from the various holdings of oil pioneer Josh Cosden and others. Gasoline marketing under the Diamond brand name began about 1920 and by the mid-1920s, Mid-Continent operated a large number of stations throughout the central United States. A super-premium fuel Diamond D-X was introduced about 1933, and by 1940 stations were branded as Diamond D-X stations. After WWII the brand name became simply D-X. In 1955 Mid-Continent merged with Sunray Oil Company and the corporate name became Sunray D-X Oil Company, revised in 1962 to D-X–Sunray Oil Company. In 1968, D-X-Sunray merged with Philadelphia-based Sun Oil Company and many dual-logo Sunoco–D-X items were introduced at this time. D-X globes had been phased out by the time of the merger. Shortly after the merger, the Sunoco brand name replaced D-X in states where Sunoco already marketed. The D-X brand was retained in other areas until after 1980, when Sunoco began gradually replacing D-X. As of this writing only small areas of D-X branding remain, primarily jobber-operated stations that just haven't yet been converted.
NEVR NOX GASOLENE
(4)   1920s   One-piece etched $900-$1,400
White globe with black logotype "NevrNox" across face. Black-and-white-outlined red arrow below logotype, with white "GASOLENE" on arrow.
NEVR NOX GASOLENE DIAMOND PRODUCT
(4)   1920s   One-piece etched $1,000-$1,600
Same as above, with red "DIAMOND" arched around top, "GASOLINE" around bottom.
NEVR NOX "PEPPY POWER"
(5)   1920s   One-piece etched   No Listing
White globe with red outline around face. Black-and-white-outlined black "NevrNox" logotype across face, with red arrow below. White "GASOLINE" on red arrow. Red "PEPPY POWER" arched around top, "IN EVERY DROP" around bottom.
NEVR NOX GASOLENE NON-POISONOUS
(4)   1925-1930   One-piece etched $1,000-$1,500
White globe with red diamond outline at center of face. Black "NevrNox" logotype inside diamond. Red arrow below logotype, with white "GASOLINE" on arrow. Small black "NON-POISONOUS" below arrow. Likely created in response to the national "scare" about "poison" Ethyl gasoline.
DIAMOND NITRO GASOLINE
(5)   1920s   One-piece etched   No Listing
White globe face with outline ring around globe face. Large "NITRO" across center, with "DIAMOND" arched around top and "GASOLINE" around bottom.
DIAMOND
(4)   1920s   One-piece etched $450-$750
White globe with red outline ring around face. Solid red diamond in center, with large "DIAMOND" across diamond.
DIAMOND GAS/OIL
(5)   1925-1930   15in Metal   No Listing
White globe face with red outline ring. Solid red diamond in center, with large black "DIAMOND" lettering across diamond. Black-outlined red "GAS" arched around top, "OIL" around bottom.
DIAMOND
(3)   1925-1933   One-piece etched $500-$700
White globe with red diamond in center of face. White and red diamond outlines around center diamond. Black "DIAMOND" lettering across diamond logo.
DIAMOND
(5)   1930-1933   13.5in Glass $200-$325
White globe face with red outline ring. Red diamond in center outlined by white diamond and red diamond bands. Black "DIAMOND" lettering across white band and red center diamond.
DIAMOND D-X LUBRICATING (tan)
(3)   1933-1936   13.5in Banded Glass $225-$375
Tan globe face with red outline ring. Red diamond outline with tan center in center of globe face. Large black-outlined tan "D-X," with black dropshade superimposed over diamond outline. Black "DIAMOND" lettering arched over top, black "chevron" below diamond, with tan "LUBRICATING MOTOR FUEL" on chevron.
DIAMOND D-X LUBRICATING MOTOR FUEL
(2)   1933-1936   13.5in Glass $250-$400

DIAMOND D-X LUBRICATING MOTOR FUEL
(2)   1933-1936   13.5in Banded Glass $250-$400
Same as above, with white globe face and lettering.
NEVRNOX ETHYL
(4)   1933-1936   13.5in Glass $225-$350
NEVRNOX ETHYL
(4)   1933-1936   13.5in Banded Glass $225-$375
White globe face with red outline ring. Black-outlined red logotype
"NevrNox" arched around top. Black and white Ethyl (EGC) logo, with
red rays below globe in plain black and white, without the yellow let-
tering and info box.
D-X LUBRICATING MOTOR FUEL (white)
(3)   1936-1946   13.5in Banded Glass $225-$375
D-X LUBRICATING MOTOR FUEL (white)
(3)   1936-1946   13.5in Glass $225-$350
Same as DIAMOND D-X LUBRICATING MOTOR FUEL above, with-
out "DIAMOND" arched above logo.
D-X ETHYL LUBRICATING MOTOR FUEL
(4)   1936-1946   13.5in Banded Glass $250-$400
D-X ETHYL LUBRICATING MOTOR FUEL
(4)   1936-1946   13.5in Glass $250-$350
White globe face with red outline ring. Red diamond outline with
white center in center of globe face. Large black "D-X" superimposed
over diamond. Black-outlined white band below "D-X," with red
"ETHYL" on band. Black "chevron" below logo with white "LUBRI-
CATING MOTOR FUEL" on chevron.
POWER (tan)
(4)   1933-1936   13.5in Banded Glass $225-$350
Tan globe face with red diamond outline, with tan center in center of
globe face. Red outline ring around face. Black "POWER" across dia-
mond logo.
POWER (white)
(3)   1936-1940   13.5in Glass $200-$325
POWER (white)
(3)   1936-1940   13.5in Banded Glass $200-$300
Same as above, with white globe face and center of diamond.
POWER "G" (white)
(4)   1940-1946   13.5in Banded Glass $200-$350
Same as POWER above, with large black italic "G" at lower edge of di-
amond.
D-X LUBRICATING GASOLINE
(2)   1946-1957   13.5in Capco $125-$175
Tan globe face with red outline ring. Red and black "D-X" logo at top
of globe face. Black script "Lubricating" above red "GASOLINE" below
logo.
Tan globe face with red outline ring. Red and black "D-X" logo at top
of globe face. Black oval with tan "ETHYL" above black "Lubricating
Gasoline" below logo.
D-X DIESEL
(4)   1946-1955   13.5in Capco $150-$225
Tan globe face with red outline ring. Red and black "D-X" logo at top
of face. Black script "Diesel" below logo.
D-X BORON w/line
(2)   1955-1957   13.5in Capco $100-$150
White globe face with thin red and thicker black line diagonally down
from left side and curved across bottom. Red and black "D-X" logo with
tan center at top of globe face, above red italic "BORON."
D-X BORON w/line w/"rocket" frame
(5)   1955-1956   13.5in Capco   No Listing
Same as above, enclosed in a cutout "rocket" frame designed to fit
around Capcolite globe.
D-X LUBRICATING GASOLINE–1957 logo
(2)   1957-1968   13.5in Capco $100-$150
White globe face with large red, white, and blue 1957 "D-X" logo above
blue "LUBRICATING/GASOLINE."
D-X BORON–1957 logo
(2)   1957-1968   13.5in Capco $75-$150
Same as above, with red italic "BORON" replacing
"LUBRICATING/GASOLINE."
D-X DIESEL–1957 logo
(3)   1957-1968   13.5in Capco $75-$150
Same as above, with blue italic "DIESEL" replacing "LUBRICAT-
ING/GASOLINE."
D-X MARINE–1957 logo
(5)   1957-1968   13.5in Capco $250-$475
White globe face with red outline ring. Red, white, and blue "D-X" logo
at top. Two blue wave lines across globe face below logo, with two blue
boats and "MARINE" above top line and "GASOLINE" between lines.

Sunray Oil

Sunray, a midcontinent area producer and refiner dating back to
the 1920s, was historically very involved with production and unbranded marketing, with very little attention paid to branded Sunray
marketing. Gasoline was sold under the company name through a
small number of jobbers and due to the limited branded marketing,
the globes listed are rare. Sunray Oil merged with Mid-Continent Petroleum in 1955 and the D-X brand was added to Sunray logos at existing Sunray stations. In about 1962, those few stations became simply D-X stations.
SUNRAY
(5)   1930-1940   Orange Gill Ripple $900-$1,500
SUNRAY
(4)   1935-1940   13.5in Orange Capco $400-$600
White edge of globe face with large black-and-white-outlined octagon
covering most of globe face. Upper 3/4 of octagon is orange, with large
yellow sun and rays extending outward. Lower 1/4 is green. Large
black "SUNRAY" is arched below sun across rays.
SUNRAY GASOLINE
(5)   1940-1955   Orange Gill Ripple $900-$1,500
SUNRAY GASOLINE
(3)   1950-1955   13.5in Orange Capco $400-$600
Similar to above, with black area around octagon, smaller rays extending from sun, and "SUNRAY" arched upward instead of downward. Black "GASOLINE" in lower green area.
SUNRAY ETHYL (EC)
(5)   1940-1955   Orange Gill Ripple $900-$1,500
SUNRAY ETHYL (EC)
(3)   1950-1955   13.5in Red Capco $400-$600
Same as above, with yellow circle on lower green area. Ethyl (EC)
with black rays on circle.

Premier, Longview, Texas

An independent Texas refiner with stations in Texas, Oklahoma,
Arkansas, and Louisiana. In 1964 the company merged with Sunray
D-X. Some stations were spun off to Vickers, while D-X retained the
Premier name. Some unsuccessful D-X stations were later converted
to Premier, and the brand survived at a small number of locations
until D-X rebranded Sunoco in the 1980s.
PREMIER REGULAR
(3)   1935-1955   13.5in Glass $200-$325
PREMIER REGULAR
(3)   1950-1965   13.5in Capco $75-$150
White globe face with blue and red outline rings. Red "PREMIER,"
with blue dropshade across upper globe face, with blue script "REGU-
LAR" below "PREMIER."
PREMIER MOTOR
(4)   1935-1940   13.5in Glass $200-$350
Same as above, with blue script "MOTOR" replacing "REGULAR."
PREMIER ETHYL (EGC)
(4)   1935-1955   13.5in Glass $200-$350
Same as above, with Ethyl (EGC) logo with yellow rays below "PRE-
MIER."
PREMIER ETHYL (EC)
(3)   1941-1955   13.5in Glass $200-$325
PREMIER ETHYL (EC)
(3)   1950-1965   13.5in Capco $75-$150
Same as above, with Ethyl (EC) logo.
PREMIER DIESEL FUEL
(4)   1950-1965   13.5in Capco $100-$175
Same as above, with blue script "DIESEL/FUEL" replacing "REGU-
LAR."
PREMIER WHITE MARINE
(5)   1950s   13.5in Capco $175-$300
Description not available.

Barnsdall Refining Company, Barnsdale, Oklahoma

One of the oldest oil refiners in the business, Barnsdall began re-
tail gasoline marketing in 1921. At one time one of the largest midcon-
tinent marketers, Barnsdall was reorganized during the depression as
Barnsdall Refining and in 1940, the Bareco brand name replaced the
Barnsdall brand. In 1952 Bareco closed their last refinery to concen-
trate on wax production, and the gasoline marketing was sold off to
Mid-Continent Petroleum. Mid-Continent eventually phased out the
Bareco brand after the merger with Sunray.
BARNSDALL (small globe, 4in base)
(5)   1910s   One-piece etched   No Listing
White globe with red "BARNSDALL REFINING" arched around top,
"GASOLINE" around bottom, wth red "B" in black square in center.

Red "BE" above square and "SQUARE" below square.
BARNSDALL (domed globe)
(5)   1920s   One-piece etched   No Listing
White "pylon" domed top globe with etched details. Blue "BARNS-DALL" across top of globe face, blue "B" in center outlined in square, and blue "GASOLINE" across bottom.
BARNSDALL BE SQUARE GAS
(4)   1920s   One-piece etched $1,100-$1,600
White globe with black outline ring around face. Large blue "B" outlined in a square in center of face, with small "BE" just above square and "SQUARE" just below. Red "BARNSDALL" arched around top, "GASOLINE" around bottom.
BARNSDALL SUPER GAS
(5)   1920s   One-piece etched $1,000-$1,500
White globe with large blue "SUPER-GAS" across face. Red "BARNS-DALL" arched around top, "ANTI-KNOCK" in straight line below "SUPER-GAS."
BARNSDALL MOTOR FUEL
(4)   1930-1941   13.5in Glass $250-$350
White globe face with blue outline ring. Red square in center, with white and blue squares outlining it. Red "BARNSDALL" arched around top, "GASOLINE" around bottom.
BARNSDALL MOTOR FUEL (flat face)
(5)   1930-1935   13.5in Glass $250-$375
Same design as above. Flat face for special body.
BARNSDALL/BE/B/SQUARE/GASOLINE
(3)   1930-1941   13.5in Glass $225-$350
White globe face with blue outline ring. Blue "B" in blue square outline in center. Small "BE" above square, small "SQUARE" below. Red "BARNSDALL" arched around top. "GASOLINE" around bottom.
BARNSDALL/SUPER-GAS/ANTI-KNOCK
(4)   1930-1933   13.5in Balcrank $250-$375
White globe face with blue outline ring. Red "BARNSDALL" arched around top, blue "SUPER-GAS" across center, and red "ANTI-KNOCK" across bottom.
BARNSDALL/SUPER-GAS/ETHYL (EGC)
(4)   1933-1940   13.5in Glass $225-$350
White globe face with blue outline ring. Red "BARNSDALL" arched around top, blue "SUPER-GAS" across center, and Ethyl (EGC) logo below.
BARECO/BE/B/SQUARE/GASOLINE
(3)   1940-1955   13.5in Glass $250-$375
White globe face with blue outline ring. Blue "B" in blue square outline in center. Small "BE" above square, small "SQUARE" below. Red "BARECO" arched around top, "GASOLINE" around bottom.
BARECO/SUPER-GAS/ETHYL (EGC)
(4)   1940-1955   13.5in Glass $225-$350
White globe face with blue outline ring. Red "BARECO" arched around top, blue "SUPER-GAS" across center, and Ethyl (EGC) logo below.
SUPER GAS/BE/B/SQUARE/PREMIUM
(4)   1940-1955   13.5in Glass $200-$350
White globe face with blue outline ring. Blue "B" in blue square outline in center. Small "BE" above square, small "SQUARE" below. Red "SUPER-GAS" arched around top, "PREMIUM" around bottom.

Monarch Manufacturing Company,
Council Bluffs, Iowa

Owner of the famous MonaMotor trademark, Monarch began gasoline marketing about 1920 and merged into Barnsdall about 1929.
MONAMOTOR GASOLINE
(5)   1920s   One-piece etched $900-$1,600
MONAMOTOR GASOLINE
(5)   1920s   One-piece baked   No Listing
White globe with red face. Black-and-white-outlined white diamond in center, with black logotype "MonaMotor" across diamond and white-outlined black "GASOLINE" arched around bottom.
MONAMOTOR GASOLINE
(5)   1920s   Oval One-piece etched   No Listing
Oval globe with same design as above.
MONAMOTOR BENZOL
(5)   1920s   One-piece etched   No Listing
Same as above, with "BENZOL" replacing "GASOLINE."
MONAMOTOR HI-TEST
(5)   1920s   One-piece etched   No Listing
Same as above, with "HI-TEST" replacing "GASOLINE."

Hawkeye Oil Company
Waterloo, Iowa

An Iowa marketer operating stations under the Hawkeye and Parco brand names. The company was purchased by Mid-Continent about 1930.

PARCO GAS
(5)   1910s   15in Metal   No Listing
Perforated metal globe face. Solid dark color with white outline ring and white "PARCO/GAS" across face.
PARCO RED BALL GASOLINE
(5)   1920s   15in Metal   No Listing
Yellow globe face with red circle in center. Black "PARCO" with red dropshade arched around top, "GASOLINE" around bottom, with "RED" to left of circle and "BALL" to right.
RED BALL GASOLINE
(5)   1920s   15in Metal   No Listing
Yellow globe face with black-and-white-outlined red circle in center. White-outlined black "RED BALL" arched around top, "GASOLINE" around bottom.
HAWKEYE OILS
(5)   1920s   15in Metal $375-$500
White globe face with large black triangle-red thunderbird IOMA logo in center. Black "HAWKEYE" arched around top, "OILS" around bottom.

EXXON and Affiliates
STANDARD OIL COMPANY OF NEW JERSEY,
New York, New York

Esso is, of course, Standard Oil of New Jersey, largest of the Standard companies to emerge from the 1911 breakup of Standard Oil. Standard (NJ) began marketing in several eastern seaboard states and in Tennessee, Louisiana, and Arkansas through Standard of Louisiana, a subsidiary assigned to them with the 1911 breakup. The Esso brand was first introduced in 1926 as an Ethyl grade gasoline, and in 1933 replaced Standard as the company's brand name. Esso marketing expanded to include stations in nineteen states with marketing after WWII, added throughout the country under various brand names detailed below. In 1959, all domestic marketing was grouped under the subsidiary Humble Oil and Refining, formerly an independent company that Standard purchased in 1919. Under Humble, the Esso brand name was retained in the East and South. Enco was introduced to replace the various other regional brands and Humble was used in Ohio when Sohio objected to both Esso and Enco. In 1972 the brand name Exxon was introduced to replace Esso, Enco, and Humble, although Enco remained in use in the upper Midwest region until that area was abandoned several years later. Exxon continues to market through its more than 11,000 stations in forty states.
STANDARD MOTOR GASOLINE (chimney top)
(5)   1912-1918   One-piece etched   No Listing
White globe with red Standard "S" logo covering face. Red "STAN-DARD" in top of "S," "GASOLINE" below, with white "MOTOR" on red center of "S."
STANDARD MOTOR GASOLINE (flat sides)
(5)   1917-1923   One-piece etched   No Listing
Same logo as above, except globe has flat sides and no chimney top.
STANDARD MOTOR GASOLINE
(5)   1918-1923   16.5in Metal $400-$700
STANDARD MOTOR GASOLINE
(4)   1918-1923   15in Metal $350-$650
White globe face with red Standard "S" logo covering most of globe face. Red "STANDARD" in top of "S," "GASOLINE" below, with white "MOTOR" on red center of "S."
STANDARD (red and black)
(5)   1918-1923   15in Metal   No Listing
Same as above, with "STANDARD" and "GASOLINE" in black instead of red.
STANDARD BENZOL
(5)   1920s   15in Metal   No Listing
Red globe face with white "S" logo (opposite from above). White "STANDARD" and "GASOLINE" and red "BENZOL" replacing "MOTOR."
"STANDARD"
(5)   1923-1924   16.5in Metal $300-$450
"STANDARD"
(4)   1923-1924   15in Metal $275-$425
White globe face with blue outline ring broken at sides, where lettering extends to edge, and at bottom for "REG.U.S.PAT.OFF." Red "STANDARD" (in quotes) across globe face.
"STANDARD" ETHYL (EGC) GASOLINE
(5)   1924-1926   15in Metal   No Listing
Wide red outer ring with white and blue outlines. White center circle. White "STANDARD" (in quotes) arched around top, "ETHYL GASO-LINE" around bottom, with large Ethyl (EGC) logo in white center circle with blue rays.

"STANDARD" WHITE
(5)   1924-1930   16.5in Metal $300-$500
"STANDARD" WHITE
(4)   1924-1930   15in Metal $250-$450
White globe face with blue "'STANDARD'" (in quotes) above "WHITE" across center.
STANDARD (Upper/lower case)
(5)   1924   16.5in Metal $275-$475
STANDARD (Upper/lower case)
(5)   1924   15in Metal $275-$450
White globe face with red lines forming white band across center ,and red half-circles above and below (referred to throughout this text as bar-and-circle). Blue "Standard" on crossbar.
STANDARD (bar and circle)
(3)   1924-1933   16.5in Metal $250-$475
STANDARD (bar and circle)
(3)   1924-1933   15in Metal $250-$425
Same as above, with "STANDARD" (all upper case) across bar.
STANDARD (bar and circle reverse)
(4)   1924-1933   16.5in Metal $300-$550
STANDARD (bar and circle reverse)
(4)   1924-1933   15in Metal $275-$500
Same as above, with red and blue reversed.
STANDARD (bar and circle) AVIATION
(5)   1924-1933   15in Metal   No Listing
Same as above, with "AVIATION" arched around top, "GASOLINE" around bottom.
ESSO (script)
(4)   1926-1933   16.5in Metal $325-$550
ESSO (script)
(4)   1926-1933   15in Metal $325-$525
ESSO SCRIPT
(5)   1926-1933   15in fired on milk glass lens   No listing
White globe face with thick red and thin blue outline rings. Blue script "Esso" diagonally across face.
ACTO
(3)   1933-1939   16.5in Metal $275-$450
ACTO
(3)   1933-1939   15in Metal $250-$375
White globe face with black-outlined green "ACTO" across face. Green line forming half-circles above and below.
ESSO
(2)   1933-1962   16.5in Metal $250-$400
ESSO
(2)   1933-1962   15in Metal $225-$350
ESSO
(4)   1950-1972   13.5in Glass $200-$275
White globe face with "ESSO" logotype in red across center of face.
ESSOLENE
(3)   1933-1939   16.5in Metal $250-$450
ESSOLENE
(3)   1933-1939   15in Metal $250-$375
White globe face with red Standard style bar-and-circle. Blue "Essolene" in crossbar.
NEW ESSO
(5)   1938 Decal   16.5in Metal   No Listing
NEW ESSO
(5)   1938 Decal   15in Metal   No Listing
Essolene "bar-and-circle" globe described above, with decal over crossbar. Script blue "NEW" to left of red "ESSO" logotype on decal.
NEW ESSO EXTRA
(5)   1938 Decal   16.5in Metal   No Listing
NEW ESSO EXTRA
(5)   1938 Decal   15in Metal   No Listing
Description not available.
ESSO EXTRA
(3)   1939-1952   16.5in Metal $250-$425
ESSO EXTRA
(3)   1939-1952   15in Metal $250-$375
ESSO EXTRA
(4)   1950-1952   13.5in Glass $175-$300
ESSO EXTRA
(5)   1939-1952   18in Metal band neon   No Listing
White globe face with "ESSO" logotype in blue over blue "EXTRA."
ESSO EXTRA (underlined)
(3)   1952-1962   16.5in Metal $250-$425
ESSO EXTRA (underlined)
(3)   1952-1962   15in Metal $250-$375
ESSO EXTRA (underlined)
(4)   1952-1972   13.5in Glass $175-$300

Same as above, with red line under "EXTRA."
ESSO AVIATION
(5)   1933-1962   16.5in Metal $550-$900
ESSO AVIATION
(5)   1933-1962   15in Metal $550-$900
ESSO AVIATION
(5)   1950-1972   13.5in $450-$750
White globe face with red "ESSO" logotype over blue "AVIATION." Small blue wings at top, red dot at bottom.
ESSO KEROSENE
(4)   1940-1962   16.5in Metal $225-$400
ESSO KEROSENE
(4)   1940-1962   15in Metal $225-$375
White globe face with red "ESSO" logotype over red "KEROSENE."
ESSO DIESEL
(4)   1940-1962   15in Metal $225-$400
White globe face with red "ESSO" logotype over blue "DIESEL."
ESSO PLUS
(4)   1962-1962   13.5in Glass $175-$250
White globe face with red "ESSO" logotype over blue "PLUS."

Exxon

The Exxon brand name was introduced in the fall of 1972, replacing Esso in nineteen eastern states, Humble in Ohio, and Enco elsewhere. When Exxon was introduced, the Enco brand name remained in use in a limited number of stations in the Chicago marketing area that had already been scheduled for abandonment about 1976.
EXXON
(4)   1972-1980   13.5in Capco $100-$150
White globe face with red "EXXON" logotype across face.
EXXON PLUS
(4)   1972-1975   13.5in Capco $100-$150
Same as above, with blue "PLUS" below "EXXON."
EXXON EXTRA
(4)   1972-1980   13.5in Capco $100-$150
Same as above, with blue "EXTRA" below "EXXON."
EXXON DIESEL
(4)   1972-1980   13.5in Capco $100-$150
Same as above, with blue "DIESEL" below "EXXON."

Standard Oil Company of Louisiana

Standard Oil of Louisiana was the marketing affiliate assigned to Standard (NJ) at the 1911 breakup of Standard Oil. Stanocola, as it was called, operated stations in Tennessee, Arkansas, and Louisiana under the Stanocola brand until 1923 when the Standard bar-and-circle image was introduced throughout the marketing territory.
STANOCOLA
(5)   1918-1923   One-piece etched   No Listing
White globe with green-outlined red outer ring around face. White center with large red, green, black, and yellow "STANOCOLA" shield in center. White lettering on red outer ring "STANDARD OIL COMPANY" arched around top, "OF LOUISIANA" around bottom.
STANOCOLA
(5)   1918-1923   15in Metal $800-$1,300
White globe face, with same description as above.
STANOCOLA IN THIS PUMP
(4)   1920-1923   15in Metal $600-$1,100
White globe face with black outline ring. Red band across center of globe face, with blue and white lettering "STANOCOLA/Gasoline." Full-color "STANOCOLA" shield at top of globe face. Black "IN THIS/PUMP" in lower white area below band.
STANOCOLA POLARINE
(5)   1920-1923   15in Metal   No Listing
White-outlined globe face with white center band and dark upper six lower areas. Stanocola shield and outline logo on upper globe face, with "STANOCOLA" over script "Polarine" on center band. White "The 'STANDARD' Motor Oil" on lower area. Known only in old photos.

Humble Oil and Refining, Houston, Texas

Houston-based producer, refiner, and marketer purchased by Standard (NJ) in 1919. The Humble brand was used in Texas and New Mexico from 1919 until 1961. In 1959 all US marketing came under the subsidiary Humble Oil and Refining, and "Humble" was added to stations of each brand then in use, although each retained its own regional brand name (Esso, Carter, Oklahoma, and so on). In 1961, Enco replaced Humble as the station brand in Texas and Oklahoma. The Humble brand was introduced in Ohio when both Esso and Enco were blocked by Sohio, and remained in use in Ohio until converted to Exxon in 1972.

Purol 15in insert on metal body (top), Derby 13.5in insert on metal reproduction body (middle), and Derby one-piece etched globe (bottom). Walt Feiger

Dixie Oils Gasoline one-piece etched globe.

Diamond one-piece etched.

Diamond NevrNox Gasolene one-piece etched globe.

NevrNox Gasoline Non-Poisonous Gasoline one-piece etched.

Miscellaneous Dixie globes. R. V. Witherspoon

Diamond Nitro Gasoline one-piece etched globe.

Standard Motor Gasoline (Standard Oil Company of New Jersey) one-piece etched, chimney cap. Sam McIntyre

Standard Motor Gasoline 15in inserts on metal body, Standard Oil of New Jersey; and Quayle Bird Gasoline 15in inserts on metal body. Gary Hildman

HUMBLE GASOLINE/HUMBLE OILS GEAR
(4)   1925-1932   13.5in Glass $250-$400
This globe face is actually a window lens used in gas station buildings.
They fit a standard 13.5in glass or plastic body and are frequently
found assembled into a complete globe. White globe face with blue outline ring and blue "gear" in center. Red "HUMBLE" arched around
top, "GASOLINE" around bottom, with red "HUMBLE/OILS" across
center of gear, white "HUMBLE OIL and REFINING CO." arched
around top of gear, "HOUSTON, Texas" around bottom.
HUMBLE OIL AND REF/HUMBLE OILS
(4)   1919-1932   15in Metal $750-$1,200
Blue outer area of globe face, with large white gear covering most of
face. Red "HUMBLE/OILS" across center of face, with blue "HUMBLE
OIL and REFINING CO." arched around top, and "HOUSTON, Texas"
arched around bottom.
FLASHLIKE ETHYL
(4)   1929-1932   15in Metal $250-$425
White globe face with red "FLASHLIKE" diagonally across upper face,
above large Ethyl (EGC) logo.
HUMBLE (bar and circle)
(4)   1932-1935   15in Metal $350-$650
Same as Standard bar-and-circle above, with blue "HUMBLE" on
crossbar.
HUMBLE
(4)   1935-1961   15in Metal $300-$500
White globe face with red, white, and blue outline rings. Red "HUM-
BLE" across center.
THRIFTANE
(4)   1939-1947   15in Metal $250-$400
White globe face with thick blue ring around outer edge. Red, white,
and blue rings around center white circle. Red script "Thriftane" diagonally across globe face.

Texas Pacific Coal and Oil, Fort Worth, Texas
An independent Texas marketer that sold out to and rebranded
Humble in 1945.
TP PRODUCTS
(4)   1930-1945   15in Metal $1,200-$1,800
White globe face with two black outline rings separated by red spacers
around face. Large red and black teepee in center, with black "TP"
across and black "PRODUCTS" below.
TP ETHYL
(5)   1930-1945   15in Metal $750-$1,200
White globe face with red outline ring. Red and white lines forming
teepee in center, with red "T" to left and "P" to right and Ethyl (EGC)
logo in center. Red "GASOLINE" below teepee.

Colonial Beacon Oil Company, Boston, Massachusetts
Formed in a late 1920s merger between Boston-area-based Colonial Oil Company and Beacon Oil. Colonial Beacon, an innovative
marketer with stations throughout New England, sold out to Standard (NJ) in 1930. The Colonial name, as a subsidiary, survived until
the end of WWII, although products were branded Esso in 1933. Colonial influenced the entire industry with the introduction of service
bays at stations and the marketing of tires, batteries, and automotive
accessories (known as TBA in the trade) through their stations. Colonial was instrumental in the formation of the Atlas Supply Company
to supply the various Standard companies that participated in the
program TBA line.
COLONIAL GAS
(5)   1920-1930   Octagon Metal $400-$700
Square lenses in metal frame with cut corners forming octagon-
shaped globe. White globe face with logotype black "Colonial/Gas" on
globe face.
COLONIAL ETHYL
(5)   1926-1930   Octagon Metal $400-$700
Same as above, with "Ethyl" replacing "Gas."
COLONIAL MOTOR
(5)   1925-1930   16.5in Metal $275-$475
White globe face, with black logotype "Colonial/Motor" on face.
COLONIAL (bar and circle)
(4)   1930-1933   15in Metal $250-$425
White globe face, with red bar-and-circle design similar to Standard
bar-and-circle above. Black-outlined green "COLONIAL" on bar.

Powerline Oil Company, Denver, Colorado
Denver-based refiner and marketer. Purchased by Standard (NJ)
in 1938, the Powerine name was retained until the end of WWII, when
it was replaced by Oval-E.
POWERINE
(4)   1925-1935   15in Metal $250-$425

Red globe face with black-outlined white bar-and-circle band across
center. Black-outlined red "POWERINE" on band.
POWERINE'S CRYSTAL GAS
(5)   1930s   15in Metal   No Listing
White globe face with black "POWERINE'S" arched around top, above
large black script "Crystal." White "GAS" on black extension from "L"
in "Crystal."

Northwest Refining Company, Cut Bank, Montana
Marketed Grizzly gasoline. The company was purchased by Standard in 1942, and was rebranded Carter in 1945.
GRIZZLY DUBBS CRACKED
(5)   pre-1946   13.5in Glass $800-$1,200
White globe face with black outline ring. Detailed standing brown
bear in center of face. Black "GRIZZLY" arched around top, "GASO-
LINE" around bottom, with small red "DUBBS/CRACKED" to left of
bear.

Yale Oil Company, Billings, Montana
Marketed Litening gasoline. Purchased by Standard (NJ) in
1946, the company rebranded Carter.
LITENING
(5)   1930-1946   15in Metal $250-$375
White globe face with black-outlined red "LITENING" in jagged logotype lettering across face.

Oval-E
Name was introduced in 1946 to replace Powerine. It was
changed to Carter in 1950.
OVAL-E
(5)   1946-1950   13.5in Red Capco $200-$300
White globe face with red logotype "E" in blue oval in center.
OVAL-E EXTRA
(5)   1946-1950   13.5in Blue Capco $250-$350
Same as above, with red "EXTRA" below oval.

Carter Oil Company, Tulsa, Oklahoma
Long a Standard production subsidiary, the Carter brand name
was introduced in 1945 to replace Grizzly and Litening. In 1950,
Carter replaced Oval-E to bring all of Standard's western marketing
under the Carter brand. The Carter brand was replaced by Enco in
1961.
CARTER
(5)   1946-1950   15in Metal $250-$450
CARTER
(4)   1950-1962   13.5in Red Capco $150-$225
White globe face with red "Carter" across face.
CARTER EXTRA
(4)   1950-1962   13.5in Blue Capco $175-$300
White globe face with blue "Carter" over red "EXTRA" across face.

Enco
Introduced in 1960, first in the Oklahoma-Pate marketing territory as a replacement for those brand names and expanded to Carter
and Humble territories in 1961, Enco (from the slogan America's
Leading ENergy COmpany), was to be Standard's primary brand
name in all areas where Esso could not be used. Replaced by Exxon in
1972, except in select areas where Standard planned to withdraw
from marketing. Used as late as 1980 in those areas.
Note: No Enco globes are known to exist.

Pate Oil Company, Milwaukee, Wisconsin
Founded in Milwaukee in 1933, Pate operated over fifty stations
when purchased by Standard in 1956. The Pate brand was replaced by
Enco in 1960.
PATE OIL CO. GASOLINE w/shield
(5)   1933-1950   15in Metal   No Listing
White globe face with detailed red, white, and blue Pate shield in cen-
ter, with "PATE OIL COMPANY" arched around top and "GASO-
LINE" around bottom.
PATE CHALLENGE
(5)   1950-1961   13.5in Capco $150-$225
Description not available.
PATE AIR GLIDE
(4)   1950-1961   13.5in Capco $150-$225
White globe face with blue outline ring. "PATE" in small red letters
offset to upper left of face. Red "AIR/GLIDE" offset to lower right.
PATE ULTRA AIR GLIDE
(4)   1956-1961   13.5in Capco $150-$225
Same as above, with red "ULTRA" with blue underline added at top.

Oklahoma Oil Company, Chicago, Illinois

A Chicago area discount marketer that Standard (NJ) purchased in 1956. Almost immediately another Chicago discounter, Perfect Power, was purchased and rebranded Oklahoma. The Gaseteria-Hoosier Pete operation was added in 1957 and also rebranded Oklahoma. The Enco name was first introduced to replace Oklahoma in 1960.

OKLAHOMA REGULAR
(5)   1930s   One-piece painted   No Listing
White globe with series of concentric circles. "OKLAHOMA" across center and smaller "REGULAR" below.

OKLAHOMA WHITE
(5)   1930s   One-piece painted   No Listing
White globe with orange outline ring. Black "OKLAHOMA" arched around top, with orange script "White" across center of face.
Note: Other Oklahoma globes are known to exist, but no details are available.

Gaseteria Oil Company, Indianapolis, Indiana

Founded prior to World War II in Indianapolis, Gaseteria operated the Bonded stations throughout Indiana and Kentucky. In the mid-1950s Bonded opened stations in Ohio. They also purchased the remnants of Johnson Oil Refining-Brilliant Bronze, as well as Hoosier Petroleum in 1956. In 1957 Standard purchased Gaseteria and rebranded the operation Oklahoma, and the Ohio locations were spun off as an independent company, based in Springfield, Ohio.

BONDED 68
(4)   1940-1946   13.5in Glass $300-$500
White globe face with large gold border, with blue detail around eight-point blue seal. White Old English "Bonded" across upper seal, with large red "'68'" in single quotes covering lower seal and lower globe face.

BONDED 98
(4)   1946-1955   13.5in Glass $300-$500
Same as above, with "'98'" replacing "'68.'"

BONDED ETHYL
(4)   1940-1955   13.5in Glass $275-$475
Similar to above, with white circle on lower seal. Ethyl (EC) logo on circle.

BONDED REGULAR
(4)   1955-1958   One-piece plastic $125-$250
White formed plastic faces assembled back-to-back with yellow seam. Rounded end rectangular, with pointed bottom and half-circle on top. Probably the most unusually shaped gas pump globe. Blue and gold seal in upper half-circle, with gold script "Quality" on seal below red band. White "REGULAR" on band. Blue "BONDED" across rectangular area of globe.

BONDED ETHYL
(4)   1955-1958   One-piece plastic $125-$250
Same as above, with "ETHYL" replacing "REGULAR."

Johnson Oil Refining Company, Chicago, Illinois

A midcontinent refiner and marketer that marketed gasoline under the Johnson, Jo-Re-Co, and Brilliant Bronze brand names. Gaseteria purchased Johnson in 1956 and sold the refinery operation to Deep Rock. The company rebranded Oklahoma with the 1957 purchase of Gaseteria by Standard (NJ).

JOHNSON TIME TELLS GASOLENE
(4)   1930s   15in Metal $900-$1,600
JOHNSON TIME TELLS GASOLENE
(4)   1930s   13.5in Glass $350-$600
Series of black and orange outline rings around black outer ring and orange center circle. Detailed hourglass in center circle, with black and white wings to either side. Black "TIME" and "TELLS" on wings. White "JOHNSON" arched around top, "GASOLENE" around bottom.

JOHNSON TIME TELLS ETHYL GASOLENE
(4)   1930s   15in Metal $550-$900
JOHNSON TIME TELLS ETHYL GASOLENE
(3)   1930s   13.5in Glass $350-$600
Similar to above, with white center circle and Ethyl (EGC) logo in circle.

JO-RE-CO TIME TELLS GASOLENE
(4)   1940s   13.5in Glass $400-$700
Same as JOHNSON TIME TELLS above, with "JO-RE-CO" replacing "JOHNSON."

JOHNSON WINGED 70 TIME TELLS GASOLENE
(4)   1934-1940   13.5in Glass $350-$600
Series of black and orange outline rings around black outer ring and orange center circle. Black-outlined white "Winged" over "70" across center of face. Black-outlined white wings to either side of "70," with

"TIME" and "TELLS" on wings. White "JOHNSON" arched around top, "GASOLENE" around bottom.

JOHNSON WINGED 70 GASOLENE
(4)   1940s   13.5in Glass $275-$500
White globe face with black and orange outline rings. Black-and-white-outlined orange rectangle above large black shield. Black "JOHNSON" on orange rectangle, white "WINGED" on upper shield, above white "70" with orange wings. White "GASOLINE" below.

JOHNSON (black/white/orange)
(3)   1940s   13.5in Capco $100-$150
Black outline ring around globe face, with upper half white and lower half orange. Black-and-white-outlined black band across center, with white "JOHNSON" on black band.

BRILLIANT BRONZE
(3)   1950-1956   13.5in Capco $150-$250
White globe face with large red burst at top. Black "brilliant/bronze" in logotype lettering covering most of globe face below burst.

BRILLIANT ETHYL T/T GASOLINE
(4)   1950-1956   13.5in Capco $250-$400
Similar to JOHNSON TIME TELLS above, with "brilliant" replacing "JOHNSON" and white "ETHYL" added above hourglass that is positioned low in center circle.

Hoosier Petroleum Corporation, Indianapolis, Indiana

An Indiana marketer purchased by Gaseteria in 1956.

HOOSIER PETE 100
(4)   1950-1958   13.5in Glass $275-$450
Mint green globe face with lower 1/3 black. Red "HOOSIER PETE" arched around top, above large white "100" positioned over color split. Green "REGULAR" below 100, and small white "GASOLINE" arched around bottom.

HOOSIER PETE ETHYL
(5)   1950-1958   13.5in Glass $275-$450
Same as above, with "ETHYL" replacing "REGULAR" and small white on black Ethyl logo below.

HOOSIER PETE FUEL OIL
(5)   1950-1958   13.5in Glass $300-$550
Mint green globe face with lower 1/3 black. Red "HOOSIER PETE" arched around top, above black "HEATER OIL." Green "FILTER-PURE PROCESSED" arched around bottom, with red flame above. Green "BTU" on flame.

Ryan's

Hoosier Pete affiliate.

RYAN'S JET HI-TEST
(4)   1950s   13.5in Glass $225-$350
White globe face, with blue shield outline with blue stars at top. Blue and white stripes forming bottom of shield at bottom. Red "RYAN'S" over blue "JET" over red "HI-TEST" across center of shield design.

RYAN'S JET KEROSENE
(5)   1950s   13.5in Glass $225-$350
Same as above, with "KEROSENE" replacing "HI-TEST."

Senco, Incorporated, Atlanta, Georgia

Formed after WWII as Clark's Oil Company, with signage similar to Milwaukee-based Clark Oil. The company rebranded Senco about 1956, and was purchased by Standard (NJ) in 1962 and rebranded Esso.

SUPER SENCO GASOLINE
(5)   1950-1962   13.5in Glass $125-$200
Orange globe face with white band across center. "SENCO" on center band, with "SUPER" above and "GASOLINE" below.

Southern Oil Company, Miami, Florida

Purchased by Standard (NJ) in 1962 and rebranded Esso.

DEEM
(5)   1955-1962   13.5in Capco $125-$200
Red globe face with large black-outlined white "DEEM" across face. Lettering is three-dimensional, with black and yellow dropshading.

Sun-Flash Oil Company, Columbus, Ohio

Purchased by Standard (NJ) in 1961 and rebranded Humble.

SUN-FLASH
(5)   1950s   13.5in Capco   No Listing
Description not available.

Alert Oil Company, Wilmington, Delaware

Formed in the late 1960s as an Esso secondary brand.
Note: No Alert globes are known to exist.

FINA and Affiliates
AMERICAN PETROFINA, Dallas, Texas

American Petrofina is the Dallas, Texas, based subsidiary of Belgium's PetrofinaSA. American Petrofina has been formed almost entirely by mergers and buyouts, beginning with the purchase of Panhandle Oil Corporation of Wichita Falls, Texas, in October 1956. Subsequent purchases, where an entire company's marketing was purchased and converted, are listed below. Fina currently operates stations throughout the central and southeastern United States.

Note: No US Fina brand globes are known to exist.

Panhandle Oil Company, Wichita Falls, Texas

Operated stations in Texas until selling out to and rebranding Fina in 1956.

PANHANDLE
(3)   1930s   15in Metal $500-$850
White globe face with red triangular Panhandle logo, with longhorns covering most of face.

PANHANDLE
(5)   1950s   13.5in Plastic   No Listing
Description same as above.

PANHANDLE OCTAGNE
(5)   1940s   15in Metal $400-$750
White globe face with large black-outlined red octagon covering most of face. White script "Octagne" diagonally across octagon, with small black and white Panhandle logo at top.

PANHANDLE SPECIAL
(5)   1940s   15in Metal $500-$850
White globe face with brown-outlined yellow octagon covering most of face. Brown "Special" with underline diagonally across octagon, with small brown and white Panhandle logo at top.

PANHANDLE NOXLESS
(5)   1940s   15in Metal $500-$850
White globe face with green rough-edged design similar to a circular saw blade covering most of face. White-and-black-outlined white "Noxless" diagonally across face, with small black and white Panhandle logo at top.

American Liberty, Dallas, Texas

Formed in the 1930s from oil holdings of the Murchison family. The company sold out to Fina in October 1957.

AMERICAN LIBERTY REGULAR
(4)   1940s   13.5in Glass $325-$600
White globe face with red outline ring. Blue "AMERICAN LIBERTY" arched around top with red, white, and blue Statue of Liberty head in center. Red script "Regular" below statue.

AMLICO PREMIUM
(5)   1950s   13.5in Capco $75-$125
Mint green globe face with dark green outline ring. Dark green "AMLICO," with white dropshade diagonally across face with dark green "PREMIUM" below, right of center.

Petro-Atlas, El Dorado, Kansas

A consolidation of the old Eldorado Refining and K-T Refining. The company sold out to Fina in March 1958.

THE ELDORADO/ELRECO/REFINING COMPANY
(4)   1930-1946   Gill $250-$425
White globe face with black outline ring forming sawtooth border around outer edge of face. Red upper and lower half-circles split by white diagonal band across center of face. Small black "THE EL DORADO" above large "ELRECO," above "REFINING CO." on diagonal band.

SPECIAL/THE EL DORADO/ELRECO/REFINING CO./GASOLINE
(4)   1930-1946   Gill $275-$425
Same as above, with white "SPECIAL" in upper red half-circle, "GASOLINE" in lower half-circle.

ELRECO REFORMED ETHYL
(4)   1930-1946   Gill $250-$400
Red globe face with white band across center. White "ELRECO" with black dropshade arched around top, with black "Re-Formed" on band. Small Ethyl (EGC) logo in white circle at bottom.

ELRECO PREMIUM
(4)   1930-1946   Gill $225-$400
White globe face with red band across center. Red "ELRECO" with black dropshade arched around top, "GASOLINE" around bottom, with white "Premium" on center band.

BUY MILES NOT GALLONS/ELRECO
(3)   1946-1955   Gill $250-$400
White globe face with round red, black, and white "ELRECO" logo in center. Red "Buy miles-Not gallons" arched around top.

BUY MILES NOT GALLONS/ELRECO/REGULAR
(3)   1946-1955   Gill $250-$400
Same as above, with "REGULAR" arched around bottom.

BUY MILES NOT GALLONS/ELRECO/PREMIUM
(3)   1946-1955   Gill $250-$400
Same as above, with "PREMIUM" arched around bottom.

BUY MILES NOT GALLONS/ELRECO/WHITE
(4)   1946-1955   Gill $250-$400
Same as above, with "WHITE" arched around bottom.

ELRECO
(5)   1955-1958   Plastic One-piece Oval $175-$275
White plastic formed oval halves cemented back-to-back. Black and white outline around red center circle split by diagonal white band. Black "ELRECO" across globe face on band. Oval version of earlier round logo.

Petroleum Marketing Company, Tulsa, Oklahoma

Petroleum Marketing Company, or Pemco, is a Tulsa-based independent that rebranded Fina about 1960.

REGULAR PEMCO GASOLINE
(2)   1950s   13.5in Capco $75-$135
White globe face with red and blue outline rings. Blue-and-red-outlined white rectangular box across center, with large blue "PEMCO" in box. Red "REGULAR" arched around top, "GASOLINE" around bottom.

PREMIUM PEMCO GASOLINE
(2)   1950s   13.5in Capco $75-$125
Same as above, with "PREMIUM" replacing "REGULAR."

Golden Rule, St. Louis, Missouri

St. Louis, Missouri, based independent that branded Fina about 1960.

GOLDEN RULE
(5)   1940s   13.5 Glass $175-$250
White globe face with red outline ring. Large yellow bar-and-circle design covers most of face, with black-outlined red "GOLDEN/RULE" superimposed over design.

Cosden Petroleum, Big Spring, Texas

Cosden Petroleum was founded about 1925 by Josh Cosden after he lost controlling interest in Mid-Continent Petroleum which he had founded in 1916. Cosden was operating a Big Spring,Texas, refinery and petrochemical company and marketing through stations in six states when they merged with American Petrofina in April 1963. Cosden stations were rebranded Fina shortly after the merger.

COSDEN GASOLINE OILS
(5)   1925-1930   One-piece etched   No Listing
White globe with solid blue etched face. White "COSDEN" arched around top, "OILS" around bottom, with script "Gasoline" underlined across center of face.

COSDEN LIQUID GAS
(5)   1930-1946   13.5in Glass $250-$375
Orange globe face with white center circle and white band across center. White "COSDEN" with black dropshade arched around top, "OILS" at bottom, with green "LIQUID GAS" on band.

COSDEN ETHYL (EGC)
(4)   1930-1946   13.5in Glass $100-$175
Red globe face with white center circle. White "COSDEN" arched around top, "GASOLINE" around bottom, with Ethyl (EGC) logo in circle.

COSDEN
(3)   1946-1960   13.5in Capco $100-$175
Green globe face with red and white outline rings and white-red-and-white-outlined red band diagonally from lower left to upper right across face. White "COSDEN" in band.

COSDEN
(4)   1960-1963   13.5in Capco $75-$150
White globe face with red outline ring. Red-and-white-outlined red band diagonally from lower left to upper right across face. White "COSDEN" on band.

Col-Tex

As best as can be determined, Col-Tex was sold off to Cosden after Apco purchased and rebranded Kanotex, greatly expanding the Apco brand from its original Oklahoma marketing territory. When Apco became the primary brand name, Col-Tex stations were either converted to Apco or sold off with the Col-Tex brand to Cosden, who operated the Col-Tex stations as a secondary brand until 1963.

COL-TEX
(3)   1954-1963   13.5in Capco $125-$175

White globe face with black outline ring and red-and-white-outlined red diagonal band from lower left to upper right. White "COL-TEX" in band.

COL-TEX ETHYL
(5)   1950s   13.5in Capco $125-$175
Description unavailable.

Onyx

Texas independent that sold out to Cosden and became a Cosden secondary brand.

ONYX PETROLEUM PRODUCTS
(5)   1920s-1930s   15in Metal   No Listing
White globe face with red outline ring and red lines forming white horizontal band across center. Red "PETROLEUM" arched across top, "PRODUCTS" across bottom, with brown woodgrain "ONYX" in center band.

ONYX AEROPLANE GASOLINE
(5)   1920s-1930s   15in Metal   No Listing
Description not available.

ONYX
(3)   1950s   13.5in Capco $75-$125
White globe face with thick black outline ring. Black outline of Texas in center of globe, with red "ONYX" across map.

ONYX ETHYL
(4)   1950s   13.5in Capco $75-$125
White globe face with thick black outline ring. Black lines offsetting white horizontal band above center. Red "ONYX" in band, small Ethyl (EC) logo in black circle below.

Wides Oil Company, Murphysboro, Illinois

Murphysboro, Illinois, based independent bought by Fina about 1972 and converted to the Fina brand after 1977.

SAVE WITH/WIDES/GAS FOR LESS
(3)   1940s   13.5in Glass $250-$350
White globe face with red outline ring. Red circle in center split lower left to upper right by diagonal white band. Blue "SAVE WITH" arched around top, "WIDES" with speed lines in center band, and "GAS FOR LESS" arched around bottom.

WIDES OIL CO. REGULAR (w/triangle)
(5)   1960s   13.5in Capco $100-$175
Description not available.

FLYING A/GETTY
TIDEWATER OIL COMPANY, New York, New York

Founded in New York in 1887, Tidewater is best known for their world-famous motor oil brand Veedol. Tidewater entered the gasoline market about 1915 and by 1920 was marketing all along the eastern seaboard under the Tydol brand. During the 1930s control of Tidewater fell into the hands of Standard Oil of New Jersey, which set up Mission Corporation as a subsidiary to operate Tidewater and Skelly.

J. Paul Getty purchased control of Mission in 1937 and merged Tidewater with California's Associated Oil Company in 1938. Associated had introduced the Flying A brand in 1932 for its premium gasoline and with the creation of Tidewater Associated Oil Company, stations in the West became Associated Flying A stations, and stations in the East became Tydol Flying A stations. In 1956, the Tydol and Associated designations were dropped and the brand became simply Flying A. In 1966 stations in the former Associated territory, including the secondary Seaside operation, were sold to Phillips Petroleum and rebranded Phillips 66. Also in 1966 the Tidewater name was dropped in favor of Getty Oil Company, Getty having completed the purchase of Mission in 1951 and having operated Tidewater Associated and Skelly as separate subsidiaries since that time.

The Getty brand first appeared in 1970, replacing Flying A at stations in the northeast. In 1983 Getty also began replacing the Skelly brand with Getty; however, before the changeover could be completed Texaco purchased Getty Oil and the Getty marketing in the northeast was sold off to New England independent Power-Test. The former Skelly locations were rebranded Texaco or sold off and Power Test, renamed Getty Oil Marketing and based in Jamestown, New York, continues to operate Getty brand stations from Maine to Virginia.

TYDOL
(5)   1910s   One-piece cast $700-$1,100
White globe with black outline ring around orange outer ring, and black ring around white center circle. Black "TYDOL" (large "T") across center of globe face.

TYDOL Cast FACES
(3)   1925-1930   15in Metal $450-$750
Cast face with black outline ring around orange outer ring, and black outline ring around white center circle. Black "TYDOL" (large "T") across center of globe face.

TYDOL T/W/O Cast FACES
(3)   1920-1930   15in Metal $450-$800
Cast face same as above, with interlocking "T/W/O" on lower globe face.

TYDOL ETHYL Cast faces (EGC)
(4)   1927-1930   15in Metal $550-$850
Cast face same as above, with cast Ethyl (EGC) logo on lower globe face.

TYDOL ETHYL (Cast face baked) ETHYL
(5)   1927-1930   15in Metal $550-$750
Cast face same as above, with baked-on Ethyl (EGC) logo on lower globe face.

TYDOL
(2)   1925-1942   16.5in Metal $225-$425
TYDOL
(2)   1925-1942   15in Metal $225-$400
TYDOL
(4)   1925-1942   14in Gill $250-$375
TYDOL
(2)   1925-1942   Gill $225-$350
TYDOL
(2)   1935-1942   13.5in Glass $225-$325
Black outline ring around orange outer ring, and black outline around white center circle. Black "TYDOL" (large "T") across center of globe face.

TYDOL T/W/O
(4)   1925-1930   15in Metal $250-$425
Same as above, with interlocking "T/W/O" on lower globe face.

TYDOL WITH ETHYL
(2)   1927-1935   15in Metal $250-$425
Same as above, with small "WITH" over larger "ETHYL" below "TYDOL."

TYDOL ETHYL (EGC)
(2)   1927-1935   15in Metal $250-$400
Same as above, with small Ethyl (EGC) logo below "TYDOL."

TYDOL ARCHED OVER ETHYL (EGC)
(3)   1935-1942   16.5in Metal $250-$475
TYDOL ARCHED OVER ETHYL (EGC)
(3)   1935-1942   15in Metal $250-$450
TYDOL ARCHED OVER ETHYL (EGC)
(3)   1935-1942   Gill $250-$400
TYDOL ARCHED OVER ETHYL (EGC)
(3)   1935-1942   13.5in Glass $200-$375
Same as above, with black "TYDOL" arched over large Ethyl (EGC) logo with blue rays.

TYDOL ARCHED OVER ETHYL (EC)
(3)   1942 only   13.5in Glass $225-$350
Same as above, with newer Ethyl (EC) logo.

TYDOL w/Flying A decal
(4)   1939-1941   15in Metal   No Listing
Same as TYDOL above, with red "FLYING/A" decal on lower globe face.

TYDOL A w/orange band
(4)   1941-1942   13.5in Glass $225-$375
Black outline ring around orange outer ring. Black outline around white center circle. Black "TYDOL" across upper globe face, with orange over black band across lower face. Black-outlined white "A" in center, with black-outlined white wings to either side.

TYDOL "A" red and black
(3)   1941-1954   Gill $225-$375
White globe face with black outline ring. Black "TYDOL" across upper globe face. Red over black horizontal band across lower face, with black-outlined red "A" in center. Black-outlined white wings extending out from "A."

TYDOL FLYING A red and black
(3)   1941-1954   Gill $225-$350
Same as TYDOL "A" above, with small black "FLYING" above "A."

TYDOL FLYING A red and black
(3)   1941-1954   Plastic $125-$250

TYDOL ETHYL w/airplane
(4)   1941-1946   Gill $350-$600
White globe face with black outline ring. Large black "TYDOL" over smaller "ETHYL" across face. Red airplane diagonally at top of globe, with streak extending down through "L" in "TYDOL."

TYDOL ETHYL (black/red)
(3)   1946-1950   Gill $225-$325
White globe face with black outline ring. Black "TYDOL" on upper globe face, with smaller red "ETHYL" offset to right below "TYDOL."

TYDOL FLYING A ETHYL red and black
(3)   1950-1954   Gill $225-$375
Same as TYDOL FLYING A above, with small black "ETHYL" below "A."
TYDOL AVIATION
(5)   1940s   Gill $400-$700
Description not available.
TIDEX
(3)   1935-1941   16.5in Metal $250-$475
TIDEX
(2)   1935-1941   15in Metal $250-$400
TIDEX
(3)   1935-1946   Gill $200-$350
TIDEX
(3)   1935-1946   13.5in Glass $200-$325
Navy blue globe face with black-outlined white band across center and vertically, forming cross. Black "TIDEX" on band.
TIDEX PLAIN
(4)   1946-1950   Gill $200-$300
White globe face with black outline ring. Black "TIDEX" across center of face.
TYDOL A w/green band
(3)   1950s   13.5in Glass $200-$350
White globe face with black outline ring. Green band across lower face. Black "TYDOL" on upper face. Black-outlined "A," with black-and-white wings on center of band.
TYDOL A DIESEL FUEL
(4)   1950s   13.5in Glass $225-$350
Same as above, with small black "DIESEL FUEL" below "A."
TYDOL FLYING A w/green band
(3)   1950s   13.5in Glass $225-$350
Same as above, with small black "FLYING" above "A."
Note: During the 1940s and 1950s, Tidewater Oil used a square white glass globe with attachable rounded corner lenses, about the size of ad glasses in gas pumps in that era. The following listings are descriptions of the various known lenses designed to fit these unusual globes.
TYDOL "A"
(4)   1940s   Square Glass $250-$450
White globe face with black "TYDOL" over red, over black band. Black-outlined red "A," with black and white wings at center of colored band.
TYDOL ETHYL
(4)   1940s   Square Glass $250-$450
White globe face with black "TYDOL" over small red "ETHYL."
TYDOL FLYING A
(4)   1950s   Square Glass $250-$450
    White globe face with green band across lower face. Black "TYDOL" over small black "FLYING" above band. Black-outlined red "A" with black six white wings on green band.
FLYING A GASOLINE
(4)   1956-1960   Square Glass $250-$450
White globe face with black-outlined red "A," with red wings in center. Red "FLYING" above "A," "GASOLINE" below.
FLYING A SUPEREXTRA
(5)   1956-1960   Square Glass $300-$500
Red globe face with black-outlined white "A," with black-outlined white wings in center. White "FLYING" above "A," white "SUPER" to left below, and "EXTRA" to right below "A."

Associated Oil Company, San Francisco, California

Founded in 1901, Associated was a West Coast integrated oil company that was marketing gasoline by 1915. In 1932 they introduced the Flying A brand as a premium grade gasoline and after the 1938 merger with Tidewater, Flying A became the company's primary brand name. Associated also operated stations under the Seaside brand as a secondary operation. Flying A stations in the Associated territory, as well as Seaside, were sold to Phillips in 1966.
ASSOCIATED GASOLINE
(4)   1915-1932   15in Metal $1,200-$2,000
Red globe face with white, green, and white outline rings. White "ASSOCIATED" arched around top, "GASOLINE" around bottom, with green-outlined white gasoline can in center. Red "MORE/MILES/TO THE/GALLON" on can.
ASSOCIATED FLYING A "ASSOC AERO TYPE"
(5)   1932-1933   15in Metal $600-$900
Red globe face with white, green, and white outline rings. Large winged "A" with green dropshades in center of face. White "FLYING" with green dropshade across top. White "ASSOCIATED" arched around bottom to left, "GASOLINE" to right, with small "AERO TYPE" in between.

ASSOCIATED FLYING A "AERO TYPE"
(4)   1933-1940   15in Metal $600-$900
Same as above, with white "AERO-TYPE GASOLINE" arched around bottom.
ASSOCIATED GASOLINE w/Ethyl (EGC)
(5)   1926-1932   15in Metal $450-$650
Red globe face with green outline ring. White circle in center, with large Ethyl (EGC) logo on circle. White "ASSOCIATED" arched around top, "GASOLINE" around bottom.
ASSOCIATED AVIATION ETHYL
(4)   1932-1940   15in Metal $450-$750
Red globe face with soaring eagle at top of globe face. Ethyl logo with black rays in yellow circle at top, to left of eagle wing. Small white "ASSOCIATED" over larger "AVIATION/ETHYL" on lower globe face.
ASSOCIATED GREEN AND GOLD
(5)   1930-1935   15in Metal $400-$650
Red outer band with red upper 1/4 background. "ASSOCIATED" in red at top, "GREEN GOLD" in green in center, "GASOLINE" in red at bottom. Lower 1/4 face green.
ASSOCIATED WHITE GOLD GASOLINE
(3)   1920s   15in Metal $350-$600
Mint green globe face with large white burst covering most of face. Large black "WHITE/GOLD" on center of face, with smaller black "ASSOCIATED" above and "GASOLINE" below.
ASSOCIATED AROTANE
(4)   1940s   15in Metal   No Listing
Red globe face, with large white "AROTANE" with black and white wings extending across from "A" at top of face. Black "HIGH OCTANE QUALITY" below "AROTANE" above white "GASOLINE."
FLYING A GASOLINE (R/W large type)
(4)   1940-1946   15in Metal $300-$550
FLYING A GASOLINE (R/W large type)
(2)   1946-1956   Gill $225-$375
FLYING A GASOLINE (R/W large type)
(2)   1946-1956   13.5in Glass $225-$350
White globe face, with large black-outlined red "A" with red wings and black details on center of face. Red "FLYING" above "A," "GASOLINE" below.
FLYING A ETHYL (blk) GASOLINE (white)
(4)   1940-1946   15in Metal $350-$650
FLYING A ETHYL (blk) GASOLINE (white)
(3)   1946-1956   Gill $275-$450
FLYING A ETHYL (blk) GASOLINE (white)
(3)   1946-1956   13.5in Glass $250-$425
Red globe face, with large black-outlined white "A" with white wings and black details positioned above center of face. White "FLYING" above "A," with white-outlined black "ETHYL" below. White "GASOLINE" below "ETHYL."
FLYING A GASOLINE (R/W small type)
(4)   1946-1956   13.5in Glass $225-$350
White globe face with black outline ring. Black-outlined red "A" with red wings and black details in center of face. Small red "FLYING" over "A," "GASOLINE" below.
FLYING A ETHYL GASOLINE (W/R small type)
(3)   1946-1956   13.5in Glass $250-$425
Red globe face with white outline ring. Black-outlined white "A" with white wings and black details on center of face. Small white "FLYING" above "A," "ETHYL GASOLINE" below "A."
FLYING A GASOLINE
(2)   1956-1970   Gill $250-$375
White globe face, with large black-outlined "A" with red wings and black details in center. Red "FLYING" horizontally over "A," "GASOLINE" arched around bottom.
FLYING A SUPER EXTRA
(2)   1956-1970   Gill $250-$400
Red globe face, with large black-outlined white "A" with white wings and black details in center. White "FLYING" horizontally over "A," "SUPER EXTRA" arched around bottom.
FLYING A DIESEL
(5)   1950s   Gill   No listing
Description not available.
FLYING A KEROSENE
(4)   1950s   Gill $275-$400
Same as FLYING A SUPEREXTRA above, with white "KEROSENE" replacing "SUPER EXTRA."

Seaside Oil Company, Santa Barbara, California

California refiner and marketer purchased by Tidewater Associated about the end of WW II. Seaside remained a Flying A secondary brand until the western marketing area was purchased by Phillips in

Early "Standard" (Standard Oil Company of New Jersey) 15in inserts on metal body.

Esso Aviation 13.5in inserts on glass body.

Esso one-piece etched. British globe.

Stanocola Gasoline one-piece etched globe.

Humble 15in inserts on metal body.

Johnson Time Tells 13.5in inserts on glass body.

Panhandle Special 15in inserts on metal body.

Cosden one-piece etched. Don Stinson

Tydol one-piece raised-letter globe.

Tydol 15in cast-face inserts on metal body.

Tydol Ethyl 13.5in insert for Gill body.

That Good Gulf Gasoline one-piece etched globe.

Gulf 13.5in inserts on glass body.

Gulf Kerosene one-piece etched globe.

Gulf one-piece raised-letter globe.

Gulf No-Nox Motor Fuel one-piece fired-on globe (center rear) and Various Gulf globes on glass bodies. Joe Esquival

1966. Phillips used the Seaside brand for a short time after the purchase, but by 1970 the stations were rebranded Phillips 66.
GRADE-NON CARBONIZING
(5)   1902s   THREE-SIDED Metal $350-$600
Complete description not available. Triangular metal frame designed to hold three Glass inserts.
SEASIDE GRADE
(3)   1935-1955   15in Metal $450-$750
White globe face with red triangle offset to upper left. Blue triangle offset to lower right, superimposed over red triangle. Yellow wave area at top of blue triangle, with blue script "Seaside." White-outlined red banner with white "GRADE" arched below waves on blue triangle. White "GASOLINE" and small sea gull on lower triangle.
SEASIDE GRADE PLUS
(4)   1935-1950   15in Metal $450-$750
Same as above, with white "+ PLUS" added below "GRADE" banner and above "GASOLINE."
SEASIDE SILVER GULL
(4)   1940-1950   15in Metal $450-$800
Same as above, with white "SILVER/GULL" over small white sea gull on blue triangle.
SEASIDE SILVER GULL TETRAETHYL
(4)   1935-1940   15in Metal $500-$800
Same as above, with "TETRAETHYL" arched around lower globe face.

GULF and Affiliates
GULF OIL COMPANY, Pittsburgh, Pennsylvania

The Gulf Oil Company was founded in 1901 at the Spindletop, Texas, oil fields. Very early in the company's history, they established a marketing presence throughout the South and East that was to dominate the company's direction for the next eighty years. Gulf is credited with having opened the first "built for that purpose, offstreet gasoline station in the world," having opened a small retail station in Pittsburgh in December 1913. Other stations pre-date this, but they were converted from other uses.

Gulf continued to market in twenty-eight southern and eastern states until the 1950s, when several purchases of regional chains made Gulf a coast-to-coast marketer. The gas shortages of the 1970s forced Gulf to withdraw from many areas, and the early 1980s saw Gulf in serious financial trouble. In 1984 Chevron (Standard of California) purchased Gulf Oil, converting stations in several states to Chevron and selling the southeastern marketing area to BP and the northeastern area to Cumberland Farms. Cumberland continues to operate stations under the Gulf brand.
THAT GOOD GULF GASOLINE
(5)   1914-1918   One-piece   No Listing
                        etched chimney cap
THAT GOOD GULF GASOLINE
(3)   1914-1930   One-piece cast $450-$750
THAT GOOD GULF GASOLINE
(3)   1914-1930   One-piece etched $450-$750
THAT GOOD GULF GASOLINE
(5)   1914-1930   One-piece baked $400-$650
White globe with orange ring around face. Orange circle in center, with orange lines extending out from circle to form white band across center. Black "THAT" arched around top, "GASOLINE" around bottom, and black "GOOD GULF" on center band. Note that there are minor differences in shape between the baked, etched, and cast versions, although the basic description remains the same.
THAT GOOD GULF GASOLINE
(5)   1925-1930   One-piece cast $475-$800
Wide orange area, extending around body, around white globe face. Blue outline ring in orange area. Orange circle in center, with lines extending out to each side forming white band across center. Blue "THAT" arched around top, "GASOLINE" around bottom, with blue "GOOD GULF" on center band.
THAT GOOD GULF GASOLINE
(5)   1920s   15in Metal $500-$850
Wide white border around orange outline ring. White globe face. Orange circle in center, with orange lines extending out from circle to form white band across center. Black "THAT" arched around top, "GASOLINE" around bottom, with black "GOOD GULF" on center band.
GULF NO NOX
(4)   1925-1930   One-piece cast $800-$1,300
White globe face with orange outline ring. Orange circle in center, with black "GULF" with white dropshade on circle. Black "NO-NOX" arched around top, "MOTOR FUEL" around bottom.
GULF NO NOX
(4)   1925-1930   One-piece etched $800-$1,200

GULF NO-NOX
(5)   1925-1930   One-piece baked $600-$900
White globe with black outline ring around face. Black line around orange disc logo in center. Black "GULF," with black-and-white-striped dropshade on orange disc. Black "NO-NOX" arched around top, "MOTOR FUEL" around bottom. Again, minor shape differences exist, although the basic descriptions remain the same.
GULF KEROSENE
(5)   1920-1930   One-piece etched   No Listing
White globe with orange outline ring around face. Orange circle in center, with black "GULF" arched round top, "KEROSENE" around bottom.
GULF
(2)   1930-1935   One-piece Cast $400-$650
GULF
(2)   1930-1935   One-piece Baked $350-$550
White globe with blue outline ring around orange face. Large blue "GULF" with white dropshade across face.
GULF
(1)   1935-1952   13.5in Glass $200-$350
GULF
(4)   1935-1952   Gill $250-$375
GULF
(1)   1935-1952   12.5in Glass $200-$350
GULF
(5)   1935-1952   18in Metal band neon No listing
Orange globe face with blue and white outline rings. Large blue "GULF" with white dropshade across face.
GOOD GULF
(5)   1930s   12.5in Glass   No Listing
Orange globe face with blue outline ring. Blue lettering "GOOD/GULF" across face.
NO-NOX ETHYL
(5)   1930s   12.5in Glass   No Listing
Orange globe face with blue outline ring. Blue "NO NOX" above Ethyl (EGC) logo on face.
TRAFFIC
(5)   1930s   12.5in Glass   No Listing
Orange globe face with blue outline ring. Blue "TRAFFIC" across face.
TRAFFIC BENZOL
(5)   1930s   13.5in Glass   No Listing
White globe face with blue outline ring and blue "TRAFFIC/BENZOL" on face.
MARINE WHITE-SPECIAL FOR MARINE USE
(3)   1940-1947   13.5in Glass $300-$600
White globe face with blue outline ring. Blue ring around small orange Gulf disc in center. Blue "MARINE WHITE" arched around top, small blue "SPECIAL/FOR MARINE/USE" below logo.
GULF DIESEL
(3)   1946-1952   12.5in Glass $200-$350
Blue globe face with orange and white outline rings. Gulf orange disc logo at top of face. Orange-outlined white band across face below logo. Orange "DIESEL/FUEL" on band.
GULF DIESELECT
(4)   1946-1952   12.5in Glass $300-$500
Same as above, with orange "DIESELECT" replacing "DIESEL/FUEL."
GULF MARINE WHITE GASOLINE
(4)   1946-1952   12.5in Glass $300-$550
White globe face with blue outline ring and wide blue band across center. Blue "GULF" in upper white area, "GASOLINE" on lower, with white "MARINE/WHITE" on center band.

Wilshire Oil Company, Los Angeles, California
Wilshire, a West Coast refiner and marketer dating from the 1910s, was purchased by Gulf in 1957. In 1965, the Wilshire brand was replaced by Gulf.
POLLY GAS
(4)   1930s   15in Metal $1,800-$3,000
Black globe face with white outline ring. White-outlined yellow "POLLY" arched around top, "GAS" around bottom. Detailed green and orange parrot in center, perched on orange-outlined yellow sign with black lettering "POLLY/GAS." Black "PROPERTY OF WILSHIRE OIL CO. INC." very small around bottom.
ECONOMY GAS WILSHIRE OIL CO.
(4)   1930s   15in Metal $350-$600
White globe face. Dark green outline rings around mint green "tombstone" shaped area covering most of face. Dark green "ECONOMY" arched around top of tombstone, with interlocking Woco logo below "ECONOMY." Red script "Anti-Knock" in white band below logo. Dark green "GASOLINE" on mint green area below band. Green "RE-

FINED BY WILSHIRE" below tombstone area. Small "PROPERTY OF WILSHIRE OIL CO. INC." around bottom.

Superior Oil Company, Des Moines, Iowa
A Des Moines-based marketer, dating from the mid-1930s. The company merged with Carpenter Oil Company in the early 1960s. About 1968, Gulf purchased Superior and rebranded the stations Gulf.

SUPERIOR 400 GASOLINE			
(3)	1932-1946	13.5in Glass	$225-$350

SUPERIOR 400 GASOLINE			
(3)	1946-1968	13.5in Capco	$100-$175

White globe face with red outline ring. Black "SUPERIOR" arched around top, "GASOLINE" around bottom, with large red "400" in center.

SUPERIOR ETHYL (EC) GASOLINE			
(4)	1950s	13.5in Capco	$100-$175

Same as above, with Ethyl (EC) logo replacing "400" in center.

SUPERIOR 400 FUEL OIL			
(5)	1950s	13.5in Capco	$100-$175

Same as SUPERIOR 400 GASOLINE above, with "FUEL OIL" replacing "GASOLINE."

Carpenter Oil Company, Lincoln, Nebraska
Founded in the 1930s (possibly earlier) as L. L.Coryell and Sons, Carpenter owned the Coryell brand by the early 1950s and operated stations throughout Nebraska. In the early 1960s they merged with Superior Oil of Des Moines, which was bought out by Gulf in 1968.

CORYELL 70 SUPER			
(4)	1950s	13.5in Capco	$125-$200

Black outline around red outer ring and around white center circle. White "CORYELL" arched around top, "GASOLINE" around bottom, with large "70" in center.

CORYELL ETHYL SENIOR (EC)			
(4)	1950s	13.5in Capco	$125-$200

Same as above, with white "SENIOR" replacing "GASOLINE," and large Ethyl (EC) logo in center.

Bulk Petroleum Company, Chicago, Illinois
Another old Chicago private brand that sold out to a major oil company during the market expansion in the 1950s to 1960s. Gulf purchased the operation and branded it Bulko in 1968. Most of the Chicago area stations were converted to Gulf, but some unsuccessful Gulf locations around the country were operated as Bulko stations in the 1970s.

BULKGAS ALWAYS LESS			
(5)	1930s	Gill	$300-$450

White globe face with red outer ring. Large red and yellow burst covering most of center white area. White "BUY MORE QUALITY" arched around red ring at top, "AT OUR LOW PRICES" around bottom, with white "BULKGAS/ALWAYS/LESS" with black dropshade on red burst in center.

HESS and Affiliates
AMERADA HESS, New York, New York
Hess. The only oil company that is better known for its annual promotion than for its products. Chances are, if you collect gasoline memorabilia, the only thing you know about Hess is that they've produced and sold a toy truck, a replica of one of their tankers or other company vehicles, every Christmas since 1964. The company's belief in absolute silence to the public and to the press has prevented much more than information about the trucks from ever being made public. The extensive research for this book has uncovered bits of information that we will attempt to consolidate here.

Hess began operations as a coal yard-service station in Asbury Park, New Jersey, about 1925. They evolved from coal into fuel oil during the depression, and from fuel oil into heavy residual oils for boiler fuels. Terminal facilities at Perth Amboy, New Jersey, were added after World War II, and the company opened its first Hess branded retail service stations about 1959. In 1963 they purchased the independent refiner Delhi-Taylor, which owned a majority of Billups Eastern as well as Southern Oil out of Fort Lauderdale, Florida. Southern stations were converted to Hess, and in 1965 Hess purchased the remaining portion of Billups Eastern and rebranded the stations Hess.

Along the way, Olixir, an Albany, New York, area chain, was purchased and rebranded Hess. In 1964, the first of the Christmas trucks were sold, branded Billups or Hess. Since that time there has been a promotional truck sold nearly every year at Christmas time, and these have become very desirable collectibles. In 1968 Hess Oil and Chemi-

cal merged with Amerada Petroleum, a production-exploration company with operations around the world. Hess currently markets through over 500 branded outlets in fifteen states, as well as supplying several strong southern private brands.

Hess-Perth, Amboy, New Jersey
No Hess globes are known to exist.

Olixer, Green Island, New York
New York independent that sold out to Hess in the early 1960s.

OLIXIR			
(3)	1930s	15in Metal	$275-$375

Yellow globe face with black outline. Black reverse-bowtie "OLIXIR" across globe face.

OLIXIR LUBRICATED GAS			
(4)	1930s	15in Metal	$300-$450

OLIXIR LUBRICATED GAS			
(5)	1930s	16.5in Metal	$350-$500

Yellow globe face with black outline ring and black band across center. Black elongated "OLIXIR" in upper half, "GAS" in lower half, with yellow "LUBRICATED" across band.

Southern Oil Company, Fort Lauderdale, Florida
Florida private brand that had been purchased by Delhi-Taylor in the late 1950s. When Hess purchased Delhi-Taylor in 1963, the Southern stations were rebranded Hess.

SOUTHERN			
(4)	1950s	13.5in Capco	$100-$150

White globe face with blue bands across, above and below center. White stars on blue bands. Red "SOUTHERN" on white between bands.

Billups Eastern Petroleum, Jacksonville, Florida
When Billups was broken up in 1959, control of Billups Eastern passed to independent refiner Delhi-Taylor. Hess purchased Delhi-Taylor in 1963, and in 1965 the company purchased the remaining portions of Billups Eastern. Billups stations from Delaware to Florida were then rebranded Hess. (See SIGNAL and AFFILIATES for listing of Billups globes.)

HUDSON and Affiliates
HUDSON OIL COMPANY, Kansas City, Kansas
Hudson Oil Company's storied history began in 1930 when Mary Hudson married Wayne Driver and moved to Kansas City. Driver went to work with Mary's brothers at a Kansas City oil marketer operating under the Silver King name. The family was involved in two gas stations in Kansas City when, in 1933, Driver was killed in an accident with a fuel oil truck. Mary quickly sold off the two stations but within a year had purchased another station, at 25th and Broadway in Kansas City and, at age twenty-one, was selling gasoline under the Hudson name. By 1937 the chain consisted of five stations, the original Kansas City location and stations at Leavenworth, Kansas, Norfolk and Omaha, Nebraska, and Moberly, Missouri.

In the late 1930s, Mary formed a partnership with her brothers and Hudson Oil was formed. The chain expanded coast to coast, with hundreds of locations by the time family members went their separate ways in 1968, with the Hudson brothers operating competing service stations under the Highway (Workingman's Friend) and Fisca (First In Service Company of America) brands. The 1977 purchase of a Cushing, Oklahoma, refinery led to a long downward spiral for Hudson and in 1985, the Mary Hudson operation was bankrupt. More than 300 Hudson brand stations closed, leaving only a dozen or so in operation today. Hudson Affiliates Highway and Fisca continue to market across the country.

Silver King, Kansas City, Kansas
A predecessor to Hudson.

SILVER KING			
(5)	EARLY 1930s	15in Metal	$500-$800

White globe face with large "SILVER" arched around top, "KING" arched around bottom, and large "SK" with arrow passing through it in center.

SILVER KING			
(5)	Early 1930s	15in Metal	$400-$550

White globe face with green outline ring. Large red "Silver-" over " King" across face.

SILVER KING			
(5)	Early 1930s	15in Metal	$400-$550

White face with green outline ring. Large red "Silver-" over "-King" across globe face.

Hudson Oil Company, Kansas City, Kansas

Introduced in 1933.
HUDSON GASOLINE
(4)   1933-1962   Gill $400-$750
Globe face has black outline and white outer ring. Orange-red center circle split by black band across center, with graduated black horizontal lines in upper half of circle. Black and white 1930s transport truck "HI-OCTANE GAS" on center band. Red-outlined black "HUDSON" arched at top, "GASOLINE" at bottom. "GASOLINE" at bottom has red rays through lettering, as if center circle is sun.
HUDSON TRANSPORT GASOLINE
(4)   1933-1946   Gill $450-$900
Same basic design as HUDSON GASOLINE above, except "HUDSON OIL CO." replaces "HUDSON" in upper ring, "TRANSPORT/GASOLINE" below black band with truck.
HUDSON REGULAR
(4)   1946-1962   13.5in Glass $350-$800
HUDSON REGULAR
(3)   1955-1962   13.5in orange Capco $300-$675
Same as HUDSON GASOLINE, except "REGULAR" replaces "GASOLINE."
AAA-1 ETHYL
(5)   1938-1946   Gill $350-$500
Same as Hudson's AAA-1 Ethyl (below) except word "HUDSON'S" does not appear at top of globe. Has Ethyl (EGC) logo.
HUDSON'S AAA-1 ETHYL
(4)   1946-1950   13.5in Glass $250-$400
HUDSON'S AAA-1 ETHYL
(4)   1946-1950   13.5in Capco $150-$250
Yellow globe face with black outline and black 1/3 lower area. Large black-and-white-outlined red "AAA-1" across most of yellow area, with small black "HUDSON'S" arched around top and script white "New" just above "AAA-1." Small Ethyl (EC) logo in black-outlined white circle offset to right at color line. White script "Lubricated" over yellow "GAS" on lower black area.
HUDSON ETHYL (EGC)
(5)   1950-1962   13.5in Glass $350-$750
Same as HUDSON GASOLINE, with black-outlined red "HUDSON" arched around top, "GASOLINE" around bottom, with large ETHYL (EGC) logo superimposed over truck in center circle. Yellow rays around Ethyl logo.
HUDSON ETHYL (EC)
(3)   1955-1962   13.5in red Capco $300-$650
Same as HUDSON ETHYL above, except with newer Ethyl (EC) logo.
HUDSON ETHYL (EC)
(5)   1955-1962   Plastic $300-$650
Same as above, except with "ETHYL" written around bottom instead of "GASOLINE."
HUDSON KEROSENE
(4)   1950s   13.5in Glass $275-$450
HUDSON KEROSENE
(4)   1950s   13.5in Capco $150-$250
White globe face with light blue outline and blue outline around red flame in center. Red "HUDSON" arched around top, blue "KEROSENE" around bottom.

HORNET OIL COMPANY, Tulsa, Oklahoma

Tulsa-based affiliate that rebranded Hudson in 1958.
HORNET GASOLINE
(3)   1950s   13.5in Capco $100-$150
Yellow globe face with black outline ring and black interlocking squares placed randomly around globe face. Large black interlocking squares in center, with white center area. Black "HORNET"on white area, black "GASOLINE" on yellow below large squares.

Major's

Major's globe is identical to the Hudson globe. The relationship between the two companies is unknown, but it is assumed that Major's was operated by one of the Hudson family members.
Note: Truck was labeled "T. MAJORS."
MAJORS REGULAR
(5)   1950s   13.5in Capco $400-$700
Identical to HUDSON REGULAR above, with red-outlined black "MAJOR'S" replacing "HUDSON."
MAJORS ETHYL (EC)
(5)   1950s   13.5in Capco $350-$650

Identical to HUDSON ETHYL above, with black-outlined red "MAJOR'S" replacing "HUDSON."

Highway Oil Company

Hudson affiliate marketing under the Highway, Hi-Lo, and Workingman's Friend brands.
Note: No Highway globes are known to exist.

Fisca Oil, Kansas City, Kansas

Hudson affiliate with stations coast-to-coast today. Fisca is an acronym for First In Service Company of America.
Note: No Fisca globes are known to exist.

HUSKY OIL COMPANY, Cody, Wyoming

Husky was originally a brand name of Western Oil and Fuel, Minneapolis, Minnesota. About 1954 Western acquired H. Earl Clack, an independent marketer in Cody, Wyoming. Western assigned the Husky brand to the H. Earl Clack subsidiary and expanded the Husky Hi-Power brand throughout the Rocky Mountain region. Western continued marketing under the Mileage name in the upper Midwest, but some dealers in that area were using the Husky name as late as 1960.

When Conoco purchased Western in the late 1950s, H. Earl Clack, renamed Husky Oil, was reorganized as a separate company. Husky Oil of Cody, Wyoming, merged with Frontier Oil in 1968. Frontier had earlier (about 1960) bought Western States Petroleum of Salt Lake City, Utah. The Husky name replaced Frontier and Beeline about 1970, and Husky expanded into Canada. In 1984 Husky Oil sold off its US marketing to concentrate on Canadian marketing. In 1990 a Denver-based marketer revived the Frontier brand name and "Rarin' to Go" trademark, and currently operates a chain of stations under the Frontier trademark.

Western Oil and Fuel Husky Globes

See CONOCO for other Western brand globe listings.
HUSKY "QUALITY PETROLEUM PRODUCTS"
(5)   1935-1940   13.5in Glass   No Listing
Same as below, except dog is black, white, and red, and red horizontal line separates northern lights from lower blue area. Black "QUALITY PETROLEUM PRODUCTS" arched above dog. Much more detail in dog.
HUSKY w/northern lights
(4)   1940-1960   13.5in Glass $500-$800
Globe face has blue outline ring around upper white area. Lower 1/3 is dark blue. Blue, grey, white, and red husky dog head with good detail, with orange and yellow "northern lights" design on upper globe face. Yellow "HUSKY" in lower blue area.

H. Earl Clack, Incorporated, Cody, Wyoming

Operated stations and truck stops under the Hecco brand until 1954, when Western purchased Clack and rebranded the stations Husky.
HECCO
(5)   1930s   15in Metal $400-$650
Good details not available. White globe face with orange "HECCO" arched around top, "GASOLINE" around bottom, with diamond in center.
HI-POWER GASOLINE-HECCOLENE OIL
(5)   1930s   15in Metal $400-$650
White globe face with dark green and orange outline rings. Dark green "HI-POWER" arched around top, "GASOLINE" around bottom, with orange and white circle in center. White diamond logo with "HECCOLENE/OIL" around border, and orange center with white "HECCO."
HI POWER ETHYL
(5)   1930s   15in Metal $325-$500
Orange globe face with dark green outline ring. Dark green "HI-POWER" diagonally across top, over smaller "Ethyl." Small Ethyl (EC) logo in black-outlined white circle with blue rays near bottom.

Husky/Hi-Power, Incorporated, Cody, Wyoming

When Western purchased H. Earl Clack, Western's Husky brand was combined with Clack's Hi-Power brand to form Husky Hi-Power.
HUSKY HI-POWER
(4)   1954-1960   15in Metal $900-$1,600
HUSKY HI-POWER
(5)   1954-1960   13.5in Glass $500-$850
Blue globe face with red outline ring. Upper white area has blue and white standing husky dog. White "HUSKY" over smaller "HI-POWER" in lower blue area.

HI POWER ETHYL
(4)   1954-1960   15in Metal $325-$500
Red-orange globe face with black outline ring. White-outlined black "HI-POWER" diagonally across, over small black "Ethyl." Small Ethyl (EC) logo in black-outlined white circle, with blue rays near bottom.

Frontier Oil, Denver, Colorado

Denver-based refiner and marketer founded in the mid-1930s. Frontier operated a chain of stations in the Rocky Mountain region. About 1960 they purchased Western States Petroleum, and operated Beeline stations on the western slope of the Rockies. In 1968, Husky Oil purchased Frontier Oil and replaced both the Frontier and Beeline brands with Husky about two years later. In 1990, a Denver marketer reintroduced the Frontier brand name on a chain of retail stations in Colorado.

FRONTIER GAS
(3)   1937-1955   13.5in Glass $275-$450
Black outline around red outer ring and around center white circle. Large black-outlined white "FRONTIER" arched around top, "GAS" around bottom, with two stars to either side. Black and white raring horse with rider in center circle, with red "RARIN' TO GO!" offset below horse.

FRONTIER RARIN' TO GO
(5)   1937-1955   Gill   No Listing
Same as above, with gold detail in horse.

FRONTIER RARIN' TO GO
(5)   1937-1955   Gill   No Listing
No red outer band, no "GAS"–large rearing horse and man.

FRONTIER ETHYL
(4)   1937-1955   13.5in Glass $200-$350
Same as above, with large Ethyl (EC) logo replacing raring horse in center white circle.

FRONTIER DIESEL
(4)   1937-1955   13.5in Glass $425-$625
Same as above, with "DIESEL" replacing "GAS."

FRONTIER RARIN' TO GO
(3)   1955-1969   13.5in Capco $175-$300
Globe face with red lower half and white upper half. Black-outlined white "FRONTIER" across lower red area just below center, with white "RARIN'-TO-GO" arched underneath. Black silhouette of raring horse and rider in upper white area.

FRONTIER FLEET FUEL DIESEL
(4)   1955-1969   13.5in Capco $100-$175
Black outline around mint green globe face. Red "FRONTIER" arched around top, "DIESEL" arched around bottom, with red "FLEET FUEL" with speed lines and black dropshade across center.

Western States Petroleum, Salt Lake City, Utah

Dating from after World War II, Western States operated the Beeline stations on the western slope of the Rockies. They merged with Frontier Oil about 1960, but the Beeline name remained in use until replaced by Husky about 1970.

BEELINE GASOLINE
(3)   1946-1965   13.5in Capco $300-$500
Bright yellow globe face with black outline ring. Black logotype script "Beeline" across center of globe, with small black "GASOLINE" below. Red dot at top with detailed black, yellow, and white bee flying across dot.

BEELINE DIESEL
(4)   1946-1965   13.5in Capco $275-$500
Same as above, with "DIESEL FUEL" replacing "GASOLINE."

IOMA
INDEPENDENT OIL MEN OF AMERICA (IOMA), Chicago, Illinois

The Independent Oil Men of America was formed in 1925 in Chicago, Illinois, to offer independent jobbers and gas-oil marketers a marketing organization and nationwide trademark to ensure recognizable quality. The trademark selected was "Red Hat," registered in June 1925. The logo consisted of a large red hat with a black band and white stars. Standard Oil of Indiana, having long used the "Red Crown" trademark, sued for trademark infringement and in 1929, the IOMA lost the right to use this valuable trademark. After that time their trademark consisted of the organization logo, the red "thunderbird" on a black triangle, the corporate logo that had been in use since 1925 but only as a secondary trademark.

TRI-STAR RED HAT GASOLINE
(5)   1925-1932   One-piece etched $1,500-$2,800

KIMMEL RED HAT GASOLINE
(5)   1925-1932   One-piece etched $1,500-$2,800

BRANDT RED HAT GASOLINE
(5)   1925-1932   One-piece etched $1,500-$2,800

S.M. OIL CO. RED HAT GASOLINE
(5)   1925-1932   One-piece etched   No Listing

TRAFFIC RED HAT GASOLINE
(5)   1925-1932   One-piece etched $1,500-$2,800
The above globes are of this design: white globe with red or black outline ring around face. Large red top hat with black hatband in center of globe. Three white stars on black hatband. Small black triangle-red thunderbird IOMA logo below hat. Company or brand name, as listed, arched in black letters around top, "GASOLINE" around bottom, with "RED" to left of hat and "HAT" to right.

TRI-STAR RED HAT GASOLINE
(5)   1925-1932   15in Metal $1,200-$1,600

HOME OIL CO. RED HAT GASOLINE
(4)   1925-1932   15in Metal $1,200-$1,600

KIMMEL RED HAT GASOLINE
(4)   1925-1932   15in Metal $1,200-$1,600

WEEKS OIL CO.,INC. RED HAT GASOLINE
(5)   1925-1932   15in Metal $1,200-$1,600

MC QUARTER RED HAT GASOLINE
(5)   1925-1932   15in Metal $1,200-$1,600
The above globes are of this design: white globe face with large red top hat with black hatband in center. Three white stars on black hatband. Small black triangle-red thunderbird IOMA logo below hat. Company or brand name, as listed, arched around top, "GASOLINE" around bottom, with "RED" to left of hat, "HAT" to right.

RED HAT GASOLINE
(4)   1925-1932   15in Metal $1,200-$1,600
Same as above, with no company name at top.

MOTOR OIL/GASOLINE RED HAT
(4)   1925-1932   15in Metal $1,300-$1,800
White globe face with wide black ring around outer edge. Large red top hat with black hatband in center. Three white stars on black hat band. Black "RED" to left of hat, "HAT" to right, with small IOMA logo below. White "MOTOR OIL" arched around top in black ring, "GASOLINE" around bottom.

REGULAR GASOLINE RED HAT
(5)   1930-1932   13.5in Capco $450-$750
Similar to Red Hat globes above, with "REGULAR" arched around top.

Independent Oils

Not all IOMA members chose to use the Red Hat brand. The brands listed below identified their products with the IOMA black triangle-red thunderbird logo. This does not indicate that a globe with the IOMA logo as opposed to the Red Hat brand is from after the 1932 discontinuance of the Red Hat.

BLAKE OIL CO. GASOLINE
(5)   1920s   One-piece etched $1,200-$1,800

PETERSENS OIL CO. GASOLINE
(5)   1920s   One-piece etched $1,200-$1,800
The above globes are of this design: white globe with black outline ring around face. Large black triangle with red thunderbird IOMA logo in center of globe face. White "INDEPENDENT" above bird, "OILS" below. Black Company or brand name, as listed arched around top, "GASOLINE" around bottom.

CONSUMERS OIL CO. WINCHESTER, TENN
(5)   1920s   One-piece etched $1,300-$2,000
Same as above, with "WINCHESTER, TENN" replacing "GASOLINE."

"A GAS CO." GASOLINE
(5)   1920s   One-piece etched   No Listing

POMIAC GASOLINE
(5)   1920s   One-piece etched   No Listing
Same as above. Small globes with 4in base.

HAWKEYE GASOLINE
(4)   1925-1935   15in Metal $400-$700

PENN VALLEY GASOLINE
(4)   1925-1935   15in Metal $400-$700

PETERSENS OIL CO. GASOLINE
(4)   1925-1935   15in Metal $400-$700

DOBSON BROS. OIL CO. GASOLINE
(5)   1925-1935   15in Metal $400-$700

H. S. GOODELL
(5)   1925-1935   15in Metal $400-$700
The above globes are of this design: white globe face with black triangle IOMA logo in center. Red thunderbird on black triangle. White

"INDEPENDENT" over bird, "OILS" below. Black company or brand, as listed, arched around top, "GASOLINE" ached around bottom.
FREI-ULRICH
(5)   1925-1935   15in Metal   No Listing
Same as above, except no "GASOLINE" around bottom.
INDEPENDENT OIL CO. SEYMOUR, MO
(3)   1925-1940   15in Metal $500-$800
Same as above, with "SEYMOUR, MO." replacing "GASOLINE."

High Hat
IOMA trademark offered as an alternative to the Red Hat brand.
HIGH HAT GASOLINE w/hat and logo
(5)   1920s   15in Metal $1,300-$2,000
White globe face with large red top hat, with black hat band and vertical red and black stripes above band. Black "HIGH" to left of hat, "HAT" to right, with black "GASOLINE" arched below.
JONES BROS. HIGH HAT
(5)   1920s   15in Metal $1,300-$2,000
Same as above, with black "JONES BROS" arched around top.

Royal and Royal 400, Fort Dodge, Iowa
ROYAL GASOLINE
(5)   1920s   One-piece etched $1,300-$2,000
White globe with black outline ring around face. Black circle around IOMA black triangle-red thunderbird logo in center. White "GASO-LINE" arched around top of circle, "MOTOR OILS" around bottom, with red "ROYAL" arched above logo and "GASOLINE" below.
ROYAL 400 GASOLINE (EMB OF DEP)
(5)   1920s   One-piece etched $1,400-$2,100
White globe with black outline ring around face. Black circle around IOMA thunderbird logo in center. White "THE EMBLEM OF" arched around top of black circle, "DEPENDABILITY" arched below, with red "ROYAL 400" arched above logo and "GASOLINE" below.
ROYAL 400 GASOLINE (bird on black)
(5)   1920s   One-piece etched $1,400-$2,000
White globe with solid black circle in center of face. Red thunderbird from IOMA logo on circle. Red "ROYAL 400" arched around top, "GASOLINE" around bottom.
ROYAL 400 RED HAT GASOLINE
(5)   1930s   13.5in Glass $600-$900
White globe face with black outline ring. Large red top hat with black hatband in center. Three white stars on hatband. Black triangle-red thunderbird IOMA logo below hat. Company or brand, as listed, arched around top, "GASOLINE" around bottom.
Note: There are probably other metal or one-piece independent globes similar to the above globes. Prices would be similar as well.

KENDALL OIL, Bradford, Pennsylvania
Kendall Refining was founded as a lubricants manufacturer and refiner in Bradford, Pennsylvania, in 1881. The company had been well established in motor oils when the first venture into gasoline came in 1922. Kendall supplied stations in Pennsylvania and New York until the first gas shortage in 1973, when the decision was made to concentrate on lubricants. The last Kendall branded station closed in 1976.
KENDALL SPHERE SHAPE
(4)   1922-1925   One-piece etched $300-$600
White sphere-shaped globe with red "KENDALL/GASOLINE" across globe.
KENDALL
(5)   1922-1928   One-piece etched $450-$700
White globe with "KENDALL" lettering across face.
KENDALL GASOLINE w/airplane
(5)   1926-1935   15in Metal   No Listing
White globe face with red and black "Spirit of St.Louis" type airplane in center. Red "KENDALL" arched around top, "GASOLINE" around bottom.
KENDALL ETHYL (EGC)
(4)   1926-1935   15in Metal $275-$450
White globe face with black outline ring and black outline around white center circle. Black-outlined red "KENDALL" arched around top, "GASOLINE" around bottom, with large Ethyl (EGC) logo with blue rays in center.
KENDALL
(3)   1935-1946   Gill $250-$350
White globe face with black-outlined red "KENDALL" in tall, thin lettering.

KENDALL ETHYL
(4)   1935-1936   Gill $275-$375
White globe face with black outline ring and black outline around white center circle. Black-outlined red "KENDALL" arched around top, "GASOLINE" around bottom, with large Ethyl (EGC) logo with blue rays in center.
KENDALL DELUXE (EARLY THIN TYPE)
(4)   1936-1946   14in Gill $275-$400
White globe face with blue-outlined red tall, thin "KENDALL" over small blue script "DeLuxe."
KENDALL DELUXE (THICKER TYPE)
(2)   1946-1970   Gill $225-$350
KENDALL DELUXE (THICKER TYPE)
(2)   1946-1970   13.5in Glass $200-$325
KENDALL DELUXE (THICKER TYPE)
(3)   1946-1970   13.5in Capco $100-$150
White globe face with blue-outlined red thicker lettering "KENDALL" over larger blue script "DeLuxe."
KENDALL POLLY POWER
(2)   1946-1970   Gill $225-$350
KENDALL POLLY POWER
(2)   1946-1970   13.5in Glass $200-$325
KENDALL POLLY POWER
(3)   1946-1970   13.5in Capco $100-$150
White globe face with large black-outlined red "KENDALL" over black script diagonal "Polly Power."

KERR MCGEE OIL INDUSTRIES,
Oklahoma City, Oklahoma
Kerr McGee was founded in the Oklahoma City oil fields as Anderson-Kerr Drilling Company in 1929. Through the early years they operated a single Oklahoma City service station, branded Phillips 66, which closed during the gas rationing days of World War II. In 1946 the corporate name was changed to Kerr McGee, shortly after the company had entered retail gasoline marketing, having purchased Oklahoma City based Harrell Brothers. The Harrell Bros. Yellow Cab gasoline trademark was replaced by the Kermac brand.
This was the extent of KM's gas station involvement until 1955, when they purchased Deep Rock Oil Company. Deep Rock had been founded in the Cushing, Oklahoma, oil fields in 1913 and had been through a stormy existence, having sold out to Shaffer Oil and Refining of Chicago in the late 1920s and again been in receivership by the late 1930s. At the time of the KM merger, the Deep Rock brand appeared on over 1,000 stations in sixteen midcontinent states. In 1957 Kerr McGee acquired Triangle Refineries, a primarily wholesale operation that had been founded in 1935. Knox Industries of Texas also sold out to KM about this time, and the Knox brand survived into the 1960s. Triangle was active in purchasing Southern private brand operations, which Kerr McGee operated well into the eighties, including Peoples Oil of Nashville, 1959; Illinois-based Mileage Mart in 1959; Trackside Gasoline Stations of Gulfport, Mississippi, 1962; Wallace Service Stations of Atlanta, 1962, along with Power Oil Company of Macon, Georgia, Coast Oil Company of Shreveport, Louisiana, and Tan-Kar Stations of Birmingham, Alabama.

Deep Rock Oil Company
Founded in the Cushing, Oklahoma, field in 1913, Deep Rock had a series of financial problems and existed under several owners before being purchased by Kerr McGee in 1955. The Kerr McGee name was added to Deep Rock stations about 1960, and the "brand" Kerr McGee was introduced in 1965. Deep Rock stations were gradually converted to the KM name, nearing completion by 1985. The Deep Rock brand survives in some areas, but this is thought to be due to jobbers who simply haven't updated signage at smaller locations.
Note: Arrows (><) in text are indicators of lettering that appears in bowtie design.
DEEP ROCK CUSHING, OK
(5)   1920s-1930s   15in Metal   No Listing
Description not available.
GASOLINE/DEEP ROCK/MOTOR OIL
(4)   1920-1928   One-piece etched $800-$1,200
GASOLINE/DEEP ROCK/MOTOR OIL
(5)   1925-1930   One-piece Baked $600-$850
White globe with red "DEEP><ROCK" across center. Reverse-bowtie blue "GASOLINE" at top, "MOTOR OILS" at bottom.
EASY STARTING/KANT NOCK/GASOLINE
(5)   1920-1928   One-piece Baked $850-$1,300
White globe with blue "KANT><NOCK" across center. Reverse-bowtie red "EASY STARTING" at top, "GASOLINE" at bottom.

Gulf No-Nox Motor Fuel one-piece etched globe.

Superior Gasoline 15in inserts on metal body. Kyle Moore

Olixir 15in inserts on metal body.

Husky 13.5in inserts on glass body.

Peterson's Gasoline one-piece etched globe.

Peterson's Gasoline 15in inserts on metal body.

Kimmell Red Hat Gasoline one-piece etched globe. Kyle Moore

Independent Oil Company 15in inserts on metal body.

Gibson Brothers Oil Company 15in inserts on metal body.

Deep Rock Gasoline one-piece fired-on globe.

Deep Rock one-piece etched.

Trackside Economy 15in inserts on metal body.

Lion Gasoline one-piece etched globe. John Phippen

Marathon Mile-maker 13.5in inserts on glass body.

Various Republic 13.5in inserts on plastic bodies. R. V. Witherspoon

GASOLINE/DEEP ROCK/GREASES
(5)   1920s   15in Metal $350-$650
Same as above, except "GREASES" replaces "MOTOR OILS."
GASOLINE/DEEP ROCK/MOTOR OIL
(5)   1928-1936   15in Metal $350-$600
GASOLINE/DEEP ROCK/MOTOR OIL
(3)   1928-1936   13.5in Glass $225-$350
White globe face with red "DEEP><ROCK" across center. Reverse-bowtie blue "GASOLINE" at top,"MOTOR OILS" at bottom.
KANT NOCK WITH ETHYL (EGC)
(5)   1928-1932   15in Metal $275-$450
KANT NOCK WITH ETHYL (EGC)
(4)   1928-1932   13.5in Glass $225-$350
White globe face with red "KANT><NOCK" at top and red "GASO-LINE" at bottom, with large Ethyl (EGC) logo in center with thick yellow rays extending out from logo.
SUPER KANT NOCK GASOLINE
(4)   1932-1936   13.5in Glass $200-$350
White globe face with red "KANT><NOCK" across center. Narrow black band above and below "KANT><NOCK," with white "SUPER" in top band and "GASOLINE" in bottom band.
DEEP ROCK w/rings
(4)   1932-1936   13.5in Glass $200-$325
White globe face with thick blue outline ring and three concentric thinner blue rings. Large blue-outlined red "DEEP><ROCK" across globe face.
REGULAR/DEEP ROCK/GASOLINE
(3)   1932-1936   13.5in Glass $200-$350
White globe face with red "DEEP><ROCK" across center. Blue "REG-ULAR" at top, "GASOLINE" at bottom.
DEEP ROCK SUPER GASOLINE
(3)   1936-1950   13.5in Glass $200-$325
White globe face with red "DEEP><ROCK" lettering at top and "GASOLINE" at bottom. Yellow circle in center, with white band across center with black "SUPER" on band.
DEEP ROCK ETHYL GASOLINE
(3)   1936-1950   13.5in Glass $200-$325
Same as above, with small Ethyl (EC) logo in center.
DEEP ROCK GREEN GASOLINE
(3)   1936-1940   13.5in Glass $200-$325
Same as above, with green circle and "GREEN" in center.
DEEP ROCK
(1)   1950-1965   13.5in Capco $75-$125
White globe face with large yellow and blue Deep Rock rectangle logo.
DEEP ROCK WITH ARROWS
(5)   1965-up   13.5in Capco $100-$150
Same as above, with red diagonal arrow.

Kermac, Oklahoma City, Oklahoma

In 1945, when Kerr McGee purchased the former Yellow Cab gas stations of Harrell Brothers Oil Company, the several stations were rebranded Kermac. Kerr McGee was more involved in production and refining than in marketing, however, and the Kermac brand never appeared on more than a few stations.
KERMAC REGULAR
(5)   1947-1955   13.5in Capco   No Listing
Light blue globe face with white "KERMAC" arched around top. Script "Regular" across lower face.
Note: Premium globe probably exists today.

Kerr McGee

The Kerr McGee name was added to Deep Rock stations about 1960 and the Kerr McGee brand, standing alone, first appeared on a group of Oklahoma City stations in 1965. The KM brand and logo eventually replaced Deep Rock and continues in use today.
KERR MCGEE
(4)   1965-up   13.5in Capco $75-$125
White globe face with red-and-blue Kerr McGee "KM" shield at center.

Triangle Refineries

Founded in 1935, Triangle Refineries operated stations under the Hiotane brand, as well as Triangle and Cloverleaf, and supplied various unbranded marketers. Kerr McGee purchased Triangle in 1957, and all of the private brand KM affiliates operated through Triangle.
TRIANGLE NEW NAVY GASOLINE
(4)   1935-1940   15in Metal $250-$450
White globe face with blue "TRIANGLE/GASOLINE" arched around top and bottom, with "NEW/NAVY" in center.
TRIANGLE w/clover
(4)   1950s   13.5in Glass $225-$325

White globe face with black "TRIANGLE" arched at top, "REFINER-IES" at bottom. Green outline triangle with green four-leaf clover in center.
CLOVERLEAF GASOLINE
(4)   1950s   13.5in red Capco $200-$375
White globe face with red outline ring. Large green-outlined white triangle covering most of globe face, with smaller green-outlined triangle inside. Green four-leaf clover in smallest triangle, with red "CLOVER-LEAF" above small triangle inside larger one.
HIOTANE
(3)   1940s   13.5in Glass $325-$600
HIOTANE
(3)   1950s   13.5in Capco $200-$425
Orange globe face with black and white interlocking border ring. Sunrise scene with white pointed tower in center of face. Black lettering vertically on tower "HIOTANE." Black and white script arched around top "As new as Tomorrow."
SOUTHPORT REGULAR GASOLINE HIOTANE
(5)   1940s   13.5in Glass $225-$350
Description not available.

Mileage Mart

Illinois-based early gasoline convenience store operation bought out in 1959 and rebranded Deep Rock.
SAVE GO MILEAGE MART
(4)   1955-1962   13.5in Capco $225-$350
White globe face with red ring outline and red lower 1/3. Black, white, and red owl on upper globe face, with white "SAVE" lettering. White "BE SMART" on upper red ring, white script "Go MILEAGE/MART" on lower 1/3.

Trackside Service Stations, Gulfport, Mississippi

Trackside was just that—an early trackside discount operation, founded in Gulfport in the early 1930s. Kerr McGee, through Triangle, purchased Trackside in 1962 and continued to operate the chain under the Trackside name until the late 1980s.
TRACKSIDE/ECONOMY/MOTOR
(5)   1930s   15in Metal $250-$450
White globe face with blue "TRACK-SIDE" arched at top of face. Blue-outlined yellow diamond at center with blue "ECONOMY" across it, over curved blue "MOTOR."
TRACKSIDE ROCKET w/tank car
(5)   Postwar   13.5in Glass $400-$650
White globe face with green and yellow octagon-shaped border around black rail tank car, with yellow "TRACKSIDE" on it over red "ROCK-ET/ANTI/KNOCK."
TRACKSIDE REGULAR
(4)   1955-1965   13.5in Glass $225-$350
White globe face with blue "TRACKSIDE" arched at top of globe face over red script "Regular," with curved blue "GASOLINE" around bottom of face.
TRACKSIDE SUPER ETHYL
(4)   1955-1965   13.5in Glass $225-$350
Similar to above, with red "SUPER/ETHYL" across center.
Note: It can be assumed that other Trackside globes do exist.

Peoples Oil Company, Nashville, Tennessee

Another mid-South discount operation, Peoples dates from the 1930s and was purchased by Triangle in 1959. Many of the stations were rebranded Kerr McGee by the 1980s.
PEOPLES REGULAR
(4)   1950s   13.5in Capco $100-$150
White globe face with red "REGULAR" arched around top, "GASO-LINE" around bottom, and script "Peoples" across center.
PEOPLES ETHYL
(4)   1950s   13.5in Capco $100-$150
White globe face with red "PEOPLES" arched around top over Ethyl (EC) logo.

Other Triangle Brands:

They include Tan-Kar, Power, Coast, and Walco. No globes are known to exist from these brands.

Mutual Oil Company, Birmingham, Alabama

Mutual, another private brand from the 1930s, was purchased by Kerr McGee in 1985 and stations were rebranded Kerr McGee.
MUTUAL
(3)   1936-1957   15in Metal $300-$500
MUTUAL
(3)   1957-1970   13.5in Glass $275-$400

MUTUAL
(3)   1957-1970   13.5in Capco $200-$325
White globe face with arched red lettering "MUTUAL" at top of face.
Large blue jumping rabbit at center of face, over red and blue ribbon
with "GASOLINE," near bottom of face.
MUTUAL ETHYL
(4)   1936-1957   15in Metal $300-$500
MUTUAL ETHYL
(4)   1957-1970   13.5in Glass $275-$400
MUTUAL ETHYL
(4)   1957-1970   13.5in Capco $125-$200
White globe face with arched red lettering "MUTUAL" at top of face.
Large outlined Ethyl (EC) logo at center of globe face, over curved red
"GASOLINE" near bottom of face.
Note: It is assumed that a 15in metal Mutual Ethyl (EGC) globe ex-
ists.

Sparky
A Triangle-supplied brand that operated in Alabama in the
1950s.
SPARKY DYNAMO ETHYL
(5)   1950s   13.5in Capco $100-$175
White globe face with small black "SPARKY" at top of face over black
"DYNAMO," with yellow in lines over outlined Ethyl (EC) logo.

LION OIL COMPANY, El Dorado, Arkansas
Lion Oil Company was founded in 1921 in the south Arkansas oil
fields. Primarily an exploration and drilling company and an early innovator in petrochemicals, Lion was operating a few service stations
by the early 1920s. From the 1920s until the early 1950s, gasoline
marketing was limited to Arkansas, Mississippi, western Tennessee,
and northern Alabama and Louisiana, although Lion Naturalube
Motor Oils were distributed throughout the United States. In 1954 the
Monsanto Chemical Corporation purchased Lion and began to expand
the marketing territory throughout the south central United States,
expanding as far west as central Kansas and as far north and east as
Bristol, Virginia. In 1959 Lion introduced the jumping lion logo, replacing the "lion and mound" logo that had been in use since the
1920s.
During the 1960s, the Monsanto name appeared on gas pump signage along with the Lion brand, and some St. Louis, Missouri, area
stations added Monsanto signage alongside the Lion signs, creating
speculation that the Lion name would be replaced. The experiment
was short-lived, however, as Monsanto decided to get out of retail
gasoline. In 1971 they sold the petroleum divisions of Lion to The Oil
Shale Company (TOSCO), retaining the petrochemical divisions. Lion
branded marketing was discontinued in 1981, although Tosco-Lion is
still involved in unbranded marketing.
LION
(4)   1924-1930   One-piece etched $400-$650
Black "LION" on white globe.
LION One-piece w/lion
(5)   1926-1930   One-piece etched   No Listing
White globe with black "LION" arched around top of globe face,
"GASOLINE" around bottom, with detailed brown standing lion, fac-
ing to right, in center of globe face.
LION GASOLINE
(4)   1930-1946   13.5in Glass $350-$600
Black-outlined white outer ring with black "LION" arched at top,
"GASOLINE" at bottom with orange center circle. Small black mound
with black and white lion on center circle. White "LION" and red "PE-
TROLEUM PRODUCTS" on base of mound.
LION ETHYL (EGC)
(4)   1930-1946   13.5in Glass $225-$375
Black-outlined white outer ring with orange "LION" at top, "GASO-
LINE" at bottom, and large Ethyl (EGC) logo with yellow rays in
white center.
LION
(3)   1946-1956   13.5in Glass $325-$575
Orange globe face, with large black mound and black and white lion
on top. Large white "LION" lettering on mound.
LION KNIX KNOX
(4)   1946-1956   13.5in Glass $325-$600
Black-outlined white outer ring with black "LION" at top, "KNIX
KNOX" at bottom. Orange center of globe with small black mound in
center, with black and white lion on top. White "LION" lettering on
mound, red "PETROLEUM PRODUCTS" on base of mound.

MARATHON and Affiliates
MARATHON OIL CORPORATION, Findlay, Ohio
The Ohio Oil Company was founded in 1887 when several northern Ohio oil production firms joined together to market their crude oil,
primarily to Standard Oil. So much so, in fact, that in 1889 Standard
purchased Ohio Oil and operated the company as a production subsidiary until the breakup of Standard in 1911. After the breakup Ohio
Oil continued as before with oil exploration and production, satisfied
to sell their product as crude oil and leave the refining and marketing
to others.
Ohio Oil first ventured into marketing with the June 1924 purchase of Lincoln Oil Refining Company of Robinson, Illinois. Lincoln
Oil operated a refinery and about twenty retail gasoline stations in
the Robinson-Terre Haute area at the time of the purchase by Ohio
Oil. With an ensured source of crude oil supply for the small refinery,
the Linco brand began to expand. By 1930 Ohio Oil had expanded the
Linco brand throughout most of the current Marathon territory—
Ohio, Indiana, Illinois, Michigan, and Kentucky.
In the meantime, Ohio Oil had been involved in numerous successful oil production ventures, and found they needed even more outlets for their products. In 1930 Ohio Oil purchased Transcontinental
Oil, a refiner and marketer that had marketed gasoline under the
Marathon trademark since about 1920. They had acquired the brand
from a Pittsburgh operation, Riverside Oil Company, that we believe
to be a forerunner of Republic Oil Company, which will be mentioned
later. Transcontinental sold gasoline under the Marathon trademark
across the Midwest and South, from North Carolina to New Mexico.
Transcontinental can best be remembered for a significant first
when in 1929 they opened several Marathon stations in Dallas, Texas,
in conjunction with Southland Ice Company's "Tote'm" stores (later 7-
Eleven), creating the first gasoline-convenience store tie-in. The
Marathon brand proved so popular that by WWII, the name had replaced Linco at stations in the original five-state territory. During the
war, the widespread Marathon territory couldn't be properly supplied
and marketing operations outside the Great Lakes area were sold, primarily to Tydol. Concentrating their marketing in a smaller territory
allowed Marathon to expand within the terrritory, and the late 1950s
brought the first of many acquisitions—Tower Oil Company of Cincinnati, Ohio, which would expand the company's marketing presence.
Numerous other purchases are detailed in the listings below, with a
group of marketing companies brought together by the 1980s under a
subsidiary, Emro Marketing. Ohio Oil, renamed Marathon Oil in
1962, was purchased by US Steel (now USX) in 1981 and continues to
market through dealer and jobber outlets under the Marathon name
in the north central states and through Emro Marketing under several brand names, primarily Speedway and Starvin Marvin, throughout
the South and East.

Lincoln Oil Refining Company, Robinson, Illinois
Purchased by Ohio Oil in 1924. Linco served as the company's
primary brand until about 1939.
LINCO GASOLINE/OILS
(5)   1924-1925   One-piece etched $850-$1,400
White globe with red, white, and blue Linco "crossed Linco" logo in
center of face. Blue "GASOLINE" arched around top, "OILS" around
bottom.
LINCO GASOLINE
(5)   1924-1926   One-piece etched $800-$1,100
Description not available.
GASOLINE LINCO OILS
(5)   1924-1934   15in Metal $450-$700
White globe face with blue and white Linco logo in center. Red
"LINCO" crossed vertically and horizontally in center of logo. Blue
"GASOLINE" arched around top, "OILS" around bottom.
LINCO
(4)   1934-1939   13.5in Glass $200-$325
White globe face with red outline ring. Blue "LINCO" across center of
globe face.
LINCO ETHYL (EGC)
(5)   1934-1939   13.5in Glass $200-$350
White globe face with red outline ring. Large Ethyl (EGC) logo in cen-
ter. Blue "LINCO" arched around top, "GASOLINE" around bottom.
LINCO BENZOL
(5)   1934-1935   13.5in Glass $250-$400
White globe face with red outline ring and blue "LINCO/BENZOL"
across center of face.
LINCO BLUE
(5)   1934-1938   13.5in Glass $250-$350
White globe face with blue "BLUE" across face.

LINCO AVIATION
(5)   1934-1939   13.5in Glass $450-$700
Description not available.

Red Fox Oil Company, Fort Wayne, Indiana
Regional marketer purchased by Linco in 1928 and rebranded Linco at that time.
(RED FOX) BENZOL GASOLINE
(5)   1910s-1920s   One-piece etched   No Listing
White globe with outline around center circle on face. "BENZOL" arched around top, "GASOLINE" around bottom, with detailed fox head in center circle. Colors unknown.

Transcontinental Oil Company, Tulsa, Oklahoma
Purchased by Ohio Oil in 1930, the Transcontinental-Marathon marketing was kept separate from Linco marketing until about 1937, and Marathon had completely replaced Linco by WWII.
MARATHON
(2)   1920-1938   15in Metal $500-$800
White globe face with orange silhouette of runner covering center of face. Black-outlined green "MARATHON" in logotype lettering across runner.
MARATHON ETHYL (EGC)
(4)   1926-1938   15in Metal $1,000-$1,600
White globe face with small flesh-colored runner at top of globe. Green "MARATHON" arched around top, split between "A" and "T" by runner. Orange-outlined black "ETHYL" below runner above Ethyl (EGC) logo.
MULTIPOWER
(3)   1928-1935   15in Metal $275-$400
White globe face with orange-outlined black "MULTIPOWER" across face. Orange and black line below, and extended "T" crossbar from band across center.
MARATHON MULTIPOWER
(5)   1935-1938   15in Metal $1,200-$2,200
White globe face with orange-outlined black "MULTI" "POWER" across center of globe face, split by detailed runner. Green "MARATHON" arched around top, "GASOLINE" around bottom.

The Ohio Oil Company, Findlay, Ohio
MARATHON (green letters)
(4)   1930s   13.5in Glass $300-$600
White globe face with orange runner in center of face. Green "MARATHON" across center of globe face.
MARATHON w/runner logo
(4)   1938-1954   13.5in Glass $350-$600
White globe face with red outline ring. Red, white, and black Marathon runner "Best in the Long Run" logo top center of globe face. Black "MARATHON" below logo.
(MARATHON) ETHYL w/runner logo
(4)   1938-1946   13.5in Glass $350-$500
Same as above, with "ETHYL" replacing "MARATHON."
MULTIPOWER (red on white)
(4)   1938-1954   13.5in Glass $225-$325
White globe face with black-outlined red "MULTIPOWER" across face.
MARATHON MILE MAKER
(3)   1946-1962   13.5in Glass $300-$500
White globe face with red, white, and dark blue "Best in the Long Run" logo in center. Dark blue "MARATHON" arched around top, red "MILE-maker" arched around bottom.
MARATHON SUPER M
(3)   1954-1962   13.5in Glass $300-$500
Blue globe face with white-outlined red, white, and blue "Best in the Long Run" logo in center. White "MARATHON" arched around top, "SUPER-M" around bottom.
MULTIPOWER (blue on white)
(4)   1954-1962   13.5in Glass $225-$325
White globe face with blue "MULTIPOWER" across face.
MARATHON DIESEL #1
(4)   1946-1962   13.5in Glass $100-$175
White globe face with green dot in center. Black "MARATHON" arched around top, green "Diesel Fuel" around bottom, with white "1" in green dot in center.
MARATHON DIESEL #2
(3)   1946-1962   13.5in Glass $100-$175
Same as above, with "2" in green dot.
MARATHON REGULAR MILE MAKER
(1)   1962-1970   13.5in Capco $100-$150
White globe face with small red, white, and blue Marathon "Big M" logo at top, above small blue "REGULAR." Larger red "MILE-maker" below "REGULAR."

MARATHON PREMIUM SUPER-M
(1)   1962-1970   13.5in Capco $100-$150
Same as above, with blue "PREMIUM" above blue "Super-M."
MARATHON DIESEL FUEL
(4)   1962-1970   13.5in Capco $100-$175
Same as above, with blue "DIESEL" over smaller red "FUEL."

Tower Oil Company, Cincinnati, Ohio
Cincinnati-based marketer that sold out to, and rebranded Marathon in 1958.
TOWER GASOLINE
(4)   1940s   13.5in Glass $300-$600
Globe face with black outline. Upper half is yellow with large black and white "tower" logo. Green band around lower half, above lower black area. White lettering "TOWER" with black dropshade on green band. Yellow script "Gasoline" in lower black area.
HI TOWER ETHYL
(2)   1940s   13.5in Glass $225-$350
White globe face with black outline. Green band across center, with black-outlined white tower logo above band. Yellow "-HI-" with black dropshade across tower, "TOWER" on band. Small Ethyl (EC) logo in circle at bottom of globe face.

Aurora Gasoline Company, Detroit, Michigan
Detroit refiner marketer that introduced the Speedway brand in the early 1930s. The company's premium product, Speedway 79 Stratofuel, was introduced before WWII. The primary brand name used from the end of the war until 1962 was Speedway 79. In 1959, Marathon purchased the Aurora Gasoline Company and the Speedway 79 logo was redesigned. Gas pump globes were eliminated at this time. The Speedway 79 brand was replaced by Marathon in 1962; however, in 1975, the Speedway brand name was reintroduced at several company-owned retail "gas only" stations as Marathon began buying up regional private brands and consolidating them under Emro Marketing with the Speedway brand name. As of this writing, the Speedway name appears on petroleum products retailed at hundreds of Emro "Starvin Marvin" convenience stores.
SPEEDWAY GASOLINE
(5)   1930s   15in Metal   No Listing
Blue globe face with yellow ring around face near edge. Large yellow "Speedway," with speed lines across globe and yellow "GASOLINE" below.
SPEEDWAY OIL CO. w/flag
(5)   1938-1946   13.5in Glass $350-$650
White globe face with blue outline rings. Large blue and white checkered flag covering most of face. Red "SPEEDWAY" below flag, over smaller "OIL COMPANY."
SPEEDWAY 79 STRATOFUEL
(5)   1938-1946   13.5in Glass   No Listing
Red globe face with white "SPEEDWAY," with blue dropshade arched just above center. Checkered flag and speed lines above "SPEEDWAY." Large white "'79,'" with blue dropshade in center, above white "STRATOFUEL" with blue dropshade.
SPEEDWAY 79 red/blue
(4)   1946-1955   13.5in Capco $125-$200
Globe face split by white line across center. Upper half blue, lower half red. Large white "SPEEDWAY" with distorted lettering in upper blue area, white "'79" in lower red area.
SPEEDWAY 79
(3)   1955-1962   13.5in Glass $200-$350
Red globe face with white band across, above center. Blue "SPEED-WAY" on band, with white "'79" in lower red area offset to right.
SPEEDWAY EXTRA
(4)   1955-1962   13.5in Glass $200-$350
Blue globe face with white band across, above center. Red "SPEED-WAY" on band, with white "EXTRA" in lower blue area.

Old Dutch Refining Company, Muskegon, Michigan
Founded in Muskegon about 1930, the Old Dutch brand appeared on a small number of stations, primarily jobber operated, in the Muskegon area. As best as can be determined, Aurora Gasoline Company purchased Old Dutch Refining in the late 1950s, although jobbers kept the Old Dutch brand alive well into the 1970s.
OLD DUTCH
(4)   1930-1946   Gill $450-$700
White globe face with progressively fading blue band across center of face. Dark blue windmill on upper globe face, with small dark blue "Old" to left of windmill and larger dark blue "Dutch" below windmill.
AROSPEED
(4)   1930-1946   Gill $225-$325

White globe face with red-outlined bar-and-circle area across center of globe face. Blue arrow "through" bar-and-circle. Blue "ARO-SPEED," with large "S" in bar-and-circle.

OLD DUTCH ECONOMY
(5)   1930-1935   15in Metal   No Listing
OLD DUTCH ECONOMY
(4)   1930-1946   Gill $450-$700
Same as OLD DUTCH above, with blue "ECONOMY" below "DUTCH."

OLD DUTCH QUALITY
(4)   1930-1946   Gill $450-$700
Same as OLD DUTCH above, with red "QUALITY" below "DUTCH."

AROSPEED
(5)   1930-1946   Glass Oval $275-$400
White globe face with blue-and-red-outlined bar-and-circle area across center of face. Blue arrow "through" bar-and-circle. Blue "ARO-SPEED," with large "S" in bar-and-circle.

OLD DUTCH
(4)   1946-1974   13.5in Capco $350-$500
White globe face with red outline ring. Blue line across center of globe face with progressively thinner red lines above. Blue windmill on upper face, with blue "Old" to left and blue "Dutch" below.

Republic Oil Company, Pittsburgh, Pennsylvania

Dating from the early 1920s and believed to be a successor to Riverside Oil Company (originator of the Marathon trademark), Republic supplied branded and unbranded jobbers throughout the Southeast. Republic marketing was concentrated in small areas and no attempt was made at complete statewide coverage in the states where they marketed. By the 1950s the corporate name was Plymouth Oil Company, and Marathon purchased the operation in 1962. Concentrating on the extensive unbranded market, the Republic brand name was eventually phased out, although some jobbers continue to use the brand name today.

REPUBLIC
(4)   1922-1946   One-piece Cast $750-$1,200
One-piece cast shield-shaped globe with three faces. Upper 1/3 of shield is blue, with three white stars and white "REPUBLIC." Lower 2/3 is red and white vertical stripes.

REPUBLIC ETHYL
(5)   1930-1946   One-piece Cast   No Listing
Same as above, with script "Ethyl" across red and white stripes.

REPUBLIC SHIELD
(3)   1946-1958   13.5in Glass $225-$350
White globe face, with red, white, and blue Republic shield covering most of face. Blue lettering "REPUBLIC" extends past sides of shield.

REPUBLIC POWER PAK'D
(2)   1958-1970   13.5in Capco $100-$175
Red globe face, with large blue-and-white-outlined red and white shield covering most of face. Red "POW'R/PAK'D," with blue dropshade and red speed lines on white band on shield.

REPUBLIC HI-T
(2)   1958-1970   13.5in Capco $100-$175
White globe face, with large red, white, and blue "HI/T" shield covering most of face.

REPUBLIC HI-WAY
(4)   1946-1950   13.5in Capco $100-$175
White globe face with blue outer ring. Blue dot in center, with white "HI-WAY" diagonally across dot. White "REPUBLIC" arched around top in blue area, "GASOLINE" around bottom.

REPUBLIC SUPERIOR GASOLINE
(5)   1950s   13.5in Capco   No Listing
White globe face with blue "SUPERIOR" arched around top, "GASO-LINE" around bottom. Double red diamond in center, with "REPUB-LIC" in red across diamond. Small "REPUBLIC PRODUCT" around bottom edge of diamond in blue letters.

HI-WAY
(3)   1950-1958   13.5in Capco $100-$175
White globe face with blue dot in center. White "HI-WAY," with blue outline diagonally across dot.

HI-WAY
(3)   1958-1970   13.5in Capco $100-$175
Blue globe face, with white band horizontally across, below center. Red lettering "HI-WAY," with blue and white lines extending up to point.

Bonded, Springfield, Ohio

The Springfield, Ohio, based affiliate of Gaseteria-Bonded of Indianapolis dates from after World War II. Bonded of Ohio remained independent after Gaseteria-Bonded sold out to Esso's Oklahoma division in 1957. Marathon purchased Bonded in January 1975, and al-

though many locations were converted to Speedway-Starvin-Marvin, the Bonded brand has remained in use at many locations.

BONDED 68
(4)   1940s   13.5in Glass $275-$375
White globe face with blue outline ring. Gold and blue eight-point star with blue center. Old English "Bonded" at top of blue center area. Large red "68" below "Bonded."

BONDED 98
(4)   1946-1955   13.5in Glass $275-$375
Same as above, with "98" replacing "68."

BONDED ETHYL
(4)   1946-1955   13.5in Glass $275-$350
Same as above, with script "Ethyl" and small Ethyl (EC) logo replacing "68."

BONDED 98 in laurel wreath
(5)   1955-1968   13.5in Glass $275-$425
White globe face with laurel wreath around outer edge of face. Blue Old English "Bonded" over large red "98" across center of face.

BONDED ETHYL in laurel wreath
(5)   1955-1968   13.5in Glass $275-$425
Same as above, with script "Ethyl" and small Ethyl (EC) logo replacing "98."

Consolidated, Oshkosh, Wisconsin

A Wisconsin discount operation from the postwar era that operated about thirty stations throughout the state. Consolidated was purchased by Marathon in July 1972, and rebranded Speedway about 1982.

CONSOLIDATED
(4)   1946-1960   Oval Glass $275-$400
White globe face with black-outlined green and black "Consolidated" oval across face.

CONSOLIDATED ETHYL
(4)   1946-1960   Oval Glass $275-$400
Same as above, with small Ethyl (EC) logo in circle at lower center of globe face.

Cheker Oil Company, Chicago, Illinois

Cheker was a suburban Chicago collection of private brands, the Cheker name originally replacing Chief and Road Chief about 1968. No globes are known from these brands. Cheker purchased the Sun-Glo operation in Indiana about 1970 and converted those stations to the Cheker brand. In 1976 Cheker, then 50 percent owned by Exxon, purchased the Imperial Refineries operation. Imperial, founded in St. Louis in 1915, was in its earliest days as an intergrated oil company with production, refining, and marketing. After the war, Imperial resumed marketing as a discount chain operation, eventually operating stations in nearly twenty states. Cheker operated Imperial Refineries as a separate brand until the September 1983 merger with Marathon-Emro, and Emro replaced most of the Imperial brand with Ecol after the 1984 purchase of this Jackson, Mississippi, independent.

Note: No Cheker globes are known to exist.

Sun Glo

Purchased by Cheker about 1970.

SUN GLO
(5)   1950-1970   13.5in Capco $125-$200
White globe face with large red circle in center. Blue "SUN-GLO" arched around top, "GASOLINE" around bottom.

Imperial Refineries, Clayton, Missouri

Founded in 1915 as a refiner and marketer, Imperial operated discount stations throughout the Midwest and South until the early 1980s.

IMPERIAL w/large old shield
(5)   1920-1930   16.5in Metal $800-$1,300
White globe face with large Imperial tan and maroon shield in center. Tan lions to either side, with banners arched above and below. Unique typestyle "IMPERIAL" in upper banner, "REFINERIES" in lower banner.

IMPERIAL REFINERIES SMALL SHIELD
(5)   1930-1946   16.5in Metal $750-$1,250
White globe face with small tan and maroon Imperial shield at top, and distinctive "IMPERIAL" across face.

IMPERIAL REFINERIES ETHYL
(5)   1930-1946   16.5in Metal $350-$600
Description not available.

IMPERIAL
(2)   1946-1982   13.5in Glass $200-$325

IMPERIAL
(1)   1946-1982   13.5in Capco $75-$125

White globe face with black outline ring. Yellow and red Imperial shield covers most of face, with black "IMPERIAL" across shield and small yellow "Refineries" below.

IMPERIAL ETHYL (EC)
(2)   1946-1965   13.5in Glass $225-$350
IMPERIAL ETHYL (EC)
(3)   1946-1965   13.5in Capco $125-$175
Yellow globe face with black outline ring and black outline around white center circle. Red "IMPERIAL" arched around top, "Refineries" around bottom, with small Ethyl (EC) logo in center.

IMPERIAL PREMIUM
(3)   1965-1982   13.5in Capco $100-$150
White globe face, with small red, yellow, and black Imperial shield at top of face and italic red "PREMIUM" across lower face.

IMPERIAL NO LEAD
(2)   1975-1982   13.5in Capco $75-$125
Same as IMPERIAL ETHYL above, with large black "NO LEAD" replacing "IMPERIAL," black crosses in white circles around bottom, and Imperial shield logo in center.

IMPERIAL DIESEL
(4)   1950-1965   13.5in Capco $100-$150
Same as IMPERIAL above, with "DIESEL" below "Refineries."

IMPERIAL STOVE OIL
(4)   1950-1965   13.5in APCO $125-$200
Same as IMPERIAL ETHYL above, with red "STOVE OIL" arched around bottom and large blue "1" in center circle. Black circle-red cross logo beside "1."

IMPERIAL 50 YEARS
(5)   1965   13.5in Glass   No Listing
White globe face with black outline ring. Gold metal and ribbon design in center, with black "50th" in center and black "1915" and "1965" to either side. Black "OUR" arched around top, "ANNIVERSARY" around bottom.
This unique globe was used at Imperial stations for one year, 1965, to commemorate their fiftieth anniversary. They are very rare.

Johnson Oil Company, Mount Pleasant, Michigan

Founded in 1926 in Lakeview, Michigan, and currently operating as the Imperial Oil Company of Mount Pleasant, Michigan, Johnson Oil was apparently an Imperial jobber during the time Imperial Oil had refineries and a jobber marketing network. They continue to market in Michigan and Indiana under the Imperial name. This company is not related to Marathon marketing, and is listed here only because of its ties to Imperial.

IMPERIAL OF MICHIGAN
(4)   1946-1970   13.5in Glass $225-$350
White globe face with large, flat-top yellow and red Imperial shield on face. Black "GASOLINE" across lower shield.

Rock Island Refining, Indianapolis, Indiana

Founded in Duncan, Oklahoma, in the 1920s, Rock Island was a midcontinent area marketer until the Second World War. Having shifted to wartime refining and virtually abandoning retail gasoline, the company was purchased by the Koch family in 1946 and moved to Indianapolis, where it became a major source of unbranded gasoline for independent marketers.
Over the years the company acquired several Indiana and Michigan marketers, including Colonial-Progressive of Fort Wayne, Tulsa of Detroit, United of Indianapolis, Naph-Sol of Muskegon, and Golden Imperial (not listed below) of Indianapolis. By the mid-1980s United had become the primary brand, replacing the others where convenient. In 1989 Marathon's Emro Marketing purchased Rock Island, and many United locations have converted to the Speedway brand.

ROCK ISLAND GASOLINE
(5)   1930-1946   15in Metal $800-$1,300
Red and white outlines around blue outer ring. Red and white rings around white center circle. White "ROCK ISLAND" arched around top, "GASOLINE" around bottom, with red line drawing of the Rock of Gibraltar in the center.

ROCK ISLAND NUNBETTER
(5)   1930-1946   15in Metal $350-$650
Same as above, with red-outlined white band diagonally across plain white center (no rock). Red "NUNBETTER" in center band.

ROCK ISLAND ROCKILENE
(4)   1930-1946   15in Metal $350-$600
ROCK ISLAND ROCKILENE
(4)   1940-1946   13.5in Glass $300-$450
Same as above, with "ROCKILENE" in center band.

ROCK ISLAND ANTI-KNOCK
(5)   1930-1946   15in Metal $300-$375
Same as above, with "ANTI-KNOCK" in center band.

ROCK ISLAND ETHYL
(5)   1930s   15in Metal   No Listing
Description not available.

ROCK ISLAND GASOLINE
(5)   1940-1946   13.5in Capco   No listing
White globe face with blue outline ring and blue outlines around white center circle. Red "ROCK ISLAND" arched around top. "GASOLINE" around bottom with blue Rock of Gibralter scene with green ocean in center.

ROCKILENE ETHYL GASOLINE
(5)   1940-1946   13.5in Capco $250-$350
Blue globe face with red/white outline rings and red outline around white center circle. White "ROCKILENE" arched around top, "GASO-LINE" around bottom with large Ethyl (EGC) logo in center circle.

ROCK ISLAND w/rock
(4)   1946-1960   13.5in Capco $325-$500
Bright yellow globe face with maroon "ROCK" across top, "ISLAND" across bottom, and maroon rock and water picture in center.

ROCK ISLAND ETHYL (EGC)
(4)   1946-1960   13.5in Capco $225-$325
Same as above, with small Ethyl (EGC) logo in white circle superimposed over rock in center.

ROCK ISLAND w/rock
(4)   1946-1960   13.5in Capco $300-$500
Same as above, with white globe face, red lettering, and blue rock.

Colonial-Progressive, Fort Wayne, Indiana

Independent marketer founded in the 1930s that operated Colonial stations in Indiana and Progressive stations in Michigan. Sold out to Rock Island in the 1960s.

COLONIAL
(3)   1950-1965   13.5in Glass $200-$325
Orange upper and lower halves with black-outlined white band across center. White band widens left-to-right. Black speed lines above and below white band. Black "COLONIAL" in progressively larger type on center band.

PROGRESSIVE
(3)   1950-1965   13.5in Glass $200-$325
Same as above, with "PROGRESSIVE" replacing "COLONIAL" in center band.

O-70
(5)   1950s   13.5in Glass $250-$375
Same as above, with large, distinctive lettering "O-70" on center band.

Tulsa Oil Company, Detroit, Michigan

Tulsa is an old Detroit independent brand that sold out to Crystal Refining in the early 1970s and was in turn purchased by Rock Island about 1978. The United brand name replaced Tulsa in 1985.

TULSA
(5)   1940s   15in Metal   No Listing
Identical in design to early Tydol globes. Orange ring around outer edge, with black line around white center circle. Black "TULSA" (oversize "T") across white center.

TULSA 95
(4)   1950-1970   13.5in Capco $125-$175
White globe face with yellow outline ring. Red "TULSA" with black dropshade across top of face. Red "95" (in quotes) in center, above yellow and black stylized cow head and horns.

TULSA 100
(3)   1950-1970   13.5in Capco $125-$175
Same as above, with "100" replacing "95."

TULSA HI-TEST
(3)   1950-1970   13.5in Capco $125-$200
Same as above, with "HI-TEST" replacing "95."

TULSA DIESEL
(4)   1950-1970   13.5in Capco $125-$200
Same as above, with "DIESEL" replacing "95."

Duro Oil Company, Detroit, Michigan

Detroit-based independent that merged with Tulsa in the 1970s.

DURO "D" GASOLINE
(4)   1950s   13.5in Glass $225-$325
Red and white outline ring around green globe face. White circle in center. White "DURO" arched around top, "GASOLINE" around bottom, with large red "D" with green dropshade in center.

United, Indianapolis, Indiana

United was an Indianapolis-based discount marketer with stations throughout Indiana and a few in Michigan. In 1985 United was purchased by their primary supplier, Rock Island, and became the brand name used to consolidate all of Rock Island's marketing. Most of

Imperial Stove Oil 13.5in inserts on yellow plastic body.

Zephyr High Octane oval lenses on oval plastic body.

Pair of Zephyr globes 13.5in inserts on Gill red ripple bodies. R. V. Witherspoon

Socony one-piece etched globe.

Socony Motor Oils one-piece etched globe.

Socony Ethyl 16.5in inserts on metal body.

Socony 16.5in milk glass inserts on metal body.

White Eagle one-piece "blunt nosed" eagle-shaped globe.

White Eagle one-piece "detailed" eagle-shaped globe.

White Eagle Gasoline 15in inserts on metal body.

White Eagle one-piece etched globe.

Wadhams Metro 15in inserts on metal body. James Bernard

White Star Gasoline 15in inserts on metal body.

Gilmore Ethyl Gasoline 15in insert for metal body. Dick Bennett

Gilmore Gasoline 15in inserts on metal body.

the United stations were rebranded Speedway in 1990, but some locations remain United.

UNITED HI-TEST w/arrow
(5)   1940s   13.5in Glass $275-$400
Blue-outlined red globe face with blue-outlined white bar-and-circle across center of globe. White "UNITED" arched in upper red area, "GASOLINE" below, with blue "HI TEST" in white center area. Red arrow passing through "HI TEST."

UNITED ETHYL red/black
(5)   1940s   13.5in Glass $225-$350
White globe face with black-outlined white circle in center. Red "UNITED" arched around top, "GASOLINE" around bottom, with black triangles to either side. Red and black stylized Ethyl logo in center.

UNITED FUEL OIL w/flame
(5)   1940s   13.5in Glass $350-$550
Light blue outline around red outer ring. Light blue outline around white center circle. White "UNITED" arched around top, "FUEL OIL" around bottom, with red, white, and tan detailed flames in center and black and blue band across flames. White script on black band "GUARANTEED QUALITY."

UNITED
(3)   1950s   13.5in Capco $100-$150
White globe face with thick red band arched across center. White "UNITED" on red band.

UNITED REGULAR
(3)   1965-1980   13.5in Capco $100-$150
White face with red band arched across most of face. Large white "UNITED" on red band. Blue "REGULAR" below band on lower globe face.

UNITED ETHYL
(3)   1965-1980   13.5in Capco $100-$150
Same as above, with blue band and red "ETHYL" below band.

Naph-Sol Refining Company, Muskegon, Michigan

Naph-Sol entered the gasoline market with the introduction of Zephyr gasoline in 1932. Marketing continued through jobbers and independent dealers in Michigan and Wisconsin until 1989, when Naph-Sol was bought out by Rock Island Refining. Several Michigan jobbers continue to use the Zephyr brand.

INDEPENDENT ZEPHYR GASOLINE
(4)   1936-1957   13.5in Glass $225-$350
White globe face with thick blue outline ring and blue lines forming white band across center. Blue "INDEPENDENT" arched around top, "GASOLINE" around bottom, with red "ZEPHYR" in band.

ZEPHYR
(4)   1936-1957   13.5in Glass $225-$350
Same as above, without "INDEPENDENT" and "GASOLINE."

ZEPHYR ETHYL
(4)   1936-1957   13.5in Glass $225-$350
Same as above, with narrower center band. Red "ETHYL" at top, "ZEPHYR" in band, and small Ethyl (EC) logo below.

ZEPHYR w/shield
(2)   1957-1970   13.5in Capco $125-$175
White globe face with blue-outlined red rounded triangle Zephyr logo covering most of face. White "ZEPHYR" over blue "GASOLINE" in logo.

(ZEPHYR) BLU-FLAME FUEL OIL
(3)   1960s   13.5in Capco $150-$250

(ZEPHYR) BLU-FLAME FUEL OIL
(3)   1950s   13.5in Glass $225-$350
Yellow globe face with black outline ring. Light blue and white flame design covering most of face, with blue "BLU-FLAME" across flames.

Osceola Refining Company, Reed City, Michigan

Independent refiner and marketer purchased by Zephyr in the 1970s.

OSCEOLA PREMIUM
(4)   1960s   One-piece plastic $200-$275
White plastic-formed trapezoidal halves assembled back-to-back. Blue "OSCEOLA" logotype across top, with red Indian head in blue area below. Red "PREMIUM" to right of Indian head.

OSCEOLA ETHYL
(4)   1960s   One-piece plastic $200-$275
Same as above, but exact description not available.

MARTIN & AFFILIATES
MARTIN OIL COMPANY, Carbondale, Illinois
MARTIN OIL SERVICE, Blue Island, Illinois

Martin, an Illinois-based trackside discounter dating from the early 1930s, was actually a collection of several family-owned operations within the Martin chain. In the earliest days dual headquarters–Chicago and Carbondale,Illinois–were listed on products and later the Chicago division was moved to Alsip and still later Blue Island, Illinois. About 1956 the chain separated into two distinct operations, the Chicago (Alsip) division becoming Martin Oil Service, while the Carbondale division remained Martin Oil Company.

Martin Oil Service expanded coast-to-coast, operating over 200 gas stations by the 1970s while Martin Oil Company concentrated marketing through a small number of stations in the south central states. Cut off from supplies during the 1973-74 gas shortage, Martin Oil Service retreated to their home base, currently operating less than 50 stations in Illinois and Indiana. Martin Oil Company sold out to J. D. Street of Maryland Heights, Missouri, in 1977, and the stations were rebranded with J. D. Street's Zephyr brand. In the 1980s J. D. Street became a branded jobber for several majors, and today the Zephyr brand remains in use on only a small number of stations.

Martin Oil Stations, Carbondale, Illinois

Operated stations in the south central states from the 1930s until purchased in 1977 by J. D. Street.

MARTIN'S ALLWEATHER GASOLINE
(5)   1930s   15in Metal $300-$550
White globe face with blue "MARTIN'S" arched around top, "GASOLINE" around bottom, with red "ALLWEATHER" across center.

MARTIN w/tank car
(5)   1935-1946   13.5in Glass $450-$800
White globe face with repeating red, white, and blue outline rings. Large red-and-white-outlined red railroad tank car across center of face, with blue-outlined white "SUPER" on tank car. Old English red-outlined blue "MARTIN'S" arched around top, red-outlined blue block "REGULAR" around bottom.

MARTIN SUPER REGULAR
(4)   1946-1966   13.5in Glass $225-$350
Red, white, and blue repeating outline rings around outer red area. Outline rings around white center circle. Red "MARTIN" across upper face, extending into outer red area. Blue "Super" diagonally over red "Regular" on lower face.

MARTIN XTRA SPECIAL
(4)   1946-1966   13.5in Glass $225-$350
Red, white, and blue repeating outline rings around white globe face. Blue "MARTIN" arched around top, "SPECIAL" horizontally across bottom, with blue-outlined red "XTRA" diagonally across face. Outline rings around "X" in "XTRA."

MARTIN ETHYL PREMIUM
(4)   1946-1958   13.5in Glass $225-$350
Red, white, and blue outline rings around blue outer area of globe. Outline rings around white center circle. Large Ethyl (EC) logo in center, with white "MARTIN" arched around top, "PREMIUM" around bottom.

J.D. Street, Maryland Heights, Missouri

Founded in 1884 as a lubricants distributor, J. D. Street entered the retail petroleum market with the introduction of the Zephyr gasoline brand in 1939. J. D. Street purchased Martin Oil Company in 1977 and converted their stations to the Zephyr brand. J. D. Street currently serves as a jobber for several major brands, as well as operating a few remaining Zephyr brand stations.

ZEPHYR
(2)   1939-1954   Gill $225-$375
White globe face with red lines forming white diagonal band across face. Red increasing-width spiral around face. Red "ZEPHYR," with speed lines and blue dropshade on band.

ZEPHYR ETHYL
(3)   1939-1954   Gill $225-$375
Same as ZEPHYR above, with black-outlined white circle, with Ethyl (EGC) logo offset to right below band.

ZEPHYR HIGH OCTANE
(3)   1954-1960   Oval Capco $150-$200
Blue globe face with blue and white outline ring. Red-outlined white diagonal band across center. Red "ZEPHYR," with speed lines and blue dropshade on band. White "HIGH OCTANE" in upper blue area, "GASOLINE" below.

ZEPHYR ETHYL
(3)   1954-1960   Oval Capco $150-$200
Same as ZEPHYR HIGH OCTANE above, with "SUPREME" replac-

ing "HIGH OCTANE" and white circle with Ethyl (EC) logo replacing "GASOLINE."
ZEPHYR
(2)   1960-1975   Oval Capco $150-$200
Much lighter blue oval, with red "ZEPHYR" on white diagonal band. No lettering in blue area.

Martin Oil Service, Alsip, Illinois

Martin Oil Service is the division that expanded coast-to-coast beginning in the late 1950s. Currently, Martin operates forty-three stations in Illinois and Indiana.
MARTIN SUPER REGULAR
(3)   1958-1962   13.5in Glass $250-$350
White globe face with grey lines, forming a large "M," screened in the background. Series of alternating blue and red lines across lower face, bent in a right angle to a point at the bottom of the face. Large blue "MARTIN" over red script "Super" over blue "REGULAR," superimposed over screened "M" on globe face.
MARTIN PREMIUM ETHYL
(3)   1958-1962   13.5in Glass $250-$350
Similar to MARTIN SUPER REGULAR above, with lines at bottom notched for black-outlined circle and Ethyl (EC) logo. Blue "MARTIN" over red script "Premium" on upper globe face.
MARTIN PURPLE MARTIN
(5)   1958-1962   13.5in Glass $225-$400
White globe face with blue "PURPLE" arched around top. Red, yellow, and red lines around lower face. Small blue bird under arch of "PURPLE," above red "MARTIN" over yellow script "The Finest," over red "ETHYL" over yellow script "of all." Small Ethyl (EC) logo in circle at end of "of all"
MARTIN SUPER REGULAR
(3)   1962-1970   13.5in Capco $100-$125
White globe face with parallel red lines across upper face. Red-outlined Martin blue "M" logo superimposed over lines. Large blue "SUPER" over smaller red "REGULAR" on lower face.
MARTIN EXTRA SPECIAL ETHYL
(3)   1962-1970   13.5in Capco $125-$175
Similar to above, with blue lines and blue-outlined Martin logo. Blue-outlined red "XTRA SPECIAL" arched below logo over red "ETHYL" and small Ethyl (EC) logo.
MARTIN PURPLE MARTIN ETHYL
(3)   1962-1970   13.5in Capco $150-$250
Similar to above, with purple lines across top and purple outline around Martin logo. Small purple bird just below logo, with purple-colored "PURPLE" to left and "MARTIN" to right of bird. Large red "ETHYL" and small Ethyl (EC) logo on lower globe face.
MARTIN DIESEL #2
(4)   1962-1970   13.5in Capco $100-$150
Similar to above, with green lines and green outline around Martin logo. Green "DIESEL" over large red "2," with green "NO." to left and "H.I." to right on lower face.
MARTIN DIESEL #1
(4)   1962-1970   13.5in Capco $100-$150
Same as above, with "1" replacing "2."
MARTIN RANGE OIL
(5)   1962-1970   13.5in Capco $100-$175
Similar to above, with green lines and green outline around Martin logo. Green "RANGE/OIL" on lower globe face.

MOBIL and Affiliates
MOBIL OIL CORPORATION, FAIRFAX, VIRGINIA
Standard Oil Company of New York/Socony, New York, New York

Founded in 1882 as the administrative division of the Standard Oil Trust, Socony eventually became involved in refining and later marketing in New York and New England. With the breakup of Standard in 1911, Socony was assigned its refining and marketing properties, but left without crude oil production. Exploration began, but most of the crude oil production came through acquisition of Magnolia Petroleum in 1918 and General Petroleum in 1926. Socony expanded its marketing through Magnolia and General (and White Eagle) as well, marketing from coast-to-coast by 1930.

In 1931 Socony merged with another Standard affiliate, Vacuum Oil, the new corporate entity to be named Socony-Vacuum Oil Company. Socony-Vacuum mated Socony's shield and flying horse with Vacuum's "Mobilgas" trademark, and expanded the Mobilgas brand to all of the affiliated companies by the end of WWII. In 1955 the company was renamed Socony-Mobil, and in 1966 Mobil Oil Corporation. See the SOCONY-VACUUM listing below for more information.

Note: The Socony "SONY & Shield" logo, which will be referred to in the following descriptions, is a blue circle with a large white-and-red-outlined five-point shield positioned to the lower edge of the circle. A red line crosses the shield about 1/3 of the way down, with red "SOCONY" above the line and red "MOTOR GASOLINE" below the line. Small blue lettering "STANDARD OIL CO. OF NEW YORK" around the bottom edge of the shield. Distorted white "S" and "O" in the blue area above the shield, and an elongated "N" to left and "Y" to right of shield. Refer to this description from the globe text below.
SOCONY MOTOR GASOLINE
(5)   1915-1932   One-piece etched $1,000-$1,900
White globe with blue-and-white-outlined SONY & Shield logo, as described above, on face.
SOCONY MOTOR GASOLINE
(4)   1915-1926   16.5in Milk glass $400-$800
                        lenses on Metal
SOCONY MOTOR GASOLINE
(3)   1915-1926   15in Milk glass $400-$750
                        lenses on Metal
SOCONY MOTOR GASOLINE
(5)   1925-1926   14in Milk glass $450-$800
                        lenses on Metal
Milk glass globe face with white outline ring around SONY & Shield logo, as described above.
SOCONY MOTOR GASOLINE
(5)   1915-1926   16.5in Metal $350-$650
SOCONY MOTOR GASOLINE
(4)   1915-1926   15in Metal $350-$600
SOCONY MOTOR GASOLINE
(5)   1920-1926   14in Porcelain $450-$800
                        lenses on Metal
SOCONY MOTOR GASOLINE
(5)   1920-1926   15in Cast lenses on Metal $600-$1,200
Globe has white outline rings around SONY & Shield, as described above.
SOCONY
(3)   1926-1934   16.5in Metal $250-$450
SOCONY
(3)   1926-1934   15in Metal $250-$400
White globe face with red "SOCONY" with blue dropshade across center.
SOCONY
(3)   1926-1934   16.5in Metal $250-$450
SOCONY
(3)   1926-1934   15in Metal $250-$450
White globe face with red "SOCONY" with blue dropshade across center—red lettering with white lines.
SOCONY SPECIAL
(4)   1922-1926   16.5in milk Glass inserts on Metal
$350-$675
SOCONY SPECIAL
(4)   1922-1926   15in milk glass inserts on metal
$350-$650
White milk glass globe face with red "SOCONY" arched around top, "GASOLINE" around bottom, with blue "SPECIAL" across center.
SOCONY ETHYL (EGC)
(3)   1926-1934   16.5in Metal $275-$500
SOCONY ETHYL (EGC)
(3)   1926-1934   15in Metal $275-$450
White globe face with red "SOCONY" with blue dropshade across center. Black-outlined white circle at top of globe face, with small Ethyl (EGC) logo. Red "ETHYL" with blue dropshade below "SOCONY."
SOCONY ETHYL (w/lines)
(3)   1926-1934   16.5in Metal $275-$525
SOCONY ETHYL (w/lines)
(3)   1926-1934   15in Metal $275-$525
Same as above, with blue outline ring and blue line under "ETHYL."
SOCONY MOTOR OILS
(5)   1915-1920   One-piece etched $750-$1,100
SOCONY MOTOR OILS
(5)   1915-1920   One-piece Baked $600-$750
One-piece globe with blue "SOCONY" over "MOTOR OILS" on face.
SOCONY BURNING OIL
(4)   1934-1940   16.5in Metal $400-$800
White globe face with small flying red horse at top. Blue "SOCONY BURNING OIL" on lower face.
STANDARD KEROSENE
(4)   1934-1940   15in Metal $325-$500
White globe face with small red flying horse at top. Blue "STANDARD" over "KEROSENE" on lower face.

Magnolia Petroleum, Dallas, Texas

A Texas oil producer, refiner, and marketer dating from 1911, Magnolia sold 45 percent interest to Socony in 1918. Socony completed the purchase in 1925. The Magnolia brand name was replaced by Mobilgas about 1934, after the Socony-Vacuum merger. Magnolia remained a separate, named subsidiary, primarily involved in pipeline transportation, until 1960.

MAGNOLIA GASOLINE
| (5) | 1915-1920 | One-piece etched | No Listing |

White globe with red "MAGNOLIA" arched around top, "GASOLINE" around bottom of face.

MAGNOLIA GASOLINE (w/flower)
| (4) | 1920-1926 | 16.5in Metal | $1,100-$1,700 |

White globe face with red outline ring. Blue-outlined red "MAGNOLIA" arched around top, "GASOLINE" around bottom, with detailed green leaf-white flower magnolia blossom in center.

MAGNOLIA MAXIMUM MILEAGE
| (3) | 1926-1934 | 16.5in Metal | $1,000-$1,600 |

White globe face with blue outline ring. Blue-outlined red "MAGNOLIA" arched around top, "GASOLINE" around bottom, with small detailed green leaf-white flower magnolia blossom in center. Blue "MAXIMUM" to left of flower, "MILEAGE" to right.

MAGNOLIA ANTI-KNOCK
| (5) | 1922-1926 | 16.5in Metal | $1,000-$1,700 |

Description not available.

MAGNOLIA ETHYL (EGC)
| (4) | 1926-1934 | 16.5in Metal | $400-$750 |

Blue outline ring around red globe face. White and blue outline around white center circle. White "MAGNOLIA" arched around top, "GASOLINE" around bottom, with small Ethyl (EGC) logo in center.

General Petroleum Corporation, Vernon, California

A pioneer California oil producer and refiner, General was founded in 1910. In 1926 Socony purchased General Petroleum and maintained the General brands until the end of World War II, gradually replacing them with Mobilgas. As with Magnolia, General remained a separate, named subsidiary until 1960.

GENERAL GASOLINE
| (4) | 1928-1934 | 15in Metal | $275-$450 |

White globe face with red line above and below center. Script blue "GENERAL" above blue "GASOLINE" between red lines.

GENERAL VIOLET RAY GASOLINE
| (5) | 1928-1932 | 15in Metal | $800-$1,500 |

White globe face with large green diamond covering most of face. White band across center of diamond, with red-outlined purple "VIOLET RAY" on band. White "GENERAL" and purple lightning bolt in upper area of diamond. Red "ANTI-KNOCK" in lower area of diamond, above wide white band. Red "GASOLINE" extending beyond edge of diamond on lower band.

GENERAL ETHYL
| (3) | 1926-1934 | 15in Metal | $500-$750 |

Red upper globe face with green lower face. Large red-outlined white triangular shield covers most of face, with red, white, and green checkerboard pattern at top of shield, small Ethyl (EGC) logo on lower shield.

GENERAL PETROLEUM ETHYL GASOLINE
| (5) | 1942 Special | 13.5in Glass | $225-$400 |

White globe face with blue outline ring. Red "GENERAL" arched around top, "PETROLEUM" around bottom, with small Ethyl (EC) logo in center and small blue "GASOLINE" below logo.

White Eagle Oil and Refining, Kansas City, Missouri

Midcontinent producer, refiner, and marketer, with gas stations in eleven midwestern states. Chief White Eagle was a leader of the Ponca Indians in Oklahoma. White Eagle was first used as a corporate name in 1916, when L. L. Marcell founded the White Eagle Petroleum Company. That same year the new company built a refinery at Augusta, Kansas, having a capacity of 2,000 barrels per day.

In 1919 the White Eagle Petroleum Company was reorganized and the name changed to the White Eagle Oil and Refining Company. This reorganization was in reality a merger of six independent oil companies, and within a few years the new company enjoyed second position in the distribution of petroleum products in the Midwest.

A second refinery was built at Casper, Wyoming, and a third was purchased at Fort Worth, Texas.

The poised White Eagle was adopted as an emblem because of its dignity and general significance, particularly in their territory and because it was in keeping with the company name. As a service station identification, this emblem—the big iron eagle in front of the station and the illuminated glass eagles on the pumps—was very effective.

In January 1930, the White Eagle Oil and Refining Company was purchased by the Standard Oil Company of New York (Socony), at which time the name was changed to the White Eagle Oil Corporation. When Socony and Vacuum merged in 1931, White Eagle Oil Corporation became a subsidiary company. In 1935, the White Eagle Oil Corporation was dissolved and the operation became the White Eagle division of Socony-Vacuum Oil Company, Incorporated.

WHITE EAGLE GASOLINE
| (4) | 1918-1920 | One-piece etched | No Listing |

White globe with black and white perched eagle in center of face. Red "WHITE EAGLE" arched around top, "GASOLINE" around bottom.

WHITE EAGLE GASOLINE AND OILS
| (4) | 1920-1925 | 15in Metal | $600-$900 |

White globe face with black octagonal outline. Black-outlined red circle in center of black-and-white-outlined black band across center. White "WHITE EAGLE" in band, white "GASOLINE" arched around top of red circle, "AND OILS" arched around bottom.

WHITE EAGLE blunt nose
| (3) | 1924-1932 | One-piece Eagle | $650-$950 |

Cast white eagle with very little detail and blunt nose.

WHITE EAGLE slit throat
| (3) | 1924-1932 | One-piece Eagle | $650-$950 |

Same as above, with casting line around throat.

WHITE EAGLE pointed nose, some detail
| (3) | 1930-1932 | One-piece Eagle | $750-$1,200 |

Cast white eagle, with more feather detail and pointed nose.

WHITE EAGLE pointed nose, good detail
| (4) | 1932 | One-piece Eagle | $850-$1,500 |

Cast white eagle, with very good feather detail and pointed nose.

Vacuum Oil Company, Rochester, New York

Founded as a lubricants manufacturer in 1866, Vacuum had developed an extensive line of specialty lubricants when Standard Oil purchased the company in 1879. During the Standard era, Vacuum's lubricants, under the Gargoyle and later Gargoyle Mobil Oil brands, were sold by the various Standard marketing firms. With the breakup of Standard in 1911, Vacuum was left to market its oils through independent channels worldwide. They became involved with gasoline marketing, under the Mobilgas brand, in the late 1920s and expanded the gasoline venture with the purchase of Lubrite Refining Company of St. Louis, Missouri, in 1929. The following year Vacuum purchased Wadhams Oil Corporation of Milwaukee, and the Vacuum Mobilgas name was added to Wadhams' extensive product line. Also in 1930, Vacuum purchased White Star Refining of Detroit and added over 1,500 outlets for Mobilgas. In 1931 Socony and Vacuum merged to form Socony Vacuum Oil Company, and after a two-year reimaging program, the Mobilgas brand name became the company's primary brand, although several of the regional marketers retained their own identities until after the war.

MOBIL
| (5) | 1920s | One-piece etched | No Listing |

Mobil across center in red.

MOBILGAS–PROGRESSIVE red and white
| (4) | 1928-1930 | 16.5in Metal | $400-$650 |

MOBILGAS–PROGRESSIVE red and white
| (4) | 1928-1930 | 15in Metal | $400-$600 |

MOBILGAS–PROGRESSIVE red and white
| (5) | 1928-1930 | 13.5in Glass | $300-$450 |

MOBILGAS–PROGRESSIVE red and white
| (5) | 1928-1930 | 15in fired on milk glass lens | No listing |

Red globe face with series of increasing-width white horizontal lines above and below white center band. Black "MOBILGAS" across band.

MOBILGAS–blue lettering w/ red line
| (2) | 1932-1933 | 16.5in Metal | $275-$400 |

MOBILGAS–blue lettering w/ red line
| (2) | 1932-1933 | 15in Metal | $275-$350 |

MOBILGAS–blue lettering w/ red line
| (3) | 1932-1933 | 13.5in Glass | $200-$325 |

White globe face with thin red line positioned above and below center, so as to form a white band across the center of face. Dark blue "MOBILGAS" in band.

MOBILGAS–green lettering w/red line
| (5) | 1932-1933 | 15in Metal | $350-$600 |

White globe face with thin red line positioned above and below center, so as to form a white band across the center of face. Bright green "MOBILGAS" in band.

MOBILGAS ETHYL
| (3) | 1928-1933 | 16.5in Metal | $275-$425 |

MOBILGAS ETHYL
| (3) | 1928-1933 | 15in Metal | $250-$400 |

White globe face with small Ethyl (EGC) logo at top of face. Black "MOBILGAS" across center, above black "ETHYL."

MOBILGAS ETHYL
(3) 1930-1933 16.5in Metal $275-$450
MOBILGAS ETHYL
(3) 1930-1933 15in Metal $250-$425
MOBILGAS ETHYL
(3) 1930-1933 13.5in Glass $200-$350
White globe face with small Ethyl (EGC) logo at top of face. Dark blue "MOBILGAS" across center, above red "ETHYL."

GARGOYLE MOBILOIL (large)
(3) 1920-1935 One-piece Oval Cast $800-$1,400
Oval one-piece cast globe with red outline ring. Detailed red and black gargoyle logo, with black "GARGOYLE" arched over top of logo. Black "MOBILOIL" across lower globe face below logo.

GARGOYLE MOBILOIL (small; raised border)
(3) 1920-1935 One-piece Oval Cast $800-$1,400
Smaller globe similar to above, with raised red outline ring.

GARGOYLE MOBILOIL (small; recessed border)
(3) 1920-1935s One-piece Oval Cast $800-$1,400
Smaller globe similar to above, with recessed red outline ring.

Lubrite Refining Company, St. Louis, Missouri

Lubrite was a St. Louis-based refiner/marketer with retail service stations in Missouri, Illinois, Iowa, and southern Indiana. In 1929, Vacuum Oil bought Lubrite in its first expansion of the Mobilgas brand name away from its own small number of stations.

LUBRITE
(5) 19235-1929 15in Metal No listing
Description not available.
LUBRITE SKY HIGH
(5) 1925-1929 15in Metal No listing
Description not available.

Wadhams Oil Corporation, Milwaukee, Wisconsin

Founded in the 1870s as a lubricants manufacturer, Wadhams was a pioneer in gasoline marketing, operating Wadhams stations throughout Wisconsin prior to 1920. Wadhams was briefly affiliated with the Independent Oil Men of America in about 1925, and expanded with the 1929 purchase of Milwaukee competitor Bartles-McGuire Oil Company. Noted for its Chinese pagoda-style stations, Wadhams had developed a first-class gasoline marketing organization when the company was purchased by Vacuum in 1930. Vacuum's Mobilgas trademark was added to the Wadhams brands, and finally replaced the Wadhams name about 1939.

WADHAMS w/can
(5) 1910s One-piece etched No Listing
White globe with black "WADHAMS" and red gasoline can on face.
WADHAMS TRUE GASOLINE
(5) 1910s One-piece etched No Listing
White globe with red "WADHAMS" (large "W") across center of face. Small black "TRUE GASOLINE" below "WADHAMS."
WADHAMS 370
(5) 1920-1925 15in Steel face on Metal $375-$525
White reflective steel face with black "WADHAMS" across top. Red "370," with black dropshade across center over red circle. Black "W" on red circle.
WADHAMS ANTI-KNOCK
(4) 1920-1925 15in steel face on metal No Listing
White reflective steel face with black "WADHAMS" across top. Red "ANTI-KNOCK" with black dropshade arched across center, over red bar. Black "W" superimposed over bar.
WADHAMS "INDEPENDENT" IOMA
(5) 1925-1929 15in Metal No Listing
White globe face with red outline ring. Red semi-circle at top of face. Black "WADHAMS" across center, with black triangle-red thunderbird IOMA logo at bottom of globe face.
WADHAMS RED HAT
(5) 1925-1929 15in Metal No Listing
"WADHAMS" and "RED HAT" independent logo showing red hat. No other details known.
WADHAMS ETHYL (EGC)
(3) 1929-1932 15in Metal $275-$450
White globe face with red outline ring. Yellow bar with black "W" at top of globe face. Black "WADHAMS" across center, with large black-and-red-outlined white circle on lower globe face. Large Ethyl (EGC) logo in circle.
WADHAMS MOBILGAS
(4) 1929-1932 15in Metal $325-$525
Red globe face similar to MOBILGAS–PROGRESSIVE RED AND

WHITE above, with black "WADHAMS" above "MOBILGAS" in upper red section.

WADHAMS METRO "W"
(4) 1929-1932 15in Metal $275-$450
WADHAMS METRO "W"
(3) 1932-1940 13.5in Glass $225-$350
White globe face with yellow outline ring. Black "WADHAMS" across upper globe face, above large black "METRO." Red bar with black "W" on lower globe face.
WADHAMS ETHYL
(3) 1932-1940 13.5in Glass $225-$350
White globe face with red outline ring. Red bar with black "W" at top of face, over black "WADHAMS." Black-yellow-and-black-outlined white circle on lower globe face, with large Ethyl (EGC) logo on circle.
WADHAMS GIANT
(5) 1932-1935 13.5in Glass $250-$375
White globe face with red outline ring. Black "WADHAMS" across upper face, with red "GIANT" with black dropshade arched across center. Red bar with black "W" on lower globe face.
WADHAMS GIANT ETHYL
(5) 1938-1940 13.5in Glass No Listing
Description not available.

Bartles-McGuire Oil Company, Milwaukee, Wisconsin

Large Wisconsin marketer that merged with Wadhams in 1929, shortly before Vacuum purchased Wadhams.

BARTLES WHITE EAGLE GASOLINE
(5) 1920s One-piece etched oval No Listing
White oval One-piece etched globe with small eagle design in center. Red band across center, with white-colored "WHITE" to left of eagle and "EAGLE" to right. Black "BARTLES" arched around top, "GASO-LINE" around bottom.
BARTLES BONDED GASOLINE
(4) 1921-1929 15in Metal $300-$550
White globe face with large red "B" covering most of face. Red arrow diagonally through "B." White "BARTLES" in upper area of "B," "BONDED" in lower area, with white "GASOLINE" on diagonal arrow.

White Star Refining Company, Detroit, Michigan

Also added to Vacuum's Mobilgas marketing was Detroit's White Star Refining. White Star operated more than 1,500 stations in Ohio, Indiana, and Michigan when purchased by Vacuum in 1930. Mobilgas replaced the White Star brand almost immediately, but former White Star outlets used a special Mobilgas shield sign with a small blue circle and white star at the bottom until after World War II.

WHITE STAR GASOLINE
(5) 1918-1920 One-piece etched No Listing
White globe with blue face. Large white star in center, with blue band across center of star. White-colored "WHITE STAR/GASOLINE" on center band, with white-colored "WHITE STAR REFINING CO." arched around top and "A/QUALITY/PRODUCT" below star.
WHITE STAR etched milk glass faces
(5) 1920-1926 15in Metal $900-$1,600
Blue globe face with large white star in center. Blue band across star, with white-colored "WHITE STAR/GASOLINE" on band. White-colored "WHITE STAR REFINING CO." arched around top, "A/QUALI-TY/PRODUCT" below star.
STAROLINE GASOLINE IS BETTER
(4) 1922-1926 15in Metal $450-$750
Blue globe face with white outline ring. Small white-outlined blue circle with white star at top. Script white "Staroline" across center, with white "GASOLINE/IS BETTER" below.
STAROLINE GASOLINE IS BETTER
(5) 1922-1926 15in Metal $450-$750
Blue globe face with large white star covering most of face. White outlined blue band superimposed across center of star. White script "Staroline" on center band with white "WHITE STAR REFINING CO." arched around top, "GASOLINE/IS BETTER" below star at bottom.
STAROLINE GASOLINE IS BETTER
(5) 1922-1926 15in Metal $450-$750
Blue globe face with large white star covering most of face. White outlined blue band superimposed across center of star. White script "Staroline" on center band with white "WHITE STAR REFINING CO." arched around top, "GASOLINE/IS BETTER" below star at bottom.
WHITE STAR GASOLINE
(4) 1926-1930 15in Metal $400-$750
Blue globe face with white outline around blue center circle. White

star in center circle, with white-colored "WHITE STAR" arched around top and "GASOLINE" around bottom.
WHITE STAR ETHYL
(4)   1926-1930   15in Metal $350-$650
Blue globe face with white-and-blue-outlined white center circle. Large Ethyl (EGC) logo in center circle. White-colored "WHITE STAR" arched around top, "GASOLINE" around bottom.
STAROLINE AND WHITE STAR ETHYL
(4)   1926-1930   15in Metal $400-$700
Blue globe face with small white circle at top. Small Ethyl (EGC) logo in circle. White script "Staroline" across center, above small white "AND," above white-colored "WHITE STAR." Yellow "ETHYL" below "WHITE STAR."
WHITE STAR GASOLINE
(4)   1930-1934   15in Metal $500-$800
White globe face with red circle in center. White star in red center circle. Blue "WHITE STAR" arched around top, "GASOLINE" around bottom.
WHITE STAR GASOLINE
(4)   1930-1934   15in Metal $500-$800
Red globe face with blue circle in center. White star in blue circle. White-colored "WHITE STAR" arched around top, "GASOLINE" around bottom.

Independent Oil Company of Pennsylvania, Altoona, Pennsylvania

Purchased by Socony-Vacuum in 1934 and rebranded Mobilgas.
INDEPENDENT (w/3 men)
(4)   1925-1934   15in Metal $1,600-$2,500
White globe face with black "INDEPENDENT" arched around top. Black-outlined white circle on lower globe face, with multicolored scene with colonial soldiers and drummer.
INDEPENDENT GASOLINE (w/3 men)
(5)   1925-1934   15in Metal   No Listing
Yellow globe face with black-outlined white circle in center. Multicolored scene with colonial soldiers and drummer in center circle. Black "INDEPENDENT" arched around top, "GASOLINE" around bottom.

Metro, Jamestown/Olean, New York

Small New York marketer purchased by Socony-Vacuum in 1934. The Mobilgas brand was added at Metro stations (note the red, white, and green "Mobilgas" globe in the Vacuum section), and Metro became a low-grade product sold at Mobil stations in the various marketing territories until after the war.
METRO GASOLINE/green lines
(4)   1925-1933   15in Metal $225-$400
White globe face with thin green line positioned above and below center. Large green "METRO" over smaller green "GASOLINE" between the lines across center of globe face.
METRO GAS GARGOYLE MOBILOIL
(5)   1933-1935   16.5in Metal $1,200-$1,700
METRO GAS GARGOYLE MOBILOIL
(5)   1933-1935   16.5in Metal $1,200-$1,700
White globe face with red, white, and blue lines across center. Blue "Metro" arched over "Gas" on upper half, red and black gargoyle logo, with black "GARGOYLE" with red stripe arched above over black "Mobiloil" on lower globe face.
METRO green/green on white/green
(3)   1935-1940   16.5in Metal $225-$400
METRO green/green on white/green
(3)   1935-1940   15in Metal $225-$400
METRO green/green on white/green
(3)   1935-1940   13.5in Glass $200-$350
Green globe face with white band across center. Large green "METRO" over smaller green "GASOLINE" on center band.
METRO red/green on white/red
(2)   1940-1955   15in Metal $250-$375
METRO red/green on white/red
(2)   1940-1955   13.5in Glass $200-$325
METRO red/green on white/red
(2)   1940-1955   13.5in Capco $100-$150
Red globe face with white band across center. Red-outlined green "Metro" across center on band.

Gilmore Oil Company, Los Angeles, California

Founded in 1900, Gilmore entered gasoline marketing in 1923. The company established an elaborate network of dealers in California, Oregon, and Washington, totaling more than 3,500 outlets at its peak in the late 1930s. In 1940 Socony-Vacuum purchased control of Gilmore and assigned Gilmore marketing to the General Petroleum subsidiary. Transition from Gilmore to Mobilgas began in 1942 and was completed in 1945, just after World War II.

GILMORE GASOLINE
(5)   1923-1925   One-piece etched   No Listing
White globe with red "GILMORE" arched across top of face, "GASOLINE" across bottom.
GILMORE "ROAR WITH GILMORE"
(4)   1925-1942   15in Metal $2,000-$3,200
Yellow globe face with black outline ring. Large red and black jumping lion at top of face, with black "ROAR" over black script lettering "with" beside lion. Black-outlined red "GILMORE" over black and white checkered flag below lion.
GILMORE BLU-GREEN GASOLINE
(4)   1925-1933   15in Metal $2,500-$4,000
Yellow globe face with black outline ring and black outlines around white semi-circles in center. Large multicolored lion's head in center superimposed over semi-circles. Black-outlined red "GILMORE" arched around top, "GASOLINE" around bottom, with blue-colored "BLU" to left of lion and "GREEN" to right.
GILMORE ETHYL
(5)   1926-1942   15in Metal $900-$1,600
Yellow globe face with black outline ring around white center circle. Small Ethyl (EGC) logo with red rays in center circle, with black script lettering "with" above. Black-outlined red "GILMORE" arched around top, "GASOLINE" around bottom.
GILMORE RED LION w/tetraethyl
(4)   1933-1942   15in Metal $2,200-$3,500
Yellow globe face with black outline ring. Large red and black lion at top of face. Black-outlined red "GILMORE/RED LION" over black script "plus," with black "TETRAETHYL" arched around bottom.
GILMORE FLEET w/flag
(5)   1933-1942   15in Metal   No Listing
Yellow globe face with black outline ring. Black-outlined red "GILMORE" across center over italic black "FLEET." Small black and white checkered flag at top of globe face.

Mobilgas/Socony-Vacuum

As was noted earlier, Socony and Vacuum merged in 1931. By 1934 it was decided to join the Socony shield and flying horse with Vacuum's Mobilgas to create a single brand name for all the affiliates. Several, including Magnolia and White Eagle, readily converted to the new Mobilgas identity. Others, including General and Wadhams, combined the Mobilgas brand with their own brand names, at least for the first few years. Conversion was nearly complete when the war interrupted, and was completed as soon as possible after the war.

Please note, however, that many manufacturers were involved in making the following globes and color variations, including some that are certain to exist but not listed, exist as well as typestyle and size variations. A complete listing would be nearly impossible, but two years of research have resulted in the following compilation. Note also that their are no differences in value between black and blue lettering, so if your blue-lettering globe is not listed, for instance, the value can be determined by comparing it with the same black-lettering globe. The "Mobilgas" designations for products was changed to Mobil in 1962, and all of the older globes were replaced at that time.
MOBILGAS w/horse black letters
(3)   1934-1962   16.5in Metal $275-$525
MOBILGAS w/horse black letters
(3)   1934-1962   15in Metal $275-$525
MOBILGAS w/horse black letters
(3)   1934-1962   13.5in Glass $225-$375
White globe face with flying red horse at top of globe face. Black "Mobilgas" across lower globe face.
MOBILGAS w/horse blue letters
(2)   1934-1962   16.5in Metal $275-$525
MOBILGAS w/horse blue letters
(2)   1934-1962   15in Metal $275-$500
MOBILGAS w/horse blue letters
(2)   1934-1962   13.5in Glass $225-$375
MOBILGAS w/horse blue letters
(4)   1934-1962   Gill $250-$400
MOBILGAS w/horse blue letters
(2)   1955-1962   13.5in Capco $175-$250
Same as above, with blue "Mobilgas."
MOBILGAS ETHYL w/horse
(3)   1934-1936   16.5in Metal $300-$550
MOBILGAS ETHYL w/horse
(3)   1934-1936   15in Metal $275-$525
White globe face with flying red horse at top of face. Black "Mobilgas" over red "ETHYL" on lower globe face.
MOBILGAS SPECIAL black letters
(3)   1936-1962   16.5in Metal $275-$500

Mobilgas Marine 16.5in inserts on metal body—no outline on horse.

Mobilgas Aircraft 15in inserts on metal body.

Mobilgas Marine 15in inserts on metal body. John Phippen

Gargoyle oval one-piece raised-letter oil cabinet globe.

Pennzoil one-piece etched globe.

Pennzoil Safe Lubrication one-piece etched globe.

Pennzip Ethyl 13.5in inserts on glass body.

Empire Gas one-piece fired-on globe.

Empire Ethyl one-piece fired-on globe.

Keystone 14in glass inserts on Gill body.

United one-piece fired-on globe.

Phillips 77 13.5in inserts on glass body.

Phillips 66 Ethyl 13.5in inserts on glass body.

Phillips 66 15in inserts on metal body.

Purol Pep 15in inserts on metal body.

Pure Xcel 15in inserts on metal (white porcelain) body.

MOBILGAS SPECIAL black letters
(3)   1936-1962   15in Metal $275-$475
MOBILGAS SPECIAL black letters
(3)   1936-1962   13.5in Glass $250-$375
White globe face with flying red horse at top of globe face. Black "Mobilgas" over red "SPECIAL" on lower globe face.
MOBILGAS SPECIAL blue letters
(2)   1936-1962   16.5in Metal $275-$500
MOBILGAS SPECIAL blue letters
(2)   1936-1962   15in Metal $275-$475
MOBILGAS SPECIAL blue letters
(2)   1936-1962   13.5in Glass $250-$375
MOBILGAS SPECIAL blue letters
(4)   1936-1962   Gill $250-$400
MOBILGAS SPECIAL blue letters
(2)   1955-1962   13.5in Capco $175-$275
White globe face with flying red horse at top of face. Blue "Mobilgas" over red "SPECIAL" on lower globe face.
MOBILGAS SPECIAL large "SPECIAL"
(4)   1946-1950   13.5in Glass $225-$375
MOBILGAS SPECIAL large "SPECIAL"
(4)   1946-1950   Gill   No Listing
White globe face with small flying red horse at top of face. Small blue "Mobilgas" over large red "SPECIAL" on lower globe face.
MOBILGAS/MOBILGAS SPECIAL dual
(5)   1955-1962   13.5in Capco   No Listing
White globe face with small flying red horse at top of face. Thin blue line across center of globe, with blue vertical line down from midpoint of horizontal line. Blue "Mobilgas" to one side of vertical line, with red arrow pointing down diagonally with blue "Mobilgas" over red "SPECIAL," with red arrow on other side of vertical line. Note that faces would be opposite for opposite sides of the pump. Very rare globe for 1950s dual pump.
MOBILFUEL DIESEL blue letters
(5)   1935-1962   16.5in Metal $300-$575
MOBILFUEL DIESEL black letters
(4)   1935-1962   15in Metal $300-$575
MOBILFUEL DIESEL black letters
(4)   1935-1962   13.5in Glass $225-$400
White globe face with flying red horse at top. Black "Mobilfuel" over red "DIESEL" on lower face.
MOBILFUEL DIESEL blue letters
(3)   1935-1962   15in Metal $300-$575
MOBILFUEL DIESEL blue letters
(3)   1935-1962   13.5in Glass $225-$400
Same as above, with blue "Mobilfuel" replacing black.
MOBILGAS MARINE w/nonoutlined horse
(5)   1930s   16.5in Metal $650-$900
White globe face with flying red horse at top. Early, locally made globe with poorly drawn horse. Black "Mobilgas" over red "MARINE" on lower globe face.
MOBILGAS MARINE w/horse
(4)   1950-1962   15in Metal $625-$900
White globe face with flying red horse at top. Black "Mobilgas" over red "MARINE" on lower globe face.
AERO MOBILGAS w/horse
(4)   1935-1950   15in Metal $700-$1,250
White globe face with flying red horse at top. Blue "AERO" offset to left over blue "Mobilgas."
MOBILGAS AIRCRAFT w/horse
(4)   1935-1962   16.5in Metal $700-$1,200
MOBILGAS AIRCRAFT w/horse
(4)   1935-1962   15in Metal $700-$1,200
MOBILGAS AIRCRAFT w/horse
(3)   1935-1962   13.5in Glass $400-$650
White globe face with flying red horse at top. Black "Mobilgas" over red "AIRCRAFT" on lower face.
MOBILGAS AIRCRAFT italic letters
(4)   1935-1962   13.5in Glass $400-$650
Same as above, with blue "Mobilgas" over red italic "AIRCRAFT."
STOVE/MOBILHEAT/OILS
(4)   1940-1955   15in Metal $350-$700
White globe face with black "Mobilheat" across center of face. Red "STOVE" above "Mobilheat," "OILS" below.
MOBILHEAT STOVE OIL w/horse
(5)   1955-1962   13.5in Capco $175-$300
White globe face with flying red horse at top. Blue "Mobilheat" above red "STOVE OIL" on lower face.
MOBIL/KEROSENE w/horse
(5)   1950-1966   15in Metal $300-$550

MOBIL/KEROSENE w/horse
(4)   1950-1966   13.5in Glass $250-$400
MOBIL/KEROSENE w/horse
(5)   1950-1966   13.5in Capco $175-$275
White globe face, with blue-outlined flying red horse positioned upper right of center. Blue "Mobil/Kerosene" positioned lower right.

Mobil

Although the Mobil name replaced Mobilgas as the primary station identification on a gradual basis between 1955 and 1958, gasoline brands remained Mobilgas and Mobilgas Special until 1962 when they were replaced with Mobil Regular and Mobil Premium. Mobil again reimaged in 1966, replacing the elongated Mobil shield with the modern "red O" logo. No US globes are known with the 1966 logo.
MOBIL REGULAR
(1)   1962-1966   13.5in Capco $100-$175
White globe face with red, white, and blue "1958" flat "Mobil" shield above "Regular" in blue.
MOBIL PREMIUM
(1)   1962-1966   13.5in Capco $100-$175
Same as above, with "Premium" in red.
MOBILFUEL DIESEL
(2)   1962-1966   13.5in Capco $100-$175
Same as above, with blue "Mobilfuel" over "Diesel."

PENNZOIL and Affiliates
PENNZOIL COMPANY,
Houston, Texas/Oil City, Pennsylvania

Pennzoil traces its orgins to the founding of South Penn Oil Company, a production unit of the Standard Oil Trust. When South Penn became independent with the breakup of Standard in 1911, they remained primarily a production operation. In 1925 they purchased control of the Pennzoil Company, an Oil City refiner and lubricants marketer that had in 1921 opened the first of a small chain of branded Pennzoil stations. The gasoline marketing was rebranded "Pennzip" in 1936 and remained such until 1958, when the Pennzoil brand was reintroduced for gasoline.

South Penn purchased the remaining interest in Pennzoil in 1955, and the company was renamed Pennzoil Company in 1963. Numerous purchases detailed below greatly expanded the scope of the company and today the company sells gasoline through more than 600 stations in five states, as well as marketing Pennzoil lubricants around the world.
PENNZOIL
(5)   1921-1928   One-piece etched $1,400-$2,000
PENNZOIL
(4)   1926-1931   One-piece Baked $900-$1,400
White globe with gold bell, with black details in center of face. Black-outlined red "PENNZOIL" diagonally across bell.
PENNZOIL ETHYL (EGC)
(5)   1926-1928   One-piece etched   No listing
PENNZOIL ETHYL (EGC)
(4)   1926-1928   One-piece Baked $600-$900
White globe with black outline ring around face and around center circle. Large Ethyl (EGC) logo with black rays in center. Large red "PENNZOIL" arched around top, smaller "GASOLINE" around bottom.
PENNZOIL SAFE LUBRICATION
(4)   1921-1928   One-piece etched $1,600-$2,500
PENNZOIL SAFE LUBRICATION
(5)   1926-1928   One-piece Baked $1,200-$1,700
White globe with gold bell, with black details in center of face. Black-outlined red "PENNZOIL" diagonally across bell. Black "SAFE LUBRICATION" arched around bottom of globe face.
PENNZOIL 100% PURE PENNSYLVANIA/SAFE LUBRICATION
(5)   15in Metal $750-$1,400
Yellow globe face with small red bell in center. Black "PENNZOIL" diagonally across bell. Black "100% PURE PENNSYLVANIA" arched around top, "SAFE LUBRICATION" around bottom.
PENNZOIL milk glass etched faces
(5)   1920s   15in Metal   No Listing
White globe face with gold bell, with black details in center. Black-outlined red "PENNZOIL" diagonally across bell.
PENNZOIL red/gold on white
(4)   1928-1936   15in Metal $700-$1,100
White globe face with gold bell, with black details in center. Black-outlined red "PENNZOIL" diagonally across bell.

PENNZOIL ETHYL GASOLINE (EGC)
(5)   1928-1936   15in Metal $350-$650
See one-piece description above.
PENNZOIL ETHYL GASOLINE (EGC)
(4)   1928-1930   15in Glass body $450-$700
See one-piece description above.
PENNZIP w/brown bell
(5)   1936-1958   13.5in Glass $350-$600
Yellow globe face with brown detailed bell in center. Red-outlined black "PENNZIP" diagonally across bell.
PENNZIP w/red bell
(3)   1936-1958   13.5in Glass $300-$500
Yellow globe face with black outline ring. Large red bell with black details in center of face, with black "PENNZIP" diagonally across bell.
PENNZIP ETHYL (EGC)
(3)   1936-1940   13.5in Glass $250-$350
Yellow globe face with black outline ring, with black outline ring around white circle offset slightly below center. Large Ethyl (EGC) logo with yellow rays in circle. Red-outlined black "PENNZIP" arched around top, "GASOLINE" around bottom.
PENNZIP ETHYL (EC)
(3)   1940-1958   13.5in Glass $250-$350
Same as above, with Ethyl (EC) logo in circle.
TRANSPORT GASOLINE
(4)   1946-1958   13.5in Glass $250-$350
White globe face with blue outline ring. Blue and white outlines around blue center circle. Large blue "TRANSPORT" arched around top, "GASOLINE" around bottom.

Wolverine-Empire Refining Company, Oil City, Pennsylvania

Founded in 1879 as Empire Oil Works, Wolverine-Empire was primarily a lubricants manufacturer. They entered the gasoline market under the Empire brand about 1928 and rebranded Wolf's Head, after their famous motor oils, about 1940. In 1963 Pennzoil purchased Wolf's Head and continued to operate the Wolf's Head stations as a secondary brand into the 1980s.
EMPIRE GAS
(5)   1920s   One-piece baked $750-$1,200
White globe with dark green outline ring around face. Dark-green-outlined white half-circles at top and bottom of globe face. Red "EMPIRE" across center, with dark green dropshade. Black "WOLVERINE-EMPIRE/REFINING CO./OIL CITY, PA." in upper half-circle, "GAS" on lower half-circle.
EMPIRE ETHYL
(5)   1920s   One-piece Baked $550-$800
White globe face with black, orange, and black outline rings. Red "EMPIRE" with black dropshade arched around top, below black design. Black-outlined circle on lower globe face, with Ethyl (EGC) logo with black rays in circle.
EMPIRE GAS
(4)   1930s   13.5in Banded Glass $300-$500
Similar to EMPIRE GAS one-piece above.
EMPIRE
(5)   1930s   13.5in Banded glass $350-$600
White face with orange circle in center, black "EMPIRE" diagonal across orange circle.
WOLF'S HEAD "WOLVERINE-EMPIRE OIL CO."
(4)   1940s   13.5in Banded Glass $325-$550
White globe face with red and black outline rings. Small wolf head logo at top, above large red "WOLF'S/HEAD." Black "WOLVERINE-EMPIRE REFINING CO." arched around bottom.
WOLF'S HEAD "WOLF'S HEAD OIL CO."
(3)   1950s   13.5in Glass $300-$500
WOLF'S HEAD "WOLF'S HEAD OIL CO."
(4)   1960s   13.5in Capco $200-$325
Same as above, with "WOLF'S HEAD OIL REFINING COMPANY, INC." arched aound bottom.
WOLF'S HEAD ETHYL (EC)
(4)   1950s   13.5in Glass $250-$425
WOLF'S HEAD ETHYL (EC)
(4)   1960s   13.5in Capco $200-$325
White globe face with black outline ring. Small wolf head logo at top, above red "WOLF'S HEAD" in bowtie lettering. Black-outlined white circle on lower globe face, with Ethyl (EC) logo in circle.

Elk Refining Company, Charleston, West Virginia

Refiner and marketer that operated the Keystone stations in West Virginia and Pennsylvania. South Penn purchased control of Elk in 1952, and the remaining portion in 1963. South Penn-Pennzoil sold off the Keystone marketing to United Refining in the 1970s. United,

an independent listed below, continues to operate a few stations under the Keystone brand.
KEYSTONE
(4)   1930-1935   15in Metal $300-$500
KEYSTONE
(4)   1935-1955   14in Gill $275-$400
KEYSTONE
(3)   1935-1955   13.5in Glass $250-$375
White globe face with large red keystone covering most of face. Blue "KEYSTONE" across keystone logo.
KEYSTONE outlined
(4)   1955-1963   13.5in Capco $125-$175
White globe face with smaller red keystone on center of face. Blue band across center of keystone, with yellow outline around keystone and band. Yellow "KEYSTONE" on band.
KEYSTONE red & black
(5)   1935-1955   13.5in Capco   No Listing
White face with black outline ring. Large red Keystone in center with black band across Keystone. White "KEYSTONE" in black band.
KEYSTONE ETHYL (EGC)
(4)   1935-1941   13.5in Glass $250-$350
White globe face with red "KEYSTONE" arched around top and large Ethyl (EGC) logo on lower face.
KEYSTONE ETHYL (EC)
(4)   1941-1963   13.5in Capco $125-$175
Same as above, with Ethyl (EC) logo.

United Refining Company, Warren, Pennsylvania

Independent refiner and marketer that purchased the Keystone stations from Pennzoil in the 1970s. Many of the former Keystone locations were converted to United's "Kwik-Fill" brand; however, as of this writing a few Keystone brand stations remain.
UNITED
(5)   1930s   One-piece Baked $450-$750
White globe with series of red concentric circles around red dot in center. White-outlined blue band across center of globe face, with white "UNITED" on band.
UNITED
(4)   1955-1963   13.5in Glass $225-$350
White globe face with blue outline ring and series of red concentric circles around red dot in center. Blue band across center, with white "UNITED" on blue band.

Fleet-Wing Corporation, Cleveland, Ohio

Pennzoil purchased the Fleet-Wing operation from Sohio in 1970, and continues to operate a small number of Fleet-Wing brand stations today. (See SOHIO for Fleet-Wing globe listings.)

Pennsylvania Refining Company, Butler, Pennsylvania

Founded in Butler in 1878, Pennsylvania Refining, later Pennreco, marketed lubricants under the Penn-Drake brand. During the 1920s and 1930s, the company branded a small number of Penn-Drake stations in Pennsylvania. The company withdrew from gasoline marketing at the start of WWII and later, in 1973, was purchased by Pennzoil Company. They continue to market a line of specialty oils today.
PENN DRAKE
(5)   1920-1930   One-piece etched   No Listing
White globe with detailed orange, black, and white picture of Drake's well on upper globe face. Black "PENN DRAKE" across center, with orange, black, and white area on lower globe face with white "GASOLINE."
PENN DRAKE ETHYL (EGC)
(5)   1926-1930   One-piece etched   No Listing
White globe with outline ring around face and around center circle. Large Ethyl (EGC) logo in center circle, with "PENN DRAKE" arched around top and "GASOLINE" around bottom.
PENN DRAKE BLUE BLOOD
(4)   1930s   13.5in Glass $450-$800
White globe face with orange, black, and white Penn-Drake logo on lower face. Blue "BLUE BLOOD" arched around top.
PENN DRAKE BLUE BLOOD
(4)   1940s   13.5in Glass $375-$600
Grey globe face with black outline ring. Series of white lines top and bottom, increasing width toward white band across center. Black-and-white-outlined red band across white center area. Black and white Drake's well at top of globe face, white "PENN-DRAKE" on center red band, and red "BLUE BLOOD" below. Variations of black or blue lettering also exist.

PENN DRAKE ETHYL (EC)
(3)   1940s   13.5in Glass $275-$450
White globe face with black outline ring. Small grey, white, and black Drake's well logo at top, with red "PENN" arched to left and "DRAKE" to right. Black "ETHYL" arched around bottom. Black-outlined white circle in center, with Ethyl (EGC) logo with yellow rays in circle.
PENNRECO
(4)   1940s   Gill $400-$700
White globe with blue "PENNRECO" in bowtie lettering across center over design. No other details known.

PHILLIPS 66 & Affiliates
PHILLIPS PETROLEUM, Bartlesville, Oklahoma

Phillips Petroleum was founded in 1917 in Bartlesville, Oklahoma, from various production and refining companies owned by Frank Phillips and others. The company entered gasoline marketing in November 1927 when they opened a small station in Wichita, Kansas. Other stations were quickly added, and other marketing operations were purchased such that the company operated over 6,000 stations in twelve states by 1930. Details on some of the companies purchased are listed below in individual company histories.

Phillips was primarily a midcontinent marketer until 1953 when they opened their first stations in Florida, setting off a marketing chain-reaction that saw them contracting with dissatisfied jobbers from other marketers and rebranding stations to Phillips 66 as far north as Virginia. Pleased with the market expansion, Phillips' "drive to Maine" expansion began, eventually pushing the brand all the way through the north Atlantic region and on to Maine. Never before had an oil company attempted such a systematic market expansion. With the purchase of Tidewater's West Coast Flying A stations in 1966, Phillips found themselves operating stations in forty-nine states. A single unit in Alaska was opened in 1967, making Phillips the second marketer to brand stations in all fifty states at the same time (Texaco was first, and Shell has been in all fifty states, but not at the same time). The 1970s gas shortages forced Phillips to abandon many areas of the country, but currently the Phillips 66 brand appears on nearly 8,000 stations in twenty-nine midcontinent and southeastern states.
PHILLIPS
(5)   1928-1929   15in Metal   No Listing
White globe face with what is thought to be a green bar-and-circle design, with a solid center circle. "PHILLIPS" across center bar, "GASOLINE" arched around top, and "MOTOR OIL" around bottom.
PHILLIPS 66
(5)   1928-1930   15in Metal   No Listing
Mint green globe face, with blue outline ring and black-outlined cobalt blue script "Phillips" arched around upper face. Tilted "66" below "Phillips."
PHILLIPS 66
(5)   1928-1930   15in Metal   No Listing
White globe face with red outline rings and large red script "Philips" arched around upper face. Tilted "66" below "Phillips."
PHILLIPS 66 (black and white)
(5)   1929-1959   15in Metal $900-$1,500
PHILLIPS 66 (black and white)
(4)   1929-1930   13.5in Glass $450-$750
White globe face, with black outline ring and large black script "Phillips" across upper globe face. Tilted "66" below "Phillips."
PHILLIPS 66 ETHYL (EGC)
(5)   1929-1930   15in Metal $900-$1,600
PHILLIPS 66 ETHYL (EGC)
(4)   1929-1930   13.5in Glass $450-$750
White globe face, with black outline ring and small black script "Phillips" arched around top. Early-style Ethyl (EGC) logo in center. Black "66" below Ethyl logo.
PHILLIPS AVIATION
(5)   1928-1929   15in Metal   No Listing
Pale green globe face with blue outline rings. Large blue script "Phillips" above smaller blue "Aviation."
PHILLIPS 77 (black and white)
(5)   1929-1930   13.5in Glass   No Listing
Similar to PHILLIPS 66 above, with "77" replacing "66." Black letters on white.
PHILBLUE
(5)   1928-1929   13.5in Glass   No Listing
Blue globe face with blue and white outline rings. White script "Phil-Blue" across face.
PHILLIPS 66 SHIELD
(4)   1930-1959   15in Metal $500-$850

PHILLIPS 66 SHIELD
(2)   1930-1959   13.5in Glass $225-$400
PHILLIPS 66 SHIELD
(2)   1930-1959   13.5in Capco $150-$250
White globe face, with black outline ring and large orange and black "Phillips 66" shield in center.
PHILLIPS 66 WITH ETHYL (EGC)
(5)   1935-1946   15in Metal   No Listing
PHILLIPS 66 WITH ETHYL (EGC)
(3)   1935-1946   13.5in Glass $275-$450
PHILLIPS 66 WITH ETHYL (EGC)
(3)   1935-1946   13.5in Capco $175-$300
Same as PHILLIPS 66 above, with Ethyl (EGC) logo superimposed over lower area of Phillips shield.
PHILLIPS 77
(4)   1933-1935   13.5in Glass $350-$600
PHILLIPS 77
(4)   1933-1935   13.5in Capco $250-$375
Same as PHILLIPS 66 above, with "77" replacing "66" in shield.
PHILLIPS 77 AVIATION (small letters)
(4)   1933-1935   13.5in Glass $600-$900
Same as PHILLIPS 77 above, with white "AVIATION" below "77" and black wings on either side of "77."
PHILLIPS 77 AVIATION (large letters)
(4)   1933-1935   13.5in Glass $600-$900
Same as above, with larger "AVIATION" below "77."
PHILLIPS 66 ETHYL (in orange band)
(4)   1946-1953   13.5in Glass $275-$425
PHILLIPS 66 ETHYL (in orange band)
(3)   1946-1953   13.5in Capco $175-$325
White globe face with black outline ring. Small orange and black Phillips 66 shield at top of face, above orange band across globe below center. White-outlined black "ETHYL" on red band.
PHILLIPS UNIQUE
(4)   1930-1940   15in Metal $300-$550
PHILLIPS UNIQUE
(3)   1930-1940   13.5in Glass $275-$450
PHILLIPS UNIQUE
(4)   1930-1940   13.5in Capco $200-$350
White globe face with black outline ring. Large Phillips shield, with orange script "Phillips" on upper black area and orange "UNIQUE" diagonally across green lower area of shield.
PHILLIPS BENZOL-GAS
(4)   1928-1934   15in Metal   No Listing
PHILLIPS BENZOL-GAS
(5)   1928-1934   13.5in Glass   No Listing
PHILLIPS BENZOL-GAS
(5)   1928-1934   13.5in Capco   No Listing
White globe face, with large orange-red burst covering most of face. White-outlined black box across center, with white "Benzo-Gas" in box. White-outlined black logotype "Phillips" above box, "DOES WHAT GASOLINE/CAN'T" below box. Similar to BENZO GAS below, and a successor to that product.
PHILLIPS FLITE FUEL
(2)   1953-1959   13.5in Capco $150-$275
White globe face with black outline ring. Small orange and black Phillips 66 shield on upper face, above black logotype script "Flite Fuel."
PHILLIPS 66
(3)   1953-1959   Three-piece plastic shield $175-$300
White plastic shield-shaped assembled frame. Plastic globe faces. Globe face is large orange and black Phillips 66 shield.
PHILLIPS 66 FLITE FUEL
(3)   1953-1959   Three-piece plastic shield $175-$300
Same assembly as above. Orange outline around edge. Small orange and black Phillips 66 shield at top, above black logotype script "Flite Fuel."
PHILLIPS 66 DIESEL
(5)   1950s   13.5in Capco   No Listing
Description not available.
PHILLIPS 66 MARINE
(5)   1950s   13.5in Capco   No Listing
Description not available.
PHILLIPS AVIATION (lime green w/shield)
(5)   1936-1948   13.5in Capco   No Listing
Description not available.

Benzo Gas Motor Fuel Company, Kansas City, Missouri
Kansas City marketer purchased by Phillips about 1928.

THE ORIGINAL BENZO GAS
(5)   1920-1930   15in Metal   No Listing
White globe face with red outline ring. Large red "burst" in center. White-outlined black box across center, with white "Benzo-Gas" across box. Black "THE/ORIGINAL" above box, "NO-KNOCK/MOTOR FUEL" below.
UNIQUE GASOLINE
(5)   1925-1928   15in Metal   No Listing
Mint green globe face, with large red-outlined white "circle-and-cross" design covering most of globe face. Red-outlined white line arched above and below circle. Red "UNIQUE" arched around top of circle, "GASOLINE" through center of cross in circle, and "Without an Equal" arched around bottom.
UNIQUE
(4)   1928-1930   15in Metal $375-$525
UNIQUE
(3)   1938-1930   13.5in Glass $200-$325
Green globe face with orange outline ring. Two orange bars across globe so as to form green center band. Orange "UNIQUE" in band.

Independent Oil and Gas Company, Tulsa, Oklahoma

Successors to Waite Phillips Oil Company, merged into Phillips Petroleum in 1930.
PHILLIPS VIM-PEP
(5)   1920-1925   15in Metal $400-$650
Description not available.
PHILLIPS PENN
(5)   1920-1925   15in Metal   No Listing
White globe face with red-outlined half-circles to left and right of center. Red "PHILLIPS" arched around top, "GASOLINE" around bottom, with red "PENN" vertical between half-circles.
INDEPENDENT
(4)   1925-1930   15in Metal $250-$400
INDEPENDENT
(4)   1928-1930   13.5in Glass $200-$300
White globe face, with red irregular border and white and red outline rings around white center circle. Large blue "I" in center, with red "INDEPENDENT" superimposed over "I."
INDEPENDENT ETHYL
(5)   1928-1930   13.5in Glass $200-$325
White globe face, with red irregular border and white and red outline rings around white outer ring. Red ring around white center circle. Blue "INDEPENDENT" arched around top, "GASOLINE" around bottom, with large Ethyl (EGC) logo in center.

Manhattan Gasoline Company, St. Paul, Minnesota

Manhattan originated the motor oil trademark "Trop Artic" in 1912 and marketed Trop-Artic oils through Manhattan stations in the north central states until Phillips purchased Manhattan in 1934. Stations were at that time rebranded Phillips 66, but Phillips adopted the Trop-Artic motor oil brand and continues to use it today.
MANHATTAN
(5)   1920s   One-piece etched $700-$1,300
White globe face, with black concentric squares forming diamond on globe face. Black-outlined box across diamond, with red "MANHAT-TAN" in box.
MANHATTAN
(5)   1920s   15in Metal $500-$750
White globe face, with black and red concentric squares forming diamond on face. Black-outlined red box across diamond, with black "MANHATTAN" in box.
MAN-GO GAS
(5)   1920s   15in Metal   No Listing
White globe face with red outline ring. Small red, white, and black "MANHATTAN" logo at top, with black-and-white-outlined red "Man-Go/Gas" with speed lines on lower globe face.
MAN-GO RED
(5)   1920s   15in Metal   No Listing
White globe face with black, white, and red "MANHATTAN" concentric squares logo on lower face. Red script "Man-Go" arched around top, with small "RED" in center.

Quaker Oil Company, St. Louis, Missouri

Quaker Oil sold the Paraland gasoline brand from the early 1930s until after World War II. The brand shifted to Paraland Oil Company of Omaha, Nebraska, by the 1950s and it is not known if Phillips owned the company at that time. By the early 1960s it became known that Paraland was Phillips' "secret" secondary brand. In later years, unsuccessful Phillips stations were converted to Paraland. The brand was last used about 1972.

PARALAND orange/blue
(4)   1930s   13.5in Glass $300-$425
Description not available.
PARALAND GASOLINE
(4)   1930s   13.5in Glass $300-$500
Yellow face with black band across center. Black outlined white circle at top with small black tree. Small black "THE QUAKER PETROLEUM COMPANY, INC." above center band. Yellow "PARALAND" across center band, black underlined "GASOLINE" on lower globe face.
PARALAND w/large tree
(5)   1935-1946   13.5in Glass $350-$600
Yellow globe face with black outline ring. Black band across face, with black and white lines below band. White circle in center, splitting lines, with black tree and "STABILITY" in circle. White "PARALAND" with yellow dropshade on center band.
PARALAND w/small tree
(4)   1935-1946   13.5in Glass $325-$500
Same as above, with small tree "STABILITY" logo in center.
PARALAND
(3)   1946-1954   13.5in Capco $150-$225
Same as above, without lines under black band or tree logo in center.
PARALAND ETHYL
(3)   1946-1954   13.5in Capco $150-$225
Yellow globe face with black band diagonally across upper face. White "PARALAND" with yellow dropshade on band. Black-outlined white circle on lower globe face, with Ethyl (EC) logo in circle.
PARALAND Oval
(3)   1954-1972   Oval Capco $125-$175
Yellow globe face with black outline ring. Black outlines above and below white band across center. Black "Paraland" on band.

Wasatch Oil Company, Salt Lake City, Utah

Wasatch was a Salt Lake City based collection of refining and marketing companies that branded stations under the Wasatch trademark in Utah, Idaho Chief in Idaho, and Washington Chief in Washington. Phillips purchased Wasatch in 1947, and stations were rebranded Phillips 66 at that time.
CHIEF GAS
(5)   1920s   One-piece etched   No Listing
Description not available.
CHIEF ANTI-KNOCK GASOLINE
(5)   1920s   15in Metal $1,600-$2,800
White globe face with wide blue ring around outer edge. Yellow circle in center, with detailed brown, black, and green Indian. Blue "Chief" arched around top, "Gasoline" around bottom, with "ANTI-KNOCK" arched vertically to either side.
WASATCH
(4)   1935-1947   13.5in Capco $400-$850
White globe face with blue outline ring. Red, white, and blue Indian head in full headdress covers most of globe face. Red band across lower face, with white "WASATCH" on band.
WASATCH ETHYL
(5)   1935-1947   13.5in Capco $450-$900
Same as above, small Ethyl (EGC) logo below red band.
IDAHO CHIEF GASOLINE
(5)   1935-1947   13.5in Capco $400-$800
White globe face with blue outline ring around red outer ring. Red band across lower face. Detailed red, white, and blue Indian head above band, with white "IDAHO CHIEF" on band and red "GASOLINE" arched in white area below. Small white "IDAHO" arched on red outer ring at top.
IDAHO ETHYL
(5)   1935-1947   13.5in Capco $350-$750
Yellow globe face with blue outline ring and red band across lower face. Detailed red, white, and blue Indian head above band, with white "IDAHO" on band and red italic "ETHYL" below.
WASHINGTON CHIEF
(5)   1935-1947   13.5in Capco $400-$850
White globe face, with blue outline ring and blue ring around large white center circle so as to form white outer ring. Red band across lower globe face with detailed red, white, and blue Indian head above band. White "WASHINGTON" on band, with red "CHIEF" in white area below. Blue "WASHINGTON" arched in outer ring at top.

Red X Oil Company, Cameron, Missouri

Missouri jobber operation that rebranded Phillips 66 after the Second World War.
RED X
(4)   1940-1959   13.5in Red Capco $175-$300

White globe face with red outline ring and large red "X" in center. Red-colored "RED" across center of "X." Blue-colored "RED X OIL CO." (with red "X") arched around top, "GASOLINE" around bottom.

PURE & Affiliates
THE PURE OIL COMPANY USA, Chicago, Illinois

Pure Oil was founded in 1891 as the Producers Oil Company in Oil City, Pennsylvania. The name was changed to The Pure Oil Company in 1895. Gasoline marketing began in 1914, and in 1917 ownership of the company passed to the Dawes family who operated public utility companies in Ohio and elsewhere. By the early 1920s, the utilities had been sold off and the company was firmly in the gasoline business.

In the 1920s, Pure grew through a series of mergers with other regional marketers including Wofford Oil Company of Atlanta, Georgia; Sherrill Oil Company of Pensacola, Florida; Seaboard Oil Company of Jacksonville, Florida; and the American Oil Company of Hattiesburg, Mississippi. Also in the late 1920s, the company introduced their famous "cottage" service station design that was to dominate Pure marketing forever and influence the competition until after the war. In 1965, Pure Oil merged with Union Oil of California and began a five-year program to replace the Pure brand with Union 76. The last of the Pure signs came down in 1970, thus passing into history one of the most distinctive images in gasoline marketing.

PUROL red/yellow one-piece
(5)   1914-1915   One-piece etched   No listing
White globe with black-outlined detailed white arrow across center. Red area extending back from point of arrow in triangle, with yellow area to right of red. Black-outlined white "Purol" logotype above arrow, "GASOLINE" below arrow.

PUROL (small blue and white)
(5)   1916-1920   One-piece etched $1,400-$2,100
White globe with dark-blue-outlined white logotype "Purol" on upper face, "GASOLINE" on lower face, with detailed arrow across center.

PUROL (large blue and white)
(5)   1916-1920   One-piece etched $1,700-$2,200
Larger version of globe described above.

PUROL (blue and white oval)
(5)   1916-1920   One-piece etched Oval   No Listing
Oval version of globe described above.

PUROL (blue and white)
(5)   1927-1930s   One-piece Baked $1,100-$1,600
Round baked version of larger design described above.
Note: All of the following globes listed as 15in metal bodies are white porcelain on metal bodies. Only the Pure Oil Company used these porcelain bodies. Prices listed include porcelain body.

PUROL red/yellow
(5)   1914-1916   15in Metal   No Listing
Globe face with detailed arrow across center. Red area extending back in triangle from point of arrow. Yellow area to right of red area. White "Purol" logotype above arrow, "GASOLINE" below.

PUROL (white arrow on blue)
(5)   1916-1920   15in Metal $500-$900
Blue globe face with detailed white arrow across center. White "Purol" logotype above arrow, "GASOLINE" below arrow.

PUROL (blue arrow on white/plain)
(3)   1920-1927   15in Metal $450-$700
White globe face with blue outline ring. Detailed blue arrow across center. Blue "Purol" logotype above arrow, "GASOLINE" below.

PUROL (blue arrow on white/plain w/o border)
(3)   1920s   15in Metal $450-$700
Same as above, without blue outline ring.

PUROL (blue and white cast face)
(5)   1920s   15in Metal   No Listing
Same as above, with cast milk glass face.

PUROL (blue arrow on white)
(3)   1927-1930   15in Metal $450-$750
PUROL (blue arrow on white)
(5)   1927-1930   15in fired on   No listing
     milk glass face
Same as above, with "THE PURE OIL COMPANY U.S.A." arched around bottom.

PUROL PEP GASOLINE (early design)
(5)   1927-1930   15in Metal $450-$750
White globe face, with blue outline ring and blue 1/3 areas top and bottom. Red "half-moon" and white arched area in upper and lower blue areas. Blue "Purol-/Pep" logotype across center white area, with blue "THE PURE OIL COMPANY" in upper white arch and "GASO-LINE" in lower arch.

DETONOX
(4)   1926-1929   15in Metal $500-$750
White globe face with red oval across center. White "DETONOX" on red oval. Blue "THE PURE OIL CO." arched around top, "GASO-LINE" around bottom.

ENERGEE TRUE GASOLINE
(4)   1929-1930   15in Metal $350-$525
White globe face, with large logotype "Energee" with speed lines across upper face. Small "True" over larger "Gasoline" below logotype.

ENERGEE DETONOX
(4)   1929-1930   15in Metal $375-$600
White globe face with red outline oval in center. Red "DETONOX" inside oval outline. Blue "Energee" with speed lines above oval, "GASO-LINE" below oval.

PUROL
(3)   1930-1932   15in Metal $300-$500
White globe face with blue "seal" border. Blue logotype "Purol" across globe face. Small blue "THE PURE OIL" arched around top inside seal, "COMPANY, U.S.A." around bottom.

PUROL PEP SOLVENIZED
(5)   1930-1932   15in Metal $400-$700
Same as PUROL PEP, with yellow "SUPER-SOLVENIZED" arched around top replacing "THE PURE OIL," and "KEEPS CARBON OUT" arched around bottom replacing "COMPANY U.S.A."

PUROL PEP
(3)   1932-1939   15in Metal $300-$550
PUROL PEP
(5)   1932-1939   13.5in Glass $250-$400
White globe face with blue "seal" border. Large blue "Purol-/Pep" logotype across center, with red half-moons above and below "Purol-/Pep." Small "THE PURE OIL" arched around top between seal border and red area. "COMPANY U.S.A." arched around bottom.

PUROL ETHYL
(3)   1932-1939   15in Metal $325-$525
PUROL ETHYL
(3)   1932-1939   13.5in Glass $250-$325
White globe face with blue "seal" border. Blue logotype "Purol" across top of face, above large Ethyl (EGC) logo in center. Blue "THE PURE OIL CO. U.S.A." arched around bottom.

(PURE) XCEL
(4)   1934-1937   15in Metal $350-$650
Blue globe face with white "seal" border. Large white script "Xcel" logotype across face, with white "THE PURE OIL CO. U.S.A." arched around bottom.

(PURE) MOTOR GASOLINE
(5)   1932-1934   15in Metal $300-$550
White globe face with blue "seal" border. Red "MOTOR/GASOLINE" in center of seal.

(PURE) US NAVY GAS
(4)   1932-1934   15in Metal $300-$500
White globe face with blue "seal" border. Red "U.S./NAVY/GAS" covering center of seal.

PURE ETHYL
(5)   1939-1940   15in Metal   No Listing
Same as PUROL ETHYL above, except "PURE" replaces "PUROL." Rare.

PURE "PRODUCTS OF THE PURE OIL CO."
(3)   1939-1961   15in Metal $250-$500
PURE "PRODUCTS OF THE PURE OIL CO."
(3)   1939-1961   13.5inGlass $250-$400
PURE "PRODUCTS OF THE PURE OIL CO."
(5)   1939-1961   18in Metal band neon   No listing
White globe face with blue "seal" border. Blue "PURE" across face, with small blue "PRODUCTS OF THE" arched around top inside seal and "PURE OIL COMPANY" around bottom.

PURE
(3)   1954-1961   13.5in Glass $250-$475
PURE
(3)   1954-1961   13.5in Capco $125-$175
White globe face with blue "seal" border. Blue "PURE" across face.

Wofford Oil Company, Atlanta, Georgia

In 1925, Pure Oil merged with Wofford Oil Company of Georgia and Wofford Oil Company of Alabama. Wofford had marketed Woco-Pep, a benzol blend, for a number of years and had used the seal-type logo that Pure Oil adopted in 1930. Purol-branded stations throughout the South continued to market Woco-Pep until World War II.

WOCO PEP
(5)   1920s   One-piece Baked   No Listing
Description not available.

Pure Energee! True Gasoline 15in inserts on metal (white porcelain) body.

Purol Pep (early style logo) 15in inserts on metal porcelain body.

Purol Gasoline 15in inserts on metal porcelain body.

Pure 15in inserts on porcelain metal body.

Purol 15in inserts on porcelain metal body.

Hi Speed Aviation one-piece etched. Bruce Hastedt

Fyre Drop one-piece etched globe. Kyle Moore

Quaker State one-piece etched globe.

Richfield 15in inserts on metal body.

Miscellaneous Richfield globes. R. V. Witherspoon

Shamrock Polymerine Gasoline 15in inserts on metal body.

Shamrock 15in inserts on metal body.

Shell one-piece etched globe.

Super Shell one-piece etched globe.

Shell one-piece recessed-letter shell-shaped globe.

WOCO PEP MORE MILES LESS CARBON
(5)   1920-1926   15in Metal $450-$800
White background, red letters. Yellow and black outline ring.
WOCO PEP MORE MILES LESS CARBON
(5)   1920-1926   15in Metal $400-$700
Yellow background, red letters.
WOCO PEP MORE MILES/LESS CARBON
(4)   1926-1930   15in Metal $450-$750
White globe face with blue seal border. Red "Woco-Pep" logotype
across globe face, with smaller red "King of Motor Fuel" below logo-
type. Blue "More Miles" across top, "Less Carbon" across bottom.
WOCO ETHYL
(5)   1926-1930   15in Metal   No Listing
Description not available.
WOCO PEP KING OF MOTOR FUEL
(4)   1930-1939   15in Metal $450-$750
White globe face with blue seal border. Large blue-outlined red "Woco-
Pep" logotype, with small red "KING OF MOTOR FUEL" across cen-
ter of face extending over seal border.
WOCO-PEP SOLVENIZED
(5)   1930-1932   15in Metal   No listing
Same as WOCO PEP KING OF MOTOR FUEL, above, with green
"SUPER-SOLVENIZED" arched around top inside seal, "KEEPS
CARBON OUT" around bottom.
PURE WOCO PEP KING OF MOTOR FUEL
(4)   1939-1942   15in Metal $425-$750
Same as above, with blue "PURE" added above logotype.

Hickock Oil Company, Toledo, Ohio

Founded in 1917, Hickock Oil Company marketed gasoline under
the Hi-Speed brand name. Pure purchased 51 percent of Hickock Oil
Company in 1928. Hickock operated the Hi-Speed stations throughout
Ohio and Michigan, and were the originators of the successful "truck
stop" concept that was greatly expanded on by Pure after the purchase
of Hickock was completed in 1951. Their stations and truck stops were
rebranded Pure.
HI-SPEED chimney top
(5)   1917-1920   One-piece etched chimney top No Listing
White globe with diagonal lettering "HI-SPEED" across face, "GASO-
LINE" across bottom. Colors unknown.
HI-SPEED GASOLINE
(5)   1920-1930   One-piece etched $750-$1,100
White globe with red half-reverse bowtie "HI-SPEED" across upper
face and "GASOLINE" across lower globe face.
HI-SPEED GYRO HIGH COMPRESSION
(5)   1927-1931   One-piece Baked   No Listing
White globe with red outline ring. Black "HI-SPEED" with speed lines
across upper globe face above large red script "GYRO." White lettering
"HI-COMPRESSION" in underline under "GYRO." Black "GAS"
across lower face.
HI-SPEED AVIATION GASOLINE
(5)   1920s   One-piece etched   No Listing
Black letters "HI-SPEED" around top, "GASOLINE" around bottom.
Script "AVIATION" in center, red letters.
HI-SPEED GYROL GAS
(5)   1930s   13.5in Glass   No Listing
Blue border, red "HI-SPEED" around top with speed lines, red "GAS"
around bottom. "GYROL" in blue, progressively larger than smaller
letters.
HI-SPEED EX-CARBON GAS
(4)   1930-1940   13.5in Glass $250-$375
White globe face with blue outline ring. Red "HI-SPEED" with speed
lines arched around top. Blue "EX-CARBON" across center, and red
"GAS" across bottom.
HI-SPEED EX-CARBON
(5)   1940-1946   13.5in Glass $250-$375
Same as above, with beige background.
HI-SPEED ETHYL
(4)   1930-1946   13.5in Glass $225-$350
White globe face with red outline ring. Red "HI-SPEED" with speed
lines arched round top, above large Ethyl (EGC) logo below.
HI-SPEED
(4)   1940-1952   13.5in Glass $200-$300
White globe face with blue outline ring and red "HI-SPEED" across
face.

HI-SPEED PREMIUM
(5)   1940-1952   13.5in Glass $250-$350
Blue border, red "HI-SPEED" across upper center, blue "PREMIUM"
below. No speed lines.
HI-SPEED DIESEL
(5)   1940-1950s   13.5in Glass $250-$375
Green border and green "DIESEL" replace "PREMIUM" in above
globe description.

W. H. Barber and Company, Chicago, Illinois

Founded in Minneapolis in the 1910s, they operated the Fyre
Drop stations and later the Meteeor stations from about 1925 on. They
introduced the Save More brand in 1940. W. H. Barber also owned the
Central West/Super Par operation at the time they were bought out by
Pure in 1945. W. H. Barber was spun off as an independent after the
Union-Pure merger in 1965, and still markets lubricants today.
IT'S FYRE DROP GASOLINE
(5)   1910s   One-piece etched $1,400-$2,000
White globe with red outline ring around face. Blue "FYRE DROP" in
bowtie lettering across center of globe face, with red sunburst between
"FYRE" and "DROP." Red "IT'S" above sunburst, "GASOLINE" across
bottom.
FYRE DROP GASOLINE
(5)   1910s   12in Metal   No Listing
Black globe face, with red "FYRE DROP" with yellow dropshade in
bowtie lettering across face. Detailed red and yellow sunburst in center. Orange "GASOLINE" with yellow dropshade across lower globe
face.
FYRE DROP GASOLINE
(5)   1920s   15in Metal $400-$650
White globe face with red "FYRE DROP" in bowtie lettering across
center of face. Smaller red "GASOLINE" below. Red-outlined yellow
sun with short rays between "FYRE" and "DROP."
IT'S FYRE DROP
(3)   1920s   15in Metal $400-$650
White globe face with blue outline ring. Yellow "FYRE DROP" with
red dropshade in bowtie lettering across face, with red and yellow sunburst in center. Red "IT'S" above "FYRE DROP," "GASOLINE" below.
METEOR "A HIGHER TEST" GASOLINE
(4)   1926-1935   15in Metal $400-$650
Yellow globe face with white outline ring. Red "Me-tee-or" logotype
arched around left side and top of face, with speed lines and white
streak below lettering. Red "A HIGHER TEST" in white streak. Red
"GASOLINE" below logotype.
METEEOR 80 GASOLINE
(4)   1935-1950   13.5in Glass $275-$400
Blue globe face with red and white outline rings. Blue and white lines
offsetting white center band across globe. Red "Meteeor" in progressively smaller lettering across band, with blue "80" below narrow end.
Blue star with red speed lines to left of "80."
METEEOR ETHYL GASOLINE
(5)   1935-1950   13.5in Glass   No listing
White face with blue outline area around upper half, red around lower
half. Large Ethyl (EGC) logo in center circle. White "ME-TEE-OR"
arched around top. "ETHYL" around bottom.
(METEEOR) DIESEL
(5)   1946-1950   13.5in Glass $175-$300
Same as above, with red logotype "Diesel" on center band. No company identification.

Save More

W. H. Barber discount brand introduced in 1940 for company-operated locations.
SAVE MORE REGULAR
(3)   1940-1965   13.5in Glass $250-$350
Blue globe face with red outline ring. White circle in center. Large red
"$" in center circle, with red-outlined white band across center of globe
face. White "SAVE MORE" arched around top, "SYSTEM" around bottom, with blue "REGULAR" in center.
SAVE MORE ETHYL
(3)   1940-1965   13.5in Glass $250-$350
Same as above, with blue "ETHYL" in center.

Central West Oil Company, South Bend, Indiana

A subsidiary of W. H. Barber. Operated the Super Par and Wisco 99 stations.
SUPER PAR REGULAR 100
(5)   1946-1960   13.5in Capco $250-$350
White globe face, with black outline ring and black outline around white center circle. Small airplane in center circle. Black-outlined band across lower center circle, with black "REGULAR" in band. Red "Super Par" arched around top, "100" below lower band.
SUPER PAR ETHYL
(5)   1946-1960   13.5in Capco $250-$350
Description not available.

Pacer Oil Company, South Bend, Indiana

Super Par affiliate.
200 PACER HI-TEST
(4)   1950s   13.5in Glass $250-$350
Globe face is red on upper 2/3 and black on lower 1/3. Large "PACER" on upper red area, with small "200" above. "HI-TEST" in lower black area.
400 PACER ETHYL
(4)   1950s   13.5in Glass $250-$350
Similar to above, with "400" replacing "200" and small Ethyl (EC) logo on lower black area.

Dickey, Incorporated, Parkwood, Iowa

Independent jobber that became a branded Pure jobber in the 1950s and continues to market Union 76 products.
DICKEY 570 GASOLINE
(4)   1940s   Gill $275-$450
Red-outlined white globe face, with black outline around red center circle. Black "DICKEY" arched around top, "GASOLINE" around bottom, with white "lightning bolt" design in red center. Black "570" in center of lightning bolt.
DICKEY 720 GASOLINE
(4)   1940s   Gill $275-$450
Same as above, with "720" in center.

QUAKER STATE
QUAKER STATE OIL REFINING COMPANY,
Oil City, Pennsylvania

In 1931 Sterling Oil Company of St. Mary's, West Virginia, Quaker State Oil Refining Company of Oil City, Pennsylvania, and sixteen other independent oil producers, refiners, lubricant compounders, and marketers joined together to form Quaker State Oil Refining Corporation. It was decided that Sterling would remain the gasoline brand, as Sterling was the only company involved with any significant gasoline marketing. The primary motor oil brand would be Quaker State, originally introduced in 1914 and distributed nationwide through lubricant jobbers, often jobbers of competing gasoline brands. The merger was the first time the famous motor oil brand name had been tied to any particular gasoline brand, and it was thought that marketing gasoline under a different name would lessen the problems associated with gasoline jobbers selling a "competitors'" motor oil. Sterling would remain the gasoline brand name until after 1960, when stations were rebranded Quaker State. Quaker State gasoline is currently sold through a small number of stations in Pennsylvania and Ohio.

Quaker State

Globes listed are for motor oil cabinets.
QUAKER STATE MOTOR OIL
(5)   1920-1931   One-piece etched $1,100-$1,700
White globe with dark green outline ring around face. Dark green "QUAKER" arched around top, "STATE" horizontal lettering across center of globe face, and "MOTOR OIL" arched around bottom.
QUAKER STATE
(5)   1920-1931   15in Metal $300-$550
White globe face with dark green outline ring. Dark green "QUAKER/STATE" on center of face.

Sterling Oil Company, St. Mary's, West Virginia

Pennsylvania producer, refiner, and marketer that originated the Pennsylvania Grade Crude Oil Association. Sterling was involved in gasoline marketing by the early 1920s and remained the brand name for gasoline marketed by Quaker State when that company entered the gasoline market after merging with Sterling and others in 1931.
STERLING £ GASOLINE
(5)   1926-1935   One-piece etched $1,000-$1,600

White globe with red outline rings around inner and outer edge of yellow outer ring. White circle in center, with large "£" in center. Black "STERLING" arched around top, "GASOLINE" around bottom.
STERLING ETHYL
(5)   1926-1935   One-piece etched, $700-$1,100
                        flat sides
White globe with red outline rings around inner and outer edge of yellow outer ring. White circle in center, with Ethyl (EGC) logo with black rays. Black "STERLING" arched around top in yellow ring, "GASOLINE" around bottom. Flat globe face.
STERLING £ GASOLINE
(4)   1930-1935   15in Metal $300-$650
STERLING £ GASOLINE
(3)   1935-1960   13.5in Glass $225-$375
Red outline rings around inner and outer edge of yellow outer ring. White circle in center, with large red "£" in center. Black "STERLING" arched around top in yellow ring, "GASOLINE" around bottom.
STERLING £ GASOLINE w/Quaker State sign
(4)   1950s   13.5in
Glass $300-$525
Same as above, with green porcelain sign attached to top of globe. White lettering on sign "A/QUAKER STATE/PRODUCT."
STERLING ETHYL
(3)   1935-1941   13.5in Glass $225-$350
Same as above, with Ethyl (EGC) logo with blue rays replacing "£" in center circle.
STERLING ETHYL
(3)   1941-1960   13.5in Glass $225-$350
Same as above, with Ethyl (EC) logo with blue rays replacing "£" in center circle.
STERLING ETHYL w/Quaker State sign
(4)   1950s   13.5in Glass $300-$500
Same as above, with green porcelain sign described above attached to top of globe.
EMOLENE BLUE
(4)   1932-1935   13.5in Glass $200-$325
Same as above, with "BLUE" replacing "£" in center.
EMOLENE £ GASOLINE
(4)   1935-1940   13.5in Glass $200-$325
White globe face with red outline ring and red ring around white center circle. Blue "EMOLENE" arched around and in between rings, "GASOLINE" below, with large red "£" in center.

RICHFIELD & Affiliates
RICHFIELD OIL CORPORATION,
Los Angeles, California
RICHFIELD OIL COMPANY OF NEW YORK,
New York, New York

Richfield, a West Coast producer, refiner, and marketer, was founded in California about 1901. By 1915 Richfield was marketing on the West Coast. The company entered East Coast markets in the mid-1920s, and created a subsidiary, Richfield Oil Company of New York, with the 1929 purchase of Walburn Petroleum Company. During the 1930s, as detailed below, Richfield was reorganized and the eastern marketing was sold to Sinclair. The remaining West Coast operations merged with Atlantic Refining in 1966 to form Atlantic Richfield. See Atlantic section for more information.

Richfield Oil Company

Globe listings for the entire company prior to 1933 breakup. Includes both East and West Coast marketing.
RICHFIELD GASOLINE OF POWER (no eagle)
(5)   1920s   15in Metal   No Listing
White globe face with Richfield shield in center. Black outline around light blue inside border. Gold line inside border, around center dark blue area. Yellow "RICHFIELD" at top underlined by extension of "R." Light-blue-outlined yellow box, with dark blue "THE GASOLINE/OF POWER" below "RICHFIELD."
RICHFIELD "THE GASOLINE OF POWER"
(5)   1920-1929   15in Metal $850-$1,500
White globe face with larger, more detailed version of above shield. Yellow and blue eagle with wings spread between "RICHFIELD" and box with slogan.
RICHFIELD AVIATION
(5)   1924-1928   15in Metal   No Listing
Yellow-outlined dark blue ring around light blue center. Yellow "RICHFIELD" arched around top, "AVIATION" around bottom, with white-bordered shield in center. Three blue airplanes replace eagle, and blue lettering in yellow area reads "AVIATION/GASOLINE."

RICHFIELD ETHYL GASOLINE
(5)   1926-1929   15in Metal $400-$650
Blue outer ring with yellow "RICHFIELD" arched around top, "GASO-
LINE" around bottom, with large Ethyl (EGC) logo in center.
BLUE STREAK GASOLINE
(5)   1926-1928   15in Metal $400-$700
Wide blue band around face. "BLUE STREAK" in large blue letters
arched in center. "GASOLINE" in white around bottom.
RICHFIELD GASOLINE OF POWER
(3)   1929-1939   15in Metal $750-$1,200
White globe face with Richfield shield, similar to above. Blue outline
ring around white border around shield.
RICHFIELD ETHYL
(4)   1929-1939   15in Metal $800-$1,400
White globe face, with large white-bordered shield covering most of
face. Small gold eagle at top above "RICHFIELD." Yellow "Ethyl"
script across globe, with small Ethyl (EGC) logo in white circle at bottom of shield.
ROCOR (blue on white, no bird)
(4)   1932-1939   15in Metal $275-$475
White globe face, with blue outline ring and blue lines offsetting a
white center band. Short blue line above and below center band. Blue
"ROCOR" on band.

Richfield Oil Company of New York
The eastern marketing division of Richfield Oil Corporation was
formed in 1929 with the purchase of New York marketers Walburn
Petroleum Company and Acewood Petroleum Company. Richfield Oil
Company of New York was created as a "jobber marketer," and former
company-owned outlets were turned over to the new company. Richfield Oil Company of New York was purchased by Sinclair in 1933
during the Richfield bankruptcy, and operated as a secondary brand
until 1964 when all Richfield jobbers and dealers were converted to
the Sinclair brand.
RICHFIELD HI-OCTANE
(3)   1939-1964   15in Metal $275-$500
RICHFIELD HI-OCTANE
(2)   1939-1964   Gill $250-$400
RICHFIELD HI-OCTANE
(2)   1939-1964   13.5in Glass $225-$375
RICHFIELD HI-OCTANE
(3)   1956-1964   13.5in Capco $150-$275
White globe face, with yellow shield outline and dark blue background. Blue, white, and yellow art-deco (nondetailed) Richfield eagle
flying left-to-right at top of shield. Large blue "RICHFIELD" across
shield below center, above small blue "HI-OCTANE."
RICHFIELD ETHYL (red)
(3)   1939-1950   15in Metal $275-$525
RICHFIELD ETHYL (red)
(2)   1939-1950   Gill $250-$400
RICHFIELD ETHYL (red)
(2)   1939-1950   13.5in Glass $225-$375
Same as above, with red "RICHFIELD" and red "ETHYL" replacing
"HI-OCTANE."
RICHFIELD ETHYL (blue)
(5)   1950-1956   15in Metal $275-$525
RICHFIELD ETHYL (blue)
(3)   1950-1956   Gill $250-$400
RICHFIELD ETHYL (blue)
(4)   1950-1956   13.5in Glass $225-$375
Same as above, with blue "RICHFIELD" and red "ETHYL" replacing
"HI-OCTANE."
ROCOR GASOLINE (shield)
(4)   1939-1950   15in Metal $300-$600
ROCOR GASOLINE (shield)
(4)   1939-1950   Gill $250-$450
Same as RICHFIELD HI-OCTANE above, with "ROCOR" replacing
"RICHFIELD" and "Gasoline" replacing "HI-OCTANE."
RICHFIELD PREMIUM
(2)   1956-1964   13.5in Glass $225-$350
RICHFIELD PREMIUM
(2)   1956-1964   13.5in Capco $150-$250
White globe face, with yellow shield outline and dark blue back-
ground. Blue, white, and yellow art-deco (nondetailed) Richfield eagle
flying left-to-right at top of shield. Wide red band across lower globe
face below eagle. White "PREMIUM" on red band, with blue "RICH-
FIELD" just below band.
RICHFIELD DIESEL
(4)   1939-1964   15in Metal $375-$550

RICHFIELD DIESEL
(4)   1939-1964   Gill $250-$400
RICHFIELD DIESEL
(4)   1939-1964   13.5in Glass $225-$350
RICHFIELD DIESEL
(4)   1939-1964   13.5in Capco $150-$250
Same as RICHFIELD HI-OCTANE above, with red "DIESEL" replacing "HI-OCTANE."

Walburn Petroleum Company
First Ethyl marketer in the New England region. In 1929, Wal-
burn Petroleum was merged with the existing Richfield company mar-
keting and Acewood Petroleum Company to form the Richfield Oil
Company of New York.
WALBURN ETHYL
(5)   1926-1929   15in Metal $300-$525
Yellow globe face with black outline ring. Black outline around white
center circle. Large Ethyl (EGC) logo in center with black rays. Black
"WALBURN" arched around top, "GASOLINE" around bottom.

Sherwood Brothers, Baltimore, Maryland
Large Richfield-Sinclair jobber operation that had marketed
under the Betholine trademark prior to branding Richfield, and con-
tinued to dual brand Betholine-Richfield and Betholine-Sinclair until
the late 1950s.
BETHOLINE MILES OF SMILES
(5)   1930-1938   15in Metal $375-$600
White globe face with large blue "BETHOLINE" in bowtie lettering,
with oversize "O" across top. Blue script "Miles of Smiles" above
"BETHOLINE," "THE WONDER/MOTOR FUEL" below.
BETHOLINE MILES OF SMILES
(5)   1930-1983   15in Metal   No Listing
Same as above, with all orange letters except "BETHOLINE."
SHERWOOD STRAIGHT RUN GASOLINE
(5)   1920s   15in Metal   No Listing
Yellow background, dark blue horizontal band trimmed in light blue,
then black. Reversed white type "STRAIGHT RUN." "SHERWOOD"
in red above, in white pogoda-style box. "GASOLINE" at bottom in
red, in white box.
Note: Other Sherwood-Betholine globes are known to exist, but no details are available.

Lamson Oil Company, Providence, Rhode Island
Private brand that rebranded Richfield about 1929. The globes
listed below are known only in old photos.
HOW ABOUT GAS "?"
(5)   1920-1928   One-piece etched No Listing
White globe with large "HOW/ABOUT/GAS/?" on globe face.
NUN-BET-ER GASOLINE
(5)   1922-1928   15in Metal   No Listing
White globe face with "NUN-BET-ER" arched around top, "GASO-
LINE" across center, and "LAMSON OIL CO., INC." across lower face.
LAMSON AVIATION GASOLINE
(5)   1925-1928   15in Metal   No Listing
Exact description not available.
LAMSON SUPER
(5)   1928-1929   15in Metal   No Listing
White globe face with "LAMSON" arched around top, large "SUPER"
across center, and "LAMSON OIL CO., INC." across lower face.
NUN-BET-ER GASOLINE
(5)   1928-1929   Gill   No Listing
White globe face with "NUN-BET-ER" arched around top, "GASO-
LINE" across center, and "LAMSON OIL CO., INC." across lower face.

Richfield Oil Corporation
Richfield of California emerged from the bankruptcy in 1937 with
marketing throughout the western United States. Ownership of Richfield had transferred to Sinclair and Cities Service and the "new"
Richfield consolidated with Sinclair's Rio Grande marketing subsidiary. Rio Grande continued to be used as a secondary brand to the
new Richfield, as well as "Rocket" being used at some stations. In
1966, Richfield Oil of California merged with Atlantic Refining to form
Atlantic Richfield. In 1970 the brand name Richfield was replaced by
the Arco brand, and Arco continues to market today throughout the
old Richfield territory.
RICHFIELD
(4)   1937-1946   15in Metal $550-$800
Yellow globe face with light blue and red outline rings. Light blue and
red outline around yellow center circle. Dark blue band across center,
with gold serif lettering "RICHFIELD" and gold lines above and below
lettering.

RICHFIELD
(4)   1946-1960   15in Metal $500-$750
Yellow globe face with light blue and red outline rings. Light blue and
red outline around yellow center circle. Dark blue band across center,
with yellow "RICHFIELD" in plain block letters on band.

Rio Grande Oil Company

Independent California refiner and marketer purchased by Sinclair in 1932. When Richfield was reorganized in 1937, Sinclair
merged their interest in Rio Grande with the new Richfield Oil Corporation. Rio Grande continued to be a Richfield-Arco secondary brand
into the 1970s.
RIO GRANDE (shield)
(5)   1930-1937   15in Metal   No Listing
White globe face with blue outline ring. Blue-outlined blue, white, and
red "RIO GRANDE" shield covers most of face.
RIO GRANDE ETHYL
(5)   1930-1937   15in Metal $500-$750
White face with blue outlined red/white/blue Rio Grande shield covering most of face. White "RIO GRANDE" in upper blue area, "ETHYL"
in center red band and small Ethyl logo (EGC) in lower white area.
RIO GRANDE (circles)
(5)   1937-1950   15in Metal $400-$700
Red and white concentric circles covering globe face, with white band
across center. Blue "RIO GRANDE" on center white box.

Rocket

Rocket was a Richfield-Arco secondary brand.
ROCKET GASOLINE
(5)   postwar   15in Metal   No Listing
Green-and-white-outlined red globe face with small green rocket left
of center at top. White rocket trail, with red lines diagonally down to
bottom left of globe face. White-outlined green "ROCKET/GASOLINE"
across center of globe.
ROCKET GASOLINE UNEXCELLED
(5)   postwar   15in Metal   No Listing
Green globe face with green rocket at upper right, with red trail following diagonally across globe. White script "Unexcelled" above rocket
trail, white block "GASOLINE" below, with white lettering "ROCKET"
with lines on red rocket trail.

SHAMROCK & AFFILIATES
DIAMOND SHAMROCK, INCORPORATED
San Antonio, Texas

Diamond Shamrock, founded in the 1930s as Shamrock Oil and
Gas Corporation in Amarillo, Texas, is a regional marketer in the
south central and southwestern United States. Little is known about
the company's early history, but evidence of marketing from the mid-
1930s and later exists. In 1967 Shamrock Oil and Gas merged with
Diamond Alkali Company, a chemical manufacturer, to form Diamond
Shamrock. The company has gradually expanded its market in recent
years and now brands over 1,900 locations. Shamrock has historically
marketed through jobbers, several including Sigmor (purchased by
Shamrock in 1983) and Cliff Brice, which have became large market-
ing organizations in themselves.
SHAMROCK GASOLINE
(4)   1930s   15in Metal $350-$550
White globe face with green "SHAMROCK" arched around top,
"GASOLINE" around bottom, and large green three-leaf clover in cen-
ter.
SHAMROCK WITH ETHYL
(5)   1930s   15in Metal   No Listing
Description not available.
SHAMROCK POLYMERINE GASOLINE
(4)   1930s   15in Metal $375-$600
White globe face with green outline and green outline around white
center circle. Large three-leaf clover in center, with white "Polymer-
ine" across clover. Green "SHAMROCK" arched around top, "GASO-
LINE" around bottom.
SHAMROCK
(3)   1946-1965   15in Metal $275-$450
White globe face, with green three-leaf clover in center and white
"SHAMROCK" across clover.
SHAMROCK
(1)   1946-1965   13.5in Capco $100-$150
White globe face, with green three-leaf clover in center and white
"SHAMROCK" across clover.
SHAMROCK oval
(1)   1965-1985   Capco Oval $125-$225

White globe face, with green three-leaf clover in center and white
"SHAMROCK" across clover.
SHAMROCK (oval w/red line border)
(3)   1965-1985   Capco Oval $125-$200
Same as above, with red outline ring around globe face.

Cliff Brice, Pueblo, Colorado
Cliff Brice is a Pueblo, Colorado, based Shamrock regional jobber operating dual-branded Cliff Brice-Shamrock stations.
CLIFF BRICE glass oval
(4)   1950-1970   Glass Oval $350-$525
White area around large Cliff Brice logo covering most of globe face.
Oval logo has green wave border around yellow outline ring around
solid red oval. White logotype "Cliff/Brice" with green dropshade on
upper oval, with small yellow logotype "Quality" white "GAS" and yellow logotype "ForLess" below "Cliff/Brice."
CLIFF BRICE Oval
(3)   1970-current   Capco oval $150-$250
Red globe face with black white outline. White "Cliff/Brice," with black
lines in unusual type covering face.

SHELL
SHELL OIL COMPANY, Houston, Texas

Shell Oil Company, a unit of the British-Dutch "Royal Dutch
Shell," entered US markets with the purchase of a terminal in Washington state in 1912. In 1917, Shell purchased St. Louis-based Roxana
Petroleum and by 1929 was marketing in all forty-eight states. Since
that time, Shell has proven to be an innovative marketer, often leading the way in new gasoline marketing concepts. Several Shell "firsts"
include the 1947 introduction of internally lit plastic signage, the 1957
introduction of landscaped "rancher" style stations, and one of the first
franchised Auto Care programs. Shell discontinued using globes at
most locations with a 1957 reimaging. Today, the company continues
to market through company direct and jobber operated locations in
forty-one states and around the world.
SHELL GASOLINE
(4)   1915-1920   15in Metal   No Listing
Red outer ring around globe face with yellow center. Detailed white
shell with black detail lines in center circle. Yellow "SHELL" arched
around top, "GASOLINE" around bottom, with dots on outer ring to
either side at center.
SHELL MOTOR OIL
(5)   1915-1920   15in Metal   No Listing
Yellow outer ring around globe face with red center. Detailed yellow
shell with red detail lines in center circle. Red "SHELL" arched
around top, "MOTOR OIL" around bottom.
400 AVIATION DRY GAS
(5)   1928-1930   15in Metal   No Listing
Yellow globe face with black outline ring and black airplane nose
down from top. Black "400" above left of airplane, "DRY" below right,
with yellow "AVIATION" across plane on wing. Black "GASOLINE"
arched around bottom.
SHELL (East Coast)
(4)   1920-1927   15in Metal $700-$1,500
White globe face with large red-outlined yellow Shell logo covering
most of face. Logo has red detail lines down from top and up from bottom, but they do not continue behind lettering. Red "SHELL" lettering
across center.
SHELL (West Coast)
(4)   1920-1927   15in Metal $800-$1,600
White globe face with large red-outlined yellow Shell logo covering
most of face. Logo has red detail lines top to bottom and arched line
across, below white-outlined red-colored "SHELL."
SHELL GASOLINE
(5)   1920-1925   15in Metal   No Listing
White globe face similar to SHELL (West Coast) above, with no
arched line, and lettering in two lines "SHELL/GASOLINE."
SHELL AVIATION
(5)   1926-1928   15in Metal   No Listing
Same as SHELL (East Coast) above, with red "AVIATION" replacing
"SHELL" across logo.
SHELL GREEN STREAK
(5)   1934-1939   15in Metal $400-$750
Mint green globe face with dark green outline and dark green script
"Green/Streak," with speed-lines diagonally above dark green "GASO-
LINE."
SHELL
(5)   1922-1924   One-piece Etched Round $500-$800
White globe with fancy red lettering "SHELL" across face.

SHELL
(3)   1924-1930   One-piece Etched Round$400-$650
White globe with red lettering "SHELL" across face.
SUPER SHELL
(4)   1928-1930   One-piece Etched Round $1,500-$2,100
White globe with red outline and detail lines forming shell, with red
italic "Super" with speed lines diagonally across top of logo and red
lettering "SHELL" across center.
SHELL (small)
(5)   1910s   One-piece cast shell $900-$1,400
Small white cast shell, with red lettering "SHELL" across center.
Based design to mount on lightpost and some very early pumps.
SHELL
(1)   1925-1957   One-piece cast shell $275-$425
White cast shell-shaped globe, with red lettering "SHELL" across cen-
ter of globe.
SUPER SHELL
(4)   1930-1940   One-piece cast shell $650-$975
White cast shell-shaped globe, with red "Super" diagonally with speed
lines above red "SHELL" offset to right across globe.
SUPER SHELL ETHYL
(4)   1930-1940   One-piece cast shell $600-$900
Same as above, with "ETHYL" in red painted on surface below
"SHELL."
SUPER SHELL ETHYL
(4)   1930-1940   One-piece cast shell $600-$950
Same as above, with "ETHYL" in red in recessed lettering below
"SHELL."
SHELL (silver Shell)
(4)   1930s   One-piece cast shell $450-$750
White cast shell with no writing.
SHELL DIESEL
(5)   1940s   One-piece cast shell   No Listing
White cast shell-shaped globe, with red "DIESEL FUEL" over red
"SHELL"across globe.
SHELL
(5)   1946-1957   12.5in Glass $600-$1,200
White globe face with large red-outlined yellow Shell logo covering
most of face.
SHELL (raised or recessed letters)
(5)   1955-1957   Plastic cast shell $200-$400
White plastic cast shell, made in two pieces assembled back-to-back,
with raised red lettering "SHELL" across center of globe.
Note: Shell was one of the first oil companies to experiment with plastics in service station signage. With an intricate trademark, it is un-
derstandable why costs involved in porcelain, glass, neon, and other
materials would cause Shell marketing people to look toward plastics
as an inexpensive alternative. In 1947 the first plastic, internally lit
oil company logo, a four-foot formed Shell sign, was introduced. Station lettering was next, and finally the cast Shell globe. While other
items proved successful, heat from the light inside caused the plastic
Shell globe to become brittle, and the experiment was discontinued
with the elimination of globes in the 1957 reimaging.
Another important consideration for collectors is that Shell, being a
worldwide marketer, has used a large number of globes in other coun-
tries. Mostly variations of cast one-piece shells, the non-US globes are
distinctly different from US globes, frequently newer, and as such not
as valuable in most cases. Most are much narrower, and many are
cast in clear glass and painted on the inside. All known US globes are
cast in white glass. Due to the fact that foreign globes are often newer
(some are actually still in use), the value of these globes are much
lower than for US versions. Don't be taken in by unusually great deals
on one-piece Shell globes, as they could be foreign versions from the
1970s. Know what you are buying!

SIGNAL and SIGNAL-CHARTER BRANDS
SIGNAL and GAS, Los Angeles, California
In 1932 Signal Oil and Gas of Los Angeles, formerly a producer
and refiner, entered the retail marketplace under the Signal name.
Involved with Standard of California from its earliest days, Signal
sold its retail marketing to Standard Chevron in 1947. In 1950 they
reentered the market with the purchase of a portion of the Bankline
Oil-Norwalk operation. In 1958 Signal merged with Hancock Oil of
Long Beach, California, and bought the Houston-based Watson Oil
and rebranded the stations Hancock. The Signal brand was operated
by Chevron until about 1965, when the entire marketing network
was sold to Humble Oil and stations were rebranded Enco. Hancock,
and Norwalk. Other Signal brands were sold off beginning in 1970.
Stations in the West were sold off individually, while the southeastern market was sold to Charter Oil-Dixie Vim.

Signal Oil and Gas, Los Angeles, California
See Signal company history in introduction above.
GO SIGNAL
(4)   1932-1948   15in Metal $1,400-$2,200
Black globe face with red outline ring. Large white stoplight with red,
black, and red signals and large flag on face. Black "GO" on stoplight
flag. Yellow "SIGNAL" below stoplight, across bottom of face.
GO SIGNAL
(4)   1932-1948   15in Metal $1,300-$2,100
Same as above, with smaller "SIGNAL" lettering.
SIGNAL PRODUCTS
(5)   1932-1948   15in Metal $1,800-$2,800
Yellow globe face with orange outline ring and orange ring around
black center circle. Stoplight, same as above but without post, on center circle. Stoplight has side flag with black "GO" lettering. White-outlined black "SIGNAL" arched around top, "PRODUCTS" around bottom.

Hancock Refining Company, Long Beach, California
Founded in 1925, Hancock was a California-based refiner and
marketer with stations throughout the state. In 1958, Signal Oil and
Gas merged with Hancock Refining. Stations remained under the
Hancock brand in California, and the brand was expanded to Texas
when Signal purchased the Watson operation and rebranded the stations Hancock. Hancock brand discontinued when Signal marketing
was sold off in 1970.
HANCOCK PRODUCTS (shield)
(5)   1926-1940   15in Metal $1,400-$2,000
White globe face with black notched outline ring and orange center
circle. Black "HANCOCK" arched around top, "PRODUCTS" around
bottom, with design to either side. Hancock crest shield in center.
Three roosters and "QUALITY" on shield.
HANCOCK GASOLINE (shield)
(4)   1926-1940   15in Metal $1,400-$2,000
Same as above, with "GASOLINE" replacing "PRODUCTS."
HANCOCK-COCK O' THE WALK
(4)   1940-1959   15in Metal $1,800-$2,600
HANCOCK-COCK O' THE WALK
(5)   1940-1959   13.5in Glass   No Listing
White globe face with black, white, and orange outline rings. Large or-
ange-red and black strutting rooster covers most of face. Black "HAN-
COCK" arched around top, smaller "COCK O' THE WALK" arched
below.

Watson Oil Company, Houston, Texas
Houston-based discounter purchased by Signal about 1960 and
rebranded Hancock.
WATSON
(5)   1950s   13.5in Capco $125-$175
Red globe face with yellow oval in center. Black lettering "WATSON"
on yellow oval.

Regal
California independent purchased by Signal about 1960.
REGAL GASOLINE w/ethyl
(5)   1950s   16.5in Metal $300-$450
White globe face with black outline ring and black ring around large
white center circle. Black "REGAL" arched around top, "GASOLINE"
around bottom, with large early Ethyl (EGC) logo with yellow rays in
center.

Billups Brothers, Greenwood, Mississippi
Founded in Greenwood, Mississippi, in 1935, Billups survived as
a family-owned operation until 1959. In that year the company was
split into two operating units, Billups Eastern and Billups Western.
Billups Western was sold out to Signal Oil and operated by them until
1970, when Signal got out of retail gasoline marketing and sold the
operation to Charter Oil. A majority of Billups Eastern was sold to independent refiner Delhi-Taylor, which was bought out by Hess Oil
and Chemical in 1963. The remaining portion of Billups Eastern was
bought by Hess in 1965, and Billups stations were rebranded Hess.
See the Hess section for more details.
BILLUPS SUPREME
(4)   1940s   Gill $325-$525
BILLUPS SUPREME
(4)   1940s   13.5in Glass $275-$450
White globe face with blue outline ring and red "BILLUPS" arched
around top, and "SUPREME" around bottom, with blue outline of outstretched hand in center.

Unusual Shell Oil shell-shaped lamp post-gas globe. Bruce Miller

Shell 12 1/2in inserts on glass body. Bruce Miller

Hancock 15in inserts on metal body.

SOC 13.5in inserts on plastic bodies. Peter Capell

Dixie Vim Ethyl 13.5in inserts on Gill glass body. R. V. Witherspoon

Dixie Vim 13.5in inserts on plastic body. R. V. Witherspoon

Sinclair Gasoline one-piece etched globe.

Sinclair Gasoline one-piece fired-on globe.

Sinclair Oils one-piece etched small 12in globe.

Sinclair H-Cs 13.5in inserts on plastic bodies. Globe on left is actually an error.

Sinclair U.S. Motor Specifications one-piece globe with decal.

Sinclair H-C 13.5in inserts; old style on left. James Bernard

Sinclair U.S. Motor Specifications Gasoline 13.5in inserts on glass body.

Sinclair U.S. Motor Specifications Gasoline 13.5in inserts on glass body.

BILLUPS "YOUR FRIEND"
(4)   1950-1970   13.5in Capco $150-$250
Red globe face with white band across center. Red, white, and blue
rings around center half-circles. Blue "BILLUPS" in center band, with
white "YOUR" in upper red area and "FRIEND" in lower red area.
BILLUPS ETHYL (EC) PREMIUM
(5)   1950-1970   13.5in Capco $250-$375
Red globe face with white circle in center. Ethyl (EC) logo in white
center circle. White script "Billups" arched around top of globe face
and extending around to small airplane on each side, as if "Billups"
lettering was skywriting. Good detail on airplanes. White "PREMI-
UM" with blue shading arched around bottom.

Spar, Orlando, Florida
Originally Orlando Ice and Fuel, Spar was bought out by Billups
Eastern soon after the Billups split in 1959. After the Billups merger
with Hess, they were operated by another independent for several
years.
SPAR
(5)   1950s   13.5in Glass $150-$250
White globe face with red lettering "SPAR" across center.

Rose Oil Company, Vicksburg, Mississippi
Rose Oil Company was apparently operated by a member of the
Billups family. Exact ties cannot be determined. The "MMP" stands
for Mississippi Motor Products.
ROSE REGULAR GASOLINE
(4)   1940s   13.5in Capco $275-$425
White globe face with green outline ring. Small green-outlined oval
near top, with Billups-Rose hand logo and red "RIDE WITH ROSE"
above hand, "YOUR FRIEND" below hand, and green "GASOLINE"
and "AND OILS" at either end of hand. Large red "REGULAR" across
globe face. Green half-moon outline below, with red "GASOLINE" in
bowtie lettering below "REGULAR."
RIDE WITH ROSE REGULAR GASOLINE
(4)   1950s   13.5in Capco $250-$400
Mint green globe face with white rectangular area in center and white
semi-circles top and bottom. Red "REGULAR" in upper semi-circle,
"GASOLINE" in lower, with red "RIDE," green "WITH," red "ROSE"
in upper part of rectangle, and outstretched hand in center above red
"YOUR FRIEND."
RIDE WITH ROSE ETHYL
(4)   1950s   13.5in Capco $125-$225
Green-outlined white ring around outer globe face, with red "RIDE
WITH" arched around top and "ROSE" around bottom. Ethyl (EC)
logo in center.
ROSETANE
(4)   1950s   13.5in Capco $125-$200
White globe face with mint green outline ring. Mint green lines
around upper and lower half-circles. Mint green "REGULAR" across
center, with red "ROSETANE" in upper half-circle and "GASOLINE"
in lower half-circle.
ROSE DIESEL
(5)   1950s   13.5in Capco $100-$175
Red globe face with white band across center. Black "DIESEL" on
band. White "ROSE" in upper red area.
PREMIUM ROSE MMP
(3)   1960s   13.5in Capco $125-$200
Green-outlined white ring around outer globe face, with red "PREMI-
UM" arched around top and "MMP" around bottom. Black circle in
center with yellow "MMP."
PREMIUM ETHYL (EC) MMP
(3)   1960s   13.5in Capco $125-$225
Same as above, with Ethyl (EC) logo in center.

Supertest Oil Company, Tampa, Florida
Postwar Florida-based discounter bought out by Signal about
1960, and sold off to Charter in 1970.
Note: No Supertest globes are known to exist.

Southland Oil Company, Savannah, Georgia
In 1970 when Signal Oil sold off its retail marketing, Southland
Oil Company of Savannah, Georgia, or SOC, was sold off to its original
owners, who had remained in management since Signal's purchase of
SOC about 1960. They operated as an independent until about 1986,
when they became a branded Texaco operation.
SOC
(4)   1950-1973   13.5in Glass $225-$325
Red, white, and black outline around red border area and white sun-
burst design on globe face. Black lettering "SOC" across center of face.

SUPER SOC
(4)   1950-1973   13.5in Glass $250-$350
Same as above, except red "SUPER" in 15in box above "SOC."

Southern Oil Stores–Dixie Vim, Jacksonville, Florida
In 1970, Signal Oil again left the retail gasoline marketplace.
Charter Oil Company of Jacksonville,Florida, had purchased the
Southern Oil Stores-Dixie Vim chain the year before, and when
Billups, Supertest, and the former Watson-Hancock stations were
placed on the market, they added them to the Dixie Vim operation.
Southern Oil Stores had been an independent marketer, one of the
original trackside discount chains with approximately fifty stations.
Founded about 1929, it is listed here only to aid in understanding the
change in ownership of Billups and Supertest.
DIXIE VIM
(5)   1930-1946   13.5in Capco   No Listing
White globe face with green outlined white diamond logo covering
globe face. Green band across center with white "DIXIE VIM" w/speed
lines. Railroad tank car at top, 1930 car at bottom connected by red
line. With slogan "FROM TANK CAR" "TO CAR TANK."
DIXIE VIM REGULAR
(5)   1946-1970   Gill $500-$700
DIXIE VIM REGULAR
(4)   1946-1970   13.5in Capco $350-$500
White globe face with light green band across upper face. Yellow circle
in center with black lettering "SOUTHERN/OIL/STORES/INC.," and
white italic "DIXIE VIM" with speed lines on band. Railroad tank car
to left of center circle, with "From Tank Car" connected by red line to
1946 Studebaker on other side of circle, with lettering "To Car Tank."
Green script "Regular" at bottom of globe face.
DIXIE VIM ETHYL
(5)   1946-1970   Gill $500-$700
DIXIE VIM ETHYL
(5)   1946-1970   13.5in Capco $400-$550
Same as above, with Ethyl (EC) logo replacing center yellow circle,
and red script "Ethyl" at bottom.

SINCLAIR and Affiliates
SINCLAIR OIL CORPORATION, New York, New York
Founded in 1916 in New York from the various holdings of
founder Harry Sinclair, including the refining and marketing formerly
under the Cudahy name, Sinclair was a huge operation right from the
start. With oil production, pipelines, railcars, refineries, terminals,
bulk plants, and service stations, Sinclair was one of few oil companies to start as a completely integrated operation. Sinclair grew larger
during the prosperous 1920s in spite of Harry Sinclair's involvement
in the Teapot Dome oil scandal of President Warren Harding's admin-
istration. With several important purchases during the early 1930s,
such as Pierce, Parco, Rio Grande, and Richfield of New York, Sinclair
was marketing from coast to coast.
With the 1937 reorganization of Rio Grande into Richfield of California, Sinclair direct operations on the West Coast were discontinued,
but Sinclair continued to market from the Rockies eastward. From
1932 until 1943 the corporate name was Consolidated Oil Company,
changing back to Sinclair Oil Corporation in 1943. After World War II
Sinclair continued to expand direct operated and jobber marketing,
building thousands of service stations along the new interstate highway system. Marketing surpassed production, and the company could
no longer supply all the crude oil needed for its own branded marketing. In 1969 Sinclair merged with oil-rich and newly created Atlantic-
Richfield, selling off its East Coast marketing to British Petroleum. In
1973 Atlantic-Richfield was court-ordered to sell most of Sinclair, and
the operation was spun off as an independent oil refiner and marketer
that today operates more than 2,500 stations in twenty states.
SINCLAIR SINCO OILS
(5)   1916-1920   One-piece Etched No Listing
White globe with green outline ring around face. Green and white outline around red center circle. White "SINCO" in distinctive lettering in
center circle. Green "SINCLAIR" arched around top, "OILS" around
bottom.
SINCLAIR "SINCO" OPALINE
(5)   1916-1920   One-piece etched No listing
White globe with green globe face. White "SINCLAIR" arched around
top, "OPALINE" around bottom with white "SINCO" across center.
Note that "Opaline" was a Sinclair motor oil brand and this is likely
an old cabinet globe.
SINCLAIR GASOLINE sphere shaped
(5)   1920-1925   One-piece Etched $700-$1,000

Thin-glass white ball-shaped globe with etched red lettering "SIN-CLAIR/GASOLINE" across spherical surface.

SINCLAIR OILS
(5)   1920-1929   One-piece Cast $750-$1,200
SINCLAIR OILS
(3)   1916-1929   One-piece Etched $750-$1,200
SINCLAIR OILS
(4)   1925-1929   One-piece Baked $550-$750
White globe with green and white outline around green face. White and green outline around center circle. Green and white vertical stripes in center circle. White "SINCLAIR" arched around top, "OILS" around bottom.

SINCLAIR OILS 12in
(4)   1916-1925   One-piece Etched $650-$1,200
Same as above, except globe is small—approximately 12in in diameter and unusually wide.

SINCLAIR OILS 12in
(5)   1916-1922   One-piece Etched $650-$1,200
Same as above, with green and white colors reversed. Globe is small–12in in diameter.

SINCLAIR GASOLINE
(3)   1920-1929   One-piece Etched $600-$950
SINCLAIR GASOLINE
(3)   1925-1929   One-piece Baked $450-$650
SINCLAIR GASOLINE
(5)   1925-1929   One-piece Flat face   No Listing
Same as SINCLAIR OILS above, with white "GASOLINE" replacing "OILS."

SINCLAIR GASOLINE (small ball-shaped)
(5)   1920-1930   One-piece Baked   No Listing
Small 6in diameter spherical lightpost-type globe, with "SINCLAIR GASOLINE" striped logo.

"SINCLAIR" BENZOL MOTOR FUEL
(5)   1922-1925   One-piece Etched   No Listing
White globe with dark green "BENZOL/MOTOR/FUEL" on globe face.

SINCLAIR BENZOL GASOLINE
(5)   1922-1925   One-piece Etched   No Listing
White globe with green lettering "SINCLAIR" arched around top of face, "GASOLINE" around bottom with red "BENZOL" in center across vertical stripes.face.

SINCLAIR HC GASOLINE with stripes
(5)   1926-EXP   One-piece etched   No listing
White globe with green face. White "SINCLAIR" arched around top, "GASOLINE" around bottom with series of green and white verticle stripes in center. Stripes are interrupted by green outlined white small center circle. Green "HC" on white center circle. This logo was an experimental design used when Sinclair first introduced the "HC" product in 1926. It remained in use for a very short period of time, probably less than one year, before being replaced by the red/white/green HC logo.

SINCLAIR HIGH COMPRESSION
(5)   1929-EXP   One-piece Baked   No Listing
White globe with red outline ring around green face. Red circle in center, with white "HIGH" with green dropshade in center circle. White "SINCLAIR" arched around top, "COMPRESSION" around bottom. Dated 1929.

SINCLAIR H-C
(5)   1926-1928   One-piece Sphere Baked No Listing
SINCLAIR H-C
(3)   1926-1935   One-piece Etched $650-$1,100
SINCLAIR H-C
(3)   1926-1935   One-piece Baked $500-$850
SINCLAIR H-C
(5)   1926-1935   One-piece Flat Face   No Listing
White globe with green and white outline ring around green globe face. White outline around red center circle, with white "H-C" on red circle. White "SINCLAIR" arched around top, "GASOLINE" around bottom.

SINCLAIR H-C (small ball-shaped)
(5)   1926-1930   One-piece Baked   No Listing
Small 6in diameter spherical lightpost globe with "SINCLAIR HC" logo.

SINCLAIR AIRCRAFT
(4)   1925-1928   One-piece Etched $1,800-$3,000
White globe with green and white outline ring around green globe face. White outline around green center circle. Red and white detailed airplane in center circle, with wings extending into outer area. White "SINCLAIR" arched around top, "AIRCRAFT" around bottom.

SINCLAIR AIRCRAFT
(4)   1928-1931   One-piece Baked $1,600-$2,500
White globe with black and white outline around red globe face. White

outline around red center circle. White and black detailed airplane in center circle, with wings extending into outer area. Fifteen-inch white "SINCLAIR" arched around top, "AIRCRAFT" around bottom.

SINCLAIR AIRCRAFT
(5)   1928-1931   13.5in Glass   No Listing
Black and white outline around red globe face. White outline around red center circle. Black and white detailed airplane in center, with white "SINCLAIR" arched around top, "AVIATION" around bottom.

SINCLAIR AVIATION
(5)   1925-1931   One-piece Etched   No Listing
White globe with green and red outline around green globe face. Red outline around green center circle, with white-outlined non-detailed airplane in center. White "SINCLAIR" arched around top, "AVIA-TION" around bottom.

SINCLAIR OILS
(5)   1930-1940   15in Metal   No Listing
SINCLAIR OILS
(5)   1930-1940   13.5in Glass $650-$1,100
Green and white outline around green globe face. White and green outline around center circle, with green and white vertical stripes. White "SINCLAIR" arched around top, "OILS" around bottom.

SINCLAIR GASOLINE
(5)   1930s   15in Metal $600-$1,100
SINCLAIR GASOLINE
(4)   1930-1937   13.5in Glass $375-$625
Same as SINCLAIR OILS above, with "GASOLINE" replacing "OILS."

SINCLAIR H-C
(5)   1930s   15in Metal $650-$1,250
SINCLAIR H-C
(1)   1930-1954   13.5in Glass $275-$350
SINCLAIR H-C
(1)   1950-1954   13.5in Capco $125-$200
Green and white outline around green globe face. White outline around red center circle. White "H-C" in center circle, with white "SINCLAIR" arched around top, "GASOLINE" around bottom.

SINCLAIR GREEN
(5)   1932   13.5in Glass   No Listing
White globe face with green outline ring and green outline around white center circle. Red and white vertical stripes in center circle, with green band across center. White "GREEN" on band. Red "SIN-CLAIR" arched around top, "GASOLINE" around bottom.

SINCLAIR US MOTOR SPEC w/decal
(5)   1930   One-piece decaled $650-$1,100
White one-piece globe, with red and white "SINCLAIR/U.S. MOTOR/SPECIFICATIONS" decal on body.

SINCLAIR US MOTOR SPEC-1
(4)   1933-1935   13.5in Glass $300-$500
White globe face with red outline ring. Red "U.S. MOTOR/SPECIFI-CATIONS" across center, with red "SINCLAIR" arched around top and "GASOLINE" around bottom.

SINCLAIR US MOTOR SPEC-2
(3)   1935-1938   13.5in Glass $325-$525
White globe face with red outline ring. Green band across lower globe face, with white "U.S. MOTOR/SPECIFICATIONS" on band. Red "SINCLAIR" arched around top.

SINCLAIR US MOTOR SPEC-3
(4)   1935-1938   13.5in Glass $300-$500
Same as above, with black band instead of green.

SINCLAIR US MOTOR SPEC
(5)   1930s   13.5in Plastic   No Listing
Same as above, with green band.

SINCLAIR ETHYL (EGC)
(3)   1937-1946   13.5in Glass $300-$500
Red globe face with white outline ring. White "SINCLAIR" arched around top, large Ethyl (EGC) logo without rays on lower face.

SINCLAIR ETHYL (EGC-OUTLINED)
(3)   1946-1947   13.5in Glass $300-$500
Same as above, with black outline around white "SINCLAIR" letter-ing.

SINCLAIR ETHYL (EC-OUTLINED)
(3)   1946-1947   13.5in Glass $300-$500
Same as above, with black outline around white "SINCLAIR" lettering and newer Ethyl (EC) logo.

SINCLAIR ETHYL GASOLINE
(4)   1947-1953   13.5in Glass $300-$500
Red globe face with black outline ring. Black outline around white center circle. White "SINCLAIR" with black dropshade arched around top, "GASOLINE" around bottom, with small Ethyl (EC) logo with yellow rays in center circle.

SINCLAIR DIESEL (dark green)
(2)   1935-1955   13.5in Glass $225-$325

Dark green globe face with black outline ring. White "Sinclair" across top, large white "DIESEL" across center, and white dot on lower face.

SINCLAIR PENNANT
(3)   1930-1933   13.5in Glass $325-$550
Red globe face with thick white outline area. White pennant flag with black details across center of face. Black "PENNANT" on flag. White "SINCLAIR" across upper globe face above flag. Various shades of red background exist.

SINCLAIR FARM PRODUCTS
(5)   1930s-1940s   13.5in Glass   No Listing
Exact description not available. Tractor on globe face.

SINCLAIR POWER-X
(1)   1953-1957   13.5in Glass $200-$325
SINCLAIR POWER-X
(1)   1953-1957   13.5in Capco $125-$175
White globe face with red outline ring. Red "POWER-X" arched across center of face. Green "SINCLAIR" arched above "POWER-X," with green "THE SUPER FUEL" below.

SINCLAIR "?"
(4)   1953 SPEC   13.5in Glass $275-$400
SINCLAIR POWER-X globe, as listed above, with silver decal covering globe face. Red question mark "?" on silver decal.

SINCLAIR HC (retrofit)
(5)   1954-1959   15in Metal $600-$900
SINCLAIR HC (new-green on white)
(1)   1954-1959   13.5in Glass $200-$325
SINCLAIR HC (new-green on white)
(1)   1954-1959   13.5in Capco $100-$150
White globe face with green outline ring. Large green "H-C" across center. Red "SINCLAIR" above "H-C," with "GASOLINE" below.

SINCLAIR UPSIDE-DOWN H-C ERROR GLOBE
(5)   1950s   13.5in Capco   No Listing
One of the very few "error globes" known to exist, a collector in North Carolina owns a single Sinclair lens as described above, with the green "H-C" in the center printed upside down in relation to the red printing on the globe. Error globes are extremely rare, as most would have been discarded in production.

SINCLAIR POWER-X 100
(1)   1957-1961   13.5in Capco $125-$175
White globe face with orange outline ring. Orange "POWER-X" arched across center. Green "SINCLAIR" arched across top, green "OVER" above orange "100," above green "OCTANE" on lower face.

SINCLAIR DIESEL (light green/old letters)
(2)   1950-1959   13.5in Glass $100-$175
Light green globe face with white outline ring. White old-style block "Sinclair" over large white "DIESEL." White dot at bottom of face.

SINCLAIR H-C
(5)   1959-1961   13.5in Capco   No Listing
White globe face with green outline ring. Large green "H-C" across center of face. Orange italic "Sinclair" (new-style "dino" lettering) across upper globe face, "GASOLINE" across lower face.

SINCLAIR DINO POWER-X
(2)   1959-1961   13.5in Capco $125-$175
White globe face with green outline ring. Green, white, and orange Sinclair logo with dinosaur at top of face. Orange "POWER-X" arched across center of face over orange "GASOLINE."

SINCLAIR DINO GASOLINE
(1)   1961-1970   13.5in Capco $75-$125
White globe face with green outline ring. Large green "DINO" arched across center of face. Green, white, and orange Sinclair logo with dinosaur at top of face. Orange "GASOLINE" below "DINO."

SINCLAIR DINO SUPREME
(1)   1961-1970   13.5in Capco $75-$125
White globe face with green outline ring. Green "DINO" arched across center of face. Green, white, and orange Sinclair logo with dinosaur at top of face. Orange "SUPREME" below "DINO."

SINCLAIR DIESEL
(2)   1959-1970   13.5in Capco $100-$175
Light green globe face with white outline ring. White italic "Sinclair" (new-style "dino" lettering) across upper face. Large white "DIESEL" across center. White dot on lower face. Color variations exist.

SINCLAIR SUPER FLAME KEROSENE
(4)   1959-1970   13.5in Capco $200-$350
Green globe face with black and white outline rings. Red "flame" in center, with white "SuperFlame" across flame. White italic "Sinclair" (new-style lettering) across top, "KEROSENE" across bottom.

SINCLAIR MARINE
(4)   1950-1959   13.5in Capco $150-$225
White globe face with green outline ring. Green "MARINE" across center of face. Red "SINCLAIR" across, above "MARINE," with small red "GASOLINE" below.

SINCLAIR MARINE
(4)   1959-1970   13.5in Capco $150-$200
Same as above, with orange italic "Sinclair" (new-style lettering) across upper globe face and orange "GASOLINE" below.

SINCLAIR HI-TEST H-C
(5)   1953 EXP.   13.5in Glass   No Listing
Experimental for 1953. White globe face with red outline ring. Red "SINCLAIR" arched around top in lettering like on POWER-X globe. Green "Hi-Test" arched across center, above red circle on lower face. White "H-C" on circle.

SINCLAIR 3-check H-C
(5)   1956 EXP.   13.5in Glass   No Listing
Part of a 1956 marketing experiment that included reimaging stations in several select markets, including Morristown, Tennessee, and Macon, Georgia, that used the Triple-Check theme in signage and pump imaging. By the 1950s the "HC" image was becoming very out-of-date, and the Triple-Check was the first step toward the 1958-59 "Dino" reimaging.
Globe details include a white globe face with very dark green area at top of globe. Three check marks–red, white, and light green– on dark green area. Red "SINCLAIR" across, below dark green area, with green "H-C" on lower globe face over red "GASOLINE."

SINCLAIR 3-check POWER X
(5)   1956 EXP.   13.5in Glass   No Listing
Same as SINCLAIR 3-CHECK HC above, with red "POWER-X" arched below "SINCLAIR" and green "THE SUPER FUEL" across lower globe face.

Pierce Petroleum Corporation, St. Louis, Missouri

Primarily a production and refining affiliate of the Standard Oil Trust, Pierce Petroleum operated as Waters-Pierce Oil Company prior to 1920. The company did extensive gasoline marketing in Mexico. It entered gasoline marketing in the south central states in the early 1920s. Pierce was purchased by and rebranded Sinclair in 1930.

PIERCE PENNANT
(4)   1920-1930   One-piece Etched $1,400-$2,000
PIERCE PENNANT
(4)   1920-1930   One-piece Baked $900-$1,400
White globe with orange and green outline rings around face. Large green pennant flag across center of face, with white-outlined orange "PENNANT" on flag. Green "PIERCE" arched around top, "GASOLINE" around bottom.

PIERCE PENNANT (square)
(5)   1925-1930   Square metal band $750-$1,000
Large rectangular metal-frame globe with flat faces. Light green and black outlines around olive-green globe face. Large 15in light green pennant flag, with dark green "PENNANT" on flag on upper face. Fifteen-inch light green "GASOLINE" below flag. Light green "PIERCE PETROLEUM CORPORATION" across lower face.

PENNANT GAS AND OIL w/heart
(5)   1920s   15in Metal   No Listing
Description not available.

Producers and Refiners Oil Company, Independence, Kansas

Producers and Refiners Oil Company, or Parco, was a Rocky Mountain refiner and marketer partially owned by Prairie Oil and Gas. When Sinclair purchased Prairie in the early 1930s, they also acquired part ownership of Parco. They purchased the remaining portions in 1934 and the operation was rebranded Sinclair.

PARCO
(4)   1920-1929   One-piece Etched $850-$1,400
White globe with red-ripple-outlined circular logo covering most of globe face. Blue "PARCO" in circle. Blue "GASOLINE" arched below logo.

PARCO
(4)   1925-1929   15in Metal $350-$550
White globe face with large red-ripple-edged and outlined logo covering most of face. Blue "PARCO" across logo.

PARCO
(4)   1929-1934   13.5in Glass $225-$350
White globe face with large red-ripple-edged and outlined logo covering most of face. Blue "PARCO" across logo.

PARCO ETHYL
(4)   1929-1934   13.5in Glass $200-$350
Red globe face with blue outline ring. Blue outline around white center circle. White "PARCO" arched around top, "GASOLINE" around bottom, with large Ethyl (EGC) logo in center.

Little America Refining Company, Little America, Wyoming

Wyoming refiner and marketer Little America Refining Company, or Larco, had ties to Fletcher Oil Company. The Larco brand was purchased by Sinclair in 1955. Larco marketed under the Covey brand name in the 1950s.

LARCO GASOLINE w/bird
(4)   1930s   15in Metal $500-$850
White globe face with large grey-outlined blue chevron-shaped shield covering most of face. White "LARCO" across top and white "GASO-LINE" across bottom, with blue-outlined white bird flying toward lower left center of shield. Light blue bands extend upward from bird's wings.

COVEY REGULAR
(4)   1950s   13.5in Capco $300-$650
Globe face features Bonneville Race Car—no other details known.

COVEY ETHYL
(4)   1950s   13.5in Capco $300-$650
Globe face features Bonneville Race Car—no other details known.

Simpson Oil Company, St. Louis, Missouri

Missouri marketer purchased by Sinclair in 1961. The Simpson Super A brand survived as a Sinclair secondary brand until 1965.

SIMPSON OIL CO. GASOLINE/OILS
(5)   1930-1940   15in Metal $350-$525
White globe face with large black script "Simpson" across top. Underline under "Simpson" in black, with white "OIL CO." on underline. Red "GASOLINE" arched around top, "OILS" around bottom.

SIMPSON OIL CO. PREMIUM GASOLINE
(3)   1940-1955   13.5in Capco $100-$150
White globe face with red script "Simpson" across center of face, above red "OIL CO." Blue "PREMIUM" arched around top, "GASOLINE" around bottom.

SIMPSON'S PREMIUM ETHYL (EC)
(2)   1946-1955   13.5in Capco $100-$150
White globe face with blue outline ring around white center circle. Large Ethyl (EC) logo in center, with red "SIMPSON'S PREMIUM" arched around top, "ETHYL" around bottom.

SUPER A HI-OCTANE GASOLINE
(2)   1955-1964   13.5in Glass $225-$350
White globe face with blue outline ring. Large red "A" in center, with blue script "Super" arched across "A." Red "HI-OCTANE" arched around top, blue "GASOLINE" around bottom.

SUPER A ETHYL (EC)
(2)   1955-1964   13.5in Glass $225-$350
White globe face with blue outline ring. Large red "A" positioned above center, with blue script "Super" across "A." Small Ethyl (EC) logo in 15in circle at bottom of globe face.

Stoll Refining Company, Louisville, Kentucky

Louisville refiner and marketer founded in 1896. Stoll was involved in kerosene and lubricants in the early years of this century. The company entered gasoline marketing in the 1920s and continued supplying stations until 1948, when Stoll was purchased by Sinclair. Their "Golden Tip" stations were rebranded Sinclair about 1952.

SILVER TIP
(5)   1920s   One-piece Baked $1,000-$1,600
White globe face with green "STOLL'S" arched around top, "GIVES WINGS TO YOUR CAR" arched around bottom, with large red script "SilverTip" over red "GASOLINE" in center.

STOLL "S"
(5)   1920-1930   15in Metal   No Listing
White globe face with gold and blue outline rings. Large gold-outlined blue "S" with detailed wings top and bottom covering most of globe face. Blue-outlined gold "STOLL" across center of globe face.

STOLL'S GOLDEN TIP GASOLINE
(5)   1930s   15in Metal $450-$750
White globe face with black "STOLL'S" arched around top, "GASO-LINE" around bottom, with large black arrow in center. Blue-outlined yellow arrowhead on arrow, and white lettering "GOLDEN TIP" on body of arrow.

GOLDEN TIP ETHYL
(5)   1930s   15in Metal $375-$600
Golden-yellow globe face with black outline ring. Large blue "ETHYL" across center, with smaller blue "GOLDEN-TIP" arched around top. Fifteen-inch white circle at bottom, with small Ethyl (EGC) logo in circle.

STOLL'S SILVER TIP
(5)   1930s   15in Metal $750-$1,000
White globe face with green "STOLL'S" arched around top, "GIVES

WINGS TO YOUR CAR" arched around bottom, and large red script "SilverTip" over red "GASOLINE" in center.

GOLDEN TIP GOES
(4)   1940-1952   13.5in Glass $275-$450
GOLDEN TIP GOES
(5)   1940-1952   13.5in Capco $200-$325
Golden-yellow globe face with blue lower 1/3. Large blue arrow across upper area, with yellow "GOLDEN TIP" on arrow. Yellow "GOES" in blue area below.

GOLDEN TIP ETHYL
(4)   1940-1952   13.5in Glass $275-$450
Golden-yellow globe face with black outline ring. Large blue "ETHYL" across center, with smaller blue "GOLDEN-TIP" arched around top. Fifteen-inch white circle at bottom, with small Ethyl (EGC) logo in circle.

SILVER TIP
(4)   1940-1952   13.5in Glass $250-$375
SILVER TIP
(5)   1940-1952   13.5in Capco $200-$325
Blue globe face with black outline ring. Yellow upper 1/3 of face. Blue circle on upper yellow area, with yellow "STOLL" "S" and wings on circle. White script "SilverTip" across lower blue area, above white "GASOLINE."

Okaw Valley Oil Company

Sinclair marketer—no details known.

OKAW VALLEY SINCLAIR GAS
(5)   1930-1935   15in Metal   No Listing
White globe face with red "OKAW VALLEY" arched around top over design. Red "OIL CO." arched around bottom, with black "SIN-CLAIR/GAS" across center of face.

Richfield Oil Company of New York

Although they are Sinclair affiliates, Richfield of New York, Sherwood-Betholine, and Rio Grande are listed under RICHFIELD for clarity.

SKELLY OIL COMPANY, Tulsa, Oklahoma

Skelly Oil Company was founded in Tulsa, Oklahoma, in 1919 from the holdings of oil trader William Grove Skelly. The company was involved in gasoline marketing from the beginning, and actively purchased chains of service stations throughout the midcontinent area during the early years. During the depression Skelly defaulted on loans, and control of the company fell into the hands of Standard Oil of New Jersey (Exxon), which formed the Mission Corporation to operate its interest in Skelly and Tidewater Oil.

J. Paul Getty, in an attempt to gain control of Tidewater, purchased control of Mission in 1937, only to find that he had also gained control of Skelly. Getty retained majority interest in Skelly until the 1960s, when the remaining interests were purchased and Skelly was merged into Getty, along with Tidewater. The company continued to operate somewhat independently throughout the 1970s, and in 1983 Skelly began a gradual changeover to the Getty brand. Getty's purchase by Texaco halted the rebranding, however, and most Skelly locations were rebranded Texaco by 1985. See the Flying A section for more information.

SKELLY One-piece
(3)   1919-1928   One-piece Baked $400-$700
White globe, with red-outlined red, white, and blue "SKELLY" diamond logo covering most of face.

SKELLY One-piece Inverted
(4)   1919-1928   One-piece Baked $250-$400
Same as above, with design inverted for globe to be used as under canopy light globe.

SKELLY
(5)   1919-1928   15in Metal $600-$1,000
White globe face with large "SKELLY" diamond logo covering most of face.

SKELLY IT'S BETTER
(5)   1919-1928   15in Metal $650-$1,100
White globe face with smaller "SKELLY" diamond logo in center. Black "IT'S BETTER" arched around top, "GASOLINE" around bottom.

SKELLY AROMAX
(3)   1928-1940   13.5in Glass $225-$350
Red globe face with blue outline ring. Large blue-outlined blue diamond logo covering most of face, with red logotype lettering "ARO-MAX" replacing "SKELLY" in center band of diamond. Center white band extends beyond diamond to edge of globe face.

SKELLY AROMAX ETHYL
(3)   1928-1936   13.5in Glass $250-$450
White globe face with red outline ring and red circle in center. Blue "SKELLY" arched around top, "AROMAX" around bottom, with Ethyl (EGC) logo with yellow rays on center red circle.
SKELLY POWERMAX
(3)   1936-1940   13.5in Glass $225-$350
White globe face with blue outline ring. Red-outlined blue Skelly diamond logo covers most of face. Red "POWERMAX" replaces "SKELLY" in center band of diamond.
SKELLY FORTIFIED
(3)   1940-1950   13.5in Glass $225-$350
Red globe face with blue and white outline rings. Red, white, and blue "SKELLY" diamond in center, with small white star to either side. White "FORTIFIED" arched around top, "GASOLINE" around bottom.
SKELLY FORTIFIED PREMIUM
(3)   1940-1950   13.5in Glass $225-$350
White globe face with blue outline ring. Red, white, and blue "SKEL-LY" diamond logo in center, with small red star to either side. Red "FORTIFIED" with blue dropshade arched around top, "PREMIUM" around bottom.
SKELLY MOTOPOWER DIESEL
(4)   1940-1956   13.5in Glass $200-$350
White globe face with red outline ring. Red, white, and blue "SKEL-LY" diamond logo in center. Red "MOTOPOWER" with speed lines arched around top, blue "DIESEL FUEL" arched around bottom.
SKELLY
(3)   1940s   13.5in Glass $225-$325
SKELLY
(4)   1940s   13.5in Capco $100-$150
White globe face with large red, white, and blue "SKELLY" diamond logo covering most of face.
SKELLY GASOLINE
(2)   1950-1956   13.5in Glass $200-$350
SKELLY GASOLINE
(3)   1950-1956   13.5in Capco $125-$175
Red globe face with blue and white outline ring. Red, white, and blue "SKELLY" diamond logo at top of face, with white "GASOLINE" arched up below sign. Three white stars below arch of "GASOLINE."
SKELLY PREMIUM
(2)   1950-1954   13.5in Glass $200-$350
SKELLY PREMIUM
(3)   1950-1954   13.5in Capco $100-$150
White globe face with blue outline ring. Red, white, and blue "SKEL-LY" diamond logo at top of face, with red "PREMIUM" arched up below logo. Three red stars below arch of "PREMIUM."
SKELLY SUPREME
(1)   1954-1956   13.5in Glass $200-$350
Same as SKELLY PREMIUM above, with red "SUPREME" with blue dropshade replacing "PREMIUM," and four blue stars replacing three red stars.
SKELLY REGULAR
(1)   1956-1972   13.5in Capco $100-$175
Red globe face with blue and white outline rings. Red, white, and blue new-style "SKELLY" diamond logo at top of face. New-style logo has smaller red "SKELLY" lettering, with white in lines and textured "S." White "REGULAR" arched up below logo, with three white stars below arch of "REGULAR."
SKELLY KEOTANE within lines
(1)   1956-1972   13.5in Capco $100-$175
White globe face with blue outline ring. Red, white, and blue new-style "SKELLY" diamond logo at top of face. Blue-outlined red "Keotane" arched up underneath logo. Four blue-outlined white stars below arch of "Keotane."
SKELLY MOTOPOWER DIESEL
(4)   1956-1965   13.5in Capco $100-$175
White globe face with red outline ring. New-style "SKELLY" diamond logo in center, with red "MOTOPOWER" with speed lines arched around top, and blue "DIESEL FUEL" around bottom.
SKELLY #1 DIESEL
(3)   1965-1972   13.5in Capco $100-$150
White globe face with large green "#1" at top, over green "DIESEL." Small red, white, and blue "SKELLY" diamond logo below "DIESEL."
SKELLY #2 DIESEL
(3)   1965-1972   13.5in Capco $100-$150
Same as above, with "#2" replacing "#1."
SKELLY HI-SPEED DIESEL
(5)   1940-1956   13.5in Capco $125-$200
"HI-SPEED" across top and "DIESEL" underneath in green. Skelly logo at bottom in red, white, and blue.

Surfco
A 1960s Skelly secondary brand. No Surfco globes are known to exist.

SOHIO and Affiliates
STANDARD OIL COMPANY OF OHIO, Cleveland, Ohio
Sohio is, of course, Standard Oil of Ohio, which traces its roots to the original formation of Standard Oil by John D. Rockefeller in Cleveland, Ohio, in 1870. Although Standard of New Jersey was to become the "main office" as such after the formation of the Standard Oil Trust in 1882, Standard of Ohio was always considered to be "the original." After the breakup of Standard Oil in 1911, Standard of Ohio was assigned marketing only in Ohio and a small refinery. Being primarily a marketing company, Sohio was a pioneer in service stations, operating a chain of company-owned stations statewide by 1920. The brand name Sohio was introduced in 1928 to identify all the company's marketing.

In their first marketing venture outside Ohio, Sohio purchased Spears and Riddle of Wheeling, West Virginia, a large regional marketer selling gasoline under the Fleet-Wing name. Fleet-Wing Corporation was formed as a subsidiary and the brand was offered to jobbers in the states surrounding Ohio. Sohio opened the first company-owned locations outside Ohio in Newport, Kentucky, in 1956, under the Boron name. Boron had first been used as a brand name for Sohio's super-premium grade of gasoline in 1954. Little was done with the Boron brand until stations were opened in western Pennsylvania in 1962.

In 1969, British Petroleum purchased a controlling interest in Sohio and BP's US marketing subsidiary was transferred to Sohio. About that time Sohio also purchased Scot Service Stations, Incorporated of McLean, Virginia. Boron and BP became Sohio's primary non-Ohio brand names. Fleet-Wing was sold to Pennzoil about 1970. In 1990 BP, having purchased the remaining portions of Sohio, began rebranding stations under the Boron, William Penn, Gas-n-Go, and Gulf (in the Southeast, purchased in 1985) to British Petroleum. Sohio stations were rebranded BP beginning in 1991, and now the entire company markets under the BP name.
RED CROWN GASOLINE
(5)   1912-1920   One-piece Etched $1,700-$2,600
Similar to one below, except with no border, and the crown detail differs. Letters are block style, in red.
RED CROWN GASOLINE
(5)   1917-1927   One-piece Etched $1,800-$2,800
White globe with red outline ring around face. Detailed elaborate red and white crown in center, with red-colored "RED CROWN" arched around top. "GASOLINE" around bottom. Lettering has pointed serifs.
RED CROWN GASOLINE
(4)   1920-1930   15in Metal $450-$1,000
White globe face with green outline ring and green ring around white center circle. Detailed elaborate red and white crown in center circle. Green-outlined red-colored "RED CROWN" arched around top, "GASOLINE" around bottom.
RED CROWN ETHYL GASOLINE
(4)   1926-1928   15in Metal $300-$500
Same as above, with large Ethyl (EGC) logo replacing crown in center circle.
RED CROWN GASOLINE
(4)   1928-1930   15in Metal $450-$850
RED CROWN GASOLINE
(5)   1928-1930   13.5in Glass   No Listing
White globe face with blue outline ring and blue ring around white center circle. Detailed elaborate red and white crown in center circle. Blue-outlined red-colored "RED CROWN" arched around top, "GASOLINE" around bottom.
SOHIO ETHYL GASOLINE
(4)   1928-1934   15in Metal $300-$550
SOHIO ETHYL GASOLINE
(5)   1928-1934   13.5in Glass $300-$450
Red globe face with blue ring around white center circle. Blue-outlined white "SOHIO" arched around top, "GASOLINE" around bottom, with dot at either side. Ethyl (EGC) logo with blue rays in white circle.
SOHIO X-70
(5)   1930-1934   15in Metal $275-$450
SOHIO X-70
(3)   1930-1950   13.5in Glass $225-$350
Globe face divided into three even horizontal bands. Red on top, white across center, and blue on bottom. Blue lettering on white center band "SOHIO/X-70."

Miscellaneous Sinclair globes. R. V. Witherspoon

Miscellaneous Sinclair globes. R. V. Witherspoon

Various Sohio 13.5in inserts on glass bodies.

Skelly Premium 13.5in inserts on glass body.

Sohio Gasoline 15in inserts on metal body.

Skelly one-piece fired-on globe, Red X Gasoline 13.5in inserts on red plastic body, and Top Octane 12.5in inserts on glass body.

Sohio X-70 15in inserts on metal body.

Sohio Extron Marine 13.5in inserts on glass body.

Sohio Pre-Mixed Outboard Marine Gasoline 13.5in inserts on glass body.

Canfield Ethyl one-piece fired-on small 8in globe, 4in base.

SOHIO ETHYL
(4)　　　1934-1939　　　13.5in Glass　　　$225-$350
White globe face with black outline ring. Blue-outlined red lettering "SOHIO/ETHYL" on upper globe face, over small Ethyl (EGC) logo with yellow rays in 15in circle at bottom.
RENOWN GREEN
(5)　　　1932-1934　　　13.5in Glass　　　$200-$325
White globe face with green outline ring. Green "RENOWN" diagonally on upper globe face, above horizontal "GREEN."
RENOWN
(4)　　　1934-1942　　　13.5in Glass　　　$200-$300
White globe face with red outline ring. Blue "RENOWN" diagonally across face.
SOHIO X-TANE
(3)　　　1940-1958　　　13.5in Glass　　　$225-$350
White globe face with red half-circles top and bottom. Blue "SOHIO/X-TANE" across center white area of globe.
SOHIO SUPREME
(3)　　　1939-1954　　　13.5in Glass　　　$200-$350
White globe face with blue vertical tapered line top and bottom. Blue-outlined red "SOHIO" above italic blue "SUPREME" across globe face.
SOHIO KEROSENE
(3)　　　1940-1970　　　13.5in Glass　　　$200-$325
White globe face with red "SOHIO" over blue "KEROSENE." Small red dot at bottom.
KEROSENE
(4)　　　1950s　　　13.5in Glass　　　$175-$275
White globe face with red "KEROSENE" across face.
SOHIO DIESEL red/white/blue
(5)　　　1946-1950　　　13.5in Glass　　　$225-$350
White globe face with red half-circle at top edged in red lines and blue half-circle at bottom edged in blue lines. Red "SOHIO" over italic blue "DIESEL" in center white band.
SOHIO DIESEL
(3)　　　1950-1970　　　13.5in Glass　　　$200-$325
White globe face with red "SOHIO" over blue "DIESEL." Small red dot at bottom.
DIESEL SUPREME
(3)　　　1950s　　　13.5in Glass　　　$200-$325
DIESEL SUPREME (Retrofit)
(5)　　　1950s　　　15in Metal　　　$250-$400
White globe face with light blue "DIESEL" over red "SUPREME." Black line between "DIESEL" and "SUPREME."
SOHIO AVIATION
(4)　　　1946-1970　　　13.5in Glass　　　$400-$650
White globe face with red "SOHIO" over blue "AVIATION." Small red dot at bottom.
SOHIO AVIATION
(4)　　　1946-1970　　　13.5in Glass　　　$400-$650
Same as above, but without the red dot.
SOHIO HEAT
(5)　　　1946-1970　　　13.5in Glass　　　$250-$400
White globe face with red "SOHIO" over blue "HEAT." Small red dot at bottom.
SOHIO MARINE GASOLINE
(4)　　　1946-1954　　　13.5in Glass　　　$375-$600
Blue globe face with white wave area at bottom. White "SOHIO/MARINE" on blue area, with red "GASOLINE" on white wave at bottom.
SOHIO PRE-MIXED OUTBOARD
(5)　　　1946-1958　　　13.5in Glass　　　$450-$650
White globe face with red and blue nautical flag on center of face. Blue-outlined red and white Sohio logo (oval and triangles) on flag. Red "PRE- ," blue "MIXED" over red "OUTBOARD" at top, red "MARINE" over blue "GASOLINE" at bottom.
BORON SUPREME
(1)　　　1954-1962　　　13.5in Glass　　　$200-$325
White globe face with diagonal red, white, and blue stripe design at top, just right of center. Blue "BORON" across center of face, with red script "SUPREME" below "BORON."
EXTRON
(1)　　　1958-1962　　　13.5in Glass　　　$200-$325
Similar to BORON SUPREME above, with red, white, and blue stripes at upper right and lower left. Blue "EXTRON" with red "X" across center of globe face.
OCTRON
(4)　　　1960s-1980s　　　13.5in Glass　　　No Listing
White globe body with red letter "OCTRON" decal across body.
BORON MARINE
(4)　　　1954-1962　　　13.5in Glass　　　$300-$475
Same as BORON SUPREME above, with blue "MARINE" replacing "SUPREME."

EXTRON MARINE
(5)　　　1958-1962　　　13.5in Glass　　　$325-$475
Same as EXTRON above, with blue "MARINE" replacing lower stripes.

Caldwell & Taylor, Cincinnati, Ohio

Cincinnati-based marketer purchased by Sohio in 1928.
CALDWELL & TAYLOR ORIGINAL BENZOL GAS
(5)　　　1910s-1920s　　　One-piece etched　　　$1,200-$2,000
White globe with black "CALDWELL" arched around top, "& TAYLOR" around bottom, and large diagonal "BENZOL" across face. Small "ORIGINAL" above "BENZOL," and "-GAS" horizontal under "BENZOL."
CALDWELL & TAYLOR GAS
(5)　　　1920s　　　One-piece Etched　　　$1,200-$2,000
Black letters, except "BENZOL" which is in red. Words are one an top of another across globe face.
CALDWELL & TAYLOR ORIGINAL BENZOL GAS
(5)　　　1920s　　　15in Metal　　　No Listing
Same description as the first one-piece above.
CALDWELL & TAYLOR ORIGINAL BENZOL GAS
(5)　　　1927-1928　　　13.5in Glass balcrank　　　No Listing
Same description as the second one-piece above.

Spears & Riddle, Wheeling, West Virginia

A large regional wholesale operation founded in the 1870s, Spears & Riddle sold gasoline under the Fleet-Wing brand name. Sohio purchased Spears & Riddle in 1928, and created the Fleet-Wing Corporation as a marketing subsidiary to brand jobbers in Ohio and surrounding states. Pennzoil purchased Fleet-Wing from Sohio about 1970, and continues to operate about a dozen stations under the Fleet-Wing name.
FLEET-WING ETHYL (EGC)
(4)　　　1928-1935　　　15in Metal　　　$375-$550
White globe face with blue "FLEET-WING" arched at top, over large Ethyl (EGC) logo with black rays.
FLEET-WING THAT'S ALL
(5)　　　1930s　　　Red Two-piece Glass　　　$450-$800
Two-piece glass halves assembled back-to-back. Red frame with blue outline ring around white face. Blue "FLEET-WING" arched at top over red oval, with blue-outlined white wings. White "THAT'S ALL" on oval.
FLEET-WING ETHYL
(5)　　　1930s　　　Red Two-piece Glass　　　$450-$800
Two-piece glass halves assembled back-to-back. Red frame with blue outline ring around white face. Blue "FLEET-WING" arched at top, over Ethyl (EGC) logo with blue rays.
FLEET-WING THAT'S ALL
(5)　　　1930s　　　13.5in Red Glass　　　$400-$750
White globe face with blue, white, and red outline rings. Blue "FLEET-WING" arched at top, over red oval with blue-outlined white wings. White "THAT'S ALL" on oval.
SAY FLEET-WING THAT'S ALL
(5)　　　1930s　　　13.5in Red Glass　　　$400-$750
White globe face with blue, white, and red outline rings. Large red bird with both wings up, on lower face. Blue "FLEET-WING" arched above bird. Red "SAY" above "FLEET-WING," red "THAT'S ALL" to right of bird.
FLEET-WING
(4)　　　1930s　　　13.5in Red Glass　　　$400-$750
White globe face with blue, white, and red outline rings. Large red bird, one wing up and one wing down, on center of face with red speed lines. Blue "FLEET-WING" superimposed over bird.
FLEET-WING ETHYL (EGC) (red bird)
(4)　　　1930s　　　13.5in Red Glass　　　$400-$750
White globe face with blue, white, and red outline rings. Smaller red bird, one wing up and one wing down, on center of face, with blue "FLEET" arched above horizontal "WING" on upper face. Small blue "-" under "E" in "FLEET." Small Ethyl (EGC) logo with yellow rays off-set right of center on lower globe face.
FLEET-WING
(4)　　　1935-1940　　　Gill　　　$375-$550
White globe face with blue, white, and red outline rings. Large red bird with blue details and red speed lines, one wing up and one wing down, on center of face. Blue "FLEET" over upper wing, "WING" over lower wing.
FLEET-WING ETHYL (EGC) (no bird)
(4)　　　1935-1940　　　Gill　　　$275-$450
White globe face with blue, white, and red outline rings. Large blue "FLEET-WING" arched at top over Ethyl (EGC) logo.

FLEET-WING ETHYL (EGC) (red bird)

(4)	1935-1940	Gill	$275-$500

White globe face with blue, white, and red outline rings. Large red bird with blue details and red speed lines, one wing up and one wing down, on center of face. Blue "FLEET-WING" arched at top, superimposed over bird wing, with small Ethyl (EGC) logo offset to lower right bottom.

FLEET-WING

(3)	1940-1965	13.5in Glass	$225-$375

FLEET-WING

(2)	1940-1965	13.5in Red Capco	$175-$300

White globe face with red soaring bird at top, above red "FLEET-WING" with blue dropshade.

FLEET-WING SUPER ETHYL (EGC)

(4)	1940-1955	13.5in Glass	$275-$450

White globe face with blue outline ring. Red soaring bird at top, above red "FLEET-WING" with blue dropshade. Blue "SUPER" with red dropshade above outlined circle, with Ethyl (EGC) logo on lower globe face.

FLEET-WING GOLDEN

(4)	1940-1955	13.5in Glass	$250-$425

White globe face with blue outline ring. Red soaring bird at top, above red "FLEET-WING" with blue dropshade. Yellow "GOLDEN" with blue dropshade above red horizontal lines on lower globe face.

FLEET-WING SUPER

(4)	1955-1960	13.5in Glass	$250-$425

White globe face with blue band on lower 1/3. Red soaring bird at top, above red "FLEET-WING" with blue dropshade. White "SUPER" on lower blue area.

FLEET-WING GOLDEN

(4)	1955-1960	13.5in Glass	$250-$425

White globe face with blue band on lower 1/3. Red soaring bird at top, above red "FLEET-WING" with blue dropshade. White "GOLDEN" on lower blue area.

FLEET-WING FLITE

(4)	1955-1960	13.5in Glass	$200-$300

White globe face with green outline ring and green "FLITE" with black dropshade across face. *Note:* Red bodies are Hull-type bodies. At least one example is known that has one side hollow as in a normal Hull body, and one side clear beneath the attached lens.

Refiners Oil Company, Dayton, Ohio

A Dayton, Ohio, based marketer that operated approximately 300 retail stations in Ohio and Indiana. When the General Motors Chemical Company developed the antiknock additive tetraethyl lead in early 1923, Refiners was chosen to test market the new product. The test was so successful that in September of that year, Standard Oil of Indiana signed on to be an exclusive distributor of the new additive, "Ethyl," through its marketing territory. Standard Oil of Ohio purchased Refiners Oil Company in 1930, and rebranded the stations Sohio.

REFINERS GASOLINE (old car)

(5)	1915-1925	15in Metal	No Listing

White globe face with black ring around white center circle. Orange and black car and detailed hill and sunrise scene in center circle. Black "REFINERS" arched around top, "GASOLINE" around bottom.

REFINERS BENZOL GASOLINE

(5)	1920-1925	15in Metal	No Listing

White globe face with black "REFINERS" arched around top, "GASOLINE" around bottom, and large black "BENZOL" across center.

REFINERS AERO GAS (w/plane)

(5)	1920-1925	15in Metal	No Listing

White globe face with "AERO" arched around top, "GASOLINE" around bottom, and airplane scene in center.

REFINERS ETHYL GASOLINE

(4)	1924-1927	16.5in Metal	$300-$500

REFINERS ETHYL GASOLINE

(4)	1924-1927	15in Metal	$300-$475

White globe face with black outline ring and black ring around white center circle. Black "REFINERS" arched around top, "GASOLINE" around bottom, with large Ethyl (EGC) logo with blue rays in center circle.

REFINERS (orange)

(4)	1925-1930	16.5in Metal	$325-$500

REFINERS (orange)

(4)	1925-1930	15in Metal	$325-$475

REFINERS (orange)

(5)	1920s	12in Metal	No Listing

Orange globe face with white outline ring. White bar-and-circle band across center. Black script "REFINERS" on white band.

REFINERS HIGH TEST

(5)	1928-1930	15in Metal	$350-$550

Orange globe face with white outline ring and white band across center. Black script "REFINERS" on white band. White-outlined black "HIGH" on upper orange area, "TEST" on lower orange area.

REFINERS ETHYL PIONEER DISTRIBUTORS

(5)	1927-1930	16.5in Metal	$375-$600

REFINERS ETHYL PIONEER DISTRIBUTORS

(5)	1927-1930	15in Metal	$375-$550

White globe face with black script "REFINERS" across top of face. Ethyl (EGC) logo at bottom, with black rays and black rectangle above logo. Yellow "PIONEER DISTRIBUTORS" on black rectangle.

Canfield Oil Company, Cleveland, Ohio

Founded in Cleveland in 1886, Canfield Oil was primarily a lubricants manufacturer that developed, among others, the William Penn motor oils. Canfield became involved in gasoline marketing in the late 1910s, operating stations in and around Cleveland. When Standard Oil purchased Canfield in 1945, there were over 200 branded stations at that time.

The Sohio brand name gradually replaced the Canfield name, although Canfield and William Penn motor oils continued in production. In the 1970s, after British Petroleum purchased a controlling interest in Standard Oil, many dealer-operated BP stations in the East were rebranded William Penn, continuing as such until the BP name was selected to replace all Sohio affiliate brand names in 1990.

CANFIELD GASOLINE

(5)	1920s	One-piece Etched	$900-$1,600

White globe with outline ring around face. "CANFIELD" arched around top, "GASOLINE" around bottom, with design in center.

CANFIELD ETHYL

(5)	late 1920s	12 or 16in One-piece Baked	No Listing

White globe with outline ring around face. "CANFIELD" arched around top, "ETHYL" around bottom, with Ethyl (EGC) logo in center.

CANZOL

(5)	1920s	One-piece Baked	$600-$900

White globe with black outline ring around yellow globe face and black script "CANZOIL" diagonally across face.

CANFIELD ETHYL GASOLINE

(5)	1920s	One-piece Baked	$750-$900

Small white globe with blue outline ring around face. Blue "CANFIELD" arched around top, "GASOLINE " around bottom, with small Ethyl (EGC) logo in center. Globe 8in tall with 4in base.

CANFIELD

(5)	1930s	13.5in Glass	$300-$500

Red globe face with green outline ring. Green-outlined white script "CANFIELD" across face.

SPUR and Affiliates
MURPHY OIL COMPANY, El Dorado, Arkansas

Murphy traces its origins to the banking, timber, and oil interests of founder C. H. Murphy, brought together in 1907. Oil production began in earnest in the 1920s, and the company shifted almost entirely to oil exploration after WW II. In 1957 Murphy entered the retail market with the purchase of River States Oil Company of Evanston, Illinois. Murphy then introduced the Royal brand name and was expanding successfully when the company purchased Spur Distributing in 1960. By 1962, all the former Royal stations had rebranded Spur and the company added several other marketers to the collection, replacing that operation's brand with Spur. The company brands over 500 Spur stations in fourteen states today.

River States Oil Company, Evanston, Illinois

River States, marketing in Wisconsin, Minnesota, Illinois, and Michigan, was a combination of several north central marketing firms brought together about 1955. In 1957 River States was purchased as the first marketing division of Murphy Oil and the "ROYAL" brand was introduced, replacing the earlier River States brand. In 1962, the Spur brand name replaced Royal at several hundred stations in the north central states.

RS ROYAL

(5)	1957-1962	Oval Capco	$150-$225

White globe face with red outline ring. Very pale blue "RS" screened in background, with red "ROYAL" across face.

Webb Cut Price Gas and Oil, Duluth, Minnesota

Founded about 1925, Webb operated stations in Minnesota,

Wisconsin, and Michigan until about 1957 when they either merged with or rebranded RS Royal.

WEBB'S CUT PRICE OIL/GAS
(5)   1930s   One-piece keyhole shaped No Listing
White keyhole-shaped globe similar to FORD BENZOL globe. Yellow outline around globe face, with large red "WEBB" across center. Red "CUT PRICE" arched around top, red "GAS" above "WEBB," and "OIL" below.

WEBB'S CUT PRICE GASOLINE-on yellow
(5)   1940s   13.5in yellow Capco $175-$325
Description not available.

WEBB'S CUT PRICE REGULAR
(5)   1940-1957   13.5in Capco $150-$250
White globe face with large red "W" over yellow band. Fifteen-inch white "WEBB" over "CUT RATE" on "W." Black "REGULAR" on yellow band below.

WEBB'S CUT PRICE PREMIUM
(5)   1940-1957   13.5in Plastic $150-$250
Same as WEBB'S CUT PRICE REGULAR, but with "PREMIUM" in black.

WEBB ETHYL
(5)   1940-1957   Oval Glass BODY $250-$425

WEBB ETHYL
(4)   1955-1957   Oval Capco $150-$250
White globe face with large red "W" over yellow band. Fifteen-inch white "WEBB" on "W." Black "ETHYL" in yellow band below.

Spur Distributing, Nashville, Tennessee

Founded by John Mason Houghland in Nashville in 1928, Spur Distributing was the original trackside gasoline chain. The company had 348 stations in twenty-one states when they were purchased by Murphy Oil in September 1960. Murphy, which had only recently entered the retail marketing field, marketed under various regional names (Royal, Spur, Ingram) until 1962, when the Spur brand name was chosen as the company's only brand and the others were replaced with the new oval and spur logo. Today, the company supplies about 500 branded stations in fourteen states.

SPUR ANTI-KNOCK GASOLINE
(5)   1928-1930   13.5in Glass $300-$375
Colors cannot be determined, as this globe is known only in a black and white photograph from 1930. Dark color globe face with lighter color band across center. White "SPUR" arched around top, "GASOLINE" around bottom, with "ANTI-KNOCK" on center band.

SPUR "TANK CAR" GLOBE
(4)   1930-1962   13.5in Glass $400-$750
White globe face with blue outline ring. Blue railroad tank car across center of face, with white "SPUR GAS" on tank car. Red "SPUR" arched around top, "GASOLINE" around bottom.

SPUR
(2)   1962-1970   Oval Capco $150-$225
Globe face is Spur oval logo. Blue outline ring around white globe face, with red crescent moon at right side of face. White "spur" rowel on red area. Blue "SPUR" logotype to left of red area.

Wood River Oil Company, Wood River, Illinois

Formed in 1939 as a refiner and marketer. The Ingram family was involved with Wood River from its founding, and eventually Wood River operations in the Wouth were spun off and rebranded Ingram.

WOOD RIVER
(4)   1939-1950   Gill $225-$350
White globe face with blue-outlined red ring around outer edge. Blue band across center, with white "WOOD RIVER" on band.

WOOD RIVER ETHYL (EGC)
(5)   1939-1950   Gill $225-$350
Same as above, with small Ethyl (EGC) logo in black circle below center.

WOOD RIVER
(4)   1950-1970   13.5in Glass $200-$300

WOOD RIVER
(4)   1950-1970   13.5in Capco $100-$150
Red outline ring around globe face. Red upper and lower 1/3 with white band across center. Dark blue "WOOD RIVER" on center band.

Ingram Oil, Nashville, Tennessee

Introduced at Wood River stations in the South in 1956. Murphy Oil purchased the Ingram marketing, 201 stations, in 1961 and rebranded the stations Spur.

INGRAM
(4)   1955-1962   13.5in Glass $225-$325

INGRAM
(4)   1955-1962   13.5in Capco $75-$125

Red outline ring around globe face. Red upper and lower 1/3, with white band across center. Black "INGRAM" on band.

Hempstead Oil Storage Company, Mobile, Alabama

Purchased by Murphy Oil in 1962, and rebranded Spur.

HOSCO
(5)   1950s-1960s   Oval Capco $150-$250
Description not available.

STANDARD and UTOCO
STANDARD OIL COMPANY OF INDIANA, Chicago, Illinois

Formed in 1889 as a refining and marketing division of the Standard Oil Trust, Standard of Indiana had established an extensive marketing organization by the time of the 1911 breakup of Standard. Primarily a marketer, Standard established an extensive network of gasoline stations throughout the Midwest. Involvement with Pan American and Amoco, detailed in the Amoco section of this book, explains Standard's purchase of Pan-Am in order to gain crude oil production. Midwest Oil Refining, listed below, was another producer purchased by Standard in order to keep its extensive refining and marketing operation going.

In 1961, Standard shifted all domestic marketing to the subsidiary American Oil Company. Stations in former Amoco, Pan-Am, and Utoco territory were rebranded American, while stations in the Standard territory remained Standard. In 1974 the Amoco brand replaced American and began to replace Standard, but many stations retain the Standard brand today. Standard Oil of Indiana became Amoco Corporation in 1984.

RED CROWN POLARINE GASOLINE
(5)   1910s   One-piece Etched round No Listing
White globe with no outline around face. Red California-style crown in center, with red-colored "RED CROWN" arched around top and "GASOLINE" around bottom. Small blue "POLARINE" between crown and "GASOLINE."

RED CROWN POLARINE GASOLINE
(5)   1910s   One-piece Etched Oval   No Listing
White oval globe with red-colored "RED CROWN" arched around top, "GASOLINE" with large "O" across center, and blue "POLARINE" arched around bottom. Small red crown in "O" in center.

RED CROWN GASOLINE w/chimney top
(5)   1910s   One-piece Etched   No Listing
White globe with red "RED CROWN" arched around top, "GASOLINE" around bottom, with small red crown in center. Chimney cap globe.

RED CROWN GASOLINE
(5)   1910s   One-piece Etched $1,800-$2,500
Same as above, except no chimney top.

RED CROWN GASOLINE
(3)   1918-1932   16.5in Metal $400-$850

RED CROWN GASOLINE
(3)   1918-1932   15in Metal $400-$800
White globe face with blue outline ring and blue ring around center circle. Red-colored "RED CROWN" arched around top, "GASOLINE" around bottom, with detailed red, white, and blue crown in center circle.

RED CROWN ETHYL GASOLINE
(3)   1926-1932   16.5in Metal $350-$550

RED CROWN ETHYL GASOLINE
(3)   1926-1932   15in Metal $350-$550
White globe face with blue outline ring and blue ring around center circle. Red-colored "RED CROWN" arched around top, "GASOLINE" around bottom, with large Ethyl (EGC) logo in center circle.

SOLITE A PERFECT GASOLINE
(4)   1922-1926   16.5in Metal $375-$700

SOLITE A PERFECT GASOLINE
(4)   1922-1926   15in Metal $375-$650
White globe face with blue outline ring and blue ring around center circle. Red-and-white-outlined blue solid triangle, point down, in center circle. White "A/PERFECT" on blue triangle. Red "SOLITE" arched around top, "GASOLINE" around bottom.

STANOLIND AVIATION
(5)   1925-1946   15in Metal $1,500-$2,400
White globe face with red outline ring. Red ring around Standard "SERVICE" logo in center (blue "STANDARD OIL COMPANY" arched around red center circle, with white torch and white "SERVICE"). Blue "STANOLIND AVIATION" arched around top, "GASOLINE" around bottom.

GASOLINE cast letter crown chimney cap
(5)   1917-1920   One-piece crown   No Listing

Cast one-piece crown with chimney cap. White crown with red upper crown area and green dots on uprights. Red "GASOLINE" cast around base of crown.
GASOLINE etched letter crown
(4)   1920-1926   One-piece crown $1,200-$1,800
Similar to above, with slight bodystyle variation and without chimney cap and with red "GASOLINE" etched letters around base of crown.
RED CROWN (smooth letters)
(3)   1926-1932   One-piece crown $450-$750
Cast one-piece crown with red painted details. White "GASOLINE" cast letters around base of crown.
RED CROWN (ridged letters)
(5)   1926-1932   One-piece crown $450-$800
Same as above, with ridged lettering "RED CROWN" around base of crown.
RED CROWN ETHYL
(5)   1926-1932   One-piece crown   No Listing
Cast one-piece crown with red painted details. White "RED CROWN ETHYL" cast letters around base of crown. Very rare.
RED CROWN ETHYL
(3)   1926-1932   One-piece crown $500-$850
Cast one-piece crown unpainted except for red "RED CROWN ETHYL" cast letters around base of crown.
SOLITE
(4)   1926-1932   One-piece crown $650-$1,000
Cast one-piece crown with blue painted details. White "SOLITE" cast letters around base of crown.
RED CROWN
(1)   1932-1962   One-piece crown $250-$350
Cast one-piece crown with red painted details.
WHITE CROWN
(1)   1932-1956   One-piece crown $225-$325
Cast one-piece crown, unpainted.
BLUE CROWN
(3)   1932-1948   One-piece crown $350-$550
Cast one-piece crown with blue painted details.
GOLD CROWN
(1)   1956-1962   One-piece crown $225-$350
Cast one-piece crown with gold painted details.
RED and GOLD CROWN (dual pumps)
(4)   1956-1962   One-piece crown $350-$600
Cast one-piece crown with red and gold painted details. Used for dual-product twin pumps.
GRAY CROWN–FUEL OIL
(5)   1930s   One-piece crown $350-$600
Cast one-piece crown with gray painted details.
GREEN CROWN–NAPTHA TRACTOR FUEL
(4)   1930s   One-piece crown $400-$650
Cast one-piece crown with green painted details.
ORANGE CROWN–AVIATION
(5)   1930s   One-piece crown   No Listing
Cast one-piece crown with orange painted details.
PURPLE CROWN–MOTOR GRADE
(5)   1930s   One-piece crown   No Listing
Cast one-piece crown with purple painted details.
STANDARD MARINE
(4)   1940s   13.5in Glass $225-$350
STANDARD MARINE
(4)   1950s   13.5in Capco $125-$175
White globe face with red "STANDARD" across center of face. Red "MARINE" arched around top, "GASOLINE" around bottom.
STANDARD DIESEL FUEL
(3)   1950s   13.5in Capco $100-$150
White globe face with red outline ring. Red "DIESEL" across center, with red "STANDARD" arched at top and "FUEL" at bottom.
STANDARD DIESEL FUEL
(3)   1950s   13.5in Capco $100-$150
White globe face with red "STANDARD" across face at center. Red "DIESEL" arched at top, "FUEL" at bottom.
STANDARD FLAME
(2)   1946-1961   One-piece Glass $125-$275
Cast one-piece flame for top of 1946-1961 porcelain Standard, Pan-Am, and Utoco signs. Painted red details.
STANDARD FLAME
(3)   1958-1961   One-piece Plastic $75-$150
Plastic two-piece assembled flame, internally painted, for above listed porcelain signs.

Standard Oil of Nebraska

A marketing operation founded in 1906 and long supplied by Standard of Indiana, Standard of Nebraska merged with Standard of

Indiana in August 1939. Stations retained the Nebraska identification until after the war.
RED CROWN GASOLINE
(4)   1910s-1920s   15in Metal $450-$800
White globe face with small red early Nebraska-style crown in center. Red "RED CROWN" arched around top, "GASOLINE" around bottom.
RED CROWN GASOLINE
(4)   1910s-1920s   15in Metal $450-$750
White globe face with small red early Nebraska-style crown in center. Blue "RED CROWN" arched around top, "GASOLINE" around bottom.
RED CROWN ETHYL
(4)   1920s-1930s   15in Metal $300-$500
Same as above, with 15in center circle with large Ethyl (EGC) logo in center and blue rays.
RED CROWN GASOLINE
(4)   1920s-1930s   15in Metal $450-$800
White globe face with red and black late Nebraska crown in center. Red-colored "RED CROWN" arched around top, "GASOLINE" around bottom.

Midwest Refining Company, Cheyenne, Wyoming

Midwest Refining was a Rocky Mountain producer and refiner when Standard of Indiana purchased controlling interest in the company in 1917. In 1928, Midwest entered the gasoline market, purchasing Arro Oil and Refining of Lewiston, Montana, Aero Oil Company of Cheyenne, Wyoming, and seventy-five gas stations in Colorado and New Mexico from Vickers. The Midwest brand name replaced the individual brands. In April 1930, Standard of Indiana purchased the entire Midwest Refining marketing, and rebranded the stations Standard. The Midwest Refining subsidiary, Utah Oil Refining Company, having ventured into gasoline marketing, continued to market under the Utah Oil brands.

Arro Oil Company, Lewiston, Montana

Purchased by Standard's Midwest Refining subsidiary and rebranded Midwest in 1929. See more details above.
ARRO
(5)   1925-1929   15in Metal   No Listing
Yellow globe face with white band across center and white vertical lines between letters in yellow areas. Black "ARRO" in upper yellow area, "GASOLINE" in lower area, with 15in yellow arrow across center band. Black interlocking letters in center of arrow, with black "NORTHERN MADE" to left and "FOR NORTHERN TRADE" to right.

Utah Oil Refining Company, Salt Lake City, Utah

Founded as a subsidiary of Midwest Refining in 1928, Utah Oil Refining Company marketed motor oils under the Vico name, and gasoline under the Pep 88 brand in Utah and Idaho until after WW II. The Utoco brand was introduced at the end of the war, and gradually replaced Vico-Pep 88. In 1961, when all of Standard's US marketing was assigned to the American Oil Company subsidiary, the American brand name replaced Utoco. In 1974, Amoco replaced American.
VICO
(5)   1930s   One-piece Baked $350-$550
Small white globe with red "VICO" logotype across face.
PEP-88–orange
(5)   1930s   15in Metal   No Listing
PEP-88–orange
(4)   1932-1948   13.5in Glass $250-$375
Orange globe face with white-outlined black "PEP/88" diagonally across face.
PEP-88–red
(4)   1940s   13.5in Capco $150-$275
Same as above, with red globe face.
PEP-88 ETHYL (EGC)
(4)   1932-1942   13.5in Glass $225-$375
Orange globe face with white-outlined black "PEP 88" arched around top, over 15in white circle. Ethyl (EGC) logo with yellow rays in circle.
PEP-88 ETHYL (EGC)
(4)   1932-1942   13.5in Capco $175-$325
Same as above, with red globe face.
PEP-88 ETHYL (EC)
(4)   1942-1948   13.5in Capco $175-$300
Same as PEP-88 ETHYL red above, with Ethyl (EC) logo in circle.
UTOCO
(4)   1948-1961   12.5in Glass $225-$400
UTOCO
(4)   1948-1961   13.5in Capco $150-$300

White globe face with large red, white, and blue 1946 torch and oval Utoco logo covering most of face.

Stanavo

Stanavo was formed in 1929 by Standard Oil of Indiana, New Jersey, and California as a joint venture to research aviation petroleum needs and market those products through their individual marketing outlets. Stanavo first marketed aviation gasoline in 1931. With the withdrawal of Standard of New Jersey in 1937, the other two participants decided to discontinue their efforts as well, and Stanavo was dissolved in June 1938.

STANAVO
(5)   1931-1938   15in Metal   No Listing
White globe face with outlined airplane across center of face. Red "STANAVO" across top, with "AVIATION GASOLINE" to lower right, below airplane.

Trues Oil Company, Spokane, Washington

An independent marketer with stations in Washington, Trues Oil was purchased by Standard in 1959. Stations remained under the Rainbow brand until after 1961, when most were rebranded American. Standard continues to market under the Rainbow name as a secondary brand.

RAINBOW GASOLINE/MOTOR OIL
(5)   1930s   15in Metal $2,500-$4,000
Blue globe face with red, yellow, and green rainbow arched around top, Detailed red car and green gas pump scene under arch of rainbow. White "RAINBOW GASOLINE MOTOR OIL" on lower face.

RAINBOW GAS TRUTEST MOTOR OIL
(5)   1940s   15in Metal   No Listing
White globe face with blue "RAINBOW GASOLINE" arched around top. Red, yellow, and green rainbow arched under lettering, with blue "TRUTEST MOTOR OIL" below rainbow. Blue "TRUES OIL COMPANY" arched around bottom.

STANDARD OIL
STANDARD OIL "INCORPORATED in KENTUCKY," Louisville, Kentucky

Standard Oil of Kentucky was, for fifty years, the world's largest gasoline "jobber." One of the Standard divisions spun off with the 1911 break up of Standard Oil, Standard of Kentucky (commonly called Kyso) was assigned marketing in Kentucky, Florida, Georgia, Alabama, and Mississippi, but had no oil refineries, oil production, or exploration, or oil pipeline connections. It was simply a marketing group with retail service stations in five southeastern states. As a result of this, Kyso contracted with Standard of New Jersey (Esso-Exxon) to supply their needs, and simply sold Esso and Esso Extra gasoline under the Crown and Crown Extra names until 1961. When Esso introduced the super-premium Golden Esso Extra in 1956, Kyso followed with Super Crown Extra. This neat arrangement ended in 1961, when Standard of California (Chevron) purchased Kyso outright and canceled the long-standing Esso supply agreements. Esso scrambled to establish markets in the Kyso territory, and Chevron promptly sued them to limit the use of the Standard trademark "Esso" in the five Kyso states.

Although Esso had unsuccessfully tried to market under the Esso brand name in Indiana Standard territory (St. Louis 1935-1938), they had long since begun using alternate brand names in other territories. The Southeast, however, was different with their already established brand (Kyso sold Esso motor oils), and a court battle ensued. In 1967 Esso lost the rights to the trademark in Kyso territory, and service stations signs were covered with tiger decals until they could be replaced by Enco signs. After a Supreme Court ruling in 1969 confirming this limitation, Esso began the name search process that eventually led to the Esso-Exxon brand name. (See the Esso-Exxon section for more details.) In the meantime, with the 1961 purchase by Chevron, stations were reimaged and globes were eliminated. The Chevron name replaced "Standard" at most Kyso stations in 1977, although a few stations remain Standard to protect the long-held brand.

CROWN GASOLINE One-piece round
(5)   1910s   One-piece Etched round $1,600-$2,400
"CROWN" around top, "GASOLINE" around bottom. Green letters, with red and green crown in center.

CROWN GASOLINE
(5)   1920s   One-piece cast crown   No Listing
One-piece cast crown similar to Standard of Indiana crowns, but more rounded on top. Red detailing on white crown, with white band around lower crown and red lettering "C.R.O.W.N." (letters separated by periods) on band.

CROWN GASOLINE
(4)   1920-1933   16.5in Metal $400-$750
CROWN GASOLINE
(4)   1920-1933   15in Metal $400-$725
White globe face with blue outline ring and blue inner ring around center circle. Red "CROWN" arched at top, "GASOLINE" at bottom, with red, white, and blue detailed crown in center.

CROWN ETHYL
(4)   1920s   16.5in Metal $350-$550
CROWN ETHYL
(4)   1920s   15in Metal $350-$500
White globe face with green outline ring. Large Ethyl (EGC) logo in center, with blue sunburst lines. Green "CROWN" arched at top, separated by dot on each side from "GASOLINE" arched around bottom.

CROWN/ STANDARD/ KY GASOLINE
(5)   1933-1940   15in Metal   No Listing
CROWN/ STANDARD/ KY GASOLINE
(4)   1920s   16.5in Metal $350-$600
CROWN/ STANDARD/ KY GASOLINE
(4)   1920s   15in Metal $350-$550
CROWN STANDARD/KY GASOLINE
(5)   1933-1940   18in Metal/neon   No listing
White globe face with blue outline ring. Blue line ovals forming design similar to bar-and-circle. Blue "CROWN" arched at top, "GASOLINE" at bottom, with red "STANDARD" in bowtie lettering on center bar, over small red "KY." Small blue lettering inside bottom oval "REG.U.S.PAT.OFF.S.O.INC.IN KY."

KYSO
(4)   1920s   15in Metal $225-$375
White globe face with black outline ring and large black "KYSO" across face.

KYSO GREEN
(4)   1920s-1930s   16.5in Metal $275-$450
KYSO GREEN
(4)   1930-1933   15in Metal $275-$400
White globe face with green outline ring. Large green "KYSO GREEN" on face.

CROWN STANDARD KY GASOLINE
(5)   1933-1940   13.5in Glass $275-$400
White globe face with blue outline ring. Blue line ovals forming design similar to bar-and-circle. Blue "CROWN" arched at top, "GASOLINE" at bottom, with red "STANDARD" in bowtie lettering on center bar, over small red "KY." Small blue lettering inside bottom oval "REG.U.S.PAT.OFF.S.O.INC.IN KY."

CROWN ETHYL
(4)   1926-1940   13.5in Glass $250-$350
White globe face with green outline ring. Green outline ring around Ethyl (EGC) logo in center. Green "CROWN" arched around top, "GASOLINE" around bottom.

CROWN
(3)   1940-1961   13.5in Glass $200-$300
CROWN
(4)   1940-1961   13.5in Capco $75-$125
White globe face with red outline ring. Red "CROWN" across face.

CROWN EXTRA
(3)   1940-1961   13.5in Glass $200-$300
CROWN EXTRA
(4)   1940-1961   13.5in Capco $75-$125
White globe face with red outline ring. Red "CROWN EXTRA" on face.

SUPER CROWN EXTRA
(3)   1956-1961   13.5in Capco $75-$125
Green globe face with white outline ring. White "SUPER CROWN EXTRA" in large letters on face.

STANDARD red on white
(4)   1940-1961   13.5in Capco $100-$150
       misc. use
White globe face with red outline ring top and bottom, broken at sides by notches. Red "STANDARD" across face.

STANDARD on blue
(4)   1947-1961   13.5in Capco $125-$175
       MISC. USE
White globe face with blue-and-red-outlined blue band across center of face. White "STANDARD" on band. Red double-wing logo above and below band.

CROWN DIESEL FUEL
(4)   1950s   13.5in Capco $100-$150
White globe face with red outline. Red lettering "CROWN DIESEL FUEL."

Caldwell & Taylor Original Benzol Gas one-piece etched globe, and Freedom Motor one-piece etched globe.

Miscellaneous Fleet-Wing Globes. R. V. Witherspoon

Royal oval lens on oval plastic body.

Gasoline Crown crown-shaped, etched-letter globes, Standard Oil of Indiana. Scott Anderson

Standard Solite Blue Crown crown-shaped, raised-letter globes, Standard Oil of Indiana.

Standard Red Crown Ethyl crown-shaped, raised-letters, Standard Oil of Indiana.

Standard Red Crown with flange base at top used as a light only; dealer promotional piece, circa 1970s.

Standard Flames one-piece flame-shaped sign globesl left one is plastic, right one is glass.

Sunoco Dynafuel 15in inserts on metal body.

Blue Sunoco 15in inserts on metal body.

Bay 13.5in inserts on glass (left) and Speed (Bay) 13.5in inserts on red plastic. R. V. Witherspoon

Super Speed Ethyl 13.5in inserts on red plastic body.

SUNOCO
SUN OIL COMPANY, Philadelphia, Pennsylvania

Sun Oil Company, or Sunoco, a refiner and marketer founded by the Pew family in Philadelphia in 1890, began retail gasoline marketing in 1920. Primarily a northeastern marketer, Sunoco had stations from Maine to the Chicago area south to Virginia by the early 1930s, as well as marketing in Florida. For many years Sunoco marketed only a premium grade of gasoline Blue Sunoco, but for a brief time after World War II, added a super-premium Sunoco Dynafuel. In 1956 Sunoco, in cooperation with the Wayne Pump Company, began experimenting with a multiple-grade blending system called Custom Blending that sold nine grades of gasoline through a single pump, drawing from two tanks and mixing in proper proportion. As the new equipment was installed, globes were eliminated in a reimaging and by 1959 the Custom-Blenders were in place at all Sunoco locations.

In 1968 Sun merged with Sunray D-X, and for the next twenty years marketed under the Sunoco name in the Northeast and East while retaining the D-X name in the Midwest. About 1988 Sun began reimaging in the Midwest, replacing the D-X brand with Sunoco at high-volume locations and selling off or closing the others. Some pockets of D-X branding remain, but this is primarily from jobbers who just haven't removed old signage. D-X and related brand globes can be found under the listing "D-X" in this book.

SUNOCO (Sun Oils)
(5)   1920s   15in Metal $500-$850
Yellow globe face with reddish-gold-outlined white diamond at top of face, with red-gold "SUN OILS" on diamond. Blue "SUNOCO GAS" under diamond, top of "SUNOCO" lettering arched down under diamond.
SUNOCO
(5)   1920s   15in Metal $300-$550
Yellow globe face with dark blue "SUNOCO" across face. Lettering arches down at top, forming half-bowtie.
SUNOCO "SMOKELESS"
(5)   1920s   15in Metal $300-$500
Description not available.
BLUE SUNOCO KNOCKLESS
(5)   1920s   15in Metal $300-$500
Yellow globe face, with white-outlined bright blue lettering "BLUE SUNOCO" over smaller blue-outlined white "KNOCKLESS."
BLUE SUNOCO-1
(2)   1931-1940   15in Metal $225-$400
White globe face with thick blue outline. Blue-outlined yellow diamond on center of face, with small blue-colored "BLUE" at top, over large "SUNOCO" (no outline) on diamond. "SUNOCO" lettering is bowtie design, and "S" and "O" extend at top and bottom of diamond where on later globe the "S" and "O" extend only below diamond.
BLUE SUNOCO-2
(2)   1940-1956   15in Metal $225-$375
White globe face with blue outline around edge. Large yellow diamond with fine blue outline on center of face. Small white-outlined blue-colored "BLUE" at top of diamond, with white-and-blue-outlined blue "SUNOCO" in bowtie lettering on lower area of diamond and extending beyond diamond.
SUNOCO DYNAFUEL
(3)   1946-1950   15in Metal $275-$450
White globe face with blue outline around edge. Large yellow diamond in center of face. White-and-blue-outlined blue "SUNOCO" above "DY-NAFUEL" on face. Lettering is such that wording forms shape of a bowtie.
BLUE SUNOCO
(5)   1946-1956   12.5in Glass $300-$550
White globe face with blue outline around edge. Large yellow diamond with fine blue outline on center of face. Small white-outlined blue-colored "BLUE" at top of diamond, with white-and-blue-outlined blue-colored "SUNOCO" in bowtie lettering on lower area of diamond and extending beyond diamond.

TENNECO & Affiliates, Houston, Texas

Formed in 1961 when Tennessee Gas Transmission (a pipeline company) merged with Bay Petroleum of Denver, Colorado. Bay had been in the process of buying out regional private brands throughout the Southeast.

Bay Petroleum, Denver, Colorado

Bay Petroleum was founded in McPherson, Kansas, and dates back to the late 1930s, although little is known about its early history. By the mid-1950s, the operation had shifted to Denver, Colorado, and in 1961 Bay merged with Tennessee Gas Transmission to form Tenneco. During the 1960s, Tenneco purchased several private brand operations that it continued to operate company-direct, and a short-lived network of branded Tenneco dealers was created. But most of the Tenneco stations were branded Bay.

During the 1950s, Bay had purchased several southern independents that had been converted to Bay and when Tenneco decided to get out of retail gasoline marketing, the remaining portion of the Bay brand, mostly in Georgia and Florida, was sold to Dixie Oil of Tifton, Georgia, a Tenneco-supplied independent that continues to operate Bay brand stations. A note of trivia here: The Bay shield logo, last revised about 1946, is the oldest logo ever to be associated with a major brand that is still in use today, without change.

BAY
(2)   1940s   Gill $225-$325
BAY
(1)   1940-current   13.5in Capco $50-$100
White globe face with large red, white, and black "BAY" shield in center.
BAY ETHYL
(4)   1938-1941   13.5in Gill $250-$350
White globe face with small "BAY" shield offset to upper left, with small Ethyl (EGC) logo in black circle offset to lower right.
BAY ETHYL
(3)   1940s   13.5in red Ripple Gill $500-$950
White globe face with small "BAY" shield offset to upper left, with small Ethyl (EC) logo in black circle offset to lower right.
BAY (red line border)
(3)   1940-1955   13.5in Capco $75-$150
BAY (red line border)
(3)   1940s-1950s   13.5in Red Capco $125-$175
White globe face with red outline ring. Large red, white, and black "BAY" shield in center.
BAY BRONZE
(3)   1956-1961   13.5in red Capco $125-$200
White globe face with red, white, and black "BAY" shield above gold-colored "BRONZE" on face.

Citizens Oil Company, Tallahassee, Florida

Citizens Oil had originally operated in the Atlanta-based Greyhound stations and had introduced the Citizens 77 brand logo about the end of World War II. In about 1950, Citizens merged with Atlanta-based Speed Oil Company. Citizens 77 operated dealer stations while the Speed brand was used in their direct-operated stations. With the 1957 purchase by Bay Petroleum, the Speed name was retained for several years in a transitional Bay-shaped "SPEED" shield.

CITIZENS 77
(4)   1946-1955   15in Metal $400-$700
CITIZENS 77
(4)   1950s   13.5in Capco $150-$325
White globe face with blue outline ring. Large red "CITIZENS" logotype across top of globe, underlined from extension of "C." Blue greyhound below logotype, with large "77" in quotes below greyhound.
CITIZENS ETHYL
(5)   1938-1950   15in Metal $375-$600
Same as above, with red outline ring and red "ETHYL" replacing "77."
CITIZENS DIESEL FUEL
(5)   1950s   13.5in Capco $150-$300
Same as Citizens, above, except "DIESEL FUEL" replaces "77."

Speed Oil Company, Atlanta, Georgia

Atlanta-based discounter that merged with Citizens Oil Company around 1950.
SUPER SPEED GASOLINE
(5)   1940s   13.5in Glass $200-$350
Description not available.
SUPER SPEED ETHYL (EGC)
(5)   1940s   13.5in Glass $225-$350
Description not available.
SUPER BENZOL GASOLINE
(5)   1940s   13.5in Glass $250-$400
Description not available.
SUPER SPEED w/Citizens Greyhound
(5)   1950s   15in Metal $375-$600
SUPER SPEED w/Citizens Greyhound
(5)   1950s   13.5in Capco $175-$325
White globe face with blue Citizens greyhound across lower face. Blue "SUPER" over red "SPEED" across upper face.
SUPER SPEED ETHYL
(5)   1950s   15in Metal $375-$600
SUPER SPEED ETHYL
(5)   1950s   13.5in Capco $175-$325

Same as above, with red "ETHYL" added under greyhound.
SUPER SPEED KEROSENE
(5)   1940s   15in Metal   No Listing
Description not available.
SPEED (on Bay shield)
(5)   1957-1961   13.5in Capco $100-$150
White globe face with thick red ring around edge and black outline ring around white center area. Red, white, and black "BAY" shield, with diagonal band from lower left to upper right, and black "SPEED" with speed lines on diagonal band.

Gulf Coast Oil Company, New Orleans, Louisiana

Gulf Coast was bought out by Bay Petroleum in the late 1950s and rebranded Bay.
GULF COAST OIL COMPANY
(3)   1920s-1930s   15in Metal $250-$450
Red globe face with multiple red, white, and blue outline rings. Large white "GULF" arched over smaller "COAST," with "OIL COMPANY" arched below, around bottom of face.
GULF COAST
(3)   1920s-1930s   15in Metal $250-$400
Same as above, with large white straight block lettering "GULF COAST."
GULF STATE
(4)   1920s-1930s   15in Metal $275-$425
Same as above, but with "GULF STATE."

Tenneco

The Tenneco brand name was introduced in 1961 and used on a group of dealer-operated "Class A" stations in the Southeast. In 1970 Tenneco began experimenting with combination gasoline-convenience stores and built a network of stores in southern metropolitan markets, eventually expanding the store concept to their Direct and Red Diamond locations. In the late 1980s Tenneco sold off the gasoline marketing to TOC Retail, and Tenneco-branded locations were rebranded Majik Market.
TENNECO
(5)   1961-1970   13.5in Capco $100-$150
White globe face with red, white, and blue Tenneco shield on center of face.

Direct Oil Company, Nashville, Tennessee

Direct Oil Company was founded in Nashville in 1946 by Calvin Houghland, the son of John Mason Houghland, founder of Spur Distributing. In the early years Direct acted much like a Spur jobber, distributing products through stations in eight states. Tenneco purchased the operation, totalling 132 stations, in 1962 and as of this writing in 1993, TOC retail, successors to the Tenneco marketing, continue to operate Direct stations throughout the Southeast.
DIRECT REGULAR
(4)   1947-1962   13.5in Capco $75-$125
White globe face with blue outline. Blue script "DIRECT" with red crossbar on "T." Red trapezoidal banner below lettering, with white "REGULAR."
DIRECT ETHYL
(4)   1947-1962   13.5in red Capco $75-$125
Same as above, with "ETHYL" on banner.

Red Diamond Oil Company, Pickens, South Carolina

Red Diamond Oil Company was a trackside discounter that was operating about twenty-five stations in North and South Carolina when purchased by Tenneco in the 1970s. Most of the original Red Diamond locations remain branded Red Diamond today.
Note: No Red Diamond globes are known to exist.

Dixie Oil Company, Tifton, Georgia

Dixie Oil Company of Tifton, Georgia, is an independent company supplied by Tenneco beginning in the late 1960s. When Tenneco got out of retail gasoline marketing in the late 1980s, Dixie Oil purchased most of the former Bay-branded operation in Georgia and Florida, and continues to operate the Bay stations today.
DIXIE BEST FOR LESS
(5)   1950s   13.5in Capco $375-$500
White globe face with large red, white, and blue confederate flag in center of face. Red "DIXIE" arched around top, "BEST FOR LESS" around bottom.
DIXIE SHIELD
(3)   1960-1970   13.5in Glass $200-$350
DIXIE SHIELD
(1)   1970-present   13.5in Capco $100-$150

White globe face with Dixie shield on face. Dixie shield is shaped same as Bay, with stars in blue outer border and red and white vertical stripes, with blue "DIXIE" in white band across center.
As of this writing in the spring of 1993, this globe continues to be used at virtually all of the Dixie stations!

Sunset

A Dixie secondary operation.
SUNSET
(5)   1960s   13.5in Capco $225-$400
White globe face with red ellipse at bottom, so as to represent setting sun. Sun's rays extend upward to cover entire face. Green "SUNSET" superimposed over rays, with three green stars above lettering.

TEXACO
THE TEXAS COMPANY, New York, New York

Throughout this country and around the world, the first gasoline pump most people ever saw was a Texaco pump. Founded in 1902 in Port Arthur, Texas, Texaco was early on a worldwide producer, refiner, and marketer. Their early "sales offices," set up to market oils and greases, specialty products, asphalts, and even roofing shingles, were to become the first organized network of gasoline filling stations. Promoting gasoline very heavily before 1910, they became the first marketer to establish a brand image–in 1915–and went on to become the first oil company to operate gas stations in all forty-eight (and later all fifty) states.

They continued to build and operate stations everywhere and with the coming of the Interstate Highway System in 1956 and the many new locations offered by it, Texaco eventually branded more than 40,000 gas stations in the United States. The oil shortages of the 1970s forced Texaco to pull back, however, moving out of some entire areas of the country by the mid-1980s. Texaco's purchase of Getty in 1984 added some former Skelly locations in areas Texaco had withdrawn from, but forced the company to the edge of bankruptcy when Pennzoil sued over the Getty purchase and won. Forced to scale back even more and to team up with a group of overseas investors, Texaco survived and currently markets through more than 15,000 stations in forty-eight states.
TEXACO GASOLINE/MOTOR OILS
(5)   1915-1917   One-piece Etched   No Listing
White globe with red face. White center with Texaco logo (red star with white-outlined green "T" and black "TEXACO"). White "TEXA-CO" arched around upper red ring, "GASOLINE" below, with diagonal white "MOTOR" to left of logo and "OIL and" to right. Chimney-cap globe with flat faces.
TEXACO LEADED Glass (large)
(5)   1910s   SPECIAL 22in Metal   No Listing
Globe has wide, flat-sided Metal body formed so as to hold a multi-piece stained-Glass lens. Lens is Texaco logo in white, with red star and natural color lead outlining green "T." Black "TEXACO" on logo painted on outside of lens.
TEXACO leaded glass
(4)   1912-1920   SPECIAL 20in Metal $1,800-$2,500
Same as above.
TEXACO porcelain sign globe
(5)   1920-1940   SPECIAL   No Listing
Two-sided porcelain sign mounted on black porcelain globe-type base. Used in locations with no electricity for lighting globe. Sign has black outline ring around white Texaco logo (red star with blk border around green "T").
TEXACO one-piece chimney top
(4)   1917-1920   One-piece Etched $1,200-$2,000
White globe with black outline ring around face. Texaco logo with red star and white-outlined green "T" on globe face. Chimney-cap globe with flat faces.
TEXACO large one-piece
(4)   1917-1920   One-piece Etched $800-$1.300
Same as above, without chimney cap.
TEXACO
(3)   1920-1931   One-piece Etched $600-$900
White globe with black outline ring around face. Texaco logo with red star and 15in green "T" on face.
TEXACO
(2)   1922-1931   One-piece cast $450-$750
Same as above, except details are cast in Glass instead of being Etched.
TEXACO ETHYL One-piece blk/wht
(3)   1926-1931   One-piece cast $700-$1,300
White globe with 15in Texaco logo (red star with 15in green "T") in

center. Black "TEXACO" arched around top, "ETHYL" around bottom.
TEXACO ETHYL one-piece red/wht
(5)   1931-1932   One-piece cast   No Listing
White globe with 15in Texaco logo (red star with 15in green "T") in center. Red ring around logo, with white "TEXACO" arched around top, "ETHYL" around bottom.
TEXACO AVIATION
(5)   1920s   One-piece cast   No Listing
White globe with black outline around face. Fifteen-inch Texaco logo (red star with 15in green "T") in center. Red "propeller" diagonally across globe, using logo for hub. Black "AVIATION" arched around top, "GASOLINE" around bottom.
TEXACO milk glass lenses
(5)   1925-1935   15in Metal   No Listing
White milk Glass lens with Texaco logo (red star with 15in green "T") covering globe lens.
TEXACO
(5)   1925-1935   16.5in Metal   No Listing
TEXACO
(4)   1925-1935   15in Metal $800-$1,200
White globe lens with black outline ring around globe face about 1in in from edge. Outline ring forms outline around Texaco logo (red star with 15in green "T") in center.
TEXACO ETHYL blk/wht
(4)   1926-1931   15in Metal $1,000-$1,400
White globe face with 15in Texaco logo (red star with 15in green "T") in center. Black "TEXACO" arched around top, "ETHYL" around bottom.
TEXACO ETHYL wht/red
(5)   1931-1935   15in Metal   No Listing
Red globe face with 15in Texaco logo (red star with 15in green "T") in center. White "TEXACO" arched around top, "ETHYL" around bottom.
TEXACO FIRE CHIEF HAT one-piece
(5)   1932 exp one-piece   No Listing
Three-dimensional cast globe in shape of fire hat over white rounded base. Hat is red, with 15in white Texaco logo (red star with 15in green "T") at front of hat. Red "FIRE CHIEF" logotype lettering with speed lines around base of hat. Probably experimental.
TEXACO FIRE CHIEF
(5)   1939 exp.   13.5in Glass   No Listing
White globe face with black outline ring. Fifteen-inch Texaco logo (red star with 15in green "T") offset to lower left, superimposed over detailed red fire hat. Red "FIRE CHIEF" logotype with speed lines across upper globe face. Probably experimental, as few are known to exist.
TEXACO blk border T
(1)   1932-1946   13.5in Glass $225-$375
TEXACO blk border T
(3)   1932-1946   Gill $250-$400
White globe face with black outline ring. Texaco logo (red star with 15in green "T") covering face.
TEXACO ETHYL blk border T
(4)   1932-1938   13.5in Glass $400-$750
Red globe face with 15in white Texaco logo (red star with black-outlined green "T") in center. White "TEXACO" arched around top, "ETHYL" around bottom.
TEXACO SKY CHIEF blk border T
(1)   1938-1946   13.5in Glass $225-$375
TEXACO SKY CHIEF blk border T
(3)   1938-1946   Gill $250-$400
Green globe face with black band across lower globe face and 15in white band across upper face. Series of white lines across upper globe face above band. Fifteen-inch white Texaco logo (red star with 15in green "T") on lower face, with 15in red "wings" extending out and up from logo. Red "Sky Chief" logotype lettering on upper white band.
TEXACO wht border T
(1)   1946-1968   13.5in Glass $200-$350
TEXACO wht border T
(3)   1946-1968   Gill $200-$375
TEXACO wht border T
(1)   1946-1968   13.5in Capco $100-$150
Same as TEXACO blk border T above, except green "T" in logo has white outline instead of black.
TEXACO SKY CHIEF wht border T
(1)   1946-1968   13.5in Glass $200-$350
TEXACO SKY CHIEF wht border T
(3)   1946-1968   Gill $225-$375
TEXACO SKY CHIEF wht border T
(2)   1946-1968   13.5in Capco $100-$150
Same as SKY CHIEF blk border T above, except green "T" in logo has white outline instead of black.

TEXACO DIESEL CHIEF
(5)   1936-1940   13.5in Glass   No Listing
Same as below, except thicker spray lines.
TEXACO DIESEL CHIEF
(4)   1946-1968   Gill $275-$550
TEXACO DIESEL CHIEF
(4)   1946-1968   13.5in Capco $225-$400
White globe face with black outline ring. Red 1/3 width band across lower face, with black line separating red and white and extending around red injector nozzle at center of face. Red "spray" out from nozzle, with 15in white Texaco logo (red star with white-outlined green "T") superimposed over spray. White "DIESEL/CHIEF" on lower red area.
TEXACO DIESEL FUEL
(5)   1946-1968   Gill $300-$600
TEXACO DIESEL FUEL
(5)   1946-1968   13.5in Capco $225-$450
Same as DIESEL CHIEF above, with green replacing red and white "DIESEL/FUEL," replacing "DIESEL/CHIEF."

Indian Refining Company, Lawrenceville, Illinois

Indian Refining Company was a refiner and marketer with branded gasoline stations in nineteen northeast and north central states. They are best remembered for the motor oil brand Havoline, introduced in 1906 by Havoline Oil Company of New York, which Indian Refining purchased in the late 1910s. Texaco continues to use the Havoline brand today. Texaco purchased Indian in 1931 in order to acquire the Havoline process patents, and Indian stations were rebranded Texaco, while "Indian Gas" became a Texaco economy-grade gasoline marketed until 1942.
INDIAN w/running Indian
(4)   1915-1924   One-piece Etched $1,900-$3,000
White globe with brown and black detailed running Indian in center. Black "INDIAN" arched around top, "GASOLINE" around bottom. "HAVOLINE" vertically on side.
INDIAN w/running Indian
(5)   1915-1924   One-piece Etched   No Listing
Small globe with 4in base, otherwise same as above.
INDIAN w/running Indian
(4)   1915-1924   15in Metal $1,500-$2,400
White globe face with brown and black detailed running Indian in center. Black "INDIAN" arched around top, "GASOLINE" around bottom.
INDIAN GASOLINE "IT ALSO MAKES A DIFFERENCE"
(5)   1914-1918   12in Metal   No Listing
White globe face with red "INDIAN/GASOLINE" over smaller black "IT ALSO MAKES A DIFFERENCE."
INDIAN RED BALL GASOLINE
(5)   1922-1925   One-piece Etched   No Listing
White globe with red dot in center of globe face. Blue "INDIAN" arched around top, "GASOLINE" around bottom with "RED" to left and "BALL" to right of red dot. Blue "HAVOLINE" vertical on side.
INDIAN HI-TEST w/lightning bolt
(5)   1915-1924   One-piece Etched   No Listing
White globe with large red dot in center of face. White lightning bolt across red dot. Blue "INDIAN" arched around top, "HI-TEST" around bottom. Blue "HAVOLINE" vertically on side.
INDIAN—red dot around Indian
(5)   1922-1925   One-piece Etched   No Listing
Transitional globe. White globe face with running Indian on red circular background in center. "INDIAN" arched around top, "GASOLINE" around bottom. Blue "HAVOLINE" vertically on side.
INDIAN GAS HAVOLINE
(4)   1924-1934   One-piece Etched $900-$1,500
INDIAN GAS HAVOLINE
(5)   1924-1934   One-piece baked $800-$1,300
White globe with red dot in center of face. Blue "INDiAN" arched around top, "GAS" around bottom, with blue "HAVOLINE" vertically down side of globe body.
INDIAN GAS small w/4in base
(5)   1924-1930   One-piece Etched   No Listing
Small lamppost globe, otherwise same as above.
INDIAN GAS
(4)   1924-1934   One-piece baked $650-$850
Same as above, without "HAVOLINE" on side.
INDIAN GAS
(4)   1924-1934   15in Metal $450-$750
White globe face with red dot in center. Blue "INDiAN" arched around top, "GAS" around bottom.
INDIAN GAS Etched milk Glass face
(5)   1915-1924   15in Metal   No Listing

Etched milk Glass face, otherwise same as above.
INDIAN GAS
(3)   1932-1942   13.5in Glass $325-$525
White globe face with red dot in center. Blue "INDiAN" arched around top, "GAS" around bottom.

TOTAL and Affiliates
TOTAL PETROLEUM, Alma, Michigan, and Denver, Colorado

Total Petroleum, a unit of the French government, entered the US market in 1970 with the purchase of Leonard Refineries. The more than 700 Leonard stations in Michigan were rebranded Total by 1971, and the company remained a one-state marketer until 1978 when they purchased Apco. They have since acquired Vickers Petroleum, from Esmark in 1980, and the Road Runner stations of the Truman Arnold Corporation. Currently they market in Michigan and surrounding states under the Total brand, and throughout the Midwest under Vickers and Apco.

Note: No Total Petroleum globes are known to exist.

McClanahan Oil Company, Alma, Michigan

Founded in the early 1930s in Michigan's oil region. McClanahan Oil entered the gasoline market about 1935, and the company was reorganized as Leonard Refineries in 1936. Gasoline was rebranded Leonard in 1938.
McCLANAHAN GOLD SEAL
(5)   1935-1938   13.5in Glass $200-$350
Yellow globe face with red outline ring and red and yellow outline around red center circle. Blue-outlined yellow script "Gold/Seal" in red center circle. Blue "McCLANAHAN" arched around top, "GASOLINE" around bottom.
McCLANAHAN THRIFT
(5)   1935-1938   13.5in Glass $200-$350
Cream-colored globe with blue "McCLANAHAN" arched around top, "GASOLINE" around bottom, with red "THRIFT" across center.

Leonard Refineries, Alma, Michigan

McClanahan Oil Company was reorganized in 1936 as Leonard Refineries. The Leonard gasoline brand was introduced in 1938. In 1970, Total Petroleum purchased Leonard Refineries and rebranded the stations Total. They continue to operate under the Total brand in Michigan, Ohio, and Wisconsin.
LEONARD DUBBS CRACKED
(5)   1938-1946   13.5in Glass   No Listing
Yellow globe face with blue diagonal band across logo. Blue outline ring. Red "LEONARD" arched around top, "GASOLINE" around bottom, with white "Dubbs Cracked" on band. Red lightning-bolt design behind band in center.
LEONARD THRIFT GASOLINE
(5)   1938-1946   13.5in Glass   No Listing
Same as McCLANAHAN THRIFT, with "LEONARD" replacing "McCLANAHAN."
LEONARD FLASH-1
(4)   1938-1946   13.5in Glass $225-$350
Red globe face with large yellow and white burst covering most of face. Blue banner across burst, with white-outlined yellow "LEONARD" on banner.
LEONARD ETHYL
(5)   1938-1946   13.5in Glass $225-$350
Red globe face with yellow outline ring. Yellow "LEONARD" arched around top. Large Ethyl (EGC) logo on lower globe face.
LEONARD FLASH-2
(3)   1946-1950   13.5in Glass $225-$350
Red globe face with large white burst covering most of face. Fifteen-inch white banner across burst, with black "LEONARD" on banner.
LEONARD X-TANE
(1)   1950-1967   13.5in Capco $75-$125
Red globe face with wide white band across center. Black "X-tane" on band.
LEONARD NEW SUPER X-TANE PREMIUM
(1)   1950-1967   13.5in Capco $100-$150
Red globe face with wide white band across center. Black "SUPER X-tane" on band, with white "NEW" in upper red area and "PREMIUM" in lower red area.
LEONARD DIESEL
(2)   1955-1970   13.5in Capco $75-$125
White globe face with green band across center. White "LEONARD" on band, with green "DIESEL" above and "FUEL" below.

LEONARD (red)
(1)   1960-1970   13.5in Capco $75-$125
Red globe face with narrow white band across center. Black "LEONARD" on band.
LEONARD PREMIUM 500
(5)   1968-1970   13.5in Capco   No Listing
Description not available. This globe is listed on a 1968 order form where jobbers and dealers ordered globes from Leonard. As of this writing, none have been found and although the Leonard Oil Company archives are in the hands of collectors, no photos are known of either. The product Premium 500 was introduced in 1968.

Roosevelt Oil Company, Mount Pleasant, Michigan

Michigan marketer operating under the Roosevelt brand before WW II and branding Power-Flight from 1946 until 1955. The company was purchased by and rebranded "Leonard" in 1955.
ROC MICHIGAN PRODUCT
(4)   1932-1946   One-piece baked $1,600-$2,000
White One-piece four-sided square globe domed at top. Black silhouette of President Theodore Roosevelt on two sides, with black "A" over red script "Roosevelt" over black "MICHIGAN/PRODUCT" on opposite two sides.
ROC BENZOL
(5)   1932-1946   One-piece baked $1,600-$2,200
Same as above, with "ROC" (large red "O," with small Roosevelt silhouette inside "O") over red "BENZOL" over black "GAS" on lettered sides.
ROC GREEN STAR
(5)   1938-1946   13.5in Glass $350-$600
White globe face with red outline ring. Large green star in center, with green-colored "GREEN" arched around top, "STAR" around bottom. "ROC" vertically to either side of star, with Roosevelt silhouette in "O" on either side.
POWER FLIGHT GASOLINE
(4)   1946-1955   13.5in Glass $275-$450
Yellow globe face with blue and white wing logo in center. Black rocket with red and white tail passing through wings. Black "POWER FLIGHT" with white shading across upper wing area, and red "GASOLINE" arched around bottom.
SUPER FLIGHT ETHYL
(4)   1946-1955   13.5in Glass $225-$375
Same as above, with black "SUPER FLIGHT" replacing "POWER FLIGHT," and red "ETHYL" arched around bottom.

Raleigh and Church, St. Louis, Missouri

A private brand jobber rebranded ROC Power Flight in 1946.
MICHIGAN MAID
(5)   1935-1946   13.5in green Ripple $1,600-$2,400
White globe face with red-outlined black circle in center. White, black, and green drawing of girl's head in center circle. Red "MICHIGAN" with green dropshade arched around top, "MAID" around bottom.

Mid-West Refining, Mount Pleasant, Michigan

This Michigan marketer and refiner marketed under the Mid-West brand until after World War II, when they licensed the "White Rose" trademark from National Refining. Stations were then rebranded Mid-West White Rose. Leonard purchased Mid-West in 1955 and continued to operate the White Rose stations as a secondary brand until after Total purchased Leonard in 1970. Stations were then rebranded Total.
MID-WEST
(4)   1935-1946   13.5in Glass $225-$350
White globe face with 15in red shield in center. Fifteen-inch white diagonal band across center, with black "MID-WEST" on band. Three white stars to lower right of band.
MID-WEST ETHYL
(4)   1935-1946   13.5in Glass $300-$450
White globe face with 15in red shield in center. Fifteen-inch white diagonal band across center of globe face, with black "MID-WEST" on band. Fifteen-inch white circle on lower shield, with small Ethyl (EGC) logo in circle. Fifteen-inch white "ETHYL" superimposed across Ethyl logo.
MID-WEST LUBRI-GAS w/camel
(4)   1935-1946   13.5in Glass $300-$500
White globe face with 15in red shield in center. Fifteen-inch white horizontal band across center of shield. Black "MID-WEST" across upper shield area, with black "LUBRI-GAS" on band. Small camel below band, with black "LUBRICATING MOTOR FUEL" arched around bottom of globe face.
MID-WEST WHITE
(4)   1935-1946   13.5in Glass $225-$350

White globe face with black outline ring. Large red circle in center. White-colored "WHITE" across center of circle, with black "MID-WEST" arched around top of face and "GASOLINE" around bottom.

Mid-West licensed White Rose from National Refining in 1946.
Note: This section is repeated in the /White Rose listings for clarity.
WHITE ROSE
(3)   1946-1970   13.5in Capco $125-$175
Green globe face with cream-colored box, with rounded sides in center. Red "WHITE/ROSE" in center box.
NEW/WHITE ROSE/ETHYL
(4)   1946-1955   13.5in Capco $125-$175
Same as above, with cream-colored "NEW" in upper green area and "ETHYL" in lower green area.
ETHYL/WHITE ROSE/ETHYL
(4)   1955-1970   13.5in Capco $125-$200
Same as above, with "ETHYL" replacing "NEW" in upper green area, as well as remaining in the lower green area.

Cavalier Service Stations, Incorporated, Flint, Michigan

Michigan regional marketer Cavalier sold out to Leonard Refineries in 1967. In 1968 the operation was rebranded Best, and when Leonard sold out to Total in 1970, Best was retained as a secondary brand. The stations were gradually changed to Total, with only three Best stations in operation as of this writing.
Note: No Best globes are known to exist.
CAVALIER REGULAR
(3)   1940s   13.5in Glass $225-$325
White globe face with thin red, white, and blue lines across center. Red thin-line lettering "CAVALIER" shaped to fit circle contour at top of globe, blue thin-line lettering "REGULAR" shaped to fit circle contour at bottom.
CAVALIER HI-TEST
(4)   1940s   13.5in Glass $225-$350
Same as above, with blue "HI-TEST" at bottom.
CAVALIER DIESEL
(4)   1940s   13.5in Glass $200-$325
Same as above, with blue "DIESEL" at bottom.
CAVALIER #1 FUEL
(4)   1940s   13.5in Glass $225-$325
Same as above, with blue "#1 FUEL" at bottom.
CAVALIER REGULAR Oval
(5)   1950s   Oval Glass $275-$400
Same as CAVALIER REGULAR above, but in an Oval format.
CAVALIER ETHYL Oval
(4)   1950s   Oval Glass $275-$400
Same as CAVALIER ETHYL above, but in an Oval format.
CAVALIER ETHYL-2 Oval
(3)   1960s   Oval Capco $125-$175
White globe face with series of red and white stripes across center. Fifteen-inch white circle in center, splitting stripes. Small Ethyl (EC) logo in circle. Red "CAVALIER" arched around top, "GASOLINE" around bottom.

Anderson-Prichard, Oklahoma City, Oklahoma

Founded in Oklahoma City in 1921, Anderson-Prichard was marketing gasoline under the Col-Tex brand in several midwestern states prior to 1930. In 1946 the Col-Tex stations in Oklahoma were rebranded Anderson-Prichard, while the remaining territory continued to use the Col-Tex brand. In 1952 Anderson-Prichard purchased the extensive Kanotex marketing and introduced the Apco brand to replace Kanotex and Anderson-Prichard. The Col-Tex operation was sold off to Cosden, which continued to operate Col-Tex as a secondary brand until their merger with Fina in 1963. Control of Apco passed to Ashland Oil in the late 1950s, and in 1978 Total Petroleum purchased the Apco operation. Total continues to brand dealer-operated Apco stations today.
COL-TEX w/deer
(5)   1929-1946   13.5in Glass $600-$900
Globe face has red gear-tooth edge outer ring around green center circle. Tan-detailed jumping deer in center circle. White "COL-TEX" arched around top, "GASOLINE" around bottom.
COL-TEX ETHYL (EGC)
(3)   1929-1946   13.5in Glass $200-$325
Same as above, with 15in white center circle. Large Ethyl (EGC) logo in center circle.
COL-TEX SERVICE
(3)   1946-1953   13.5in Glass $225-$350
Same as above, with yellow-outlined blue circle in center. Yellow

"SERVICE" across center, with small yellow lightning bolts above and below.
COL-TEX CHALLENGE
(4)   1946-1953   13.5in Glass $225-$350
Same as above, with white-outlined blue circle in center. White script "Challenge" across blue center circle.
ANDERSON-PRICHARD CHALLENGE
(3)   1946-1953   13.5in Glass $225-$350
Same as COL-TEX CHALLENGE above, with white "ANDERSON" arched around top and "PRICHARD" around bottom.
ANDERSON-PRICHARD ETHYL (EC)
(4)   1946-1953   13.5in Glass $225-$350
Same as COL-TEX ETHYL above, with white "ANDERSON" arched around top and "PRICHARD" around bottom. Ethyl (EC) logo in center.
ANDERSON-PRICHARD 70 OCTANE
(3)   1946-1953   13.5in Glass $225-$350
Same as COL-TEX 70 OCTANE above, with white "ANDERSON" arched around top and "PRICHARD" around bottom.
ANDERSON-PRICHARD SERVICE
(4)   1946-1953   13.5in Glass $225-$350
Same as COL-TEX SERVICE above, with white "ANDERSON" arched around top and "PRICHARD" around bottom.
ANDERSON-PRICHARD DIESEL
(5)   1946-1953   13.5in Glass $225-$350
Same as ANDERSON-PRICHARD CHALLENGE above, with white script "Diesel" across blue center circle.
APCO REGULAR
(1)   1953-1970   13.5in Capco $75-$125
White globe face with red outline ring. Red and white shield logo with red "APCO" in center. White "REGULAR" in red band across lower area of shield.
APCO PREMIUM
(1)   1953-1970   13.5in Capco $75-$125
Same as above, with "PREMIUM" replacing "REGULAR."
APCO WHITE
(1)   1953-1970   13.5in Capco $75-$125
Same as above, with "WHITE" replacing "REGULAR."
APCO DIESEL
(1)   1953-1970   13.5in Capco $75-$125
Same as above, with "DIESEL" replacing "REGULAR."
APCO KEROSENE
(1)   1953-1970   13.5in Capco $75-$125
Same as above, with "KEROSENE" replacing "REGULAR."

Kanotex, Arkansas City, Kansas

Founded as Superior Refining in Longton, Kansas, in 1905, the Kanotex trademark was first used in 1909. The company moved to Arkansas City, Kansas, in 1917 and later merged with Arkansas City-based Lesh Refining. Innovative marketers, the Kanotex trademark appeared in more than twenty midwestern states. In 1952 Anderson-Prichard purchased Kanotex and rebranded the Kanotex operation, as well as their own Anderson-Prichard stations, to Apco.
KANOTEX
(4)   1920s   One-piece Etched $1,400-$2,200
White globe with white star-yellow sunflower Kanotex logo in center of face. Red "KANOTEX" (large "O") across logo.
KANOTEX KANT-NOX
(5)   1920s   One-piece Etched   No Listing
Same as KANOTEX above, with red "KANT-NOX" arched around bottom of logo.
KANOTEX SUPER KANT-NOX
(5)   1920s   One-piece Etched   No Listing
Same as KANOTEX above, with red "SUPER" arched around top and red "KANT-NOX" arched around bottom.
KANOTEX reverse side "F&T" GAS
(5)   1920s   One-piece Etched   No Listing
Same as KANOTEX above, with red vertical Oval on reverse. White "F and T" on Oval, with small white "GAS" at bottom.
KANOTEX
(5)   1920-1925   15in Metal $750-$1,100
KANOTEX
(4)   1925-1930   15in Glass $650-$1,000
White globe face with red outline ring. Large white star-yellow sunflower Kanotex logo in center. Red "KANOTEX" across logo.
USE KANOTEX GASOLINE
(5)   1920-1925   15in Metal   No listing
Same as Kanotex, above, with red "USE" arched around top, "GASOLINE" around bottom.
SUPER/KANOTEX/KANT-NOX
(5)   1925-1930   15in Glass $750-$1,100

Koolmotor 15in insert, and Texaco white-outlined "T" 13.5in insert.

Texaco White T 13.5in inserts on Gill body, and Texaco Skychief White T 13.5in inserts on Gill body. R. V. Witherspoon

Texaco with black-outlined "T" 13.5in inserts on Hull body. Don Meyr

Texaco one-piece raised-letter globe.

Texaco Ethyl one-piece raised-letter globe.

Texaco one-piece etched globe.

Various Mid-West globes 13.5in inserts on glass bodies. Lonnie Hop

Indian Gas Havoline one-piece etched globe.

Indian Gasoline one-piece etched small globe with 4in base.

Roosevelt Michigan Product one-piece fired-on, unusual-shaped globe.

Roosevelt Benzol one-piece fired-on, unusual-shaped globe, and Diamond one-piece etched globe. Tom Proffitt

Same as KANOTEX 15in Glass above, with red "SUPER" arched around top and red "KANT-NOX" around bottom.

KANOTEX ETHYL
(5)   1926-1930   15in Metal $600-$950
KANOTEX ETHYL
(5)   1926-1930   15in Glass $650-$1,000
White globe face with small white star-yellow sunflower Kanotex logo at top. Red "KANOTEX" arched through logo around top. Large Ethyl (EGC) logo below Kanotex logo.

KANOTEX BONDIFIED
(5)   1926-1930   15in Metal $550-$900
White globe face with red outline ring. Small white star/yellow sunflower Kanotex logo arched around top of face. Large red seal design on lower face with white script "Bondified" across seal.

KANOTEX
(2)   1930-1952   Gill $250-$400
KANOTEX
(5)   1930-1952   13.5in Glass $250-$400
White globe face with red outline ring. Large white star-yellow sunflower Kanotex logo in center of face, with red "KANOTEX" across logo. Brown "REGISTERED TRADE MARK" across face below logo.

KANOTEX AVIATION
(3)   1930-1939   Gill $750-$1,200
KANOTEX AVIATION
(5)   1930-1939   13.5in Glass $650-$1,000
White globe face with red outline ring. Small white star-yellow sunflower Kanotex logo at top of face. Red "KANOTEX" arched around top across logo. Fifteen-inch yellow "AVIATION" with red in line across center of face. Yellow sun with red and black airplane on lower globe face.

KANOTEX ETHYL (EGC)
(2)   1939-1952   Gill $225-$400
White globe face with red outline ring. Small white star-yellow sunflower Kanotex logo at top of face. Red "KANOTEX" arched around top across logo. Large Ethyl (EGC) logo on lower globe face.

KANOTEX BONDIFIED
(2)   1930-1952   Gill $225-$400
White globe face with red outline ring. Small white star-yellow sunflower Kanotex logo at top of face. Red "KANOTEX" arched around top across logo. Red banner diagonally across lower globe face, with white script "Bondified" on banner. Red lightning bolts adjacent to banner.

KANOTEX SOVEREIGN
(3)   1937-1952   Gill $225-$375
Brown globe face with large white-outlined yellow shield covering most of face. Brown "SOVEREIGN/QUALITY" across shield, with small 15in white Oval at top of globe face. Kanotex logo with red "KANOTEX" in Oval.
This globe also appears under "SOVEREIGN SERVICE" in the "DERBY" section.

Lesh Refining Company, Arkansas City, Kansas
An early Kansas refiner that merged with Kanotex in 1928.
THAT GOOD LESH GASOLINE
(5)   1920-1928   15in Metal   No Listing
White Metal-perforated globe face with black "THAT GOOD" arched around top, "GASOLINE" around bottom, and script "Lesh" in center.

Vickers Petroleum Corporation, Wichita, Kansas
Founded in 1917, Vickers was a refiner and marketer operating stations in the central United States. The company remained in the Vickers family until 1968, when it was purchased by Esmark, the conglomerate that had its roots in Swift and Company, the Chicago meat packers. Under Esmark, the brand expanded into about a dozen midwestern states. Total purchased Vickers in 1980, and continues to operate stations under the Vickers brand today.

(VICKERS) HI-RATIO GASOLINE
(5)   1920s   15in Metal $300-$525
White globe face with large red seal covering most of face. Large white "V" on lower seal. White, red, and white lettering "HI-RATIO" across top, with white box below. Red "GASOLINE/FOR/HIGH COMPRESSION/MOTORS" in box.

VICKERS
(4)   1930s-1950   13.5in Red Capco $225-$350
White globe face with red outline ring and red center circle. White band across lower area of center circle, and large 15in white "V" on circle. Red "VICKERS" on band.

VICKERS ETHYL
(4)   1930s-1950   13.5in Red Capco $200-$325
Same as above, with small Ethyl (EC) logo in 15in white circle over upper area of "V."

VICKERS SQUARE
(2)   1950-1968   One-piece Plastic $150-$250
White Two-piece square Plastic globe assembled back-to-back. Large Vickers logo (black and white "V" with red crown in red-outlined white, with red band across bottom and white "VICKERS" on band) covering most of globe face.

VICKERS RECTANGLE
(1)   1968-1980   One-piece Plastic $150-$250
White Two-piece rectangular Plastic globe assembled back-to-back. Small new Vickers logo (red-outlined white with red and black "V" below black "Vickers") covering globe face.

Knight Oil Company, Springfield, Missouri
Missouri marketer purchased by Vickers about 1959. The company was rebranded Vickers in the early 1960s.
KNIGHT REGULAR
(3)   1946-1959   13.5in Capco $250-$400
White globe face with blue horse and rider in center. Rider holding blue shield with red "K." Red "KNIGHT" arched around top, "REGULAR" around bottom. Blue fern leaves to either side.

KNIGHT OIL CO. ETHYL
(3)   1946-1959   13.5in Capco $250-$400
White globe face with blue outline ring. Blue horse and rider in center. Rider holding blue shield with red "K." Red "KNIGHT OIL CO." arched around top, "ETHYL" around bottom.

KNIGHT OIL CO. DIESEL
(4)   1946-1959   13.5in Capco $250-$400
Same as KNIGHT OIL CO. ETHYL above, with red "DIESEL" replacing "ETHYL."

KNIGHT KEROSENE
(5)   1946-1959   13.5in Capco $250-$400
Same as KNIGHT REGULAR above, with red "KEROSENE" replacing "REGULAR."

KNIGHT GASOLINE
(5)   1959-1964   One-piece $150-$300
                     SQUARE Plastic
White Two-piece square Plastic globe assembled back-to-back. Red bands across top and bottom, with white in between. White "KNIGHT" on top band, "GASOLINE" on bottom, and blue horse and rider in center.

Bell Oil and Gas, Tulsa, Oklahoma
An independent refiner and marketer founded in 1918 and purchased by Vickers in the late 1960s. Bell was primarily a wholesale marketer with only a few branded stations.
BELL (BELL OIL-GAS CO.)
(5)   1930s   13.5in Glass   No Listing
Light blue globe face with black outline ring. Large bell in center. Red-outlined white "BELL OIL-GAS CO." arched around top, "GASOLINE" around bottom, with "BE" to left of bell and "LL" to right. Red-outlined white "PERFECT/QUALITY/SINCE 1918" below bell, and dark blue lettering on bell "THIS/PRODUCT IS/WARRANTED/TO GIVE ENTIRE/SATISFACTION/BY THE/DEALER AND/MANUFACTURER."

BELL (bell and derrick)
(3)   1935-1940   Gill $300-$600
Orange globe face with blue outline ring. Blue "BELL" with white dropshade across upper face, with blue bell below. White "cutaway" on bell shows oil derrick.

BELL
(3)   1940-1950   Gill $275-$550
Orange globe face with blue outline ring. Blue "BELL" with white dropshade across upper face. Blue bell with white details on lower face.

BELL REGULAR
(2)   1940-1950   Gill $300-$600
BELL REGULAR
(3)   1950-1970   13.5in Capco $250-$450
Same as BELL above, with white script "Regular" across bell.
Note: BELL REGULAR on Orange Gill Ripple would bring $900-$1,350.

BELL ETHYL
(2)   1935-1941   Gill $300-$600
Same as BELL above, with Ethyl (EGC) logo superimposed over bell.
BELL ETHYL
(3)   1941-1970   13.5in Capco $250-$450
Same as BELL ETHYL above, with Ethyl (EC) logo.

Ben Franklin Refining Company, Ardmore, Oklahoma
Oklahoma-based Ben Franklin Refining operated a few Ben

113

Franklin branded stations in the 1930s. They merged with Bell Oil prior to World War II.

BEN FRANKLIN PREMIUM REGULAR
(3)   1930s   Gill $600-$900

BEN FRANKLIN PREMIUM REGULAR
(4)   1930s   Red Ripple Gill $1,100-$1,500
Red globe face with white circle in center and white outer ring arched around bottom of face. Black and white line drawing of Ben Franklin on center circle. Fifteen-inch white "BEN FRANKLIN" arched around top, with red "REGULAR" arched in white area at bottom. Red script "Premium" across lower area of drawing in center circle.

BEN FRANKLIN ETHYL
(3)   1930s   Gill $600-$900

BEN FRANKLIN ETHYL
(4)   1930s   Red Ripple Gill $1,000-$1,500
Same as above, with no white area at bottom. Fifteen-inch white circle positioned at lower edge of center circle, with small Ethyl (EGC) logo in circle.

UNION OIL COMPANY OF CALIFORNIA

Organized in 1890 in Santa Paula, California, from the holdings of founders Lyman Stewart and Wallace Hardison and others, Union Oil Company began selling California-made gasoline to California motorists in 1913. Throughout its history a dominant West Coast marketer, Union was operating stations in twelve states at the time of the 1965 merger with Chicago-based Pure Oil. By 1970, the Union 76 brand had replaced Pure and the company was marketing coast-to-coast. The corporate name became Unocal Corporation in 1983, and the brand became Unocal 76 in 1985. As of this writing Unocal is trying to sell off southeastern marketing in much of the former Pure Oil territory to concentrate on its West Coast home base.

UNION NON DETONATING GASOLINE
(5)   1920s   15in Metal $275-$500
White globe with large red "UNION" arched around top, "GASOLINE" around bottom, with small black "NON/DETONATING" in center. Black "THIS GLOBE PROPERTY OF UNION OIL CO." arched around bottom. All Union globes have a similar statement in very small lettering at the bottom, but on this globe it is large enough to be easily read.

UNOCO on green shield
(5)   1920s   15in Metal $600-$900
White globe face with large yellow-outlined green shield covering most of face. White "UNOCO" across shield.

UNION GASOLINE–red/wht/blue shield
(5)   1925-1930   15in Metal   No Listing
White globe face with large blue-outlined shield covering most of face. Upper 1/3 of shield is blue and lower 2/3 is red and white vertical stripes. White "UNION/GASOLINE" in upper blue area.

UNION ETHYL GASOLINE red/wht/blue shield
(5)   1926-1930   15in Metal   No Listing
Blue globe face with red-outlined white shield covering most of face. Blue "UNION" arched around top, "ETHYL GASOLINE" arched around bottom, with Ethyl (EGC) shield in center.

UNION PRODUCTS 76 (blue shield)
(5)   1932-1935   15in Metal $600-$900
White globe face with yellow-outlined shield, with upper 1/3 blue and lower 2/3 orange. White "UNION" arched over small "PRODUCTS" on upper blue area. Large blue "76" on lower orange area over white "GASOLINE."

UNION 76 GASOLINE SHIELD (white)
(4)   1935-1946   15in Metal $600-$900
White globe face with blue-and-orange-outlined shield, with upper 1/3 blue and lower 2/3 orange. White "UNION" on upper blue area and large white "76" on lower orange area.

UNION ETHYL GASOLINE shield (EGC)
(5)   1932-1946   15in Metal $650-$900
White globe face with large yellow-outlined shield, with upper 1/3 blue and lower 2/3 orange. Orange "UNION" arched in upper blue area of shield. Ethyl (EGC) shield with yellow rays at center of orange area, and blue "GASOLINE" arched below.

UNION WHITE MAGIC GASOLINE shield
(4)   1932-1946   15in Metal $600-$900
White globe face with large yellow-outlined blue shield covering most of face. White "UNION" at top of shield over large white script "White/Magic." Small white "GASOLINE" at bottom.

Independent Oil Company Globes, Prices, and Histories

The globes listing in this section are from independent jobber-brand or private-brand operations. No ties to any major oil companies are known, except as noted, although no doubt many early companies have sold out to or been rebranded by a major. If it is known that a company is still in business, that fact is noted too. Listings are arranged alphabetically by *globe name* (not company name), and a cross-reference is provided when a globe is listed, out of alphabetical sequence, with others from the same brand.

AA Oil Company
Company history unknown.

AA OIL CO.
(5)   1950s   Oval Capco $125-$200
White globe face with large blue "AA" over smaller "oil company."

Accurate Measure Company
Company history unknown.

ACCURATE GAS
(5)   1920s   15in Metal $300-$550
White globe face with black "Accurate" across center. Large black "GAS" below, with "THE ACCURATE MEASURE" arched around top over "OIL/CO."

Ace High
See listing for MIDWEST in this section.

Acme
Company history unknown.

ACME REGULAR
(3)   1950s   13.5in Capco $75-$150
Orange globe face with white and black lines forming white band across center. White "SUPER" in upper orange area, "REGULAR" in lower, with black-outlined orange "ACME" in center band.

ACME ETHYL
(3)   1950s   13.5in Capco $75-$150
Same as above, with "ETHYL" replacing "REGULAR."

Aerio
Gregory Independent Oil Company, Gregory, South Dakota
Company history unknown.

AERIO GAS
(4)   1940s   13.5in Glass $850-$1,500
White globe face with black outline. Red and black single-engine airplane in center of globe face, surrounded by clouds. Red "AERIO" at top of face, "GAS" at bottom.

AERIO 70
(4)   1940s   13.5in Glass $850-$1,500
Same as above, with "70" replacing "GAS."

Aero Gas
Company history unknown.

AERO GAS–THE WONDER GAS
(5)   1920s   One-piece etched   No Listing
Description not available.

AERO HIGH TEST ETHYL (EGC)
(5)   1940s   13.5in Glass $300-$500
Orange globe face with black-outlined white "AERO" at top of face. Black wing design, with white "HIGH TEST NO KNOCK" below lettering. Ethyl logo (EGC) in white circle at bottom.

Ager
Company history unknown.
AGER GAS/OILS
(5)   1920s   One-piece etched $1,200-$1,600
White globe with red outline ring around globe face. Blue bowtie-shaped band across center, with white "AGER" in band. Red-and-white-outlined blue "GAS" in upper area, "OILS" below.

Airlight
Company history unknown.
AIRLIGHT GASOLINE
(5)   1920s   15in Metal $250-$375
White globe face with green "AIRLIGHT" over "GASOLINE."

Air-O-Test
Company history unknown.
AIR-O-TEST "TESTED BEST GASOLINE"
(5)   1920s   15in Metal   No Listing
Description not available.

Airway
Company history unknown.
AIRWAY
(4)   1950s   13.5in Capco $75-$125
White globe face with series of red, white, and black lines forming white band across center. Black "AIRWAY" with speed lines in band.
AIRWAY ETHYL
(4)   1950s   13.5in Capco $75-$125
Same as above, with small Ethyl (EC) logo in circle, added below band.

Allfire
See listing for WINGS in this section.

Allied Oil Company, Tyler, Texas
Company history unknown.
ALLIED REGULAR
(4)   1950s   13.5in Capco $100-$150
White globe face with blue outline ring and blue lines forming white center band. Red "ALLIED" in center band, with italic blue "REGULAR" below band.
ALLIED PREMIUM
(4)   1950s   13.5in Capco $100-$150
Same as above, with red "PREMIUM" replacing blue "REGULAR."

All-Pen
Bradford Oil Refining Company, Bradford, Pennsylvania
Company history unknown.
ALL-PEN GAS
(5)   1930s   15in Metal $450-$700
Description not available.
ALL-PEN GAS
(4)   1930s   13.5in Glass $275-$450
Description not available.
ALL-PEN GAS w/ethyl (EGC)
(5)   1930s   13.5in Glass $250-$400
Orange globe face with blue and white outline rings. White center circle, with white semi-circles top and bottom. Small Ethyl (EGC) logo in center circle. Blue "ALL-PEN" in upper semi-circle and "GAS" in lower. Blue "BRADFORD" arched around top, "OIL REFINING CO." around bottom.

Altitude Oil Company
Company history unknown.
ALTOMOTOR POWERFUL
(5)   1940s   13.5in yellow Capco $250-$375
White globe face with green outline ring. Detailed black and white "ALTITUDE" logo at top on yellow semi-circle. Green arrow across center, with black-outlined yellow "ALTOMOTOR" on arrow. Black "POWERFUL" arched around bottom.
ALTOMOTOR HI-CO HIGH COMPRESSION
(5)   1940s   13.5in Capco $250-$375
White globe face with yellow outline ring. Detailed black and white "ALTITUDE" logo at top on red semi-circle. Red "HI-CO" over yellow design in center, with red "HIGH COMPRESSION" arched around bottom.

American Oil Company, Morristown, Tennessee
Founded in Morristown, Tennessee, in 1921 when Barto Fisher bought a failing Texaco service station and private branded it "Ameri-

can." The American brand name was used through 1926, when Fisher acquired a Sinclair distributorship and rebranded his stations Sinclair. The company is still doing business today, as Fisher Oil Company.
AMERICAN
(4)   1922-1926   15in Metal $450-$650
Red and white vertical striped globe face, with blue band across center. White "AMERICAN" on band.

American Petroleum Company, Davenport, Iowa
Company history unknown.
RANGER GASOLINE (around eagle)
(4)   1930s   Gill $400-$750
White globe face with black outline ring. Black ring around yellow center circle. Black-outlined yellow bands to either side of circle. Black-detailed eagle in center circle. Black "RANGER" arched around top, "GASOLINE" around bottom.
U.S.MOTOR GASOLINE (around eagle)
(4)   1930s   Gill $400-$750
Same as above, with black "U.S.MOTOR" replacing "RANGER."
AMERICAN ETHYL GASOLINE (EGC)
(4)   1930s   Gill $250-$350
Yellow globe face with black outline ring and black outline around white center circle. Ethyl (EGC) logo in center circle. Black "AMERICAN" arched around top, "GASOLINE" around bottom.
AMPETCO
(4)   1940s   13.5in red Capco $150-$250
Series of red and white vertical stripes covers globe face. Blue band across center, with white "AMPETCO" on band.

American Oil & Gas, Dallas, Texas
Company history unknown. May have been a forerunner to American Liberty Oil Company.
AMERICAN w/eagle
(5)   1920s   15in Metal   No listing
White globe face with large yellow-outlined blue oval covering most of face. Detailed brown, white, and yellow eagle carrying oil can in center of oval, with red "AMERICAN" arched around top of oval, white "POWERFUL AS ITS NAME" around bottom, and red script "Gasoline" superimposed over eagle.
AMERICAN w/eagle
(4)   1930s   13.5in Glass $300-$550
White globe face with blue outline ring. Red, white, and blue detailed eagle in center carrying shield and banner. Blue lettering on banner "POWERFUL AS ITS NAME." Blue-outlined red "AMERICAN" arched around top, "GASOLINE" around bottom.
AMERICAN w/stars
(4)   1940s   13.5in Glass $225-$325
White globe face with red and blue outline rings. Red-outlined blue "AMERICAN" across center, with blue stars all around face.
BUDGET
(4)   1940s   13.5in Glass $225-$325
Same as above, with "BUDGET" replacing "AMERICAN."

American Hi Octane
Company history unknown.
AMERICAN/HI-OCTANE/OIL COMPANY
(4)   1940s   13.5in Glass $250-$350
White globe face with red outline ring. Shield in center, with blue and white vertical stripes and red stars. Red "HI-OCTANE" diagonally across shield. Blue "AMERICAN" arched around top, "OIL CO." around bottom.

Amo
Company history unknown.
AMO "NO DOPES"
(5)   1920s   15in Metal $250-$375
Description not available.
AMO "NO DOPES–NO JOKES"
(5)   1920s   15in Metal $250-$375
Description not available.

Ampec Company
Company history unknown.
AMPEC CO. AVIATION GAS
(5)   1920s   One-piece etched $900-$1,500
Description not available.

Anchor Petroleum, Atlanta, Georgia
Company history unknown.

ANCHOR GASOLINE
(5)   1930s   One-piece etched   No Listing
Description not available.
ANCHOR REGULAR w/anchor
(5)   1940s   13.5in Capco $225-$350
Yellow globe face with black outline ring. White center circle with black anchor. Red "ANCHOR" arched around top, "REGULAR" around bottom.
ANCHOR ETHYL
(5)   1940s   13.5in Capco $100-$150
Same as above, with Ethyl (EC) logo in center. Red "PREMIUM" replacing "REGULAR."

Andy-Dandy Oil Company
Company history unknown.
ANDY-DANDY OIL CO.
(5)   1930s   Gill $650-$1,000
Red globe face with black and white "attendant," with pump hose in center of globe face. Silver dollar head on attendant. White "ANDY/DANDY" to left of figure, "OIL CO." to right.

Anthony Oil Company, Fort Wayne, Indiana
Company history unknown.
ANTHONY WHITE MULE GAS–IT KICKS
(5)   1920s   One-piece etched   No Listing
White globe with red outline ring around face. Black "ANTHONY" arched around top, "GAS" around bottom, with red "WHITE/MULE" in center. Black vertical "IT KICKS" on side of globe.
ANTHONY REGULAR GAS
(4)   1930s   15in Metal $275-$375
Description not available.
WHITE MULE w/mule
(5)   1930s   13.5in Glass $400-$650
Description not available.

Apex
Company history unknown.
APEX GASOLINE w/oil well
(5)   1930s   15in Metal $1,750-$2,500
Globe face has light blue upper half and white lower half. White clouds on upper blue area, with black oil well in center. Red "APEX" with black outlines and white in lines across center, with black "GASOLINE" below.
APEX REGULAR yellow on white
(3)   1950s   13.5in Capco $75-$125
White globe face with yellow outline ring and yellow "APEX" over "REGULAR" on globe face.
APEX ETHYL
(3)   1950s   13.5in Capco $75-$125
Description not available.

Armould Oil Company
Company history unknown.
ARMOULD OIL PRODUCTS
(5)   1920s   One-piece baked $600-$850
White globe with black outline ring around face. Center circle is divided into quadrants, red and white over white and red. Black "ARMOULD OIL" arched around top, "PRODUCTS" around bottom.

Aro-Flight
Company history unknown.
ARO-FLIGHT
(5)   1950s   13.5in Capco $200-$350
Pink globe face with white outline around pink center circle. Black and white non-detailed airplane across center. Black "ARO" arched around top, "FLIGHT" around bottom.

Arrow Oil Company, New York, New York
Company history unknown.
ARROW
(5)   1920s   One-piece etched   No Listing
Description not available.
ARROW ETHYL
(5)   1920s   One-piece etched $1,100-$1,600
White globe with yellow outline around face and around white center circle. Red "ARROW" arched around top, with large Ethyl (EGC) logo in center.
ARROW GASOLINE
(5)   1930s   15in Metal $650-$1,000
Description not available.

Arrowhead Gas Company, Lynchburg, Virginia
Company history unknown.
ARROWHEAD GAS CO. w/arrowhead
(5)   1920s   One-piece etched   No Listing
White globe face with double-outlined rounded triangle covering face. Red "ARROWHEAD" arched in between upper outlines, "GASOLINE" and "COMPANY" on side outlines, with large arrowhead point-down in center. Outline white lettering "GAS" across arrowhead.

Ascot
Company history unknown.
ASCOT w/race car
(5)   1930s   15in Metal   No Listing
White globe face with red-and-green-outlined green irregular shield-shaped design covering most of face. White lettering "ASCOT" across top of shield, "GASOLINE" arched around bottom, with white oval in center. Black, white, and green detailed 1920s race car on oval.

Atlantic Pacific Service Co., Mt. Vernon, Illinois
Company history unknown.
ATLANTIC PACIFIC A-P GAS
(5)   1920s   15in Metal   No Listing
Red outer band with double border white/red. Top says "ATLANTIC PACIFIC SERVICE CO." in white, "MT. VERNON, ILL." in white at bottom. Detailed early bi-plane in center. "A.P." above plane. "GAS" below plane.

Atlas
Company history unknown.
ATLAS SUPER POWER
(5)   1950s   13.5in Glass $100-$150
White globe face with red outline ring. Red "ATLAS" in reverse-bowtie lettering across center of face. Blue "SUPER" arched around top, "POWER" around bottom.

Atomic
Company history unknown.
ATOMIC GAS w/parachute & bomb
(5)   1950s   13.5in Glass $450-$750
Description not available.

Aviation Brand
Company history unknown.
AVIATION BRAND GASOLINE
(5)   1940s   15in Metal $1,800-$2,500
Black globe face with yellow center circle. Detailed black and white passenger airplane in center, over front view of old car. Yellow "AVIATION" arched around top, "GASOLINE" around bottom, with small black "BRAND" above airplane.

B&M Oil Company
Company history unknown.
B&M POWER PACK REGULAR
(4)   1950s   13.5in Capco $75-$125
White globe face with blue outline ring and blue lines forming white band across center. Red "B&M OIL CO." on upper field, red italic "POWER PAC" with speed lines on center band, red "REGULAR" on lower field.
B&M POWER PACK ETHYL
(4)   1950s   13.5in Capco $75-$125
Same as above, with Ethyl shield (EC) in small black circle replacing "REGULAR" on lower field.

Badger Oil Company
Wisconsin independent. Company history unknown.
BADGER 60-62
(5)   1930s   13.5in Glass   No Listing
White globe face with blue, white, and black outline rings. Black-outlined blue "BADGER" over blue "60-62" across center of face, with black and green badger at top of globe face.
BADGER w/shield
(5)   1930s   13.5in Glass   No Listing
White globe face with black outline ring. Large red shield covers most of face, with black "BADGER/PETROLEUM/COMPANY" on shield. Small white wings at bottom of shield.

Band City Oil Company, South Bend, Indiana
Company history unknown.
BAND CITY SUPER ETHYL
(5)   1950s   Oval Capco $150-$250
Blue globe face with large white burst covering most of face. Red band

arched around top, with white "BAND CITY" on band. Red "SUPER/ETHYL" in burst.

Bartles & Sweeney
Company history unknown.
BARTLES & SWEENEY
(5)   1910s   One-piece etched $750-$1,250
White globe with red "BARTLES/SWEENEY" across center of face. Red "GASOLINE" arched around bottom. Small 8in globe with 4in base.

Barto
Started by John Barto, former employee of Red Fox Petroleum of Ft. Wayne, Indiana.
BARTO GASOLINE
(4)   1940s   13.5in Capco $100-$150
White globe face with blue outline ring and blue lines forming white cross inside center circle. Red "BARTO" vertically and horizontally in cross, with blue "LUBRICATED" arched around top, "GASOLINE" around bottom.

Bay Petroleum, Saginaw, Michigan
Petroleum refining and marketing division of Bay City-based Dow Chemical.
BAY
(3)   1950s   13.5in Glass $125-$200
White globe face with red, blue, and red outline rings. Blue "BAY" across center of face.

Caminol Company, Long Beach, California
California refiner and marketer purchased by Canada's Ultramar in the 1980s. The company is currently operating under both Beacon and Ultramar brand names. It also operated under the Kettleman brand in the 1930s.
KETTLEMAN KING
(4)   1920s   15in Metal $750-$1,000
Bright blue globe face with yellow-outlined red "KETTLEMAN" arched around top, "GASOLINE" around bottom, with red-outlined yellow flat hexagon in center. Blue "KING" on hexagon.
BEACON-A CAMINOL PRODUCT
(4)   1920s   15in Metal $1,800-$2,500
White globe face with detailed nighttime lighthouse scene on face. Red and blue elongated triangles form border top and bottom. White lighthouse with blue lines and yellow light on blue "rock" mound against yellow and blue ocean. Blue, yellow, and white light rays at top. Yellow "BEACON" across top of light tower, above red "GASOLINE." Red "A CAMINOL PRODUCT" on base. Super detail.
BEACON CAMINOL CO. w/lighthouse
(4)   1930s   15in Metal $1,800-$2,500
White globe face with red-outlined yellow "chevron" style shield on face. Red, white, and blue lighthouse tower to left in shield, beach scene and ocean at bottom. Red "BEACON" in blue-outlined white band across top, above blue "SECURITY" and red "GASOLINE." Small blue "A CAMINOL/PRODUCT" at bottom.
BEACON SECURITY w/lighthouse
(4)   1930s   15in Metal $1,800-$2,500
White globe face with red-outlined hexagon on face. Blue background inside hexagon, with detailed white lighthouse tower and yellow light rays. Yellow waves against blue lighthouse base. Large yellow "BEACON" over smaller red "GASOLINE" across lighthouse tower. Red "THE CAMINOL" to left of tower, "COMPANY, LTD." to right of tower.
BEACON SECURITY w/lighthouse
(4)   1930s 15in Metal $1,800-$2,500
White globe face with blue and white lighthouse tower on blue base with blue and white waves. Red and yellow light with rays out from top of lighthouse. Vertical red "BEACON" on tower. Yellow "SECURITY" over white "GASOLINE," over red "A CAMINOL PRODUCT" on blue base.
CAMINOL ETHYL w/ethyl logo
(4)   1930s   15in Metal $400-$750
White globe face with red-and-white-outlined dark blue "chevron" type shield on face. Yellow "CAMINOL" over white "ETHYL," over small yellow "GASOLINE" on shield above white circle near bottom. Ethyl (EGC) logo on white circle.

Beacon
Company history unknown.
BEACON FLASH
(5)   1930s   13.5in Glass   No Listing

White globe face with outline ring. Lighthouse tower in center, with "BEACON" arched around top, "FLASH" around bottom.
BEACON AVIATION
(5)   1930s   13.5in Glass   No Listing
White globe face with red outline. Green and white lighthouse tower in center, with red beacon light and red wings. Green "BEACON" arched at top, "AVIATION" at bottom.
BEACON SKYWAY w/tower
(5)   1940s   13.5in Glass   No Listing
White globe face with light blue mountain scene behind blue structural steel tower on blue base. Red "BEACON" vertically on tower. Red "SKY" to left of tower, "WAY" to right, with white "SIGN OF SERVICE" on blue base.

Beaver Oil Company
Company history unknown.
BEAVER GASOLINE
(5)   1920s   15in Metal $250-$350
White globe face with blue outline ring. Blue "BEAVER" arched across top, over smaller blue "OIL/COMPANY." Blue "GASOLINE" across lower globe face.

Benzola
Company history unknown.
BEN ZOLA
(5)   1940s   Gill $200-$325
Description not available.

Benzoline
Company history unknown.
BENZOLINE
(5)   1930s   15in Metal $250-$350
White globe face with black "BENZOLINE" (large red "O") in bowtie lettering across globe face. Red lightning bolts above and below.

Berry Asphalt Company, Little Rock, Arkansas
Company history unknown.
BERRY HY-GRADE PREMIUM
(4)   1950s   13.5in Capco $175-$300
Blue globe face with yellow outline ring and yellow outline of Arkansas in center of face. Yellow "BERRY" arched across top of map, with yellow "HI-GRADE" diagonally across center. Yellow "PREMIUM" across bottom of globe face.

Big Chief
Company history unknown.
BIG CHIEF
(5)   1920s   15in Metal $1,800-$2,500
White globe face with black "BIG CHIEF" arched around top. Red and black Indian on lower globe face.

Big West Oil Company, Salt Lake City, Utah
Company history unknown.
BIG WEST GASOLINE
(5)   1940s   13.5in Glass   No Listing
Black-and-white-outlined black ring around globe face with red center. Black-and-white-striped stylized "mountain" on center circle, with white rays into red area of center. White "BIG WEST" arched in top of ring, "GASOLINE" at bottom.
BIG WEST X77
(5)   1940s   13.5in Glass $300-$550
Similar to above, with orange center circle with crossbar extending into outer ring. White "77" in center, with small "x" offset to left. White "BIG WEST" at top, "GASOLINE" at bottom.
HI GRADE SPUR GASOLINE
(5)   1940s   13.5in Glass $350-$600
Identical to above, with white-outlined black "Spur" in center in unique typestyle. Black spurs to either side. White "HI-GRADE" arched around top, "GASOLINE" around bottom.

Black Charger
Company history unknown.
BLACK CHARGER w/horse
(5)   1930s   15in Metal   No Listing
Orange globe face with black and white horse, with knight in center of face. Black-colored "BLACK CHARGER" arched around top, with script "Oxygenated/Gasoline" on lower globe face.

Blendo
Company history unknown.

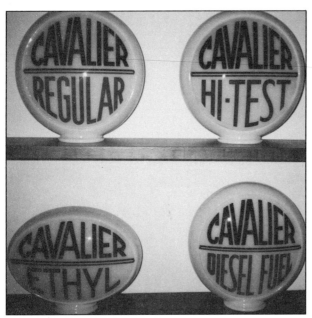

Super Kant-Nox Kanotex one-piece etched globe. Kyle Moore

Vickers Hi-Ratio Gasoline 15in inserts on metal body. Walt Feiger

Various Cavalier 13.5in inserts on glass bodies. Also, oval glass inserts on oval glass body. Lonnie Hop

Bell Regular 13.5in inserts on Gill orange ripple body and Bell Ethyl 13.5in inserts on Gill white ripple body.

Union Non Detonating 15in inserts on metal body.

Aero-Gas Anti-Knock one-piece etched globe. Gary Hildman

Ager Gas/Oils one-piece etched globe.

Super Power 15in inserts on metal body.

White Mule Gasoline one-piece etched globe. Mike Mullaly

British Petroleum one-piece globe.

Bull Dog Pep 15in inserts on metal body.

Chippewa Gasoline 15in inserts on metal body.

BLENDO-GAS
(5)   1920s   15in Metal $275-$350
Light yellow globe face with black-and-white-outlined black rectangle across center of globe face. White "BLENDO-GAS" in box.

Blue Bell
Company history unknown.
BLUE BELL
(5)   1930s   15in Metal   No Listing
Description not available.

Blue Bird Chemical Company, Los Angeles, California
Company history unknown.
BLUE BIRD INTERSTATE GAS
(5)   1920s   One-piece etched Oval   No Listing
Similar to metal-band globe below.
BLUE BIRD INTERSTATE GAS
(4)   1920s   15in Metal $650-$1,100
White globe face with large diamond in center. "BLUE BIRD" with small bird arched around top, "GASOLINE" around bottom, with "OIL/INTERSTATE/GAS" in distorted lettering in diamond.

Blue Blaze
Company history unknown.
BLUE BLAZE KEROSENE
(4)   1930s   13.5in Glass $225-$350
White globe face with red outline ring. Blue-colored "BLUE/BLAZE" with speed lines across upper globe face, above red "KEROSENE." Blue "Guaranteed/47 Gravity" (red 47) on lower globe face.

Blue Bonnet
Central Petroleum Corporation, Shelbyville, Indiana
Company history unknown.
BLUE BONNET GASOLINE
(5)   1930s   15in Metal   No Listing
White globe face with red and blue flowers in center with green leaves. Blue "BLUEBONNET" arched around top, "GASOLINE" around bottom.

Blue Ribbon
Golden Rule Oil Company, Wichita, Kansas
Company history unknown.
BLUE RIBBON GASOLINE
(5)   1920s   15in Metal   No Listing
White globe face with blue ribbon vertically in center. White arched "BLUE" over vertical "RIBBON" on ribbon, blue-colored "BLUE RIBBON" arched around top of globe face, red "GASOLINE" around bottom.

Bolene Refining Company, Enid, Oklahoma
Company history unknown.
BOLENE GASOLINE ball shaped
(5)   1920s   One-piece baked   No Listing
White sphere-shaped globe, with blue and white cross pattern around globe. White "BOLENE" vertically and horizontally around globe.
BOLENE
(5)   1920s   One-piece etched $1,000-$1,600
White globe, with blue outline ring around globe face and blue cross in center of face. White "BOLENE" vertically and horizontally on cross.
BOLENE GASOLINE round w/seal
(5)   1920s   One-piece etched   No Listing
Description not available.
BLUE SEAL
(4)   1920s   15in Metal $400-$650
White globe face with blue outline ring. Blue dot with red arrow in center, with blue-colored "BLUE" across top and "SEAL" across bottom.

Bolivar
Alleghany Refining, Incorporated
Company history unknown.
BOLIVAR GAS
(5)   1930s   15in Metal $450-$700
White globe face with small red, white, and blue flag at top. Black "ALLEGHANY REFINING" around flag. Yellow band across center, with black "BOLIVAR" in bowtie lettering on band. Black "GAS" below.
BOLIVAR GAS
(4)   1930s   13.5in Glass $300-$475
Similar to above.

BOLIVAR WITH ETHYL
(4)   1930s   13.5in Glass $275-$425
Similar to above, with Ethyl (EGC) logo replacing "GAS."

Bonded
Company history unknown.
BONDED HY
(5)   1930s   15in Metal $700-$1,000
Description not available.
BONDED UNIVERSAL
(5)   1930s   Gill $350-$650
White globe face with blue map of western hemisphere on globe face. Red-and-blue-outlined blue bowtie-shaped band across center, with white "UNIVERSAL" on band. Red "BONDED" arched down at top, "GASOLINE" up at bottom.

Bonner
Company history unknown.
BONNER GAS CO. w/arrow
(5)   1920s   12in Metal   No Listing
Description not available.

Boston
Company history unknown.
BOSTON GASOLINE
(5)   1920s   One-piece etched   No Listing
Description not available.

Browder Oil Company, Fort Worth, Texas
Company history unknown.
BROWDER REGULAR 76
(3)   1940s   13.5in Glass $250-$375
White globe face with blue outline ring. Red circle in center, with blue script "Regular" over white "76" in circle. Red "BROWDER" arched around top, "GASOLINE" around bottom.
BROWDER ETHYL (EGC)
(3)   1940s   13.5in Glass $250-$350
Same as above, with blue-outlined white circle in center. Blue and white Ethyl (EGC) logo with red rays in center circle.
BROWDER SPECIAL
(3)   1940s 13.5in Glass $250-$375
Same as above, with blue circle in center. Blue-outlined white "SPECIAL" across center of globe face.

Bruin Petroleum, Butler, Pennsylvania
Company history unknown.
BRUINOIL "BEAR OF THEM ALL"
(5)   1920s   15in Metal $2,000-$2,800
White globe face with detailed blue, white, and green mountain scene in center of face. Large bear in center, above blue "THE BEAR/OF THEM ALL." Red "BRUINOIL" arched around bottom.
BRUIN/PENNSYLVANIA PETROLEUM/PRODUCTS
(4)   1920s   15in Metal $1,750-$2,500
White globe face with seated light brown bear holding wooden keg at top of face. "BRUIN" in arched lettering below bear, over small "PENNSYLVANIA PETROLEUM/PRODUCTS."
BRUIN w/dark brown bear
(5)   1920s   15in Metal   No Listing
Same as above, with darker brown bear.

Bryco
Company history unknown.
BRYCO w/ethyl
(4)   1930s   13.5in Glass   No Listing
Description not available.

Budget
See listing for AMERICAN in this section.

Bull Dog
Company history unknown.
BULL DOG PEP
(5)   1930s   15in Metal   No Listing
White globe face with black outline ring around white center circle. Black-outlined red "BULL DOG" arched around top, "PEP" around bottom, with black and red bulldog with hat in center circle.

Buffalo
See listing for WESTLAND in this section.

Burgess

Company history unknown.

CAMPECO AVIATION

BURGESS GASOLINE ETHYL

(4)   1930s   15in Metal $250-$400

Description not available.

California Petroleum Company

Company history unknown.

CALPET

(5)   1930s   15in Metal   No Listing

White globe face with blue outline of four-leaf clover shape on face. Red "CALPET" across center. No other details known.

Cameo

Company history unknown.

CAMEO w/cameo

(5)   1920s   One-piece baked   No Listing

White globe with black outline around face and black outline around black center circle. White cameo figure in center circle. Red "CAMEO" arched around top, "GASOLINE" around bottom.

Campeco

Company history unknown.

CAMPECO AVIATION

(5)   1920s   One-piece etched   No Listing

White globe with blue outline ring and blue "CAMPECO" across center of face. Red "AVIATION" across top, "GASOLINE" across bottom.

Capitol

Company history unknown.

CAPITOL ETHYL

(4)   1930s   13.5in Glass $200-$325

Red globe face with white circle in center. Large Ethyl (EGC) logo in center circle. White "CAPITOL" arched around top, "ETHYL" around bottom.

Carrier Independent Oil Company

Company history unknown.

CARRIER INDEPENDENT OIL CO.

(5)   1920s   15in Metal $275-$375

Description not available.

Cargray

See listing for DORCO in this section.

Cascade

Company history unknown.

CASCADE GASOLINE

(5)   1940s   13.5in Glass $225-$350

Description not available.

Central Oil & Grease

Company history unknown.

CENTRAL OIL & GREASE SUPER MEDIUM

(4)   1920s   15in Metal $300-$475

Red globe face with black-outlined yellow center circle. Yellow "CENTRAL OIL" with black dropshade arched around top, "& GREASE CO." around bottom, with red "Super/Medium" in center circle.

CENTRAL OIL & GREASE SUPER HI-TEST

(4)   1920s   15in Metal $325-$500

Same as above, with "HiTest" replacing "Medium."

Certified Oil Company, Columbus, Ohio

Certified Oil currently operates more than 100 stations in Ohio.

CERTIFIED SUPER HI-TEST ETHYL

(4)   1950s   13.5in Capco $100-$150

White globe face with black script "Certified" across top of face. Red "SUPER HI TEST" across center, over small Ethyl (EC) logo in circle at bottom.

CERTIFIED HIGHEST QUALITY

(4)   1950s   13.5in Capco $100-$150

White globe face with red band diagonally across center. White "CERTIFIED" on band. Blue-outlined white banner top and bottom, with blue "HIGHEST" at top and "QUALITY" at bottom.

Certified 70

Company history unknown.

CERTIFIED 70 OCTANE

(4)   1940s   13.5in

White globe face with red outline ring. Blue script "Certified" across

center, over red "70 OCTANE" and black "GASOLINE." Black interlocked "LOGCO" at top of face.

Champion

Company history unknown.

CHAMPION GASOLINE w/race car

(5)   1920s   15in Metal   No Listing

Red globe face with white circle in center. Blue-detailed race car in center circle. White "CHAMPION" arched around top, "GASOLINE" around bottom.

CHAMPION REGULAR

(4)   1940s   13.5in Glass   No Listing

White globe face with red "Champion" over green "REGULAR" in center of face. Green lines from upper right to lower left.

CHAMPION w/Boxing Glove

(5)   1950s   13.5in Glass   No Listing

White globe with red "CHAMPION" arched around top. Yellow arm with red boxing glove and red lines in center. Red "MORE Power" across bottom.

Champion Oil Company, Madison, Indiana

Company history unknown.

CHAMPION 70 GASOLINE

(4)   1950s   13.5in Capco $125-$200

Description not available.

Chanute

Company history unknown.

CHANUTE ETHYL

(4)   1930s   Gill $200-$325

Red globe face with black-outlined white "CHANUTE" arched around top and "ETHYL" around bottom. White center circle with, Ethyl (EGC) logo in center with yellow rays.

Charm
Radiant Oil Company

Ohio marketer. Company history unknown.

CHARM GAS

(5)   1920s   One-piece etched $1,000-$1,600

Description not available. Similar to CHARM GAS below.

CHARM GAS

(5)   1930s   13.5in Glass $200-$300

White globe face with red outline ring. Blue script "Charm" over blue "GAS" on face.

Chippewa

Company history unknown.

CHIPPEWA GASOLINE w/Indian

(5)   1920s   15in Metal $1,700-$2,500

White globe face with black "CHIPPEWA" arched around top, red "GASOLINE around bottom, and red and black Indian head in center.

Cleburne Oil Company

Company history unknown.

CLEBURNE OIL CO. VELV-O-LENE GAS

(5)   1930s   15in Metal $400-$700

White globe face with large blue circle in center. White "GAS" in center circle. Blue "CLEBURNE OIL COMPANY" arched around top, red-outlined blue "VEL-VO-LINE" around bottom.

CLEBURNE OIL CO. US MOTOR GAS

(5)   1930s   13.5in Glass $225-$350

Description not available.

Climatic

Company history unknown.

CLIMATIC FLASH GASOLINE

(5)   1940s   13.5in Glass $250-$375

White globe face with "CLIMATIC" arched around top, "GASOLINE" around bottom, with italic-outlined "FLASH" with speed lines across center.

Clipper, New York

Company history unknown.

CLIPPER GASOLINE w/ship

(5)   1930s   15in Metal   No Listing

White globe face with black outline ring and black ship in center of face. Green "Clipper" arched around top, "Gasoline" around bottom, with green waves under ship.

CLIPPER HI-COMPRESSION

(5)   1930s   15in Metal   No Listing

Same as above, with "HIGH COMPRESSION" added under ship.

CLIPPER w/airplane (a Seattle company)
(4)   1940s   15in Metal $1,500-$2,200
White globe face with green and red airplane in center of face. Red "CLIPPER" with green dropshade and speed lines across lower globe face.
CLIPPER w/airplane (a Seattle company)
(4)   1950s   Oval Capco $400-$600
Same as above, except with oval format.

Clymer
Company history unknown.
CLYMER ANTI-KNOCK BLUE FIRST GRADE
(5)   1940s   13.5in Glass $275-$425
Description not available.

Coast-2-Coast Oil Company, Cleveland, Ohio
Company history unknown.
COAST 2 COAST
(5)   1920s   One-piece etched $1,000-$1,400
White globe face with black outline ring. Green "COAST 2 COAST" vertically and horizontally, crossing in center.

Coastal Petroleum Corporation, Mobile, Alabama
Company history unknown.
COASTAL GASOLINE
(4)   1932-1946   13.5in Glass $300-$450
White globe face with blue outline ring and blue circle in center. Detailed white sea gulls in center circle. Red "COASTAL" arched around top, "GASOLINE" around bottom.
COASTAL ANTI-KNOCK
(3)   1946-1960   13.5in Capco $250-$350
Same as above, with "ANTI-KNOCK" replacing "GASOLINE."
COASTAL PRODUCTS
(4)   1946-1960   13.5in Capco $250-$350
Same as above, with "PRODUCTS" replacing "GASOLINE."

Colonial Oil Company, Jacksonville, Florida
Company history unknown.
COLONIAL MINUTEMAN GASOLINE
(4)   1950-1970   13.5in Glass $275-$450
COLONIAL MINUTEMAN GASOLINE
(3)   1950-1970   13.5in Capco $175-$275
White globe face with blue and red outline rings. Blue Old English "Colonial" across center of face, over blue "MINUTEMAN" and red "GASOLINE." Red lines split by blue minuteman head at top of globe face.

Col-Tex
Indiana Home Oil Company, Indianapolis, Indiana
Company history unknown.
COL-TEX GASOLINE
(4)   1940s   13.5in Glass $125-$200
Description not available.

Colonial Oil Company, Des Moines, Iowa
Company history unknown.
COLONIAL PREMIUM
(4)   1950s   13.5in Capco $100-$150
White globe face with red "COLONIAL" in white wing logotype at top of face. Red-outlined white rectangle with red "PREMIUM" on lower globe face.

Columbia Oil Company
Company history unknown.
COLUMBIA OIL CO. COCO GASOLINE
(5)   1930s   15in Metal   No Listing
Black globe face with large white circle in center. White "COLUMBIA OIL COMPANY" arched around top of globe. Black "COCO" in center circle, with black-outlined white box across "COCO." Black "GASOLINE" in box.

Columbus
Company history unknown.
COLUMBUS GASOLINE W/COLUMBUS
(5)   1930s   15in Metal   No Listing
Description not available.

Consumers Oil Company, Nashville, Tennessee
Company history unknown.
CONSUMERS GASOLINE
(5)   1930s   15in Metal $350-$550
White globe face with blue outline around white center circle. Red chain design in center circle. Blue-outlined red "CONSUMERS" arched around top, "GASOLINE" around bottom.

Continental Refining Company, Oil City, Pennsylvania
Company history unknown.
CORECO
(5)   1910s   One-piece etched $1,600-$2,000
CORECO
(5)   1920s   15in Metal $700-$950
Yellow globe face with white-outlined red "CORECO" around top of face, "GAS" around bottom, with white-outlined black keystone in center. White "ESTABLISHED/1885" on keystone.
CORECO GAS W/PENNSYLVANIA
(5)   1920s   One-piece baked $900-$1,400
CORECO GAS w/Pennsylvania
(5)   1930s   13.5in Glass $300-$500
Yellow globe face with black map of Pennsylvania in center, with white "ESTABLISHED/1885" on map. Black-outlined red "CORECO" arched around top, "GAS" around bottom.

Corey's
Company history unknown.
COREY'S HIO 100
(4)   1950s   13.5in Capco $100-$150
White globe face with blue outline ring. Blue "H-I-O" arched around top, with red "COREY'S" across center. Blue-outlined white "100" on lower globe face.

Coronado
Company history unknown.
CORONADO WHITE
(5)   1940s   13.5in Glass   No Listing
Yellow globe face with green and white mountain scene on lower face. Red "CORONADO" arched around top. Yellow shield with red "SW" over white-colored "WHITE" on mountain scene.

Crescent Oil Company
Company history unknown.
CRESCENT
(5)   1920s   One-piece etched oval   No Listing
White oval globe with orange crescent moon in center. Black "CRESCENT" across center of globe.
CRESCENT GASOLINE
(4)   1920s   15in Metal $350-$600
Yellow globe face with orange-outlined black crescent moon forming "C" at left of face. Black "CRESCENT" arched above center, "GASOLINE" below, with orange rays extending out from moon, and black design in center.
CRESCENT OIL CO. INDEPENDENT GASOLINE
(4)   1930s   15in Metal $375-$700
CRESCENT OIL CO. INDEPENDENT GASOLINE
(4)   1930s   Gill   No Listing
White globe face with orange-outlined hexagon with orange crescent moon and star in center of face. Blue "CRESCENT OIL CO." arched around top, "GASOLINE" around bottom, with "INDEPENDENT" across center of globe face.

Cresyl
See listing for SITE in this section.

Crystal
Burford Oil Company, Pecos, Texas
Company history unknown.
CRYSTAL
(4)   1930s   One-piece baked $400-$600
White globe with black-outlined green in reverse-bowtie lettering across center of face.
CRYSTAL UPSIDE DOWN
(4)   1930s   One-piece baked $250-$350
Same as above, except with design inverted.
CRYSTAL
(5)   1930s   15in Metal $250-$350
Description not available.

Crystal Flash Petroleum, Indianapolis, Indiana
Crystal Flash is a family-owned private brand that had operations in both Indianapolis and in Grand Rapids, Michigan. The company continues to market through approximately twenty stations in Indiana.
CRYSTAL FLASH ANTI-KNOCK
(4)   1930s   16.5in $300-$525

Description not available.
CRYSTAL FLASH "DOPE FREE" ANTI KNOCK
(4)   1930s   Gill $225-$350
White globe face with blue "Crystal/-Flash" diagonally across upper face. Red "DOPE FREE" over blue "Anti-Knock" on lower face.
SUPER FLASH EXTRA POWER/HI COMP.
(5)   1930s   Gill $300-$425
White globe face with blue diagonal lines forming white band across center. Blue "SUPER FLASH" in band. Red "EXTRA/POWER" above band, "HIGH/COMPRESSION" below band.
CRYSTAL FLASH GASOLINE "JUST A LITTLE BETTER"
(4)   1946-1960   Gill $225-$325
White globe face with blue burst on upper face. White "Crystal/Flash" on burst. Red "GASOLINE" over "Just a Little Better" on lower globe face.
SUPER FLASH ETHYL (EGC)
(4)   1946-1960   Gill $275-$400
White globe face with red "SUPER/FLASH" over very early style Ethyl (EGC) logo. Despite the apparent age, this globe was in use as late as 1960.
SUPER 99
(5)   1957-1960   Gill $250-$400
Description not available.
CRYSTAL FLASH
(3)   1960s   Gill $275-$400
CRYSTAL FLASH
(4)   1960s   13.5in Capco $125-$175
White globe face with blue rectangle in center of face. White "Crystal Flash" with red lightning bolt on rectangle.
SUPER FLASH
(4)   1960s   Gill $275-$400
SUPER FLASH
(4)   1960s   13.5in Capco $125-$175
White globe face with blue-outlined white rectangle in center of face. Blue "Super Flash" with red lightning bolts on rectangle.

Cushing
Gibble Oil Company, Cushing, Oklahoma
Company history unknown.
CUSHING
(5)   1922-1930   One-piece etched $1,400-$2,000
Description not available.
CUSHING GASOLINE
(4)   1930-1940   Gill $450
White globe face with black "CUSHING" arched across top, "GASOLINE" across bottom, with red band and "C.R.G.CO." logo in center.
CUSHING ANTI-KNOCK
(4)   1930-1940   Gill $450
Same as above, with "ANTI-KNOCK" replacing "GASOLINE."
CUSHING ETHYL
(5)   1930-1940   Gill $450
Same as above, with Ethyl (EGC) logo on lower globe face. No band or logo in center.
CUSHING-GIBBLE-PREMIUM
(4)   1940-1960   13.5in Capco $250-$350
White globe face with black-outlined red line across center, split in center by black-outlined red triangle. White "GIBBLE/OIL/CO." in triangle. Black-outlined red "CUSHING" arched around top, "PREMIUM" around bottom.
CUSHING-GIBBLE ANTI-KNOCK
(3)   1940-1960   13.5in Capco $250-$400
Same as above, with "ANTI-KNOCK" replacing "PREMIUM."

Cyclo
Company history unknown.
CYCLO ETHYL
(4)   1930s   13.5in Capco $200-$300
Description not available.

Danciger Refineries, Tulsa, Oklahoma
An independent Tulsa refiner involved in gasoline marketing under the Road Runner brand.
DANCIGER ROAD RUNNER REGULAR
(4)   1930s   13.5in Glass $400-$700
White globe face with red outline ring and red circle in center. Detailed black and white road runner bird across center of face. Blue "DANCIGER/ROAD RUNNER" arched around top, "REGULAR" around bottom.
DANCIGER ROAD RUNNER ANTI-KNOCK
(4)   1930s   13.5in Glass $400-$700
Same as above, with blue "ANTI-KNOCK" replacing "REGULAR."

DANCIGER ROAD RUNNER 400
(4)   1940s   13.5in Glass $350-$500
Same as above, with "400" replacing "REGULAR."
DANCIGER ROAD RUNNER RACER
(4)   1940s   13.5in Glass $350-$500
White globe face with blue outline ring. Red circle offset to upper right of face, with speed lines arched to left. Large blue "RACER" arched over speed lines. Red "ROAD/RUNNER" across top, black and white road runner bird on lower face.

Davis
Company history unknown.
DAVIS GASOLINE
(5)   1930s   15in Metal $250-$350
Green globe face with white-outlined red band across center. White "DAVIS" on band, with "PRODUCTS" arched around top and "PETROLEUM" around bottom.

Delco
Lindsay-McMillan Company, Milwaukee, Wisconsin
Company history unknown.
DELCO MOTOR OILS
(5)   1920s   One-piece etched   No Listing
White globe with black script "Delco" diagonally across center of face. Red "LINDSAY McMILLAN CO.'s" arched around top, "MOTOR OILS" around bottom.
DELCO GASOLINE
(5)   1926-1930   One-piece baked $800-$1,300
White globe with red outline ring around face. Black script "Delco" over black "GASOLINE" in center of globe face. Small IOMA thunderbird logo under "GASOLINE." Red "AS GOOD AS GAS CAN BE" arched around top, "LINDSAY McMILLAN CO." around bottom.
DELCO BENZOL GAS
(5)   1926-1930   One-piece baked $900-$1,500
White globe with red outline ring around face. Black script "Delco" over black "BENZOL" in center of globe face. Small red and black logo below "BENZOL." Red "BETTER THAN GASOLINE" arched around top, "LINDSAY McMILLAN CO." around bottom.

Delta
See Mapco.

Denver
Company history unknown.
DENVER
(3)   1950s   13.5in Capco $75-$100
Green globe face with white band across center. Red "DENVER" in band.

Dixcel
Milton Oil Company, Sedalia, Missouri, and
Pioneer Oil Company, Carthage/Joplin, Missouri
As best as can be determined, Milton Oil Company of Sedalia, Missouri, introduced the Dixcel brand sometime around 1930. Pioneer Oil of Carthage and Joplin, Missouri, was apparently a jobber for Dixcel that sometime after WW II acquired the brand from Milton. Milton continued to operate under the Savex brand well into the 1970s, and Pioneer rebranded from Dixcel to Pioneer sometime around 1960. Current status of either company cannot be determined.
A TRIAL TELLS/GASOLINE
(5)   1930-1935   15in Metal   No Listing
A TRIAL TELLS/DIXCEL/GASOLINE
(4)   1930-1946   13.5in Glass $225-$325
White globe face with large orange circle in center. Black band across face. White "DIXCEL" on band, with black "A Trial Tells" arched around top of orange area and black "GASOLINE" arched around bottom.
MILTON OIL CO./DIXCEL/GASOLINE
(4)   1930-1946   13.5in Glass $225-$325
Orange globe face with black outline ring and black ring around white center circle. Black band across center, with white "DIXCEL" on band. White "MILTON OIL CO." arched around top, "GASOLINE" around bottom.
PIONEER OIL CO./DIXCEL/GASOLINE
(4)   1946-1960   13.5in Glass $225-$325
Same as above, with "PIONEER OIL COMPANY" replacing "MILTON OIL COMPANY."
PIONEER OIL CO./MOTOR/GASOLINE
(4)   1946-1960   13.5in Glass $225-$325
Same as above, with "MOTOR" replacing "DIXCEL."

DIXCEL PREMIUM ETHYL (EC)
(4)   1946-1970   13.5in Glass $200-$300
Orange globe face with black outline ring and black outline around
white center circle. White "DIXCEL" arched around top, "PREMIUM"
around bottom, with Ethyl (EC) logo in center.
PIONEER REGULAR blk/orange
(4)   1960-1970   13.5in Capco $100-$150
Orange globe face with black outline ring. White-outlined black "PIO-
NEER" over black "REGULAR." Black underline under "REGULAR."
PIONEER PREMIUM blk/orange
(4)   1960-1970   13.5in Capco $100-$150
Same as above, with "PREMIUM" replacing "REGULAR."
Postwar Milton Oil Company marketing
SAVE WITH SAVEX
(3)   1946-1970   13.5in Glass $250-$350
White globe face with green band across center. White "SAVEX" on
band. Black "SAVE" arched around top, over "WITH," and black
"GASOLINE" arched around bottom.
SAVEX ETHYL
(3)   1946-1970   13.5in Glass $250-$350
Green globe face with white circle in center. White "SAVEX" arched
around top, "PREMIUM" around bottom, with large Ethyl (EC) logo in
center.

Dobson
Company history unknown.
DOBSON RED DART GASOLINE
(4)   1950s   13.5in Capco $150-$200
White globe face with red outline ring. Red arrowhead with
"RED/DART" in center. Blue "DOBSON" across top, "GASOLINE"
across bottom.

Dollar Value
Company history unknown.
DOLLAR VALUE GASOLINE w/ "$"
(5)   1930s   15in Metal $300-$550
White globe face with large green-outlined orange dollar sign ($) in
center. Green-outlined red "VALUE" across dollar sign. Red-outlined
green "DOLLAR" arched around top, "GASOLINE" around bottom.

Dorchester Gas Producing Company, Amarillo, Texas
Company history unknown.
DORCO
(3)   1950s   13.5in Capco $150-$250
Black globe face with yellow, black, and yellow outline rings. Yellow
"DORCO" diagonally across center. Yellow and black circle design
with wings at top of face.
CARGRAY ETHYL
(4)   1950s   13.5in Capco $125-$175
Similar to DORCO above. Description not available.
CARGRAY GOLD
(4)   1950s   13.5in Capco $125-$175
Similar to DORCO above. Description not available.

Dough Boy
Company history unknown.
DOUGH BOY w/shield
(5)   1920s   15in Metal   No Listing
White globe with red, white, and blue striped shield in center of face.
Red "DOUGH BOY" arched around top, "GASOLINE" around bottom.

Drakes Refinery Stations, Incorporated
Drakes is an independent Michigan discount service station oper-
ation that continues to operate six stations today.
HI-OCTANE DRAKES REGULAR w/bird
(4)   1950-1970   13.5in Capco $200-$325
White globe face with black script "Drakes" across center. Black "HI
OCTANE" arched around top, with grey, black, and yellow duck in
flight across lower face. Black-outlined yellow "REGULAR" superim-
posed over duck.
SUPER DRAKES ETHYL (EC)
(5)   1950-1970   13.5in Capco $150-$225
White globe face with black script "Drakes" across center. Black
"SUPER" arched around top, with Ethyl (EC) logo on lower face.

E
Company history unknown.
E-ETHYL
(5)   1950s   15in Metal $150-200
White globe face with blue outline ring. Large orange "E" in center,
with blue "ETHYL" across "E."

Economy
Company history unknown.
BUY ECONOMY GAS
(5)   1930s   15in Metal $300-450
White globe face with green bowtie "ECONOMY" across center. Red
"BUY" at top, "GASOLINE" across bottom.
ECONOMY OILS (w/three stars)
(5)   1930s   15in Metal $325-$600
Black globe face with red band across center. Red "ECONOMY"
arched around top, "OILS" around bottom, with three white stars and
black "QUALITY SERVICE ECONOMY" on center band.

Eddy Refining Company, Houston, Texas
Company history unknown.
EDDY
(5)   1950s   13.5in Capco   No Listing
Description unavailable.

El Camino
Company history unknown.
EL CAMINO (w/mission scene)
(5)   1930s   15in Metal   No Listing
Detailed mission scene on globe face.

Eldred Oil Company, Warren, Pennsylvania
Company history unknown.
ELDRED GASOLINE
(5)   1920s   One-piece etched $900-$1,500
White globe with red outline ring. Black-outlined yellow triangle cov-
ers most of globe face. Red map of Pennsylvania in center, with white
"OIL" on map. Black "ELDRED" across upper triangle. "OIL" across
lower triangle. This design will be referred to as an "Eldred logo"
throughout these descriptions.
ELDRED GASOLINE
(5)   1920s   15in Metal $450-$700
White globe face with large Eldred logo in center.
BETTY BLUE THE WONDER GAS
(5)   1920s   One-piece etched $1,100-$1,800
White globe with blue outline ring around face. Blue ring around center circle, with small Eldred logo in center. Blue "BETTY BLUE"
arched around top, red "THE WONDER GAS" around bottom.
ELDRED BETTY BLUE
(4)   1930s   13.5in Glass $350-$625
ELDRED BETTY BLUE
(4)   1930s   Gill $375-$650
White globe face with black and red and black outline rings. Black and
red ring around center circle, with small Eldred logo in center. Black-
outlined blue "BETTY BLUE" arched around top, "THE WONDER
GAS" around bottom.
ELDRED BETTY BLUE (no logo)
(5)   1930s   Gill $250-$350
White globe face with black outline ring and red circle in center. Black
band across center, with white "ELDRED" in band. Blue "BETTY
BLUE" arched around top, "GASOLINE" around bottom.
ELDRED ETHYL
(5)   1920s   One-piece etched $1,200-$1,600
ELDRED ETHYL
(4)   1920s   15in Metal $375-$550
White globe face with black outline ring. Black outline around center
circle. Small Ethyl (EGC) logo in center circle. Black-outlined red "EL-
DRED" arched around top, "GASOLINE" around bottom.
ELDRED NEVRNOX
(5)   1920s   One-piece etched $1,100-$1,700
                  6in or 7in base
White globe face with red outline ring. Black-outlined red "NevrNox"
across upper globe face, above Eldred logo.
ELDRED NEVRNOX
(5)   1920s   15in Metal $400-$650
White globe face with large Eldred logo in center. Black-outlined red
"NevrNox" across top of face over logo.
ELDRED STRAIGHT RUN 68-70
(5)   1920s   15in Metal $375-$500
Red globe face with black-outlined white band across center. Black-
outlined white "ELDRED" across upper face, "HIGH TEST" on lower
face, with black "68-70 STRAIGHT RUN" across center band.
ELDRED SUPER GAS
(5)   1920s   One-piece etched $1,200-$1,900
White globe with black outline around globe face. Black-outlined orange Eldred logo in center, with black Pennsylvania map with white
"SUPER" across map. Black "HI-TEST" across top of globe face over
logo.

Clipper Gasoline 15in inserts on metal body. John Phippen

Columbus Gasoline one-piece fired-on globe.

Coreco one-piece etched globe. Kyle Moore

Coronado White 13.5in inserts on glass body.

Danciger Road Runner 13.5in inserts on glass body.

Eldred Gas one-piece etched. Kyle Moore

Eldred NevrNox 15in inserts on metal body.

Eldred Straight Run High Test 15in inserts on metal body.

EMCO one-piece etched globe.

Ethyl 15in inserts on metal body.

First National Gasoline one-piece etched globe.

Ford Benzol one-piece fired-on keyhole-shaped globe.

Fosters Supertane Regular and Ethyl 13.5in inserts on glass body. R. V. Witherspoon

Galtex one-piece etched.

Gar-vis 15in inserts on metal body. R. V. Witherspoon

ELDRED SUPER GAS
(5)   1920s   One-piece etched $1,200-$1,900
White globe with red outline around globe face. Large yellow Eldred logo in center, with white "SUPER" on red map. Black "HI-TEST" across top of face over logo.
ELDRED SUPER GAS
(5)   1920s   15in Metal $375-$600
Description not available.

Electrogas
Custer City Oil Company, Bradford, Pennsylvania
Company history unknown.
ELECTROGAS–CUSTER CITY OIL CO.
(5)   1930s   13.5in Glass $275-$400
White globe face with red outline ring. Blue "ELECTROGAS" with red lightning bolt across center. Blue "CUSTER CITY OIL CO." arched around top, "BRADFORD, PA" around bottom.

Emery Manufacturing Company
Company history unknown.
EMCO GAS
(5)   1920s   One-piece etched $750-$1,100
White globe with red "EMCO" across center. Black "EMERY MFG. CO." arched around top, "GASOLINE" around bottom.
EMCO 100% PENNA GAS
(5)   1920s   One-piece baked $650-$850
Dark green border, "100% PENNA" around top, and "GASOLINE" around bottom in dark green. Large red "EMCO" in center of face, trimmed in dark green.

Equator
Company history unknown.
EQUATOR GASOLINE
(5)   1920s   One-piece etched   No Listing
White globe with black world globe in center. Red rays surrounding globe, with red "EQUATOR" with black dropshade across globe. Red "GASOLINE" across bottom.

Erickson Oil Company, Minneapolis, Minnesota
Founded in Barron, Wisconsin, in 1931, Erickson is a pioneer discount service station operation. From 1931 until 1959 they expanded the chain of "gas only" discount stations throughout the north central states. In 1959 they launched "Holiday," a combination gasoline-convenience store that was the first of its kind.

Located in small towns throughout their marketing territory, Holiday stations supplied not only automotive needs but convenience store items and sporting goods as well. By the mid-1960s, many former Erickson "gas only" locations had been converted into Holiday Station stores. Where the primary brand for the chain's 230-plus locations today is Holiday, some stations, under control of various Erickson family members, remain branded Erickson or Erickson-Freedom.
ERICKSON'S 110 ETHYL
(5)   1935-1950   Glass oval $250-$450
White oval globe face with green "ERICKSON'S" arched around top, "ETHYL" around bottom, with large red "100" over green "HI-GRADE" in center.
ERICKSON'S RANGE OIL
(5)   1946-1950   Glass oval $250-$450
White oval globe with yellow "ERICKSON'S" arched around top, "HIGHEST QUALITY" around bottom, with blue "RANGE OIL" across center.
ERICKSON'S
(4)   1950-1965   Oval Capco $125-$200
Yellow globe face with black outline ring. Red script "ERICKSON'S" across globe face.

Esta, Reading, Pennsylvania
Company history unknown.
ESTA MOTOR FUEL
(4)   1940s   Gill $200-$350
White globe face with blue, red, and blue lines forming white diagonal band across center of globe face. Blue-outlined red "ESTA" on band. Blue "MOTOR" above band, "FUEL" below.
ESTA ETHYL
(4)   1940s   Gill $200-$350
White globe face with blue, red, and blue lines forming diagonal band across center. Blue-outlined red "ESTA ETHYL" in band.

Este Oil Company, Cincinnati, Ohio
Company history unknown.

GO ESTE
(4)   1950s   13.5in Glass $200-$325
Description not available.

Ethyl Corporation, Richmond, Virginia
In 1922 the General Motors research labs in Dayton, Ohio, discovered that tetraethyl lead could be added to gasoline to increase its anti-knock properties. Higher compression engine development had been hindered by the lack of an available motor fuel. Refiners Oil Company, a Dayton independent, was chosen to first market the blended gasoline. Ethylizers, mixing chambers that dispensed tetraethyl lead into gasoline, were added to pumps at several Refiners locations. The marketing experiment was deemed a success and in September 1923, Standard Oil of Indiana signed an agreement with General Motors to distribute the new gasoline throughout its territory. In early 1924, both GM and Standard looked at a partnership to produce and market the new product, but GM rejected Standard's offer and instead teamed up with Standard of New Jersey (Esso). Esso had also been experimenting with tetraethyl lead, and their operations complemented GM's better than anything Standard had to offer.

In August 1924, the Ethyl Gasoline Corporation was formed from GM and Esso's joint operation. In May 1925, Ethyl sales were temporarily suspended due to some lead poisoning concerns after several people involved in the manufacture of Ethyl died.

The US Surgeon General, after more than a year's research, allowed Ethyl to resume operations with the understanding that all blending would be done at the refinery and that the Ethyl mixers added to gasoline pumps would be removed. Sales resumed in June 1926, and gasoline marketers everywhere applied for an Ethyl franchise. Strict guidelines for refining gasoline to be blended with Ethyl were set up, and it was not until 1933 that tetraethyl lead could be added to a regular-grade gasoline.

In April 1942, the Ethyl Gasoline Corporation became simply the Ethyl Corporation, and the logo was redesigned at that time. The company continues to market gasoline additives today.
ETHYL GASOLINE GENERAL MOTORS
(5)   1923-1924   15in Metal   No Listing
White globe face with large black triangular Ethyl logo in center. Yellow "ETHYL GAS" on triangle, with yellow banner across lower area of logo. Black "GENERAL MOTORS PRODUCT" on banner. Blue rays surround logo.
ETHYL (EGC)
(5)   1924-1942   One-piece baked $750-$1,250
White globe with large Ethyl (EGC) logo on globe face.
ETHYL (EGC)
(5)   1924-1942   15in Metal $300-$550
White globe face with large Ethyl (EGC) logo with blue rays.
ETHYL GASOLINE
(5)   1924-1942   15in Metal   No Listing
White globe face with black outline ring and black ring around white center circle. Red "ETHYL" arched around top, "GASOLINE" around bottom, with small Ethyl (EGC) logo with blue rays in center.
ETHYL (EGC) (smaller than full face)
(5)   1924-1942   13.5in Glass $225-$325
White globe face with black outline ring around large center circle. Large Ethyl (EGC) logo with yellow rays in center circle.
ETHYL (EC)
(5)   1942-1950   15in Metal $300-$600
ETHYL (EC)
(5)   1942-1965   13.5in Capco $225-$325
White globe face with black outline ring. Large Ethyl (EC) logo with yellow rays covering most of the face.

Ethylene Gasoline Company, Dallas, Texas
Company history unknown.
ANTI-KNOCK GASOLINE
(5)   1930s   15in Metal $375-$650
White globe face with black outline ring and yellow ring around white center circle. Black "ANTI-KNOCK" arched around top, "GASOLINE" around bottom with yellow/red shield with text in center.

Eureka
Bristolville Oil and Gas Company, Bristolville, Ohio
Company history unknown.
EUREKA GAS
(5)   1920s   One-piece etched $1,400-$2,200
White globe with yellow outline ring. Black "BRISTOLVILLE OIL AND GAS CO." arched around top, "EUREKA GAS" around bottom, with green four-leaf clover in center and smaller clovers placed around that.

Company

history unknown.

R EVERY DROP WORKS

_s_   One-piece etched   No Listing

obe lace with red "POWER" arched around top, "GASOLENE" around bottom, with green "EVANS OIL" over red "EVERY DROP" over green "WORKS" in center.

Excelsior
C. E. Mills Oil Company, Syracuse, New York
Company history unknown.

EXCELSIOR GASOLINE

| (5) | 1910s | One-piece etched chimney top | No Listing |

Similar to Metal globe listed below

EXCELSIOR GASOLINE

| (5) | 1920s | 15in Metal | $450-$650 |

White globe face with black banner across center. "C. E. MILLS OIL CO." in banner. Red "EXCELSIOR" arched around top, red "GASO-LINE" around bottom.

SUPERIOR GASOLINE

| (5) | 1920s | 15in Metal | $450-$650 |

Same as above, with "SUPERIOR" replacing "EXCELSIOR."

F-W
Company history unknown.

F-W GREEN

| (5) | 1930s | 15in Metal | $225-$325 |

White globe face with green band 2/3 across from left with white "F-W," small green triangle offset at end of band, above green band 2/3 across from right with white-colored "GREEN," and small green triangle offset at end of band.

F-W

| (4) | 1940s | 13.5in Capco | $75-$125 |

White globe face with large block letter "F-W" on center of face. Small green triangle above and below "F-W."

Fairplay Oil Company
Company history unknown.

FAIRPLAY OIL CO.

| (5) | 1930s | 15in Metal | $225-$300 |

White globe face with red "FAIRPLAY/OIL/CO." on face.

Falls
Company history unknown.

FALLS STRAIGHT RUN GAS

| (5) | 1920s | 15in Metal | $400-$600 |

White globe face with large black arrow across center. Red "FALLS" across top, "GAS" across bottom, with white "STRAIGHT RUN" on arrow.

Fargo
Company history unknown. Marketed in the North Atlantic area.

FARGO REGULAR

| (3) | 1950s | 13.5in Capco | $100-$150 |

White globe face with two fine red lines across center, creating a white center band. Red "FARGO" in band. Blue "REGULAR" below band.

TORNADO ETHYL

| (4) | 1950s | 13.5in Capco | $125-$175 |

White globe face with two fine blue lines across center, creating a white center band. Blue "TORNADO" in band. Blue "ETHYL" below band.

Federal Oil Company, Los Angeles, California
Company history unknown.

FEDERAL SUPER GASOLINE

| (5) | 1930s | 15in Metal | $275-$400 |

White globe face with large red "Super" across center. Smaller black "Federal" above "Super," and "Gasoline" below.

FEDERAL ETHYL GASOLINE

| (5) | 1930s | 15in Metal | $275-$425 |

Same as above, with script "Ethyl" above "Gasoline."

Fiore 100
Chicago area marketer. Company history unknown.

FIORE 100

| (4) | 1950s | 13.5in Capco | $100-$150 |

White globe face with black outline ring. Large red circle in center. Black "FIORE/100" in red circle.

First National Oil Corporation, Long Island City, New York
Company history unknown.

FIRST NATIONAL GASOLINE

| (5) | 1920s | One-piece etched | No Listing |

White globe with outline ring around face. Circle in center, with outline ring and lines forming white band across center of globe face. "NATIONAL" on center band, with "FIRST" arched around top and "GASOLINE" around bottom.

Fleet
Shelby Petroleum Company, La Follette, Tennessee
Shelby Petroleum is an independent marketer that operates discount gasoline stations in Tennessee, Kentucky, and Virginia. Stations were rebranded from Fleet to Peer about 1960. The company also operated stations under the Sail brand, and currently operates less than twenty stations, all branded Peer.

Note: No Peer or Sail globes are known to exist.

FLEET REGULAR

| (5) | 1940s | 13.5in Capco | $150-$200 |

White globe face with "FLEET" diagonally across face. "REGULAR" below "FLEET." No other details known.

FLEET ETHYL

| (5) | 1940s | 13.5in Capco | $150-$200 |

Same as above, with "ETHYL" replacing "REGULAR."

Flight
Company history unknown.

FLIGHT

| (5) | 1930s | 15in Metal | $225-$375 |

Globe face has yellow upper area and blue lower area, with blue lines offsetting white arched band across center. Red "Flight" with speed lines arched in band.

Forester New-Way Serv/Ind Oil of North Carolina, North Wilkesboro, North Carolina
Forester New-Way is an independent jobber, founded in 1928, with an elaborate station in North Wilkesboro, North Carolina. The company operated under the Fonse brand until 1953, when they became a branded Esso jobber. It continues to market Exxon products today.

FONSE

| (5) | 1928-1953 | 15in Metal | $225-$350 |

White globe face with blue lines forming white cross on face. Blue "FONSE" vertically and horizontally, in cross.

Ford Motor Company, Dearborn, Michigan
While General Motors was involved in developing the gasoline additive tetraethyl lead, Ford was promoting a benzol-based motor fuel as an alternative to the low-octane gasoline of the day. Genuine Ford Benzol was sold through select Detroit-area Ford dealers. By 1940, Ford had began promoting a benzol product to independent Michigan marketers under a franchise-type program.

FORD BENZOL

| (4) | 1925-1930 | One-piece baked | $2,200-$3,500 |

Keyhole-shaped one-piece globe. Blue globe face with white outline. White script "Ford" over white "BENZOL" on face. Some have decal with yellow "ALTERNATE FUEL" arched around top. Red line around body perimeter.

FORD BENZOL

| (5) | 1930-1935 | 15in Metal | $750-$1,350 |

Blue flat globe face with white outline ring. White script "Ford" over white "BENZOL" on face.

FORD BENZOL

| (5) | 1935-1940 | 13.5in Glass | $300-$600 |

Blue globe face with white outline ring. White script "Ford" over white "BENZOL."

BENZOL PREMIUM BLEND w/star

| (4) | | Banded Glass | |

Blue globe face with red and white outline rings. Small white star with red center dot on blue circle near top, over white "BENZOL/PRE-MIUM/BLEND."

BENZOL JR w/star

| (4) | | 13.5in Glass | $275-$425 |

White globe face with white star with red center dot on blue circle at top. Brown "BENZOL" over "JR" below star across face.

Foster Oil Terminals, Opp, Alabama
Gulf Coast wholesale operation with a few branded stations. It survived into the 1970s.

FOSTER OIL CO. (w/red star)
(5)   1920s   One-piece etched   No Listing
White globe with large red star in center. Black "FOSTER" arched around top, "OIL CO." around bottom.
FOSTER SUPERTANE
(2)   1950s   13.5in Capco $275-$450
White globe face with large blue "flame" design covering most of face. Orange script "Supertane" across flames. Blue-outlined orange "FOSTER" arched around top, "OIL COMPANY" around bottom.
FOSTER SUPERTANE ETHYL
(2)   1950s   13.5in red Capco $275-$450
Same as above, with white circle on lower flame area. Small Ethyl (EC) logo in circle.

Galtex
Deyo Oil Company, Incorporated, Galveston, Texas
Company history unknown.
GALTEX
(5)   1910s   One-piece etched $1,100-$1,600
White globe with black outline around face. Yellow bar-and-circle across center. Fifteen-inch white "GALTEX" in center bar. Fifteen-inch yellow "PALE FILTERED" arched around top, "MOTOR OILS" around bottom.
GALTEX GAS
(5)   1920s   16.5in Metal $350-$550
White globe face with red bar-and-circle across center of face. White "GALTEX" on center bar. Red "DEYO OIL CO. Inc." arched around top, "THE BETTER GASOLINE" around bottom.

Gano
Company history unknown.
GANO SPECIAL
(4)   1930s   Gill $250-$400
Description not available.

Garrett Oil Company
Company history unknown.
GARRETT OIL CO. LILY GASOLINE
(5)   1920s   One-piece etched   No Listing
White globe with black "GARRETT OIL COMPANY" arched around top. Black "LILY" over orange "GASOLINE" on lower globe face.

Gar-Vis, The Southern Oil Reclaiming Company, Anderson, South Carolina
GAR-VIS PRODUCTS
(5)   1930s   15in Metal   No Listing
Yellow globe face with dark-blue-outlined white center circle. Blue outline broken such that white center has band extending to edge of face at upper left and lower right. Red "GAR-VIS" with black dropshade diagonally across center over "PRODUCTS." Red "GAS" with black dropshade in upper center extension, "OIL" in lower extension.

Gasamat, Fort Collins, Colorado
Gasamat was founded in Fort Collins, Colorado, in 1957 when the local Phillips 66 jobber became involved in experiments with coin-operated gas pumps. By the 1960s, Gasamat had developed into a chain of drive-through self-service stations with live-in attendants. The company expanded into convenience stores and abandoned the drive-through operation in the 1970s. It operates around fifty stations today.
GASAMAT
(4)   1957-1965   Oval Capco $150-$250
White oval globe with red elongated hexagon covering most of face. Yellow logotype "Gasamat" on red hexagon.
GASAMAT "SERVE SELF"
(5)   1965-1970   13.5in Capco $100-$150
White globe face with red lines forming white shield on face. Red "Gasamat" logotype on upper shield, over red "SERVE/SELF."

Gas Stop
Company history unknown.
GAS STOP
(5)   1960s   13.5in Capco $150-$275
White globe face with blue outline ring. Blue-outlined red "Gas/Stop," with small stop sign on center of face.

Gate Petroleum, Jacksonville, Florida
Founded by former Billups executives when Hess purchased Billups, Gate Petroleum operates a chain of discount service stations throughout the Southeast.

GATE 93
(5)   1964-1967   13.5in Capco $100-$150
White globe face with large red "93" in center. Red "GATE REGULAR" arched around top. No other details known.
GATE
(5)   1967-1970   13.5in Capco $200-$300
White globe face with red, white, and blue GATE logo in center.

Gaylor
Company history unknown.
GAYLOR
(5)   1950s   13.5in Capco $125-$175
Red globe face with red-outlined yellow bowtie band across center of face. Red "GAYLOR" in band.

General Oil and Gasoline Company, Cleveland, Ohio
Company history unknown.
SUNLIGHT GASOLINE
(5)   1920s   15in Metal   No Listing
White globe face with blue area across bottom. Large orange sun with rays in center of face. Blue "GENERAL OIL and GASOLINE CO." arched around top, blue-outlined orange "SUNLIGHT" arched through rays. White "GASOLINE" across bottom of globe face, with "CLEVELAND, OHIO" arched around bottom.

General Oil Company
Company history unknown.
GENERAL MOTOR FUEL
(4)   1930s   15in Metal $400-$650
White globe face with black outline ring. Red-outlined yellow shield in center, with red "MOTOR" and "FUEL" on shield. Black band diagonally across center, with yellow "GENERAL" on band.
SER-VIS (on shield)
(4)   1930s   15in Metal $400-$600
Same as above, with "SER-VIS" on band.
GENOCO (on shield)
(5)   1930s   15in Metal $400-$650
White globe face with yellow outline ring. Red-outlined white shield in center, with yellow band diagonally across face. Black "GENOCO" in band.
ORIOLE GAS (on shield)
(4)   1930s   15in Metal $450-$750
Same as GENOCO above, with blackbird on top of shield, black "ORIOLE" replacing "GENOCO" in band, and red "GAS" below band.

G. E. Smith Oil Company
Company history unknown.
G. E. SMITH GAS–octagon chimney cap
(5)   1910s   One-piece etched   No Listing
Description not available.

Gilland Oil Company, Albuquerque, New Mexico
Company history unknown.
GILCO HIGH ALTITUDE GASOLINE
(5)   1920s   15in Metal   No Listing
Description not available.

Ginn Service Stations
Company history unknown.
GINN SERVICE STATIONS
(5)   1950s   13.5in Capco $125-$175
White globe face with orange-and-white-striped trapezoid in center of face. Black "GINN/SERVICE STATIONS" in trapezoid.

Gladiator
Company history unknown.
GLADIATOR GASOLINE US MOTOR SPEC
(5)   1930s   13.5in Glass $300-$500
White globe face with black outline ring. Black circle at top of face, with black and white swords crossed through circle. Black "GLADIATOR" across center over "GASOLINE," with black "U.S.MOTOR SPECIFICATION" arched around bottom.

Globe Oil Company, McPherson, Kansas
A midcontinent refiner and marketer operating under the Globe brand throughout the central United States.
GLOBE yellow border
(5)   1940s   13.5in Glass   No Listing
Same as below, with yellow outline area. Series of blue cars and trucks around yellow band.

GLOBE ETHYL yellow border
(4)   1940s   13.5in Glass $350-$550
Same as GLOBE ETHYL below, with yellow outline ring. No cars in border.

GLOBE GASOLINE
(3)   1930s   Gill $350-$550
White globe face with red outline area. Blue-outlined world globe, with blue grid and blue North and South America covering most of globe face. White-outlined blue band arched across map, with white "GLOBE" in band. Blue "GASOLINE" arched around bottom.

GLOBE ETHYL
(3)   1930s   Gill $350-$525
Same as above, with Ethyl (EGC) logo replacing "GASOLINE" at bottom of globe face.

UTILITY GASOLINE
(4)   1930s   Gill $350-$550
Same as GLOBE above, with red "UTILITY" replacing "GLOBE" in band.

Good Luck Oil Company, Dallas, Texas
Company history unknown.
GLOCO
(4)   1950s   13.5in Capco $225-$325
White globe face with black outline ring. Red "GLOCO," with red and white shading across center of face.

Goco
Company history unknown.
GOCO
(5)   1930s   Gill $500-$700
Service station attendant holding nozzle and hose.

Go Devil
Company history unknown.
GO DEVIL BENZOL
(5)   1920s   16.5in Metal   No Listing
White globe face with large red and black devil's head covering most of face. Black "GO DEVIL/BENZOL" across face.

Good Luck—Ohio River Refining, Cincinnati, Ohio
Company history unknown.
GOOD LUCK GASOLINE
(5)   1930s   15in Metal $400-$650
"GOOD LUCK" in green, inside arching yellow band across top. Four-leaf clover at bottom.

GOOD LUCK ETHYL (EGC)
(5)   1930s   15in Metal $400-$650
Similar to above, with Ethyl logo below clover.

Gold Bond—Sovereign Oil Company, Chicago, Illinois
Company history unknown.
GOLD BOND GASOLINE
(5)   1920s   One-piece etched $1,200-$1,800
White globe with yellow face. White circle around yellow center circle. Black "SOVEREIGN OIL CO." arched around top of white circle, "GASOLINE" around bottom. White area in center circle, with red "GOLD/TRIED AND TESTED/BOND."

GOLD BOND 70
(5)   1930s   Gill $700-$1,350
White globe face with black outline ring and black ring around yellow center circle. Fifteen-inch yellow "GOLD BOND" arched around top, "70" around bottom, with detailed yellow, black, and white mountain scene in center.

Golden
Company history unknown.
GOLDEN TOP OCTANE SUPER REGULAR
(4)   1940s   12.5in Glass $225-$350
White globe face with yellow outline ring and yellow-outlined semi-circles in center. Black "TOP OCTANE" arched around top, red "REGULAR" across center, and red "SUPER" around bottom.

GOLDEN 102 PREMIUM (EC)
(4)   1940s   12.5in Glass $225-$350
White globe face with yellow outline ring. Yellow "GOLDEN" arched around top, over red "102." Small Ethyl (EC) logo on lower face, with red "PREMIUM" arched around bottom.

GOLDEN 97 ETHYL (EC)
(4)   1940s   12.5in Glass $225-$350
Same as above, with red "97" replacing "102" and "ETHYL" replacing "PREMIUM."

GOLDEN 100+ OCTANE
(4)   1940s   13.5in Capco $225-$350
Description not available.

Golden Eagle
Company history unknown. Thought to be one of the California-based postwar self-service originators.
GOLDEN EAGLE
(5)   1946-1950   13.5in Capco   No Listing
Mint green globe face with white outline ring and white outline around red center circle. Large yellow and black eagle in center of face. Yellow "GOLDEN EAGLE" arched around top, "GASOLINE" around bottom.

Golden Gate
Company history unknown
GOLDEN GATE GASOLINE w/bridge
(5)   1930s   15in Metal   No Listing
Description not available.

Golden West Oil Company, San Antonio, Texas
Company history unknown.
GOLDEN WEST OIL CO.
(5)   1940s   13.5in YELLOW Capco $450-$750
Globe face has elaborate yellow and white sunset over blue water scene. White banner across top with black "GOLDEN WEST." Blue "OIL COMPANY" over sun in scene.

Goodrich
Company history unknown.
GOODRICH
(5)   1926-1935   15in Metal   No Listing
Yellow background, with black letters "GOODRICH" above"GASO-LINE." Large fancy "G" serves as "G" for both words.

GOODRICH ETHYL (EGC)
(4)   1926-1935   15in Metal $300-$500
White globe face with red outline ring and red outline around white center circle. Red "GOODRICH" arched around top, "GASOLINE" around bottom, with large Ethyl (EGC) logo in center.

GOODRICH A-K SPECIAL
(5)   1926-1935   15in Metal   No listing
Yellow globe face with black outline ring and black ring around red center circle. Black "GOODRICH" arched around top, "SPECIAL" around bottom with large black outlined yellow "A-K" in center red circle.

Gossettes Oil Company, Griffin, Georgia
Company history unknown.
GOSSETTS OIL CO. DIXIE GEM
(5)   1930s   15in Metal $275-$450
White globe face with red script "Dixie Gem" diagonally across face. Black "GOSSETTS OIL CO." arched around top, "GRIFFIN, GA" around bottom.

GOSSETTS OIL CO. REGULAR
(5)   1930s   15in Metal $250-$450
White globe face with red "REGULAR/GASOLINE" across center. Red "GOSSETTS OIL CO." arched around top, "GRIFFIN, GA" around bottom.

Gramps
Company history unknown.
GRAMPS
(5)   1930s   15in Metal $200-$300
White globe face with two black lines across center so as to form a white center band. Black "GRAMPS" on band.

Gurney
See listing for WNAX in this section.

Guyler—Russian Oil Company, Chicago, Illinois
Company history unknown.
GUYLER BRAND GASOLINE/MOTOR OIL
(4)   1930s   14in Gill $450-$675
Description not available.

GUYLER BRAND ANTI-KNOCK GASOLINE
(4)   1930s   14in Gill $450-$675
Red globe face with white-outlined red diamond in center. White "GUYLER" with blue dropshade diagonally across diamond, "BRAND" on lower right of diamond. White "ANTI-KNOCK" arched around top, "GASOLINE" around bottom.

GUYLER BRAND HIGH-TEST GASOLINE
(5)   1930s   Gill   No listing
Same as above, "HIGH-TEST" replacing "ANTI-KNOCK."

Hall Brothers, Dayton, Ohio
Company history unknown.
HALL BROS. SUPER 67
(4)   1950s   13.5in Banded Glass $225-$375
White globe face with blue outline ring. Red "HALL BROS." arched around top, with large red "67" in center. Blue "SUPER" across "67."
HALL BROS. SUPER 72
(4)   1950s   13.5in Banded Glass $225-$375
Same as above, with "72" replacing "67."
HALL BROS. SUPER 80 BENZOL
(5)   1950s   13.5in Banded Glass $275-$425
Same as above, with "80" replacing "67," and "BENZOL" across bottom of globe face.
HALL BROS. KEROSENE
(5)   1950s   13.5in Banded Glass $200-$350
Same as above, with blue "KEROSENE" replacing "67."
HALL BROS. FUEL OIL
(5)   1950s   13.5in Banded Glass $200-$350
Same as above, with blue "FUEL OIL" replacing "67."

Haney's
Company history unknown.
HANEY'S INDEPENDENT GASOLINE
(5)   1930s   15in Metal $550-$850
White globe face with large red "H" in center. Blue arrow through "H," with red "INDEPENDENT" arched above and "DEPENDABLE" below. Blue "HANEY'S" arched around top of face, "GASOLINE" around bottom.

Hanley
Company history unknown.
HANLEY
(5)   1940s   13.5in Glass $200-$300
Yellow globe face with geartooth border and blue outline area. Blue "HANLEY" with white dropshade across center of face.

Harmony, Monroe, Michigan
Company history unknown.
HARMONY–MUSIC TO YOUR MOTOR
(5)   1930s   Green ripple gill $1,400-$2,000
White globe face with green "HARMONY" in bowtie lettering across center of face. Red "MUSIC," "TO/YOUR," "MOTOR" across lower globe face.
UNIVERSAL
(5)   1930s   Green ripple gill $1,300-$2,000
White globe face with large 15in green triangles on upper and lower globe face forming white band across center. Red "UNIVERSAL" across center band.

Hart Oil Company
Company history unknown.
HART OIL CO. GASOLINE AND MOTOR OILS
(5)   1920s-1930s   15in Metal   No Listing
Description not available.

Hearn
Company history unknown.
HEARN
(5)   1920s   15in Metal cast faces $600-$850
Description not available.

Heart of Dixie
Company history unknown.
HEART OF DIXIE PREMIUM
(5)   1950s   13.5in Capco $150-$225
Green globe face with white outline around green center circle. Red heart in center circle, with white-outlined red "HEART OF DIXIE" arched around top, "PREMIUM" around bottom.

Hendrix Oil Company, Lineville, Alabama
Company history unknown.
HENDRIX OIL CO.
(5)   1950s   13.5in Red Capco $150-$250
White globe face with double blue lines arched above and below center, forming white center band. Large blue "Hendrix" in band, with blue "OIL CO." below band.

Dryer, Clark and Dryer, Oklahoma City, Oklahoma
Company history unknown.
HERCULES ETHYL GASOLINE
(3)   1946-1960   13.5in Glass $125-$175
Green globe face with white circle in center. White "HERCULES" arched around top, "GASOLINE" around bottom, with red "ETHYL" across center.

Hicksatomic
An Illinois marketer. Company history unknown.
HICKSATOMIC
(5)   1946-1950   Oval Glass $250-$450
HICKSATOMIC
(2)   1950-1965   Oval Capco $150-$250
White globe face with red outline ring. Red sun with rays in center. Green "HICKSATOMIC" in progressively larger letters across center of face.

Hico
Company history unknown.
HICO ANTIKNOCK HIGH COMPRESSION
(5)   1930s   15in Metal   No Listing
Yellow globe face with black outline around white center circle. Black, white, and black lines around yellow diamond in center. Fifteen-inch white "HICO" and smaller black text in center diamond. Black "ANTI-KNOCK" arched around top, "HIGH COMPRESSION" around bottom.
HICO HIGH COMPRESSION
(5)   1930s   13.5in Glass $375-$600
Description not available.

Hi Flite
Company history unknown.
HI FLITE
(4)   1950s   13.5in Glass $200-$300
Description not available.

Hi Energee
Company history unknown.
HI ENERGEE GASOLINE
(4)   1950s   13.5in Capco $100-$150
White globe face with red outline ring. Red "HI/ENERGEE" with blue underline in center of globe face. Blue "GASOLINE" above small "WSJ" at bottom of face.

Hilite
Company history unknown.
HILITE S AND L
(4)   1950s   13.5in Glass $200-$325
White globe face with black "Hilite" across center of face. Fifteen-inch interlocked squares at bottom of globe face, with red "S and L" in squares.

Hills
Company history unknown.
HILLS (w/transport)
(4)   probably 1940s   13.5in Glass   No Listing
Description not available.

Hi-O-Co
Company history unknown.
HI-O-CO
(4)   1940s   Gill   No Listing
Blue globe face with white circle in center. Green four-leaf clover in center, with blue "72" on clover. White "HI-O-CO" arched around top, "GASOLINE" around bottom.

Hi Power
Denny Klepper Oil Company, Wichita, Kansas
Company history unknown.
HI-POWER 70
(5)   1930s   Gill $250-$350
White globe face with red "HI-POWER" and lightning bolts across center of globe face. Blue "70" at top of globe face.
HI-POWER
(5)   1930s   Gill $250-$350
White globe face with red "HI-POWER" and lightning bolts across center of face.
HI-POWER ETHYL
(5)   1930s   Gill $250-$350
Description not available.

129

Harmony Music in your Motor 13.5in inserts on Gill green ripple body. Don Meyr

Hygrade 15in inserts on metal body.

Kenoco Ethyl 13.5in inserts on glass body.

Laurel Leaf neon-lighted globe and sign.

Liberty Oil Company 15in inserts for metal body (top), and Walburn Ethyl 15in insert for metal body (bottom). Tyler Rider

Liberty Gasoline 15in inserts on metal body.

MacMillan 95 Gasoline 15in inserts on metal body. Brad Lego

Marine Gasoline 15in inserts on metal body.

Mayflower 13.5in inserts on glass body. Scott Anderson

O-Gas-Co 15in inserts on metal body.

Pugh Peerless oval glass inserts on oval glass body. Lonnie Hop

Pure Penna Gas one-piece etched globe.

H. & J. Oil Company Quality Gasoline one-piece etched globe. Lonnie Hop

Hi-Power Oil Company, Forest City, North Carolina
Company history unknown.
HI-POWER w/soaring eagle
(5)   1935-1950   13.5in Glass   No Listing
Red globe face with white outline around light blue center circle. Detailed black and white eagle in flight in center circle. White "HI-POWER" arched around top, "GASOLINE" around bottom.

Hi-Way 99
Company history unknown.
HI-WAY 99 ETHYL
(5)   1930s   15in Metal   No Listing
Yellow globe face with 15in white highway shield in center. Black "99" in shield. Diagonal black line lower to upper right, across globe face. Black "HI-WAY" at top, "ETHYL" at bottom.

Holiday
Company history unknown. Not related to Erickson-Holiday.
HOLIDAY REGULAR 94 OCTANE
(5)   1950s   13.5in Capco $150-$225
Green globe face with black outline ring. Fifteen-inch yellow interstate-style shield, with green "HOLIDAY" at top and black "REGULAR 94 OCTANE" in lower area.

Home Oil Company, Maysville, Kentucky
Company history unknown.
HOME OIL CO. GAS MAYSVILLE, KY
(5)   1920s   15in Metal $250-$450
White globe face with large blue-outlined orange circle in center of face. White-outlined blue "GAS" in center circle. Blue "HOME OIL CO." arched around top, "MAYSVILLE, KY." around bottom.
HOME OIL CO. ANTI-KNOCK
(5)   1920s   15in Metal   No Listing
White globe face with blue band across center. Blue "HOME OIL CO." arched around top, "MAYSVILLE, KY." around bottom, with white-outlined blue "ANTI-KNOCK SPECIAL" on center band.
HOME OIL CO. GASOLINE (w/old house)
(5)   1920s   15in Metal   No Listing
White globe face with black outline around white center circle. Detailed brown, black, and white picture of house in center circle. Black "GASOLINE" arched around top, "HOME OIL CO." around bottom.

Home Oil Company, Baltimore, Maryland
Company history unknown.
HOMOCO (w/eagle)
(5)   1930s   15in Metal $750-$1,100
White globe face with red outline ring. Black and white perched eagle in center, with red banner across eagle. White "HOMOCO" on banner.
HOMOCO 100 SUPER
(5)   1946-1970   13.5in Capco $125-$150
White globe face with yellow outline ring. Green and white eagle at top, with yellow banner across eagle. White "HOMOCO" in banner. Large yellow "100" over green "SUPER" on lower globe face.
HOMOCO KEROSENE
(5)   1946-1970   13.5in Capco $150-$200
White globe face with red outline ring. Green and white eagle at top, with red banner across eagle. White "HOMOCO" on banner. Green "KEROSENE" across lower globe face.

Home Oil Company
Company history unknown.
THE HOME OIL CO./HOCO GAS
(5)   1920s   15in Metal   No Listing
White globe face with red-and-white-outlined red band across center. White "HOCO-GAS" in band. Red "THE HOME OIL CO." arched around top. Red script "IT HAS THE PEP" across lower face.

Home State
A Michigan marketer. Company history unknown.
HOME STATE GASOLINE
(5)   1930s   15in Metal $500-$800
Red globe face with green center circle. White "HOME STATE" arched around top, "GASOLINE" around bottom, with white map of Michigan in center circle. Black "MICHIGAN" across map.

Hoosier
Company history unknown.
HOOSIER IND. OIL GASOLINE
(5)   1930s   15in Metal $450-$700
Description not available.

Hoosier King
Company history unknown.
HOOSIER KING
(4)   1950s   13.5in Capco $175-$300
Yellow globe face with dark green outline ring. Green-outlined white map of Indiana in center, with green crown at top of map. Green "HOOSIER" over script "KING" across center of globe.

Horton's, Little Rock, Arkansas
Company history unknown.
HORTON'S
(5)   1950s   Oval Capco $125-$200
White globe face with blue outline ring. Blue "HORTON'S" across center of face, with two red uprights which along with and "HORTON'S" form an "H."

Huffman
Company history unknown.
HUFFMAN PREMIUM
(5)   1950s   13.5in Glass $200-$300
Description not available.

Hurricane
Oil Refineries, Incorporated, Shreveport, Louisiana
Company history unknown.
HURRICANE GASOLINE
(5)   1935-1942   13.5in Glass $350-$600
White globe face with red outline ring. Black script "HURRICANE" arched around top, black "GASOLINE" around bottom, with red "spinner" in center.
HURRICANE ETHYL
(4)   1935-1942   13.5in Glass $275-$500
Same as above, with large Ethyl (EGC) logo replacing spinner.

Hustol
Company history unknown.
HUSTOL
(4)   1940s   13.5in Glass $275-$375
White globe face with black "H" covering most of face. Detailed turrets on top and bottom of uprights on "H." Yellow "HUSTOL" on crossbar of "H."

Hy-Flash—Miller Oil Company, Toledo, Ohio
Company history unknown.
HY-FLASH PREMIUM
(4)   1940s   13.5in Capco $1750-$300
Blue globe face with red and white outline rings. Yellow circle in center, with large red arrowhead in white area pointed to red dot in center of yellow circle. Light blue "HY FLASH" arched around top, yellow script "PREMIUM" around bottom.

Hygrade Oil and Fuel Corporation, Buffalo, New York
Company history unknown.
HYGRADE
(5)   1930s   15in Metal $300-$450
White globe face with black outline ring. Fifteen-inch yellow bowtie band across center of face, with red "HYGRADE" in band.

Hy Pure—A. J. Carran Company
Company history unknown.
HY-PURE A. J. CARRAN CO.
(5)   1920s   15in Metal $275-$475
Blue globe face with white "bar-and-circle" design across center. Red "HY-PURE" in center bar. White "A. J. CARRAN CO." arched around top, "GASOLINE AND OILS" around bottom.

Hy-Speed
Company history unknown.
HY-SPEED LOCAL OIL GAS
(5)   1920s   One-piece etched $850-$1,400
White globe with orange band across center. White "HY-SPEED" in center band. Black "LOCAL OIL" arched around top, "GAS" around bottom.

Illinois Oil Company, Rock Island, Illinois
Company history unknown.
ILLINOIS OIL CO. TORPEDO GASOLINE
(4)   1920s   15in Metal $600-$1,000
White globe face with black outline ring, and black around white center circle. Black and white torpedo across center, with red "Torpedo."

Red "ILLINOIS OIL CO." arched around top, "GASOLINE" around bottom.

THAT GOOD TORPEDO GAS
(5)   1930s   15in Metal   No Listing
White globe face with black outline ring. Black outline of the state of Illinois covering most of face, with 15in white banner across map. Black "ILLINOIS OIL CO." in banner, with red "THAT/GOOD" above banner and "TORPEDO/GASOLINE" in unusual lettering below banner.

ILLINOIS OIL CO. CHAMPION
(5)   1930s   Gill   No Listing
White globe face with black and red outline ring. Large red map of Illinois covers most of face, with 15in white banner across upper area of map. Black "ILLINOIS OIL CO." in banner, with black "CHAMPION" below in bowtie lettering.

Independent—Racetrac Petroleum, Atlanta, Georgia

Racetrac Petroleum was founded as the Oil Well Company in Opp, Alabama, after WW II. In 1960 the company was purchased by St. Louis discounter Carl Bolch. In 1977, the Raceway brand name replaced Oil Well at independently owned stations. The company also operates stations under the Racetrac brand name. They supply over 200 stations throughout the South.

INDEPENDENT ETHYL "THE OIL WELL"
(4)   1950s   13.5in Glass $300-$500
White globe face with black oil derrick in center of face. Red "INDEPENDENT" arched around top, "The OIL WELL" around bottom, with red "REGULAR" across center.

INDEPENDENT REGULAR "THE OIL WELL"
(4)   1950s   13.5in Glass $325-$550
Same as above, with red "ETHYL" and small Ethyl (EC) logo replacing "REGULAR" across center of face.

Indian Oil Products Company, Cleveland, Ohio

Company history unknown.

INDIAN AEROLENE
(5)   1920s   15in Metal   No Listing
White globe face with black "INDIAN OIL PRODUCTS CO." arched around top, and running Indian on lower face carrying arrow. Black "AEROLENE" on arrow.

Indiana Oil Company, Lafayette, Indiana

Company history unknown.

INDIANA
(4)   1950s   13.5in Capco $100-$150
Red globe face with white outline ring and white band across center. Red "INDIANA" in center band.

INDIANA ETHYL
(4)   1950s   13.5in Capco $125-$175
Red globe face with white outline ring and white band across center. Red "INDIANA" in center band. Ethyl (EC) logo on lower red area below band.

Instant

Company history unknown.

INSTANT AVIATION
(5)   1950s   Oval Capco   No Listing
White globe face with green outline ring and large green "INSTANT" over smaller green "AVIATION." Small red airplane at top of face.

Iowa Oil Company, Dubuque, Iowa

Company history unknown.

IOWA GAS
(5)   1920s   One-piece etched $750-$1,250
White globe with red block lettering "IOWA/GAS" across face.

IOWA GAS
(4)   1920s   One-piece etched $800-$1,300
Same as above, with red "IOWA" arched over "GAS."

IOWA GAS
(5)   1930s   Gill $400-$600
White globe face with red outline ring. Red "IOWA" in reverse-bowtie lettering, nested into red "GAS" in bowtie lettering.

Iroquois

Company history unknown.

IROQUOIS CHIEF (w/Indian)
(5)   1940s   13.5in Glass $700-$1,200
White globe face with black outline ring and black ring around white center circle. Red "IROQUOIS" arched around top, "CHIEF" around bottom, with detailed multicolored Indian head in center circle.

J.B. Flowers

Company history unknown.

J. B. FLOWERS GAS
(5)   1930s   15in Metal $275-$450
Description not available.

Kaw Valley Oil Company

Company history unknown.

KVX SUPER HIGH COMPRESSION
(5)   1930s   13.5in Glass $225-$375
White globe face with large red "KVX" in center. Blue arrow through "KVX." Blue "KAW VALLEY OIL CO." arched around top over blue "SUPER," with blue "HIGH/COMPRESSION" below "KVX."

Kayo—Torch Oil Company, St. Louis, Missouri

Operated under the Kayo brand in the 1920s. No direct connection to Chattanooga-based Kayo Oil, although when the Kayo brand was introduced, they used a logotype similar to that of Torch Oil's Kayo.

KAYO TORCH GAS
(5)   1920s   One-piece etched   No Listing
White globe face with red outline ring around face and red upper half of face. Large white "KAYO" on upper red area, with red and black flame design in center. White "TORCH" on flame. Black "HIGH COMPRESSION" arched around bottom.

Kentucky Oil Company

Company history unknown.

KENOCO
(5)   1950s   13.5in Glass $200-$325
White globe face with red band across center. White "KENOCO" on red band. Blue wings at top of face.

Kettleman

See listing for BEACON in this section.

KHTA

Company history unknown.

KHTA
(5)   1930s   16.5in Metal   No Listing
Description not available.

Kilnoc

Company history unknown.

KILNOC BLUE
(5)   1930s   15in Metal $300-$550
Description not available.

King

Company history unknown.

KING PERFORMANCE PLUS BENZOL
(5)   1940s   13.5in Glass $250-$400
White globe face with red outline ring and red lines forming white band across center. Red "PERFORMANCE/PLUS" in center band, with blue "KING" above band and blue "BENZOL" below.

Kingfish Oil Company, Kannapolis, North Carolina

Company history unknown.

KING FISH HI-SPEED ANTI KNOCK
(5)   1930s   One-piece baked   No Listing
Green globe face with red band across center. White fish outline and "HI-SPEED" on center band. White "KING FISH" arched around top, "ANTI-KNOCK" around bottom.

Kno-Klick

Company history unknown.

KNO-KLICK
(5)   1930s   15in Metal   No Listing
White globe face with black outline ring. Red "KNO-KLICK" across center, with black "HI-TEST" arched around top and "GASOLINE" around bottom.

La Salle Gasoline, Burkburnett, Texas

Company history unknown.

LA SALLE GASOLINE
(5)   1930s   15in Metal   No Listing
White globe face with red outline ring. Red diamond with black rectangle in center of globe face. Red script "LaSalle" on rectangle. Black "GASOLINE" arched around top, "BURKBURNETT, TEXAS" around bottom.

LA SALLE
(4)   1940s   13.5in Glass $250-$350
LA SALLE
(4)   1950s   13.5in Capco $125-$175
White globe face with large red diamond in center. Black rectangle superimposed over diamond, with red script "LaSalle" on rectangle.
LA SALLE ETHYL
(4)   1940s   13.5in Glass $250-$375
LA SALLE ETHYL
(4)   1950s   13.5in Red Capco $150-$200
Same as above, with logo placed higher, and small Ethyl (EC) logo in circle on lower globe face.

Laurel Leaf
Company history unknown. Thought to be a Wyoming marketer.
LAURELEAF
(5)   1920s   15in Metal   No Listing
LAURELEAF
(4)   1930s   13.5in Glass $300-$550
LAURELLEAF
(5)   1930s   18in Metal band neon   No listing
White globe face with black outline ring. Detailed green leaves in center, with red "LAURELEAF" across center.

Liberty Oil Company, Mount Vernon, Illinois
Company history unknown.
LIOCO
(5)   1920s   15in Metal $800-$1,400
White globe face with black ring around white center circle. Red "LIOCO" arched around top, "GASOLINE" around bottom, with black and white Statue of Liberty in center circle. Black "LIBERTY" to left of statue, "OIL CO. INC." to right.
LIBERTY GASOLINE
(5)   1920s   15in Metal   No Listing
Orange globe face with black area on lower face. Large black and white drawing of Statue of Liberty on orange area, with white "LIBERTY/GASOLINE" below.
LIBERTY OIL CO. LIBERTY GASOLINE
(5)   1930s   15in Metal $900-$1,500
White globe face with blue Statue of Liberty in center. Blue "LIBERTY" to left, "OIL CO. INC." to right of statue, with red "LIBERTY" arched around top, and "GASOLINE" around bottom.
LIBERTY BLUE (w/liberty)
(4)   1930s   15in Metal $1,100-$1,700
Blue globe face with red Statue of Liberty in center. White "LIBERTY/BLUE" across statue. Small red "LIBERTY OIL CO. INC." arched around bottom.
LIBERTY
(5)   1940s   Gill $500-$900
White globe face with blue outline ring. Small blue Statue of Liberty at left side of globe face, with red vertical rectangle to right. White vertical "LIBERTY" on red rectangle.

Liberty Pep
Company history unknown.
LIBERTY PEP ETHYL
(5)   1930s   15in Metal $300-$550
Red globe face with black outline ring and black ring around white center circle. Large Ethyl (EGC) logo in center, with white "LIBERTY PEP" arched around top, "GASOLINE" around bottom.

Life—Barnett Oil Company
Company history unknown.
LIFE GASOLINE
(4)   1930s   13.5in Glass $750-$1,250
Red globe face with large yellow circle in center. Red, white, black, and green elf in center circle. White "LIFE" arched around top, "GASOLINE" around bottom.
LIFE ETHYL
(5)   1930s   13.5in Glass   No listing
Red globe face with white center circle. White "LIFE" arched around top, "GASOLINE" around bottom with large Ethyl (EGC) logo in center.

Lighthouse
Company history unknown, thought to be a Michigan company.
LIGHTHOUSE GASOLINE
(5)   1920s   One-piece baked   No Listing
White globe with red and white brick lighthouse in center. Black script "Lighthouse" arched around top, "Gasoline" around bottom.

LIGHTHOUSE GAS
(5)   1920s   One-piece etched   No Listing
White globe with red face. Non-detailed green, black, and yellow lighthouse in center, with white "LIGHTHOUSE" across upper area above "GAS."

Lightning
Company history unknown.
LIGHTNING MOTOR FUEL
(5)   1920s   15in Metal   No Listing
Green globe face with white outline ring and wide red band across center. Fifteen-inch white "LIGHTNING" arched across band, over smaller "MOTOR FUEL."

Liquid Lightning
Company history unknown.
LIQUID LIGHTNING NOT DOPED
(5)   1920s   15in Metal   No Listing
Description not available.

Little Oil Company, Richmond, Virginia
Founded about 1920, Little was an early Esso jobber that also marketed a low-grade gasoline under their own brand. By the 1950s Little Oil had become a large Phillips 66 jobber, and they continue in operation today.
LITTLE
(5)   1920s   15in Metal   No Listing
White globe face with black "LITTLE" across face.

Little Bear
Company history unknown.
LITTLE BEAR GASOLINE
(5)   1930s   Gill $950-$1,500
Red globe face with white circle in center. Brown bear in center circle. White "LITTLE BEAR" arched around top, "GASOLINE" around bottom.

Little Major's
Company history unknown.
LITTLE MAJOR'S REGULAR
(5)   1950s   13.5in Capco $100-$175
White globe face with black outline ring. Black "LITTLE MAJORS" arched around top, yellow rocket in center over red "REGULAR."
LITTLE MAJORS ETHYL
(5)   1950s   13.5in Capco $100-$175
Same as above with "ETHYL" replacing "REGULAR."
HI-TEST
(5)   1950s   13.5in Capco $100-$175
White globe face with black outline ring. Red "Hi-Test" and rocket over small Ethyl (EC) logo.

Lonzo
Company history unknown.
LONZO REGULAR
(5)   1950s   13.5in Capco $100-$150
Red globe face with white band across center. Blue "REGULAR" in center band, with white "LONZO" arched around top, "OIL CO." around bottom.
LONZO ETHYL
(5)   1950s   13.5in Capco $100-$150
Same as above, with "ETHYL" replacing "REGULAR."

Lunsford
Company history unknown.
LUNSFORD 78 REGULAR
(4)   1930s   13.5in Banded Glass $225-$375
White globe face with black and orange outline rings. Black "LUNSFORD" arched around top, "OIL COMPANY" around bottom, with orange "REGULAR" over black "78" in center.
LUNSFORD 88 ETHYL
(4)   1930s   13.5in Banded Glass $225-$350
White globe face with black and orange outline rings. Black "LUNSFORD OIL COMPANY" arched around top, with large Ethyl (EGC) logo in center and black "88" at bottom.

M
Company history unknown.
M (w/airplane) 1950s   13.5in Capco $175-$350
Yellow globe face with red outline ring and large red "M" in center of face. Red-outlined white airplane flying through "M."

M & H—Miller and Holmes, St. Paul, Minnesota

Founded in 1896 as a wholesale grocer, Miller and Holmes entered the gasoline market under the M&H brand in 1931. They expanded greatly in the 1950s with as many as thirty-five stations throughout the upper Midwest. Today they operate large discount-type gasoline stations, most with convenience stores.

M&H
(4)   1933-1960   13.5in Capco $75-$100
White globe face with red "M&H" across center.

M&M

Company history unknown.

M&M SUPER ETHYL
(5)   1950s   13.5in RED Capco $175-$250
White globe face, with red "M&M" with black dropshade arched around top of face. Red italic "SUPER" with speed lines across center, above small Ethyl (EC) logo.

MacMillan Petroleum, New York, New York

A lubricants manufacturer that operated a few gas stations from the 1930s until the 1980s.

MacMILLAN 95 1930s   15in Metal $500-$850
GASOLINE (w/car)
Red globe face with white, black, and white outline rings. White "MacMILLAN 95 GASOLINE" with black dropshade in center of face, with small black and white car and star at top of face.

MacMILLAN XTRA OCTANE
(5)   1930s   15in Metal   No Listing
Description not available.

MacMILLAN ETHYL
(5)   1930s   15in Metal   No Listing
Description not available.

Magic Benzol Gas

See listing for THONI'S in this section.

Magic—Geauga Oil Company, Cleveland, Ohio

Company history unknown.

MAGIC GAS
(5)   1920s   One-piece etched $900-$1,600
White globe face with blue script "MAGIC" across center of face. Red "burst" behind "MAGIC." Red "GEAUGA OIL CO." arched around top, "GASOLINE" around bottom.

Magnet

Company history unknown.

MAGNET
(5)   1950s   13.5in Capco $100-$175
White globe face with black outline ring. Large 15in red horseshoe magnet in center of face. Red-outlined black "MAGNET" across center.

Major Oil Company, Wilmington, Delaware

Company history unknown.

SUPER MAJOR ETHYL
(5)   1940s   13.5in Glass   No Listing
Description not available.

Marcus Harris

Company history unknown.

MARCUS HARRIS
(4)   1920s   One-piece etched   No Listing
White globe, with large red-outlined white "MH" in center of face over red "MARCUS HARRIS CO."

Marine Oil Company, St. Louis, Missouri

Company history is unknown for Marine Oil. Jobber-operated stations were branded Marine, while the forty or so company-operated discount stations were branded Mars. Mars stations were found from Chattanooga to California, with Marine stations within 300 miles of St. Louis.

MARINE
(5)   1940s   13.5in Glass $275-$450
Aqua globe face with blue-outlined white band across center. Band outline forms waves top and bottom. Red and white sea horse in center of face. Red "MARINE" with speed lines across band, with white "GASOLINE" below.

MARINE
(3)   1950s   13.5in Capco $225-$350
Same as above, except background is blue instead of aqua.

MARS
(3)   1950s   13.5in Capco $100-$150
White globe face with red circle in center. Blue band diagonally across circle, with white "MARS" in band.

Mayflower Oil Company, Boston, Massachusetts

Company history unknown.

MAYFLOWER
(5)   1930s   13.5in Glass $650-$1,100
White globe face with black outline ring and black ring around white center circle. Black and white ship in center circle. Red "MAYFLOWER" arched around top. "GASOLINE" around bottom.

McCord

Company history unknown.

McCORD AIRCRAFT
(5)   1930s   Gill   No Listing
Description not available.

McFarlands

Company history unknown.

McFARLANDS HUMMINGBIRD GAS (w/bird)
(5)   Late 1920s   15in Metal   No Listing
White globe face with black "HUMMINGBIRD GAS" arched across center, over detailed black and red bird. Green "McFARLANDS" arched at top, red "FOR HIGH COMPRESSION MOTORS" around bottom.

McGovern

Company history unknown.

McGOVERN PLACE
(5)   1920s   One-piece etched   No Listing
                            sq. shaped
102
Description not available.

McMurrey

Company history unknown.

McMURREY REGULAR
(4)   1940s   13.5in Capco $75-$125
White globe face with outlined band across center. "McMURREY" in band, with "REGULAR" across top and "LEADED GASOLINE" on lower face.

McMURREY SUPER GAS DUBBS CRACKED (decal)
(4)   1950s   13.5in Capco $75-$125
Red globe face with yellow McMURREY decal on face. No other details available.

Mehmken's

Company history unknown.

MEHMKEN'S EDELWEISS
(5)   1920s   15in Metal   No Listing
White globe face with red band across top. Blue script "EDELWEISS" across center, with red and blue underlines. Blue "MEHMKEN'S" across top, with red "GASOLINE" arched around bottom.

MEHMKEN'S T&T
(5)   1920s   15in Metal   No Listing
White globe face with red outline ring. Black "MEHMKEN'S" across top of globe face, with black "TOUCH 'N TRAVEL" (large Ts) across center and black "GASOLINE" arched around bottom.

Meadville Corporation, Haverford, Pennsylvania

Meadville operated large multi-pump discount stations in mid-Atlantic metropolitan areas under the Save-Way and Safe-Way brands. In the 1950s, they acquired Reading, Pennsylvania, based Merit, and continue to operate stations under the Merit brand today.

MERIT
(4)   1950s   Gill $225-$350
Red globe face with white-outlined green elongated octagon in center of face. Fifteen-inch white "MERIT" on octagon.

MERIT HI TEST
(4)   1950s   Gill $225-$375
Same as above, with yellow circle on lower globe face. Black "HI TEST" in circle.

MERIT ETHYL (EGC)
(4)   1950s   Gill $225-$350
Green globe face with white-outlined red elongated octagon in center of face. Fifteen-inch white "MERIT" on octagon. White circle with Ethyl (EGC) logo on lower globe face.

Michigan Pride
Company history unknown.
MICHIGAN PRIDE GASOLINE
(5)   1930s   15in Metal $500-$800
White globe face with orange "PRIDE" with black shading across center of face. White box with black "SUPER" across "PRIDE." Black "MICHIGAN" across top, "GASOLINE" across bottom.

Midway
Company history unknown.
MIDWAY HIGH POWER GAS
(4)   1930s   15in Metal   No Listing
White globe face with black silhouette of car across center. Red "MIDWAY" arched across top, with "HIGH POWER GAS" around bottom. White "HASN'T KNOCKED YET" on car.
MIDWAY GASOLINE (w/triangle)
(4)   1930s   15in Metal $250-$400
White globe face with red "MIDWAY" arched around top, "GASOLINE" around bottom, with red linked chain in center forming triangle. Black "POWER QUALITY UNIFORMITY" around chain.
MIDWAY KANOTEX ETHYL
(5)   1930s-1940s   13.5in Gill $250-$400
Red letters trimmed in black. "MIDWAY" around top, "KANOTEX" through center over Kanotex sunflower logo. Ethyl (EGC) logo at bottom.

Midwest Oil Company, Minneapolis, Minnesota
Dating from the early 1920s, Midwest was a large upper Midwest independent. They originally operated under the Midwest-Ace High brand, but by the late 1930s they were using just Ace High. They purchased Minneapolis-based H. K. Stahl & Company in 1958, and about that time rebranded from Ace High to Midwest. They operated stations as late as the 1980s.
MIDWEST ACE HIGH (w/airplane)
(5)   1925-1930   15in Metal $1,800-$3,000
MIDWEST ACE HIGH (w/airplane)
(5)   1928-1930   13.5in Glass   No Listing
White globe face with red "MIDWEST OIL COMPANY" arched around top, "GASOLINE" around bottom, and blue and grey biplane in center. Blue "ACE" above plane, "HIGH" below.
MIDWEST GASOLINE WITH ETHYL
(5)   1925-1930   15in Metal $300-$450
Description not available.
MIDWEST AVIO GASOLINE
(5)   1920s   15in Metal   No Listing
Similar to above, with blue "AVIO" over blue-outlined triangle replacing biplane in center. Blue "QUALITY" inside triangle outline.
ACE HIGH COMPRESSION GASOLINE
(5)   1930s   13.5in Glass $225-$350
Description not available.
AVIO
(4)   1946-1958   13.5in Capco $125-$175
White globe face with blue outline ring. Large blue "AVIO" over blue-outlined triangle in center of face. Blue "QUALITY" inside triangle. Red "GASOLINE" arched around bottom.
ACE HIGH
(5)   1930-1958   13.5in Glass $250-$375
Red globe face with black outline ring and black ring around white center circle. Black "ACE" over "HIGH" in center circle. White "GASOLINE" arched around bottom.
MIDWEST
(4)   1958-1970   Oval Capco $125-$175
White globe with large red, white, and blue MIDWEST arrow logo covering face.

H.K. Stahl & Company, St. Paul, Minnesota
Note: H. K. Stahl and Company, St. Paul, Minnesota, merged with Midwest about 1958.
TROPHY–OUR PREMIUM
(4)   1935-1958   Gill $250-$400
White globe face with blue outline ring. Purple-outlined white trophy in center, with blue "TROPHY" in bowtie lettering across center. Blue "OUR PREMIUM" below "TROPHY."
TROPHY POWER FLASH
(5)   1950-1958   Gill $250-$400
White globe face with blue outline ring and blue band across bottom. Red "POWERFLASH" with speed lines across upper face, with small red trophy just below center. Red-outlined white "TROPHY" in bowtie lettering in lower blue area.

Moco
Company history unknown.

MOCO
(5)   1940s   13.5in Glass $300-$450
Description not available.

Mohawk Oil Company
California independent refiner and marketer, company history unknown.
MOHAWK GASOLINE
(4)   1930s   15in Metal $1,400-$2,400
Red globe face with black outline ring and black outline around white center circle. White "MOHAWK" arched around top, "GASOLINE" around bottom, with red and black Indian head in center.
MOHAWK ETHYL
(5)   1930s   15in Metal   No Listing
White globe face with black outline ring and black ring around white center circle. Red "MOHAWK" arched around top, "ETHYL" around bottom, with red and black Indian head in center.

Monarch
Company history unknown.
MONARCH ETHYL
(4)   1930s   13.5in Glass $250-$375
Description not available.

Moore
Company history unknown.
MOORE GASOLINE
(5)   1920s   One-piece etched $750-$1,100
White globe face with red "MOORE" arched across top, "GASOLINE" across bottom.

Moore's
Company history unknown.
MOORE'S REGULAR SUPREME
(4)   1940s   13.5in Glass $200-$350
White globe face with green outline ring and green band across center. White "REGULAR" in center band. Green script "MOORE'S" across top, "SUPREME" across bottom.
MOORE'S ETHYL SUPREME
(4)   1940s   13.5in Glass $200-$350
Same as above, except red replaces green, and white "ETHYL" replaces "REGULAR."
MOORE'S FIRST GRADE REGULAR
(5)   1950s   13.5in Glass $225-$375
Green globe face with white band across center. White script "MOORE'S" across top, "SUPREME" across bottom, with yellow circle in center band. Red band with white "REGULAR" across circle. Green script "FIRST" and "GRADE" with lightning bolts in yellow circle.
MOORE'S ETHYL
(4)   1950s   13.5in Glass $225-$350
Same as above, except red replaces green, and small Ethyl (EC) logo replaces circle in center band.

Morco, Morrison's Cove, Pennsylvania
Sold gasoline in the 1920s, and was a local brand named after Morrison's Cove. This company was affiliated with Feather Petroleum and was sold in the 1970s.
MORCO
(5)   1920s   15in Metal   No Listing
Mountain scene with deer. Details not available, but see photo.

Motorease
Company history unknown.
MOTOREASE GASOLINE
(5)   1930s   15in Metal $300-$450
White globe face with blue outline rings. Red "MOTOREASE" arched across top, "GASOLINE" across bottom, with blue design in center.

Motor Inn
Company history unknown.
MOTOR INN GASOLINE
(5)   1920s   One-piece etched $1,200-$1,800
MOTOR INN GASOLINE
(5)   1910s   One-piece etched chimney top   No Listing
White globe with blue "THE MOTOR INN" on upper face, over blue square outline. Red price box in center where the dealer could paint in the going price. Red "GASOLINE" arched around bottom.

Moultray
Company history unknown.

Quaker Straight Run one-piece etched (left, red), and Quaker Hi Test one-piece etched (right, green).

Royal Flight Gas one-piece painted globe. Jim Welty

Royaline Gasoline 15in inserts on metal body.

Royal Rose one-piece etched globe. Preston Aust

Silver Flash one-piece raised-letter octagon-shaped globe.

Sky Trak 13.5in inserts on plastic body. Lonnie Hop

Spirit Gas one-piece painted globe. Dave Walthers

Tankar 13.5in inserts on red plastic body.

Tankar Ethyl 13.5in inserts on plastic body.

Tarzon 15in inserts on metal body.

Magic Benzol Gas 15in inserts on metal body.

Magic Benzol Gas 13.5in inserts on glass body. Don Meyr

Todd's Hygrade Gasoline one-piece etched sphere-shaped globe.

V.H.S.S. Co. Nocles 15in inserts on metal body.

Van Pick one-piece etched.

MOULTRAY
(5)   1920s   15in Metal $225-$325
White globe face with black lines above and below center, forming
white band across center of face. Black "MOULTRAY" in band.

Mountain
Company history unknown.
MOUNTAIN GAS
(5)   1920s   One-piece etched   No Listing
Orange globe face with mountain scene with "MOUNTAIN" arched
around top and "THE PEAK OF QUALITY" around the bottom. No
other details available.

Mule—Russell Oil Company, Butte, Montana
Company history unknown.
MULE GAS
(5)   1930s   15in Metal $750-$1,200
Globe face with large mule shoe in center of face. Large "MULE"
across shoe above "THE GAS." "WITH A KICK" arched around bottom.

Muskegon Oil Company, Muskegon, Michigan
Company history unknown.
MUSGO
(3)   1927-1929   One-piece baked $2,000-$3,500
Orange globe face with black outline ring, and black ring around blue
center circle. Black "MUSGO" arched around top, "MICHIGAN'S
MILE MAKER" around bottom. Detailed hand-painted Indian in center circle.
Musgo globes are actually common for a one-piece globe. More than
seventy are known to exist. Yet, because of their beauty and so few
traded among collectors, they do command a high price. Only a few
have sold at the upper price range listed, as of this writing. A couple
have sold for as much as $4,000.
SUPER ZIP (ETHYL)
(5)   1927-1929   One-piece baked $450-$650
White globe with black "SUPER/ZIP" on face. This was the Musgo
Ethyl brand name.

Navajo
Company history unknown.
NAVAJO
(5)   1950s   13.5in GREEN Capco $175-$250
Series of red horizontal bands across globe face. Blue "Navajo" across
center of face.

New State Oil Company, Oklahoma City, Oklahoma
Company history unknown.
NEW STATE 88
(4)   1950s   13.5in Capco $150-$250
White globe face with red "NEW STATE" with black dropshade arched
around top. Green "88" in center, with grey rocket diagonally through
"88."

NC Pep
Company history unknown.
NC PEP-STATE INSPECTED
(5)   1920s   One-piece etched $1,000-$1,600
White globe with blue outline ring around globe face. Large blue
"N.C./PEP" on center of face, with red arrow through "N.C." Small
"STATE INSPECTED" around bottom.

Newport
Company history unknown.
NEWPORT GASOLINE/OILS
(4)   1920s   One-piece etched $750-$1,000
White globe with black octagonal outline around orange center circle,
and black center band. Black "GASOLINE" arched in upper circle,
"OILS" in lower, white "NEWPORT" on band.
NEWPORT UPSIDE DOWN
(5)   1920s   One-piece etched $325-$550
Same as above, but made to open up for canopy light globe.

Nicolene—National Independent Oil Company
Company history unknown.
NICOLENE GASOLENE/MOTOR OIL
(5)   1920s   15in Metal $350-$650
White globe face with small Nicolene keystone shield in center. Black
ring around keystone, with white "NATIONAL INDEPENDENT OIL
COMPANY," red "NICOLENE" arched around top, "GASOLENE"

around bottom, and black "MOTOR" to left of center circle, "OILS and"
to right.
NICOLENE KEROSENE
(5)   1920s   15in Metal $400-$650
Same as above, with "KEROSENE" replacing "GASOLINE."

Nonpareil
Company history unknown.
NONPAREIL SILENT GASOLINE
(5)   1920s   15in Metal $250-$400
Description not available.

Northern Lite
Company history unknown.
NORTHERN LITE GASOLINE
(5)   1930s   13.5in Glass $650-$850
Description not available.

Northland Gasoline, Waterloo, Iowa
Primarily a lubricants manufacturer, Northland was involved
with a small number of gasoline stations in the 1920s and 1930s.
Today, the company manufactures specialty lubricants.
NORTHLAND GAS (w/IOMA logo)
(5)   1920s   15in Metal $500-$700
White globe face with black triangle-red thunderbird IOMA logo in
center. Black "NORTHLAND" arched around top, "GAS" around bottom.
NORTHLAND GASOLINE
(5)   1930s   Gill $275-$450
White globe face with red, white, and black "NORTHLAND" shield in
center. Black lettering on shield "THE BADGE OF CERTAINTY."
Black-outlined red "NORTHLAND" arched around top, "GASOLINE"
around bottom.

Northwestern Oil Company, Superior, Wisconsin
We do not believe that this is the same Northwestern Refining
that operated out of St. Paul Park, Minnesota.
NORTHWESTERN VIMAMITE GASOLINE
(5)   1920s   15in Metal   No Listing
White globe face with black outline ring and black lines forming white
band across upper face. Orange diamond in center of face, with black
"VIMAMITE" across diamond. Black "NORTHWESTERN" in band,
"Gasoline" across lower globe face.

Noxout
Company history unknown.
NOXOUT PREMIUM PRODUCTS
(4)   1950s   13.5in Glass $250-$350
Red globe face with yellow circle offset to left of center. Large white
"NOXOUT" with black dropshade expanding out from circle. White
"PREMIUM" arched around top, "PRODUCTS" around bottom.

NPC
Company history unknown.
NPC GAS (w/shield)
(5)   1930s   Gill $275-$450
Description not available.

O'Day
Company history unknown.
O'DAY REGULAR GAS
(5)   1920s   15in Metal $375-$575
White globe face with yellow circle and band outline in center. Black
"O'DAY" arched around top, "GAS" around bottom, with red "REGU-
LAR" on center band.
O'DAY ANTI-KNOCK
(5)   1920s   15in Metal $400-$650
Same as above, with "ANTI-KNOCK" replacing "REGULAR."
O'DAY AEROPLANE
(5)   1920s   15in Metal $450-$700
Same as above, with "AEROPLANE" replacing "REGULAR."
O'DAY PEP
(3)   1920s   15in Metal $400-$650
Same as above, with "PEP" replacing "REGULAR."
O'DAY CRYSTAL WHITE GAS
(5)   1920s   15in Metal $400-$650
Same as above, with red "CRYSTAL/WHITE" replacing "REGULAR."

O'Neils
Company history unknown.

O'NEILS EVERY DROP TESTED
(5)   1920s   15in Metal   No Listing
Description not available.

O-Gas-Co-Sales-Corporation
Company history unknown.
O-GAS-CO-SALES-CORP. GASOLINE
(5)   1920s   15in Metal $275-$400
Yellow globe face with red "O-GAS-CO" arched around top, "SALES CORP." around bottom, and black "GASOLINE" across center.

Octol
Company history unknown.
OCTOL 68
(5)   1940s   Gill $250-$375
White globe face with black outline ring. Black-outlined orange octagon covers most of face. Black "OCTOL" over large black "68" on octagon.

Ohio Pep
Company history unknown.
OHIO PEP
(5)   1920s   One-piece Oval etched $850-$1,300
White pointed oval globe with dark lettering "OHIO/PEP."
OHIO PEP
(5)   1920s   16.5in Metal $275-$475
White globe face with black lettering "OHIO/PEP."

Oil Creek Refining Company, Oil City, Pennsylvania
Company history unknown.
OIL CREEK JUST FINE
(4)   1910s   15in Metal/Metal faces $600-$800
Green metal globe face with letter perforations. White "JUST FINE" arched around top, "GASOLINE" across center, "OIL CREEK REFNG. CO." around bottom.
JUST FINE/OIL CREEK/GASOLINE
(4)   1920s   15in Metal $300-$550
White globe face with red "JUST FINE" arched around top, "GASO-LINE" around bottom, with blue "OIL CREEK" across center.
OIL CREEK ETHYL (EGC) GASOLINE
(4)   1920s   15in Metal $300-$500
White globe face with red outline ring and red outline ring around center white circle. Large Ethyl (EGC) logo in center with blue rays. Blue "OIL CREEK" arched around top, red "GASOLINE" around bottom.
ELIM-A-NOX/OIL CREEK/GASOLINE
(4)   1930s   15in Metal $600-$900
White globe face with orange outline ring. Green "ELIM-A-NOX" arched around top, "GASOLINE" around bottom, with orange and green Oil Creek scene logo in center.
ETHYL OIL CREEK ETHYL (EGC)
(4)   1930s   15in Metal $600-$900
White globe face with orange outline ring. Green "ETHYL" arched around top, above orange and green Oil Creek scene logo. Ethyl (EGC) shield at bottom, with yellow rays forming circle.
OIL CREEK (w/oil well)
(5)   1930s   15in Metal $500-$750
Same as above, with no wording on top or bottom.
OIL CREEK ETHYL ELIMINOX
(4)   1930s   15in Metal $600-$900
Description not available.
OIL CREEK (w/oil well and permit seal)
(5)   1930s   15in Metal $550-$800
Description not available.

Old Trusty
Company history unknown.
OLD TRUSTY
(4)   1930s   Gill $275-$450
White globe face with red outline ring and red circle in center with blue border. White band across circle. Blue-outlined red letters "Old Trusty" on center band, with lightning bolts above and below center band on red circle. Blue "MOTOR OILS" arched around top, "GASO-LINE" around bottom.

Ohio Motors
Company history unknown.
OM GASOLINE
(4)   1920s   15in Metal $250-$350
White globe face with large red-outlined blue "OM" above smaller blue "GASOLINE."

Omar Refining Company, Tulsa, Oklahoma
Company history unknown.
OMAR MAGIC
(4)   1930s   13.5in Glass $275-$400
White globe face with black outline ring. Black Old English "Omar" across center of face, with small "aladdins lamp" above and "MAGIC" below.
OMAR ETHYL
(4)   1930s   13.5in Glass $225-$350
White globe face with black outline ring. Red Old English "Omar" across top of face, above Ethyl (EGC) shield.

Oriental, Denver, Colorado
Company history unknown.
ORIENTAL POLY OCTANE
(4)   1930s   13.5in Glass $225-$350
White globe face with black and two-tone blue octagon on large green circle in center. Blue outline ring and borders of white center band. Blue "ORIENTAL" in upper white border, "COLORADO MADE" on lower, with dark blue "Poly Octane" on center band.
ORIENTAL REGULAR
(3)   1950s   13.5in Capco $100-$150
White globe face with blue "ORIENTAL" arched around top, "GASO-LINE" around bottom, "REGULAR" across center.
ORIENTAL ETHYL
(3)   1950s   13.5in Capco $100-$150
Same as above, with "ETHYL" replacing "REGULAR."
ORIENTAL BRONZE
(4)   1950s   13.5in Capco $100-$150
Same as above, with "BRONZE" replacing "REGULAR."

Oriole
See listing for GENERAL OIL COMPANY in this section.

Pacific Oil Company, Los Angeles, California
Company history unknown.
PACIFIC STATES
(5)   1930s   15in Metal $250-$450
Red globe face with white "PACIFIC/STATES" in center of face. No other details available.
PRODUCTS OF PACIFIC STATES OIL CO.
(4)   1930s   15in Metal $250-$450
Orange globe face with black-outlined white "PACIFIC/STATES" in center. Black "PRODUCTS OF" at top, "OIL COMPANY" at bottom.

Palacine
Wirt Franklin Petroleum, Ardmore, Oklahoma
Company history unknown.
PALACINE IT'S BETTER
(4)   1920s   15in Metal   No Listing
Green globe face with white outline ring and white-outlined red band across center. White "PALACINE" on center band. White "GASO-LINE" arched around top, "OILS" around bottom, with small white "IT'S BETTER" below band.
WIRT FRANKLIN PALACINE "IT'S BETTER"
(4)   1930s   15in Metal $1,800-$2,800
Red globe face with white outer ring. Multicolored standing Indian with raised hand in red center area. White "PALACINE" above Indian, "IT'S BETTER" below. Black "WIRT FRANKLIN" arched around top, "PETROLEUM CORPORATION" around bottom.
WIRT FRANKLIN PALACINE "A FRIEND"
(4)   1930s   15in Metal $1,800-$2,800
Same as above, with "A FRIEND" replacing "IT'S BETTER."
PALACINE ETHYL
(5)   1930s   15in Metal $650-$900
White globe face with black "PALACINE" arched around top, "GASO-LINE" around bottom, with large Ethyl (EGC) logo in center circle,

Pankey Oil Company, Brookfield, Missouri
A Missouri independent that began marketing about 1915. The company was known to market as late as 1970.
PANKEY (orange ball shaped)
(5)   1910s   One-piece baked   No Listing
Orange spherical globe with white "PANKEY" on globe.
PANKEY GASOLINE
(5)   1920s   15in Metal $400-$650
White globe face with red outline ring and red ring around white center circle. Red triangle with white triangle in center circle. Red "PANKEY" arched around top, "GASOLINE" around bottom, with red and white "PANKEY/OILS" in triangles in center circle.

PANKEY SWAN GASOLINE
(5)   1920s   15in Metal $400-$575
Red globe face with white outline ring and white ring around red center circle. White "PANKEY" arched around top, "GASOLINE" around bottom, with white "SWAN" in center circle.

Parade
H. L. Hunt Refining Company, Tuscaloosa, Alabama
The gasoline marketing division of the H. L.Hunt family interests. The company still operates a few stations in Alabama.
PARADE (w/map)
(4)   1947-1960   13.5in Capco $200-$300
White globe face with black outline ring. Black-outlined green and white map of southeastern United States in center of globe face, with red "PARADE" with speed lines across map.
HLH PARADE PRODUCTS
(5)   1960-1970   Oval Capco $125-$200
White globe face with blue outline ring. Red "PARADE" with speed lines across center of face, with blue "HLH" at top and "PRODUCTS" at bottom.

Paragon Refining, Toledo, Ohio
Company history unknown.
PARAGON GASOLENE
(5)   1910s   One-piece etched $650-$1,000
White globe with red "PARAGON" arched across upper face and "GASOLENE" arched below.
PARAGON GASOLENE (w/mountain)
(5)   1920s   15in Metal   No Listing
White globe face with blue, white, and black snow-covered mountain scene in center circle. Red "PARAGON" arched around top, "GASO-LENE" around bottom, with black script "Peak of Perfection" across scene.
PARAGON REFINING COMPANY
(5)   1930s   15in Metal $300-$525
White globe face with red-outlined green box across center of face. White "PARAGON" in box. Green "REFINING" arched around top, "COMPANY" around bottom.

Paramount
Company history unknown.
PARAMOUNT "THAT/FAMOUS GASOLINE"
(5)   1920s   15in Metal $300-$500
White globe face with distorted red lettering "THAT/FAMOUS" over blue "PARAGON" over red "GASOLINE" on face.

Peerless—Miller's Oil Company, Kansas City, Missouri
Company history unknown.
PEERLESS
(5)   1920s   One-piece etched $800-$1,100
White globe with red "PEERLESS" across top, "GASOLINE" across bottom.
PEERLESS/PEERLESS GASOLINE
(5)   1930s   15in Metal $275-$450
White globe face with blue center circle. Red "PEERLESS" arched around top, "GASOLINE" around bottom, with white "PEERLESS" repeated in center circle.
PEERLESS TRIANGLE
(5)   1930s   Balcrank Glass   No Listing
White globe face with black outline ring. Large red triangle, point down, in center of face, with black band across triangle. White "PEER-LESS" in band.
PEERLESS 88
(4)   1940s   13.5in Capco $100-$150
White globe face with blue outline ring. Script "Peerless" over large "88" on upper globe face, with "GASOLINE" arched around bottom.
PEERLESS oval
(4)   1950s   Oval $175-$250
White globe face with red, white, and black "PEERLESS" shield with crossed flags on face. No other details known.

Penco
Company history unknown.
PENCO GASOLINE
(5)   1920s   15in Metal   No Listing
Description not available.

Penn
Company history unknown.
PENN AIRCRAFT
(5)   1930s   Gill $300-$525

White globe face with blue outline ring and blue ring around red center circle. Blue-outlined white band diagonally across center, with blue "AIRCRAFT" with speed lines in band. Blue "PENN" arched around top, "GASOLINE" around bottom.

Pennolene—Well Brothers, Frederick, Maryland
Company history unknown.
PENNOLENE SUPER CHARGED GAS
(4)   1930s   15in Metal $550-$850
White globe face with black-outlined orange oval, with wing and burst design in center of face. Black "PENN-O-LENE" arched around top of oval, "SUPER CHARGED GAS" around bottom.
PENNOLENE SUPER BLEND GAS
(5)   1930s   15in Metal $600-$950
White globe face with blue, orange, and black oval and design similar to above. White "SUPER-BLEND GAS" replacing "SUPER CHARGED GAS" around bottom of oval.

People Choice—The Peoples Supply Company
Company history unknown.
PEOPLES CHOICE
(5)   1940s   13.5in Glass $275-$400
White globe face with red outline ring. Blue "PEOPLES/CHOICE" with red lines in center of globe face.

Pep—The Pep Boys, Philadelphia, Pennsylvania
This globe has been attributed to the Pep Boys' auto supply operation. We can find no certain evidence that the Pep Boys were ever involved in gasoline marketing.
PEP "GAS WITH A PUNCH"
(5)   1920s   15in Metal   No Listing
Orange globe face with large black "PEP" across center. Black band across, below "PEP," with orange script "The GAS with a PUNCH" in band.

Perfect
Company history unknown.
PERFECT
(5)   1920s   15in Metal $300-$450
Yellow globe face with thick blue outline ring, and blue outline above and below white bowtie band across center. Black "PERFECT" in band.
PERFECT HIGH TEST
(5)   1920s   15in Metal $300-$425
White globe face with blue outline ring. Blue "PERFECT/HI TEST" in center of globe face.

Perry Gas and Oil Company, Perry, Missouri
Company history unknown.
PERRY
(5)   1930s   15in Metal   No Listing
White globe face with blue bar-and-circle design in center. White "QUALITY" on center bar. Red "PERRY GAS and OIL CO." arched around top, "GASOLINE" around bottom.

Perry Oil Company
A Georgia marketer. Company history unknown.
PERRY HOME OWNED
(5)   1930s   16.5in Metal $275-$450
White globe face with blue lines forming band across center. Red "PERRY" in center band. Blue "PERRY" arched around top, "OIL COMPANY" around bottom, with blue "HOME" above center band and "OWNED" below.

Petroleum Solvents, Butler, Pennsylvania
Company history unknown.
PETROSOL
(5)   1930s   15in Metal $225-$375
Description not available.

Phelps
Company history unknown.
PHELPS REGULAR
(5)   1920s   15in Metal   No Listing
Description not available.
PHELPS PREMIUM
(5)   1920s   15in Metal   No Listing
Description not available.
Philadelphia Gas and Oil
Company history unknown.
PHILGO
(5)   1920s   15in Metal   No Listing

White globe face with red and black 1920s car in center. Red "PHIL-GO" arched around top, "GASOLINE" around bottom.

Piedmont
A North Carolina independent, company history unknown.
PIEDMONT TRU-VALU GASOLINE
| (5) | 1940s | 13.5in Glass | No Listing |
Description not available.

Pioneer
Company history unknown. These globes are not thought to be from the Pioneer-Dixcel operation in Missouri.
PIONEER (w/covered wagon)
| (5) | 1930s | 15in Metal | No Listing |
Red globe face with black outline ring and black ring around white center circle. Red, white, and black covered wagon detailed scene in center circle. White "PIONEER" arched around top, "GASOLINE" around bottom.
PIONEER (w/Indian and covered wagon)
| (5) | 1930s | 15in Metal | $1,800-$2,400 |
White globe face with red outline ring. Brown and black Indian looking down on wagon train in center of globe face. Red script "Pioneer" across scene, with white "GASOLINE" in underline below "Pioneer."
PIONEER MOTOR BLUE
| (5) | 1930s | 13.5in Glass | No Listing |
Description not available.
PIONEER ZIPPER
| (5) | 1940s | 13.5in Glass Banded | $300-$450 |
White globe face with black "PIONEER" above red "ZIPPER" with speed lines and lightning bolts.
PIONEER HIGH
| (5) | 1940s | 13.5in Glass | $300-$450 |
Same as above, with script red "High" below "PIONEER."

Pittman Oil Company, Chilicothe, Missouri
Company history unknown.
PITTMAN STREAMLINED GASOLINE
| (4) | 1940s | Gill | $800-$1,200 |
White globe face with red band and series of red lines on lower globe face. Blue airplane and cloud scene in center. Blue "PITTMAN" arched around top, with red script "Streamlined" in break in red lines, and white "GASOLINE" in red band at bottom.

Platolene, Carmi, Illinois
Founded in the 1930s as R. J. Oil Refining Company in Terre Haute, Indiana. It was originally marketed under the "500" brand, with "Platolene" added to the "500" after WW II. The company moved to Carmi, Illinois, in the 1970s. Several dozen stations are in operation today.
"500" R. J. OIL AND REFINING CO.
| (5) | 1935-1940 | 13.5in Glass | $350-$650 |
Red globe face with black and white outline rings. Large white "500" at top over banner, across lower face. "R. J. OIL AND REFINING CO." on banner. Black and white checked flag on left.
PLATOLENE 500
| (4) | 1940-1965 | 13.5in Glass | $275-$400 |
Similar to above, except no flag, and "PLATOLENE" replaces "R. J. OIL."
PLATOLENE 500
| (4) | 1965-1970 | Oval Capco | $150-$250 |
White globe face with red "500" on upper face. Blue outline ring and blue band on lower face, with white "PLATOLENE" on band.

Poland
Company history unknown.
POLAND NEW NAVY
| (5) | 1920s | 15in Metal | No Listing |
Steel globe face. Yellow face with blue and red ship in center. Red "POLAND" arched around top over blue bowtie "NEW NAVY." Red "GASOLINE" arched around bottom.

Polar
Company history unknown.
POLAR GASOLINE
| (5) | 1930s | Gill | $850-$1,300 |
White globe face with blue outline ring and blue rings around white center circle. Blue "POLAR" arched around top, "GASOLINE" around bottom, with blue and white drawing of polar bear in center circle.

Popular
Company history unknown.
POPULAR REGULAR
| (5) | 1940s | 13.5in Glass | No Listing |

White globe face with blue outline ring. Blue late 1930s convertible with driver and station attendant with red gas pumps in center. Excellent detail. Red "POPULAR" arched around top, red "REGULAR" across bottom.
POPULAR PREMIUM
| (5) | 1940s | 13.5in Glass | No listing |
Same as above, "NO. 1 DIESEL" replacing "REGULAR."

Powell's
Company history unknown.
POWELL'S SUPERBA
| (5) | 1930s | 15in Metal | $225-$400 |
White globe face with red "POWELL'S" arched around top, "GASOLINE" around bottom, with red "SUPERBA" across center.

Power
Company history unknown.
POWER
| (5) | 1940s | 13.5in Glass | $250-$400 |
White globe face with orange-and-white-outlined orange drawing of Montana in center of face. White "POWER" with black dropshade across map.

Powerflash
Company history unknown.
POWERFLASH INDEPENDENT GASOLINE
| (4) | 1930s | 15in Metal | $450-$800 |
White globe face with blue band across center. Blue "INDEPENDENT" arched around top, "GASOLINE" around bottom, with white script "Powerflash" in center band. Blue piston below band, with red flash extending above band.
POWERFLASH INDEPENDENT GASOLINE
| (5) | 1930s | Gill | $350-$500 |
White globe face with red outline ring and red band across center. Blue "INDEPENDENT" arched around top, "GASOLINE" around bottom, with white script "Powerflash" in center band.

Powerized
Sunburst Refining Company, Great Falls, Montana
Company history unknown.
POWERIZED GASOLINE SUNBURST REFINING
| (5) | 1930s | 15in Metal | $1,600-$2,200 |
White globe face with black outline rings and black ring around center circle. Red "POWERIZED" arched around top, "GASOLINE" around bottom, with black and white oil well scene with yellow rays in center circle. Black "SUNBURST REFINING" on lower area of scene.

Power King, Anderson, Indiana
Company history unknown.
POWER KING PREMIUM
| (4) | 1950s | 13.5in Capco | $150-$250 |
Multicolored shield. No other details available.
POWER KING ETHYL
| (4) | 1950s | 13.5in Capco | $150-$250 |
Multicolored shield. no other details available.

Power Plus
Company history unknown.
POWER PLUS "THE BETTER GASOLINE"
| (5) | 1930s | 15in Metal | No Listing |
White globe face with black and white drawing of man breaking chain on upper face. Black "POWER PLUS" below drawing, above small black "THE BETTERGAS" in outlined box.

Pride Oil Company, Knoxville, Tennessee
An eastern Tennessee private brand dating back to the late 1940s. Pride became a branded Bay jobber in the 1960s, operating dual-branded Bay-Pride stations. Still in operation as a Phillips 66 jobber today, the company brands Pride and dual Pride-Phillips 66 stations.
PRIDE REGULAR oval
| (4) | 1950s Oval Capco | $125-$200 |
White globe face with blue outline ring. Red, white, and blue shield with stars in center, with blue "PRIDE" arched around top, red "REGULAR" around bottom.
PRIDE ETHYL oval
| (4) | 1950s | Oval Capco | $125-$200 |
Same as above, with "ETHYL" replacing "REGULAR."

Primrose

Company history unknown.

PRIMROSE GASOLINE
(5)   1930s   15in Metal $350-$575
White globe face with green bowtie "PRIMROSE" across center of face. Green "SPECIAL MOTOR" arched around top, "GASOLINE" around bottom.

Protex

Company history unknown.

PROTEX GASOLINE/MOTOR OILS
(5)   1920s   One-piece etched   No Listing
White globe with red outline ring around face. Red "Protex" with underline across center of globe. White "PROTECTS YOUR MOTOR" on underline. Blue "GASOLINE" arched around top, "MOTOR OILS" around bottom.

Protoco

Company history unknown.

PROTOCO
(5)   1930s   15in Metal   No Listing
Description not available.

W. H. Pugh and Company, Racine, Wisconsin

Company history unknown.

PUGH PEERLESS
(5)   1950s   Glass oval $350-$650
White globe face with black-outlined red "Pugh" on upper face. Blue and white attendant's head at top of "P" as a characterization. Blue italic "PEERLESS" across lower globe face.

PUGH CLIPPER
(5)   1950s   Glass oval $350-$650
Same as above, with "CLIPPER" replacing "PEERLESS."

PUGH CHALLENGE
(5)   1940s   13.5in Glass $250-$350
Red globe face with geartooth edge and white outline, identical in design to an Anderson-Prichard face. Yellow circle in center, with black script "Challenge."

Pure Gold, Oklahoma City, Oklahoma

Company history unknown.

PURE GOLD
(4)   1950s   13.5in Capco $250-$350
Yellow globe face with black outline ring. Large red seal in center, with black "PURE GOLD" across center of face.

Pure Penna

Pennsylvania-based. Company history unknown.

PURE PENNA GAS
(5)   1920s   One-piece etched   No Listing
White globe with red-outlined keystone in center. Blue "PENNA" across keystone. Red "PURE" arched around top, "GAS" around bottom.

Pure Quill

Company history unknown.

PURE QUILL (w/feather)
(5)   1920s   15in Metal   No listing
"PURE QUILL" around top dark green, "GASOLINE" around bottom. Red feather in center.

Purple Flash

Company history unknown.

PURPLE FLASH
(5)   1930s   15in Metal $300-$550
Yellow globe face with yellow and black outline rings. Black-outlined purple-colored "PURPLE" arched around top above red "flash" with black speed lines.

QT—Quicktrip Stores, Tulsa, Oklahoma

Operates convenience stores in six states. Company history is unknown, but it is believed to date back to the late 1950s.

QT
(5)   1980s   13.5in Capco $75-$125
White globe face with large red square in center. White "QT" with black dropshading in red square. This is likely a globe made for use at trade shows and other similar displays.

Quaker Oil Company, Plainfield, Indiana

Company history unknown.

QUAKER STRAIGHT RUN GASOLINE
(5)   1920s   One-piece etched   No Listing
White globe with red outline ring around face, forming large "Q" with tail extending from center circle through outer ring. Red center circle. Red "QUAKER" arched in top of "Q," "GASOLINE" in bottom, with white "STRAIGHT/RUN" on center circle.

QUAKER HIGH TEST GASOLINE
(5)   1920s   One-piece etched   No Listing
Same as above, except everything red becomes green, and lettering in center is "HIGH/TEST."

Quality—H&J Oil Company

Company history unknown.

QUALITY GASOLINE
(5)   1920s   One-piece etched   No Listing
White globe with blue "H&J OIL CO." across center of face. Red "QUALITY" arched around top, "GASOLINE" around bottom.

Quality Lane

Company history unknown.

QUALITY LANE
(5)   1930s   15in Metal   No Listing
Description not available.

Quayle Bird

Company history unknown.

QUAYLE BIRD GASOLINE
(5)   1920s   15in Metal $1,400-$1,800
Red globe face with white outline ring and white and brown ring around yellow center circle. Detailed brown and white bird in center, with smaller brown birds in background. White "QUAYLE BIRD" arched around top, "GASOLINE" around bottom.

Quincy, Boston, Massachusetts

An independent Boston-area marketer founded in the nineteenth century, Quincy continues to operate stations today. It was the last marketer to use the old IOMA logo.

QUINCY POW-R-PLUS (w/eagle)
(5)   1930s   15in Metal $600-$900
Green and white outline rings around green outer ring. White center circle with green triangle-red thunderbird IOMA logo. White "QUINCY" arched in upper ring, "POW-R-PLUS" around lower ring.

Radium

Company history unknown.

RADIUM GASOLINE
(5)   1920s   15in Metal   No Listing
White globe face with orange-outlined black script "Radium" across center of face. Orange "GASOLINE" in black underline under "Radium." Detailed orange and black building pictured at top of globe, with black "FORT VENANGO" below picture.

Raimor, Greenville, Ohio

Company history unknown.

RAIMOR QUALITY
(5)   1930s   15in Metal $275-$375
Orange globe face with white outline ring and white center area. Black "SERVICE/RAIMOR/QUALITY" on white center of globe face.

Rancho

Company history unknown.

RANCHO N.A.K. GASOLINE
(5)   1930s   15in Metal   No Listing
Yellow globe face with green band across lower face. Red "Rancho" and design above band, red "GASOLINE" over green script "the spirit of power" below band, with white "N-A-K" and smaller lettering on band.

Rebel—Atlas Oil Corporation, New Orleans, Louisiana

Deep South discounter that rebranded TCR (for Texas City Refining) in the 1960s.

REBEL
(4)   1950s   13.5in Capco $125-$225
Tan globe face with red outline ring. Red-outlined dark blue "REBEL" on lower face, with crossed confederate flags and cannon barrel at top of face. When reproduced, this globe was modified to read "DIXIE."

Red Ace—Mapco, West Memphis, Arkansas

Independent refiner that purchased Nashville-based Red Ace Petroleum and Memphis-based Delta Oil in the 1970s. By 1985 most locations had been rebranded Delta, and in the late 1980s the Delta stations were converted to convenience stores and branded Mapco Express or Delta Express.

Warrior Chieftain 13.5in glass inserts on Gill body. Ace Feek

Waverly Blue Moon two-piece glass globe.

Wespeco one-piece etched globe.

White Flyer 13.5in inserts on glass body.

White Lily 15in inserts on metal body. Kyle Moore

White Rose 15in inserts on metal body.

White Rose Filtered Gasoline one-piece etched globe. Dan Shaw

Filtered Gasoline one-piece etched globe.

Filtered Gasoline one-piece etched chimney-cap globe.

Filtered Gasolene one-piece etched 8in globe with 4in base.

You See What You Get Filtered Gasoline one-piece etched chimney-cap globe. David Jackson

Full Measure one-piece etched sphere-shaped globe.

Gasolene small one-piece etched globe with arches and 4in base.

Gasoline 15in inserts on metal body.

Gasoline 15in perforated metal inserts on metal body.

Gasoline fancy "G" one-piece etched globe.

RED ACE
(4)   1950s   13.5in Glass $175-$250
Blue globe face with red and white outline rings. Large white-outlined red "X" covers most of face, with white "RED/ACE" in center of "X."
DELTA
(4)   1950s   13.5in Glass $225-$350
White globe face with black-outlined red triangle, point up, in center of face. Black-and-white-outlined black box over upper triangle, with white "DELTA" in box.

Red Arrow
Company history unknown.
RED ARROW
(5)   1920s   One-piece etched   No listing
White globe with red "RED ARROW" across upper face. Large red arrow across center of face.
RED ARROW PEP
(5)   1920s   One-piece baked   No Listing
Similar to above, with "PEP" in center and large red arrow through "PEP."
RED ARROW (w/arrow)
(5)   1930s   Gill $350-$600
Similar to etched globe above.

Red Chief
Company history unknown.
RED CHIEF ETHYL
(4)   1930s   15in Metal $300-$550
White globe face with black outline ring and black ring around white center circle. Red "RED CHIEF" arched around top, "GASOLINE" around bottom, with large Ethyl (EGC) logo in center circle.

Red Feather
Company history unknown.
RED FEATHER (w/Indian)
(5)   1930s   Gill   No Listing
White globe face with blue and white detailed Indian in center. Red-colored "RED FEATHER" arched around top of globe face.

Red Star
Company history unknown.
RED STAR GAS
(5)   1920s   One-piece etched   No Listing
White globe with large red star in center of face. Red "RED STAR" arched around top, "GAS" around bottom.

Red Streak
Company history unknown.
RED STREAK NO KNOCK/GASOLINE
(5)   1920s   15in Metal $275-$450
Description not available.

Regal Oil Refining Company, Piqua, Ohio
Company history unknown.
REGAL
(5)   1910s   15in Metal/ $400-$750
                         perforated Metal faces
Perforated steel faces with shield outline and script "Regal" over "GASOLINE/MOTOR/OILS."
REGAL
(5)   1920s   15in Metal $900-$1,600
White globe face with detailed yellow-outlined white shield in center of face. Red banner across top of shield, with yellow script "Regal." Multicolored elf in center holding upper banner. Red "MOTOR/OILS" to left, "GASOLINE/KEROSENE" to right, with red banner across lower globe face below shield. White "THE REGAL OIL REFINING CO./PIQUA, OHIO" on lower banner.

Redwine
Company history unknown.
REDWINE SUPERCHARGED
(4)   1940s   13.5in Capco $225-$375
White globe face with blue outline ring. Red circle with orange and green bands in center. White "Super/Charged" in circle. Red-colored "REDWINE" arched around top, blue "GASOLINE" around bottom, with small blue "REGULAR" below red center circle.
REDWINE ETHYL
(5)   1940s   13.5in Capco $225-$375
Multicolored globe face. Details not available.

REDWINE KEROSENE
(5)   1940s   13.5in Capco $100-$150
Description not available.
UNITED SUPERCHARGED
(4)   1940s   13.5in Capco $225-$375
Same as REDWINE SUPERCHARGED above, with "UNITED" replacing "REDWINE."

Reed Oil Company, Big Springs, Texas
Company history unknown.
REED & DEIDS
(5)   1930s   15in Metal $275-$450
Blue lettering on orange. No other details available.
REED
(5)   1940s   13.5in Glass   No Listing
Orange globe face with blue and white outline rings. Blue "REED" across center of face. Identical in design, colors, and typestyle to Gulf globe face.

Reighards, Altoona, Pennsylvania
Founded as a single station in 1920, and continues to market in the Altoona area today.
REIGHARDS
(5)   1920s   One-piece etched $800-$1,100
White globe with blue line across center of face. Blue "REIGHARDS" arched around top, red "GASOLINE" around bottom.
REIGHARDS
(5)   1920s   15in Metal $225-$325
White globe face, with blue-outlined red "Reighards" in distinctive lettering across face.
REIGHARDS MOTOR GASOLINE
(5)   1920s   15in Metal   No Listing
Description not available.

Rice Oil Company, Johnstown, Ohio
Company history unknown.
RICE OIL CO.
(5)   1920s   One-piece etched   No Listing
Description not available.
RICE OIL CO. JOHNSTOWN, O.
(5)   1920s   15in Metal $500-$800
White globe face with red ring around white center circle. Interlocked multicolored "ROCO" in center circle, with black "RICE OIL CO." arched around top, "JOHNSTOWN, O." around bottom.

Richtane
Gladewater Refining Company, Gladewater, Texas
Company history unknown.
RICH TANE MOTOR
(4)   1930s   13.5in Glass $275-$425
Red globe face with black and white outline rings. Black-outlined white "RICH-TAN" across upper face, over white script "Motor." Small black "GLADEWATER REFINING CO." arched around bottom in white outline ring.
RICH TANE REGULAR
(4)   1930s   13.5in Glass $275-$425
Same as above, with white script "Regular" replacing "Motor."
RICH TANE ETHYL
(4)   1930s   13.5in Glass $275-$425
Same as above, with small Ethyl (EGC) logo in white circle replacing "Motor" on lower globe face.

Roadio
Company history unknown.
ROADIO GASOLINE
(5)   1930s   15in Metal $250-$375
White globe face with red band across upper face and blue band across lower face. Blue "ROADIO/GASOLINE" in center white area.
ROADIO KEROSENE
(5)   1930s   15in Metal $250-$375
Same as above, with "KEROSENE" replacing "GASOLINE."

Roadking
Company history unknown.
ROADKING (w/knight)
(4)   1950s   13.5in Capco $225-$375
White globe face with red knight and horse in center. Red "ROAD KING" arched around top of globe face.

Road Supreme
Company history unknown.
ROAD SUPREME (w/horse)
(5)   1950s   13.5in Capco $300-$550
Green globe face with red outline ring and red ring around white center circle. White "ROAD SUPREME" arched around top, "GASOLINE" around bottom, with detailed brown and black horse's head in center circle. Red "A WINNER" below horse head.

Rotarline
Company history unknown.
ROTARLINE
(5)   1930s   15in Metal $225-$325
White globe face with red "ROTARLINE" across center. Black "HIGH" arched around top, "COMPRESSION" around bottom.

Royal Flight
Company history unknown.
ROYAL FLIGHT (w/eagle)
(5)   1920s   One-piece PAINTED   No Listing
White globe with black eagle in center. Black "ROYAL FLIGHT" arched around top. Black "GAS" across lower globe face.

Royaline Oil Company, Royal Oak, Michigan
Company history unknown. Still in operation.
ROYALINE GASOLINE
(5)   1920s   One-piece etched $1,800-$2,800
White globe with black face. White circle in center of face, with black "ROC" tire design in center. White "ROYALINE" arched around top, "GASOLINE" around bottom.
ROYALINE HI-TEST
(5)   1920s   One-piece etched   No Listing
Same as above, with "HI-TEST" replacing "GASOLINE."
ROYALINE GASOLINE
(5)   1930s   15in Metal $750-$1,300
Black globe face with white circle in center. Black "ROC" tire log in center circle. White "ROYALINE" arched around top, "GASOLINE" around bottom.
ROYALINE HI-TEST
(5)   1930s   15in Metal   No Listing
Same as above, with "HI-TEST" replacing "GASOLINE" and "ROYA-LINE" in script.
ROYALINE BENZOL
(5)   1930s   15in Metal $900-$1,600
Same as above, with "BENZOL" replacing "GASOLINE."

Royal Rose—Spencer and Perry
Company history unknown.
ROYAL ROSE GASOLINE–SPENCER AND PERRY
(5)   1920s   One-piece etched   No Listing
White globe with blue "GASOLINE" across center. Blue "ANTI" above and "KNOCK" below, with arrows on each side. Blue "ROYAL ROSE" arched around top, "SPENCER and PERRY" around bottom.
ROSOLENE
(5)   1920s   One-piece etched $750-$1,000
White globe with blue "ROSOLENE" across center of face. Small blue design above and below "ROSOLENE."

Rushing Oil Company
Company history unknown.
RUSH-O-LENE PREMIUM (w/cardinal)
(5)   1930s   13.5in Glass $300-$650
White globe face with detailed red and blue cardinal in center. Blue "PREMIUM" above cardinal, "GASOLINE" below. Red "RUSH-O-LENE" arched around top, "RUSHING OIL CO." around bottom.

Salyer Refining Company, Oklahoma City, Oklahoma
Company history unknown.
SALYER GASOLINE (w/goose)
(4)   1950s   13.5in Glass   No listing
White globe face with multicolored girl riding goose in center. Yellow "SALYER'S" arched around top, "STAY-READY" around bottom.

Savex
See listing for DIXCEL in this section.

Savings Products/D&H Company, Tupelo, Mississippi
SAVINGS REGULAR
(5)   1947-1965   13.5in Capco $125-$200
White globe face with red and yellow dollar signs. Red "SAVINGS/PRODUCTS" across lower globe face over "REGULAR."

144

SAVINGS ETHYL
(5)   1947-1965   13.5in Capco $125-$200
Similar to above, with "ETHYL" replacing "REGULAR."
SAVINGS GOLDEN PREMIUM
(5)   1960-1965   13.5in Capco $125-$200
Same as above, with yellow "GOLDEN/PREMIUM" replacing the word "REGULAR."

Seal-O-Co, Saginaw, Michigan
Company history unknown.
SEAL-O-CO REGULAR
(4)   1950s   13.5in Capco $125-$175
White globe face with black and yellow outline rings. Black band at bottom, with yellow "REGULAR" on band. Red "SEAL-O-CO" with black dropshade across center, with red triangular design at top of globe.
SEAL-O-CO ETHYL (EC) GASOLINE
(4)   1950s   13.5in Capco $125-$175
Black-outlined white center circle with blue ring arched around top, red ring around bottom. Large Ethyl (EC) logo in center circle. White "SEAL-O-CO" arched around top, "ETHYL" around bottom.

Sears Oil Company, Rome, New York
Company history unknown.
SEARS GASOLINE
(5)   1930s   15in Metal $250-$400
Description not available.

Sea Way
New York marketer. Company history unknown.
SEA-WAY
(5)   1950s   13.5in Capco $250-$375
White and yellow globe face with red, white, and blue nautical flag in center. Black "Sea-Way" across center of flag.

Security
Company history unknown.
SECURITY (w/anchor)
(4)   1930s   15in Metal $900-$1,600
White globe face with green outline ring and green ring around white center circle with green waves. Red anchor with waves in center circle. Red "SECURITY" arched around top, "GASOLINE" around bottom.

Seneca Chief
Company history unknown.
SENECA CHIEF GASOLINE
(5)   1930s   13.5in Glass   No Listing
Description not available.
SENECA CHIEF SENZO BENZOL MOTOR FUEL
(5)   1930s   13.5in Glass $300-$600
Red globe face with blue outline ring and white center circle. Blue "SENZO" in center circle, with blue-outlined white "SENECA CHIEF" arched around top, "BENZOL MOTOR FUEL" around bottom.

Seoco
Company history unknown.
SEOCO SPEED GAS
(5)   1930s   13.5in Glass $225-$350
White globe face with orange "SEOCO" over black "SPEED GAS" on face.

Service Oil Company
Company history unknown.
SERVICE Oil Company
(5)   1940s   13.5in Glass $200-$325
White globe face with blue outline ring and yellow script "Service" across center of face. Blue "OIL COMPANY" in yellow underline below "Service."

Service Distributing Company, Albemarle, North Carolina
North Carolina's largest independent, marketing through over 100 stations across the state. Founded with a single station in Albemarle in 1933, they introduced the Service-Plus brand at the end of World War II. The company currently operates under both Service Plus and Servco.
SERVICE PLUS REGULAR
(4)   1946-1970   13.5in Glass $200-$350
White globe face with blue outline ring and blue outline around white center circle. Red "SERVICE-PLUS" arched around top, "GASOLINE" around bottom, with red "REGULAR" across center circle.

SERVICE PLUS HI-OCTANE
(4)   1946-1950   13.5in Glass $200-$350
Same as above, with "HI-OCTANE" replacing "REGULAR."
SERVICE PLUS ETHYL
(5)   1950-1970   13.5in Glass $200-$350
Same as above, with Ethyl (EC) logo replacing "REGULAR" in center circle.
SERVICE PLUS ETHYL PREMIUM
(4)   1950-1970   13.5in Glass $200-$350
Same as above, with "PREMIUM" replacing "GASOLINE" around bottom of globe face.

Shamrock Oil Company, Winter Park, Florida
Company history unknown.
SHAMROCK (clover w/red band)
(4)   1950s   13.5in Glass $250-$400
White globe face with large black-outlined green clover in center of face. Red banner across clover, with white "SHAMROCK" in banner.

Sharlene
Company history unknown.
SHARLENE CRYSTAL
(5)   1930s   13.5in Glass $225-$350
White globe face with black outline ring. Black-outlined square in center, with black band diagonally across square. Red "SHARLENE" in band. Red "CRYSTAL" arched around top, "GASOLINE" around bottom.
SHARLENE SUPER
(5)   1930s   13.5in Glass $225-$350
Similar to above, with red outline and red "HIGH" and "OCTANE" in center box. Black "SUPER" arched around top, "GASOLINE" around bottom.

Sheroils
Company history unknown.
SHER-OILS HI POW
(5)   1930s   One-piece etched $1,000-$1,600
White globe with blue outline ring and blue "HI-POW" across center. Red script "Sher-oilS" at top, red "MOTOR FUEL" at bottom.
SHER-OILS HI POW
(5)   1930s   One-piece baked $800-$1,200
Same as above.
SHER-OILS INDEPENDENT GASOLINE
(5)   1930s   15in Metal $250-$400
White globe face with red script "Sher-oilS" across center of face. Red "INDEPENDENT" arched around top, "GASOLINE" around bottom.

Silencer—East Texas Refining Company
A Dixie Distributors affiliate. Company history unknown.
SILENCER "S-S-SH"
(4)   1930s   15in Metal $350-$525
White globe face with yellow oval across center of face. Black "SILENCER" in oval, with orange "S-S-SH" across top, "Stops Knocks" across bottom.
SILENCER ETHYL (EGC)
(4)   1930s   15in Metal $250-$375
White globe face with yellow oval across upper face. Black "SILENCER" in oval. Black-outlined white circle on lower globe face, with small Ethyl (EGC) logo in circle.
DIXIE SILENCER STOPS KNOCKS
(5)   1940s   13.5in YELLOW Capco $250-$375
White globe face with yellow oval across center. Black "SILENCER" in yellow oval. Red "DIXIE" arched across top, "Stops Knocks" across bottom.
SILENCER DIXIE ETHYL (EGC)
(5)   1940s   13.5in RED Capco $200-$325
White globe face with black-outlined white circle in center. Small Ethyl (EGC) logo in center circle. Blue "SILENCER" arched around top, "DIXIE" around bottom.

Silver Gas
Company history unknown.
SILVER GAS
(5)   1930s   13.5in Capco $150-$275
Blue globe face with white "SILVER/GAS" logotype with small white star on face.

Silver Flash—Columbus Oil Company, Columbus, Ohio
Company history unknown.
SILVER FLASH
(5)   1920s   One-piece cast $1,000-$1,600

White octagon-shaped globe with red face. White "Silver/Flash" diagonally across face between green lines.
SILVER FLASH ETHYL
(5)   1920s   One-piece cast $1,200-$1,800
White octagon-shaped globe with green face. White "SILVER FLASH ETHYL" diagonally across face between red lines.
COLUMBUS GASOLINE
(5)   1920s   One-piece baked $800-$1,200
White globe with blue outline ring and blue lines forming bar-and-circle design across center. Blue band across center, with white "THE COLUMBUS OIL COMPANY." Red "COLUMBUS" arched around top, "GASOLINE" around bottom.
COLUMBUS GASOLINE
(5)   1920s   15in Metal   No Listing
"COLUMBUS" around top, red "GASOLINE" around bottom. Detailed sketch of Christopher Columbus in center.
SILVER FLASH ANTI-KNOCK
(5)   1920s   One-piece baked $900-$1,600
White globe, with red outline ring around white face and blue center circle with red band across center. White "SILVER FLASH" in red band, with white "ANTI-KNOCK" in upper half of blue circle and "GASOLINE" below. Red "THE BEST YOU CAN GET" arched around top, "THE COLUMBUS OIL COMPANY" around bottom.
SILVER FLASH GASOLINE Metal inserts
(5)   1910s   15in Metal $500-$700
Description not available.
SILVER FLASH GASOLINE
(5)   1920s   15in Metal $500-$750
Description not available.
SILVER FLASH ANTI-KNOCK
(5)   1920s   15in Metal   No Listing
Description not available.
SILVER FLASH ANTI-KNOCK
(5)   1930s   13.5in Glass $300-$525
Description not available.

Silver Pep
Company history unknown.
SILVER PEP
(5)   1930s   13.5in Glass $250-$375
Red globe face with blue and white wing design and white "SILVER/PEP" on face.

Simms Oil Company, Dallas, Texas
Company history unknown.
SIMMS GAS (V-shaped globe)
(4)   1920s   One-piece baked $600-$900
White cone-shaped globe with red triangle outline and red "SIMMS/GAS" on face.

Sipo
Company history unknown.
SIPO CARBONLESS (w/world)
(5)   1920s   15in Metal   No Listing
Red globe face with blue world globe in center. White band around world, with black car and red "SILENT POWER." White "SIPO" with red shading across world. White "CARBONLESS" arched around top, "LUBRICATED" around bottom.

Sioux Oil Company, Newcastle, Wyoming
Company history unknown.
SIOUX PETROLEUM PRODUCTS
(5)   1930s   Gill $800-$1,600
White globe face with Indian head in center. "SIOUX" arched around top, "PETROLEUM PRODUCTS" around bottom.
SIOUX
(5)   1940s   Gill $800-$1,500
White globe face with red and black Indian head with white feathers in center of face. Black "SIOUX" arched around bottom.
SIOUX
(4)   1950s   13.5in RED Capco $375-$650
White globe face with large red arrowhead. No other details available.

Site Oil Company, Clayton, Missouri
Operated under the Cresyl brand in the 1930s and 1940s, and evolved into the chain discounter Site after WW II. They continue to operate stations under the Site brand.
CRESYL REGULAR KNOCK FREE
(4)   1940s   13.5in Glass $250-$350
White globe face with blue triangle in center. Yellow circle at bottom

of triangle, with blue "KNOCK/FREE" in circle. Yellow "CRESYL" across top, light blue "REGULAR" across center.

CRESYL 98
(4)   1940s   13.5in Glass $250-$350
White globe face with orange triangle in center. Yellow circle at bottom, with small Ethyl (EGC) logo. Yellow "CRESYL" over black "98" on upper triangle.

CRESYL 110
(4)   1940s   13.5in Glass $250-$350
White globe face with red triangle in center. White circle at bottom of triangle, with small Ethyl (EGC) logo. Red "CRESYL" over black "110" on upper triangle.

SITE
(3)   1946-1970   Oval Capco $125-$175
White oval globe face with blue rounded shield covering most of face. Yellow "SITE" across shield.

Skylark
Company history unknown.

SKYLARK ETHYL GASOLINE
(4)   1950s   13.5in Capco $125-$175
White globe face with blue outline ring and blue script "Skylark" arched around top. Yellow "ETHYL" over blue "GASOLINE" on lower globe face.

Sky Trak
Company history unknown.

SKY TRAK (red/blue)
(4)   1950s   13.5in Capco $250-$400
White globe face with blue cloud scene in center. Red "SKY TRAK" diagonally across clouds, with small red airplane.

SKY TRAK
(3)   1950s   13.5in Capco $100-$150
White globe face with red diagonal lines forming band across globe. Red "SKY TRAK" in band.

SKY TRAK
(4)   1950s   13.5in Capco $100-$150
Same as above, with green replacing red.

Smith Oil Company, Rockford, Illinois
Company history unknown.

SMITH PARAMOUNT GASOLINE
(5)   1930s   14in Glass   No Listing
White globe face with black outline ring. Black "SMITH" with red design at top of globe face, over red "PARAMOUNT/GASOLINE."

Smitholene
Company history unknown.

SMITHOLENE GASOLINE
(4)   1940s   12.5in Glass $850-$1,350
White globe face with black outline ring and red outline around blue center circle. Detailed airplane with red "BRAND" in center circle. Black "SMITH-O-LENE" arched around top, "GASOLINE" around bottom.

SMITHOLENE ETHYL
(4)   1940s   12.5in Glass $850-$1,250
Same as above, with red "ETHYL" replacing "BRAND" above airplane.

Sooner State Oils
Company history unknown.

SOONER OCTALENE
(5)   1930s   13.5in GREEN Capco   No Listing
Red globe face with white octagon in center of face. Red "OCTALENE" arched across upper area, "GAS" at bottom, with small red "SOONER STATE/OILS" with covered wagon scene in center.

SOONER ETHYL
(5)   1930s   13.5in RED Capco   No Listing
Description not available.

Southern Oil Company, High Point, North Carolina
Company history unknown.

SOUTHERN GASOLINE
(5)   1930s   16.5in Metal $250-$425
White globe face with black "SOUTHERN" arched above red reverse-bowtie "GASOLINE" across center of face.

SOUTHERN
(5)   1950s   13.5in Glass $200-$300
White globe face with red outline ring and red "SOUTHERN" across center.

SOUTHERN EXTRA
(5)   1950s   13.5in Glass $200-$325
White globe face with blue outline ring and blue "SOUTHERN/EXTRA" with red underline across center.

Southern Oil
Company history unknown.

SOUTHERN INDEPENDENT GASOLINE
(5)   1930s   One-piece baked $600-$850
Orange globe face with black outline and black lines forming orange band across center. Black "INDEPENDENT" arched around top, "GASOLINE" around bottom, with "SOUTHERN" in center band.

SOUTHERN "EAST TEXAS" GASOLINE
(5)   1930s   One-piece baked   No Listing
Same as above, with no black lines across center. Black "SOUTHERN" arched around top, "GASOLINE" around bottom, with black "EAST-TEXAS" across center.

Southern States Oil Company, Jacksonville, Florida
Company history unknown.

SOUTHERN STATES Oil Company
(4)   1950s   13.5in Glass $350-$500
White globe face with red-outlined blue triangle with white center in center of face. White "SOUTHERN STATES GASOLINE" around blue area of triangle, with blue "OILS" in white center.

Southland Oil Company, Yazoo City, Mississippi
Company history unknown.

SOUTHLAND
(4)   1950s   13.5in Glass $200-$325
White globe face with double green outline ring and double green outline rings around white center circle. Red "SOUTHLAND" across center.

Southwest
Company history unknown.

SOUTHWEST ETHYL
(5)   1950s   13.5in Capco $125-$175
White globe face with red sunburst in center. Black band arched across sunburst, with white "ETHYL" in band. Red "SOUTHWEST" arched around top, "OIL COMPANY" arched around bottom.

SOUTHWEST KEROSENE
(5)   1950s   13.5in Capco $125-$175
Same as above, with white "KEROSENE" in band.

SOUTHWEST DIESEL
(5)   1950s   13.5in Capco $125-$175
Same as above, with white "DIESEL" in band.

Sparco—Shreveport Producers and Refiners, Shreveport, Louisiana
Company history unknown.

SPARCO ANTI-KNOCK
(5)   1930s   16.5in Metal $300-$550
White globe face with red sun halves and rays top and bottom, separated by large blue "SPARCO/ANTI-KNOCK" in bowtie lettering across center.

SPARCOLENE
(5)   1930s   15in Metal $250-$400
White globe face with orange script "Sparcolene" across center. No other details known.

Spartan
Company history unknown.

SPARTAN
(4)   1930s   15in Metal $350-$550
White globe face with blue Spartan helmet above blue "SPARTAN" on center of globe face.

SPARTAN ETHYL
(4)   1930s   15in Metal $325-$600
White globe face with red Spartan helmet over red "SPARTAN/ETHYL" on face.

Speed-O
Company history unknown.

SPEED-O
(5)   1930s   15in Metal $230-$375
White globe face with black "GAS" across center. Red "SPEED-O" with speed lines across upper face, with red "ALL ENERGY" across bottom.

Speedway
United Dividend Oil Company, Canon City, Colorado
Founded in Canon City, Colorado, in 1930, United operated stations under the Speedway brand until the 1970s.
SPEEDWAY THE BETTER GAS
(4)   1930s   Gill $850-$1,350
White globe face with black car scene in center. Red "SPEEDWAY" arched around top, "THE BETTER GAS" around bottom.
SPEEDWAY EXTRA
(5)   1930s   Gill $275-$400
Yellow globe face with green outline ring. Green-outlined red "SPEEDWAY" arched around top, "GASOLINE" around bottom, with red-outlined green "XTRA" across center.

Speedwing Corporation, Alton, Illinois
A midwestern independent operating under the Speedwing and Pana brand names.
SPEEDWING 700
(5)   1950s   Oval Capco $150-$250
Blue outer border. Red upper 1/3 background with white star. White center band with blue "SPEEDWING" across center. Lower 1/3 blue background, with "700" in white.

Spirit Gas
Company history unknown.
SPIRIT GAS
(5)   1920s   One-piece PAINTED $400-$650
White globe with black script "SPIRIT" over block "GAS."

Sprinkle Gasoline, Greensboro, North Carolina
Founded in Greensboro in 1925, Sprinkle was one of the first trackside discounters, operating stations throughout North Carolina. The 1970s gas shortages forced the closing of most locations, and as of this writing only one station remains in operation.
SPRINKLE GASOLINE
(5)   1920s   One-piece etched $600-$1,000
White globe with red "SPRINKLE" arched across top, "GASOLINE" across bottom.
SPRINKLE GASOLINE
(5)   1930s   15in Metal $400-$600
White globe face with green-outlined orange circle in center. White "S" in center circle. Green "SPRINKLE" arched around top, "GASOLINE" around bottom.
SPRINKLE REGULAR
(4)   1940s   Yellow ripple Gill   No Listing
Yellow globe face with red oval in center. White center in red oval, with red "S." White "SPRINKLE" arched in top of oval, "GASOLINE" below.
SPRINKLE POWER S GASOLINE
(4)   1950s   13.5in Capco $125-$175
Red and blue globe face with large white "S" covering most of face. Blue "SPRINKLE" arched in top of "S," "POWER" in center, and "GASOLINE" below.

Spunkey's Oil Company
Company history unknown.
SPUNKEY'S OIL CO.
(4)   1950s   13.5in Glass $225-$350
White globe face with red outline ring and red lines forming white band across center. Black interlocked "SOCO" at top of globe face, with red "SPUNKEY'S" in center band. Black "OIL CO." below band.
SPUNKEYS REGULAR
(4)   1950s   13.5in Glass $225-$350
Same as above, with black script "Regular" on lower globe face.
SPUNKEYS ETHYL
(4)   1950s   13.5in Glass $225-$350
Same as above, with black script "Ethyl" on lower globe face.
SPUNKEYS ETHYL (EC)
(4)   1940s   13.5in Glass $250-$375
Same as above, with Ethyl (EC) logo on lower globe face.

Stanley Oil Company, St. Louis, Missouri
Company history unknown.
HYTONE GAS–STANLEY OIL CO.
(5)   1920s   One-piece etched   No Listing
Description not available.
STANLEY
(5)   1940s   13.5in Glass $250-$350
White globe face with red outline ring and blue-outlined white band across center. Large red-outlined "S" in center with blue "STANLEY"

on center band. Red "SUPER" arched around top, "GASOLINE" around bottom.
STANLEY LEADER GAS (w/drum major)
(5)   1950s   13.5in Capco $350-$550
Description not available.

Star Pep
Company history unknown.
STAR PEP INDEPENDENT GASOLINE
(5)   1930s   15in Metal   No Listing
Blue globe face with red and white circle in center. Large white star in center circle, with red "STAR/PEP" over "TEXAS MADE FOR TEXAS TRADE" in star. White "INDEPENDENT" arched around top, "GASOLINE" around bottom.

Stephen
Company history unknown.
STEPHEN
(5)   1930s   13.5in Glass $225-$375
Red, white, and blue globe face with multiple outline rings. Large "S" in center in blue diamond box. Red "STEPHEN" across center.

Stone Oil Company, Fitzgerald, Georgia
Company history unknown.
STONES REGULAR
(4)   1950s   13.5in Capco $100-$150
White globe face, with blue outline ring and yellow "STONES" over blue script "Regular."

Streich Oil Company, Manitowoc, Wisconsin
Company history unknown.
STREICH OIL CO. QUALITY SERVICE
(5)   1930s   15in Metal $225-$400
White globe face with blue "QUALITY" arched around top, "SERVICE" arched around bottom, with blue "STREICH OIL CO." across center.

Sunland Refining Company
Company history unknown.
SUNLAND GASOLINE "LOOK FOR THE ORANGE PUMP"
(5)   1930s   15in Metal   No Listing
Orange globe face with olive areas arched top and bottom, with olive band across center. Black "SUNLAND/GASOLINE" in center band. Black "SUNLAND REFINING CO." arched in upper area, "LOOK FOR THE ORANGE PUMP" in bottom area.
SUNLAND HIGHER OCTANE
(3)   1940s   15in Metal $275-$500
White globe face with orange-outlined white parallelogram in center of face. Black-outlined orange "HO" in center, with black-outlined white box across letters with orange "HIGHER OCTANE" in box. Black "SUNLAND" above "HO," "GASOLINE" below.
SUNLAND ETHYL (EGC)
(3)   1940s   15in Metal $275-$450
White globe face with orange-and-black-outlined shield in center of face. Black band around bottom of shield. Black "SUNLAND" over red "ETHYL" over black "GASOLINE" on upper shield. Small Ethyl (EGC) logo on lower shield. Orange "SUNLAND REFINING/CORPORATION" in lower black band.

Sunrise
Company history unknown.
SUNRISE GASOLINE
(5)   1930s   15in Metal   No Listing
Description not available.
SUNRISE NOK-LESS GAS
(5)   1930s   15in Metal   No Listing
White globe with orange sun with rays on upper half of globe. Blue "SUNRISE" across sun. Blue "NOK-LESS" on lower globe face.

Sunset Oil Company, Los Angeles, California
Company history unknown. This series of metal-band globes were first used after 1940.
SUNSET GASOLINE (w/sunset scene)
(5)   1940s   15in Metal $2,000-$3,500
Description not available.
SUNSET ETHYL
(5)   1920s   15in Metal   No Listing
White globe face with yellow-outlined green shield in center of face. White "SUNSET" over multicolored sunset scene on shield, white "ETHYL" below. Small Ethyl (EGC) logo on lower globe face.

Gasoline one-piece etched chimney-cap globe and Liberty 13.5in inserts on glass body. Tom Licouris

Gasoline small one-piece etched globe, green background.

Gasoline one-piece etched plain "G," 7in base.

Guaranteed Measure one-piece etched globe.

Guarantee Visible Pump one-piece etched 14in globe with chimney cap.

Visible Measure one-piece etched globe.

Visible Gasoline one-piece etched sphere-shaped globe.

Perry Home Owned Oil Co., 16.5in inserts on metal body.

Canzol one-piece fired-on globe.

Burrell Gasoline one-piece etched.

Crouse Clear Vision 15in metal perforated inserts on metal body. Tom Davidson

Light House Gas one-piece etched globe. Larry Starkweather

Unity Gasoline 15in inserts on metal body.

Mountain Gasoline one-piece etched globe. Kyle Moore

Eldred Hi-Test one-piece etched globe (orange triangle).

SUNSET DE LUXE
(5)   1920s   15in Metal   No Listing
Cream-colored globe face with orange-and-yellow-outlined green triangle, point down, on center of face. White "SUNSET" and multicolored
sunset scene on upper triangle over green band on lower triangle.
White "DELUXE"in band.
SUNSET MARINE (w/sunset)
(5)   1920s   15in Metal   No Listing
Black globe face same as above, with white "MARINE" in lower green
band.
SUNSET THRIFTY (w/Scotsman)
(5)   1920s   15in Metal   No Listing
Cream-colored globe face with red-and-green-outlined yellow triangle
on center of face. Green "THRIFTY" over multicolored Scotsman on
upper triangle over green band across lower triangle. White "GASO-
LINE" in lower green band.

Super 98
Company history unknown.
SUPER 98
(4)   1950s   13.5in Capco $100-$175
Globe face has red upper half and blue lower half split diagonally.
Black-outlined white "Super" in upper red area, "98" in lower blue
area.

Super Chief
Company history unknown.
SUPER CHIEF
(5)   1950s   13.5in Capco $175-$350
White globe face with black stylized Indian head in center. Red
"SUPER" arched around top, "CHIEF" around bottom.

Super Flash
See listing for CRYSTAL FLASH in this section.

Super Flash
Company history unknown.
SUPER FLASH GASOLINE
(5)   1940s   13.5in Glass $225-$375
Red globe face with white center circle. White band across center, with
blue "FLASH" in band. Large blue "S" in center circle. White "SUPER"
arched around top, "GASOLINE" around bottom.

Super Rose
Guarantee Oil Company, Indianapolis, Indiana
Company history unknown.
SUPER ROSE ANTI KNOCK
(4)   1950s   13.5in Glass $300-$650
White globe face with black outline ring and black ring around white
center circle. Red rose with green leaves in center circle. Red script
"Super" and red "ROSE" arched around top, black "ANTI-KNOCK"
around bottom.
SUPER ROSE ETHYL
(5)   1950s   13.5in Glass $225-$350
Same as above, with Ethyl (EC) logo replacing rose in center circle
and black "ETHYL" arched around bottom.

Super Oil Company
Company history unknown.
SUPER OIL CO. REGULAR GAS
(5)   1950s   13.5in Glass   No Listing
Description not available.

Star Service and Petroleum, Centralia, Illinois
A large regional independent that went out of business in 1990.
SUPER STAR
(5)   1950s   13.5in Glass $250-$375
White globe face with large red star in center. Blue "SUPER" arched
around top, "STAR" around bottom.

Super Quality
Company history unknown.
SUPER QUALITY
(5)   1950s   13.5in Glass $250-$375
White globe face with orange outline ring. Black band across center,
with orange "SUPER Q QUALITY" (large "Q") in band. Black "GUAR-
ANTEED" arched around top, "HIGH OCTANE" around bottom.

Super United
Company history unknown.

SUPER UNITED HIGH TEST
(5)   1940s   Gill $250-$350
Orange globe face with white octagon in center. Orange band across
center of octagon, with black "UNITED" on band. Black script "Super"
above band, "High Test" below band.

Super Zip
See listing for MUSGO in this section.

Superior
See listing for EXCELSIOR in this section.

Superior Oil Company, King City, Missouri
Company history unknown.
SUPERIOR GAS AND OIL
(4)   1930s   15in Metal $275-$425
White globe face with red and blue checkerboard design in center. No
other details available.

Superior
Company history unknown.
SUPERIOR GASOLINE
(4)   1930s   15in Metal   No Listing
Yellow globe face with black outline ring and white band across cen-
ter. Black-outlined red "SUPERIOR/GASOLINE" in center band.
SUPERIOR GASOLINE (w/sunburst)
(5)   1930s   15in Metal $375-$550
White globe face with red sun in center, with red rays extending out to
edge of face. Blue bowtie band across center, with white "SUPERIOR."
White "GASOLINE" arched in lower edge of sun.

Supreme
Company history unknown.
SUPREME HI TANE
(5)   1950s   13.5in Capco $150-$250
White globe face with red, white, and blue shield at top of face.
"SUPREME" on band across shield, with "HI TANE" across lower
globe face.

Sweney Gasoline and Oil Company, Peoria, Illinois
Company history unknown.
SWENEY SKY HAWK GASOLINE
(4)   1930s   15in Metal $750-$1,200
SWENEY SKY HAWK GASOLINE
(5)   1930s   14in Gill $400-$750
White globe face with red script "Sweney" across upper face. Light
green hawk below "SWENEY," above light-green-outlined dark green
"SKY HAWK." Red "GASOLINE" arched around bottom.

Sweet Wyman
Company history unknown.
SWEET WYMAN GASOLINE
(5)   1930s   15in Metal $350-$650
Green globe face with red "SWEET" with white and black backshad-
ing at top of globe face over yellow "WYMAN." Red "GASOLINE"
arched down across bottom.

Sylvan Oil Company
Company history unknown.
SYLVAN OIL CO. GAS
(5)   1920s   15in Metal $500-$900
White globe face with blue outline ring. Large blue-outlined red keystone in center of globe face, with white "SYLVAN" vertically and
"OIL CO" horizontally in keystone. Black "GASOLINE" arched around
bottom, with black "INC" at top and black arrows around to either
side.

T&T Gasoline Stations
Company history unknown.
T&T GASOLINE
(5)   1950s   13.5in Glass $225-$325
Description not available.

Tankar Stations, Norfolk, Virginia
Founded in Sheffield, Alabama, in 1933, Tankar operated a chain
of discount service stations in Virginia, West Virginia, and Alabama,
with station buildings built out of actual railroad tank cars. The company shifted headquarters to Norfolk in 1939. Tankar began operating
automatic car washes in 1966, and gradually replaced the gas stations
with car washes. The last station closed in Portsmouth, Virginia, in
1979, although they continue to operates car washes today.

TANKAR
(5)   1933-1970   13.5in RED Capco $375-$600
White globe face with detailed red and black railroad tank car in center of face, with yellow "TANKAR" on car. Yellow lines above and below tank car.
TANKAR ETHYL (EGC)
(5)   1935-1940   13.5in Capco $300-$525
White globe face with small red and black detailed railroad tank car at top of face. Yellow "TANKAR" on car. Black-outlined white circle with large Ethyl (EGC) logo on lower globe face.
TANKAR ETHYL (EC)
(5)   1940-1970   13.5in Capco $300-$525
Same as above, with Ethyl (EC) logo.

Tarzon
Company history unknown.
TARZON GAS/OIL
(5)   1920s   15in Metal $300-$500
Description not available.

Tempo
Company history unknown.
TEMPO
(5)   1950s   13.5in Capco $100-$150
White globe face with red outline ring and green-outlined red diamond on face. White-outlined green "TEMPO" across diamond.

Texas
Company history unknown.
TEXAS
(4)   1950s   13.5in Glass $225-$350
Orange globe face with black outline ring. Black "TEXAS" across globe face, with white and blue three-dimensional area behind lettering.
TEXAS MOTOR GASOLINE
(5)   1940s   Gill   No Listing
Description not available.

Texas Rose
Company history unknown.
TEXAS ROSE REGULAR
(3)   1930s   Gill $300-$550
White globe face with red outline ring. Red "TEXAS ROSE" with green dropshade arched around top. Red rose with green leaves in center, with red lines across lower globe face forming white band. Green "REGULAR" in band.
TEXAS ROSE ETHYL
(3)   1930s   Gill $300-$550
Same as above, with black-outlined white circle with Ethyl (EC) logo replacing band and "REGULAR" on lower globe face.
TEXAS ROSE REGULAR
(3)   1940s-1950s   13.5in Capco $200-$350
Same as earlier TEXAS ROSE REGULAR above.
TEXAS ROSE ETHYL
(3)   1940s-1950s   13.5in Capco $200-$350
Same as earlier TEXAS ROSE ETHYL above.

Texgas—Union Texas Petroleum, Houston, Texas
A unit of Allied Chemical, operating stations in the south central states.
TEXGAS PLATINUM REGULAR
(4)   1950s   13.5in Capco $150-$250
White globe face with blue-outlined white diamond in center. Red "Texgas" logotype across diamond. Blue band at top, with white script "Platinum" on band. Red "REGULAR" across lower globe face.
TEXGAS PLATINUM PREMIUM
(4)   1950s   13.5in Capco $150-$250
Same as above, with "PREMIUM" replacing "REGULAR."

Thermoil Lubricants, Elk City, Oklahoma
Company history unknown.
THERMOIL MOTOR OIL
(5)   1920s   15in Metal   No Listing
White globe face with red diamond and Thermoil logo in center of face. Black "THERMOIL" arched around top, "MOTOR OIL" across center over red script "Crankcase/Service/Here."

Thoni Oil/Magic Benzol Gas Stations Incorporated, Miami, Florida
Founded in the 1930s in Nashville, they were operating about fifty stations under the Thoni name throughout the South by the

1950s. They continued to operate a widely scattered chain of stations until 1990.
MAGIC BENZOL GAS
(5)   1935-1946   15in Metal $400-$600
White globe face with red banner across center. White "BENZOL" on banner. Blue script "Magic" at top of globe, with line extending from "Magic" around outer edge of globe face. Blue script "Gas" below banner.
MAGIC BENZOL GAS–THONI
(5)   1946-1950   13.5in Glass $275-$425
Same as above, with small blue "BRAND" added below "GAS," and red "THONI'S" below outline on lower globe face.
THONI'S 90
(5)   1950-1960   13.5in Glass $300-$550
White globe face with blue outline ring. Blue "THONI OIL CO." arched around top, with black rocket and red speed lines in center of face. Red "JET 90 POWER" across lower globe face.
THONI'S ETHYL
(5)   1950-1960   13.5in Glass $300-$550
Description not available.

Jack Thornton Oil Company
Company history unknown.
THORNTON
(5)   1950s   13.5in Capco $125-$175
Light blue globe face with white trapezoidal band across center. Red "THORNTON" in band, with white "JACK" above and "OIL Company" below.

Three D's
Company history unknown.
THREE D'S (w/cow)
(5)   1920s   15in Metal   No Listing
White globe face with large red cow in center of globe face. Three white "D" marks branded on cow. Black "THREE D'S PRODUCTS" arched around top, "DISTRIBUTORS INC." around bottom, with red "XTRA D" under cow.

Tidal Refining Company, Tulsa, Oklahoma
Company history unknown.
TIDAL
(5)   1920s   One-piece etched $550-$850
White globe with red "TIDAL/GAS" on globe face.
TIDAL
(5)   1920s   15in Metal $250-$375
Description not available.

Tidelands, Pensacola, Florida
Company history unknown.
THRIFTY (w/Scottie dog and blanket)
(4)   1950s   13.5in Capco $250-$425
White globe face with black outline ring. Red burst in center, with black and red Scottish terrier in center of burst. Black "THRIFTY" arched around top, "GAS" around bottom.

Thrifty
Company history unknown.
THRIFTY PREMIUM
(5)   1950s   13.5in Capco $100-$150
White globe face with red outline ring. Blue-outlined white oval in center, with blue waves. Red "THRIFTY" over blue "PREMIUM" in oval.

Tidioute
Company history unknown.
TIDIOUTE
(5)   1920s   15in Metal   No Listing
Description not available.

Tioga
Petroleum Products Company, Chanute, Kansas
Company history unknown.
TIOGA GASOLINE
(4)   1940s   13.5in Glass $1,800-$2,500
White globe face with black outline ring and black ring around yellow center circle. Black "TIOGA" arched around top, "GASOLINE" around bottom, with detailed multicolored Indian in center.
TIOGA ETHYL
(5)   1940s   13.5in Glass $300-$475
Same as above, with white circle in center. Large Ethyl (EGC) logo in center circle.

Tidewater Oil Service, Matthews, Virginia

Rural Virginia jobber that branded several dozen stations under the TIWOSER brand from 1932 until 1952. Branded Pure in 1952, they market Unocal products today.

TIWOSER
(4)   1932-1940   15in Metal $2,000-$3,500
White globe face with red outline ring. Detailed sunset at sea, with clipper ship scene on lower globe face with black "TIWOSER" arched around top over black "HIGH TEST." Red "GASOLINE" below high test, just above scene. Black "TIDEWATER OIL SERVICE" arched around bottom. This globe has long been considered one of the most detailed of all "picture" globes.

Todd's

Company history unknown.
TODD'S HYGRADE GAS
(5)   1920s   One-piece etched $450-$750
Spherical white globe with black "HYGRADE/TODD'S/GASOLINE" on globe face.

Tony's

Company history unknown.
TONY'S ECONOMY GAS/OIL
(5)   1920s   15in Metal   No Listing
Orange globe face with black "TONY'S/ECONOMY/GAS-OILS" on face.

Torpedo

See listing for ILLINOIS OIL in this section.

Tourist

Company history unknown.
TOURIST
(5)   1930s   15in Metal   No Listing
White globe face with blue outline ring. Red script "Tourist" with blue shading across globe face.

Trackage, Minneapolis, Minnesota

Company history unknown.
TRACKAGE "TANK CAR TO YOUR CAR"
(5)   1940s   13.5in Glass $375-$700
White globe face with blue outline ring. Blue railroad tank car in center of globe, with red "TRACKAGE" on tank car. Blue "TANK CAR" across top, "TO/YOUR CAR" across bottom.

Taylor Oil Company, Winston-Salem, North Carolina

Roby Taylor, Richfield jobber in Winston-Salem, North Carolina, operated the Travelers discount chain throughout central and eastern North Carolina. Some stations were rebranded Etna about 1960 and as Etna became the company's primary brand, Travelers stations were either converted or sold. Taylor Oil continues to operate under the Etna name today.

TRAVELERS
(5)   1946-1960   Gill $250-$400
TRAVELERS
(5)   1946-1960   15in Metal   No Listing
Yellow globe face with blue line across center. Blue car on line, with blue airplane above. Blue "TRAVELERS" arched around top, "GASO-LINE" around bottom.
TRAVELERS KEROSENE
(5)   1946-1960   15in Metal   No Listing
Same as above, with "KEROSENE" replacing "GASOLINE."

Travelon Oil Company, Rochester, New York

Company history unknown.
TRAVELON GASOLINE
(5)   1940s   13.5in Glass $375-$575
White globe face with red outline ring. Blue map of western hemisphere, with blue band arched across center. Red "TRAVELON" on blue band, with blue "GASOLINE" below.

Trophy

See listing for MIDWEST in this section.

Tryon Oil Company

Company history unknown.
TRYON OIL CO-PEP-PO GASOLINE
(5)   1920s   One-piece baked $400-$850
                    small globe
White globe with red "Pep-Po" across center of face. Red "TRYON

OIL" arched around top over "CO," with red "MOTOR FUEL" arched around bottom.

Tyreco

Company history unknown.
TYRECO ROADKING (w/car)
(5)   1930s   13.5in Glass   No Listing
White globe face with black outline ring. Red diagonal band across center of globe face, with blue band across bottom. Black car on top of red band. Blue "TYRECO" across top, black "ROAD KING" in red band, and white "GASOLINE" in blue band.

Union Oil Company

Company history unknown.
UNION OIL CO. UNION PRODUCTS
(5)   1930s   15in Metal   No Listing
UNION OIL CO. UNION PRODUCTS
(4)   1940s   13.5in Glass $250-$375
White globe face with blue and red outline rings. Blue band diagonally across center, with red-outlined white "UNION" on band. Blue "UNION OIL CO." arched around top, "PRODUCTS" around bottom.
UNION OIL CO. HI-TEST PRODUCTS
(5)   1940s   13.5in Glass $250-$375
Same as above, with "HI-TEST" replacing "UNION."
UNION OIL CO. FARMCO PRODUCTS
(5)   1940s   13.5in Gill $250-$375
Same as above, with "FARMCO" replacing "UNION."

United

Company history unknown.
UNITED GASOLINE
(5)   1920s   One-piece etched   No Listing
UNITED GASOLINE
(5)   1920s   One-piece baked   No Listing
Description not available.
UNITED MOTOR OILS
(5)   1920s   One-piece etched   No Listing
Description not available.
UNITED GASOLINE (w/small shield)
(5)   1920s   15in Metal   No Listing
White globe face with small shield in center. "UNITED" arched around top, "GASOLINE" around bottom.
UNITED MOTOR GAS (w/small shield)
(5)   1920s   15in Metal   No Listing
Same as above, with "MOTOR GAS" replacing "GASOLINE."
(UNITED) "HIGH TEST"
(5)   1920s   15in Metal   No Listing
White globe with plain "HIGH/TEST" on globe face.

United Products

Company history unknown.
UNITED PRODUCTS (w/pheasant)
(5)   1950s   13.5in Glass $750-$1,400
White globe face with red outline ring. Blue "UNITED" arched across top, with multicolored detailed pheasant in center. Blue "PRODUCTS" across lower globe face.
UNITED GAS (w/pheasant)
(5)   1950s   13.5in Glass $750-$1,400
Same as above, with "GAS" replacing "PRODUCTS."
UNITED BRONZE (w/pheasant)
(5)   1950s   13.5in Glass $750-$1,400
Same as above, with "BRONZE" replacing "PRODUCTS."

Unity Oil Company

Company history unknown.
OH-BOY-WHAT-A-GAS
(4)   1920s   15in Metal   No Listing
White globe face with red "OH BOY" arched around top, "GAS" around bottom, and blue "WHAT A" in center.
UNITY OIL CO. OH-BOY-WHAT-A-GAS
(5)   1920s   15in Metal $1,000-$1,600
White globe face with blue lines forming zeppelin across center. White "UNITY OIL CO" on zeppelin. Red "OH BOY" with speed lines arched around top, "GAS" around bottom, with blue "WHAT A" above "GAS."
UNITY GASOLINE
(5)   1920s   15in Metal   No Listing
Same as above, with "UNITY" arched around top, "GASOLINE" around bottom.

Universal Oil Company, Texas

Company history unknown.
UNIVERSAL GASOLINE
(5)   1920s   15in Metal $500-$900
White globe face with orange outline ring. Orange globe with grid in center, with black-outlined orange "UNIVERSAL" arched below globe. Black-outlined orange "GASOLINE" arched around bottom, "UNIVERSAL OIL CO" around top.

Universal

See listing for HARMONY in this section.

Utility

See listing for GLOBE in this section.

VS

Company history unknown.
VS
(4)   1950s   13.5in Capco $125-$175
White globe face with orange outline ring. Large block-letter orange-outlined green "VS" on globe face.
VS ETHYL
(4)   1950s   13.5in Capco $125-$175
Same as above, with small Ethyl (EC) logo added to lower left.

Valley Home Service Station Company, Bridgeport, Ohio

Company history unknown.
V.H.S.S.CO. NOC-LES
(4)   1920s   15in Metal $250-$450
Cream-colored globe face, with blue lines forming cream center band and blue lines forming half-circles above and below band. Blue-outlined red "V.H.S.S.CO." arched around top, "GASOLINE" around bottom, with red "NOC-LES" in center band.
V.H.S.S.CO. MOTOR
(5)   1920s   15in Metal $250-$450
Same as above, with "MOTOR" replacing "NOC-LES."

Vahey Oil Company, Youngstown, Ohio

Company history unknown.
VAHEY PRODUCTS
(5)   1910s   One-piece etched oval   No Listing
Description not available.
VAHEY RID-O-NOX
(5)   1920s   One-piece etched   No Listing
White globe with red, white, and black Vahey logo at top of face. "VAHEY'S/RID-O-NOX/GASOLINE" across center of face, "RID-O-NOX" in green.
VAHEY GASOLINE
(5)   1920s   One-piece baked   No Listing
White globe with black face. Large red "V" covers center of face, with white "VAHEY'S/PRODUCTS" across "V." White "ESTABLISHED/1893" arched across top, "YOUNGSTOWN, OHIO" around bottom.

Valley Oil Company, Middletown, Connecticut

Company history unknown.
VALOCO
(5)   1930s   Banded Glass $300-$525
White globe face with orange outline ring and orange lines forming bar-and-circle design across center of face. Green "VALOCO" across center band, with green "MOTOR" arched around top, "GASOLINE" around bottom. Green triangle-red thunderbird IOMA logo in upper circle area.

Vance Oil Company, Indianapolis, Indiana

Company history unknown.
VANCE BRONZE
(4)   1950s   13.5in Glass $300-$450
White globe face with red outline ring. Large gold "V" from top to bottom on face, with blue-outlined red script "Vance" across upper "V." Blue ".".-" above "Vance." Blue "HIGH QUALITY" over gold "BRONZE" across center of face.
VANCE PREMIUM ETHYL
(4)   1950s   13.5in Glass $300-$450
Same as above, with blue "PREMIUM" over blue-outlined red "ETHYL" over small Ethyl (EC) logo on lower globe face.
VANCE KEROSENE
(4)   1950s   13.5in Glass $300-$425
Same as above, with blue "HIGH TEST" over blue-outlined red "KEROSENE" on lower globe face.

VANCE HI QUALITY DIESEL
(5)   1950s   13.5in Glass $300-$425
Same as above, with blue "HIGH QUALITY" over blue-outlined red "DIESEL" on lower globe face.
VANCE BLUE FLAME FUEL OIL
(5)   1950s   13.5in Glass $300-$450
Same as above, with blue-colored "BLUE FLAME" over blue-outlined red "FUEL OIL" on lower globe face.

Van Pick

Company history unknown.
VAN PICK BETTER GASOLINE
(4)   1920s   One-piece etched $800-$1,250
White globe with black-outlined yellow shield in center of face. Black "BETTER/GASOLINE" on shield. Black "VAN" arched around top, "PICK" around bottom.

Veltex—Fletcher Oil Company, Boise, Idaho

Company history unknown.
VELTEX
(4)   1930s   15in Metal $500-$775
Orange globe face with double white outline rings around outer edge. Large white-outlined "V" in center of circle. Blue-outlined orange band across center, with blue "VELTEX" in center band.
VELTEX ETHYL
(5)   1930s   15in Metal   No Listing
Blue globe face with wide white outline area. Large orange "V" with white banner across center. Blue "VELTEX" over script "Ethyl" on band. White circle at top, with small Ethyl (EGC) logo in circle. White "GASOLINE" across lower face.

Venoco

Company history unknown.
VENOCO HI POWER
(4)   1930s   15in Metal   No Listing
White globe face with red "VENOCO" across center. Blue "-HI-" above, "POWER" below.
VENOCO HI POWER
(4)   1930s   15in Metal   No Listing
White globe face with blue lines across center and forming trapezoid top and bottom. Red "VENOCO" in bowtie lettering across center, with blue "-HI-" in top trapezoid and "POWER" in lower one.

Venus—R. M. Mays Oil Company

Company history unknown.
VENUS cast faces
(5)   1920s   15in Metal   No Listing
White cast globe face with red script "Venus" arched around top and connected to red script "Gasoline" arched around bottom. Blue "R. M. MAYS/OIL CO." in center.

Vertex

Company history unknown.
QUALITY GASOLINE/VERTEX
(5)   1930s   15in Metal   No Listing
Description not available.
QUALITY VERTEX GASOLINE
(5)   1940s   13.5in Glass $200-$300
Description not available.

Victoria

Company history unknown.
VICTORIA
(4)   1950s   Oval Capco $150-$200
White globe face with red "Victoria" (large "V") across face.

Vigor

Company history unknown.
VIGOR
(5)   1920s   15in Metal   No Listing
White globe face with blue script "Vigor" over blue "HI-GRADE/GASOLINE."

Vi-King

Company history unknown.
VI-KING
(5)   1920s   15in Metal $200-$325
White globe face with black "VI-KING" across face.

Viking—Anderson Petroleum Company, Anderson, South Carolina

Marketed in North and South Carolina under the Viking name. It was later a Dixie Distributors jobber.

VIKING
(5)   1940s   13.5in YELLOW Capco $225-$350
White globe face with small blue Viking ship at top. Red "VIKING" with black dropshade across center of globe face.

VIKING HIGH OCTANE
(5)   1940s   13.5in Capco $225-$350
Yellow globe face with black outline ring. Large red oval in center of face, with black-outlined white "VIKING" across center of oval. White "HIGH" above and "OCTANE" below "VIKING." Red "CUT-RATE" arched around top, "GAS-OIL" around bottom.

Waggoner Oil Company

Company history unknown.

WAGGONER GOLDEN FLASH GASOLINE
(5)   1930s   13.5in Glass $350-$550
White globe face with outline ring and diagonal band across center. Lightning bolts and "GOLDEN/FLASH" across band. "WAGGONER" arched around top over sun, "GASOLINE" arched around bottom.

Wake Up
J. A. Hogshire and Son, Indianapolis, Indiana

Founded in Lebanon, Indiana, in 1923, J. A.Hogshire was one of the original members of the IOMA organization. They introduced the Wake Up brand in 1937, operating discount stations throughout Indiana under the Wake Up name. They continue to operate several dozen stations today.

WAKE UP
(5)   1937-1955   Gill $400-$750
White globe face with large red rooster covering most of face. Blue "WAKE UP" across rooster.

WAKE UP ETHYL
(5)   1937-1955   Gill $400-$750
White globe with small red rooster at top of face. Blue "WAKE UP" across rooster. Ethyl (EGC) logo in circle on lower globe face.

WAKE UP 99
(5)   1955-1960   Gill $400-$750
White globe face red rooster in center of face. Blue "WAKE UP" across rooster, blue "99" at bottom of globe face.

Warelubeco, Incorporated, Jacksonville, Illinois

Founded in Springfield, Illinois, in 1930 as Ware-Rogers Oil Company, the company was an independent jobber with local stations until after WW II. After the war they began expanding and promoting their Wareco brand, and their stations became noted for excellent service with multiple attendants servicing each customer. In the early 1980s they began dual-branding, operating stations with their own Wareco name, teamed with a major. Currently they operate over 100 stations, many branded Wareco-Coastal or Wareco-Phillips 66, while most of the original forty locations retain only the Wareco brand.

WARECO REGULAR
(4)   1950-1965   Oval Capco $250-$400
White globe face with black-outlined red oval covering most of face. Black-outlined white trapezoid across center of oval, with blue "WARECO" on rectangle. Black and white detailed station attendant on upper globe face, white "REGULAR" across lower area of red oval.

WARECO ETHYL
(4)   1950-1965   Oval Capco $250-$400
Same as above, with "ETHYL" replacing "REGULAR."

WARECO NO. 1 DIESEL
(5)   1950-1965   Oval capco $250-$350
Same as above with "NO. 1 DIESEL" replacing "REGULAR."

Warrior

Company history unknown.

WARRIOR CHIEFTAN (w/Indian)
(5)   1930s   Gill $1,800-$2,500
White globe face with large multicolored Indian head in center of face. Yellow banner at top, with black "WARRIOR" and black "CHIEFTAIN" arched around bottom.

Wavaho Oil Company, Lacey Springs, Alabama

Company history unknown. Still in operation.

WAVAHO GASOLINE
(5)   1950s   13.5in Capco $300-$750
White globe face with blue outline ring. Red "WAVAHO" arched across top over red, white and blue Indian head. Blue band across center of

lower globe face, with white "GASOLINE" on band. Red design to either end of band.

Waverly Oil Works, Pittsburgh, Pennsylvania

Primarily a lubricants manufacturer. Company history unknown.

WAVERLY
(5)   1920s   One-piece etched $700-$900
Description not available.

WAVERLY MOTOR GAS
(5)   1920s   One-piece etched $800-$1,200
White globe with red script "Waverly" over "MOTOR/GAS."

WAVERLY BLUE MOON
(5)   1920s   two-piece Glass SPECIAL $400-$650
White globe with blue-and-white-outlined blue face. White script "Waverly" over white "BLUE/MOON" in center of face.

Webaco

Company history unknown.

WEBACO PURE GAS
(5)   1920s   15in Metal $275-$450
Description not available.

Weiloff's

Company history unknown.

WEILOFF'S US MOTOR GASOLINE
(5)   1930s   15in Metal $325-$550
White globe face with black-outlined red "WEILOFF'S" arched around top, "GASOLINE" around bottom. Red-outlined black "U.S./MOTOR" in center.

Welco, Chicago, Illinois

Company history unknown.

WELCO ETHYL
(5)   1950s   Oval Capco $175-$225
White globe face with series of blue stripes across center. Small Ethyl (EC) logo in black-outlined white circle at center of lines. Red "WELCO" arched around top, blue "GASOLINE" around bottom.

WELCO ETHYL
(5)   1950s   13.5in Capco $100-$150
White globe face with blue band across center. Red "WELCO" arched around top, blue "GASOLINE" around bottom with white "ETHYL" in center band.

We-No-Nah

Company history unknown.

WE-NO-NAH GASOLINE
(5)   1920s   15in Metal   No Listing
White globe face with blue "WE-NO-NAH" arched over red "GASO-LINE."

Wespeco—Western Petroleum Company of Kentucky, Chicago, Illinois

Company history unknown.

WESPECO GASOLINE
(5)   1920s   One-piece etched   No Listing
                              chimney cap
White globe with black and white mountain scene at top of face. Red band across center, with white "WESPECO/GASOLINE" on band. Black "WESTERN PETROLEUM/Company/OF KENTUCKY/INCORPORATED" on lower globe face.

Western

Company history unknown.

WESTERN (w/road scene)
(5)   1930s   13.5in Glass   No Listing
White globe face with black outline ring. Red "WESTERN" arched around top, with red and black scene on lower face.

WESTERN MOTOR
(5)   1930s   13.5in Glass   No Listing
White globe face with green outline ring. Green "WESTERN" arched around top, with green and white scene in center. Green script "Motor" on lower face.

Westland Oil Company, Minot, North Dakota

Marketed the famous Buffalo gasoline in the northern plains states.

WESTLAND GASOLINE (w/red hat)
(5)   1920s   One-piece etched $1,800-$2,800
"WESTLAND" around top, "GASOLINE" around bottom. Large red hat in center.

Eldred Hi-Test one-piece etched (yellow triangle). John Phippen

Dixie Gasoline, keyhole three-piece, Dixie Oil. John Phippen

Farmers Union of Nebraska, 15in faces on special holder. Bob Weak

Consumers Oil Co., one-piece etched. John Phippen

LOG Company Certified 70 Octane Gasoline, 13.5in glass inserts on plastic body.

Crown Gasoline, one-piece etched, Standard Oil of Kentucky.

Various 13.5in glass inserts on Gill ripple bodies. Gary Hildman

Miscellaneous Atlantic globes. R.V. Witherspoon

Various metal-frame globes 15in inserts. Gary Hildman

WESTLAND GASOLINE (w/buffalo)
(5)   1920s   One-piece etched $1,800-$2,800
Similar to above, except buffalo replaces red hat.
BUFFALO GASOLINE (w/buffalo)
(5)   1920s   One-piece etched $1,700-$2,500
White globe with black buffalo in center of face. Red "BUFFALO"
arched around top, "GASOLINE" around bottom.
WESTLAND GASOLINE (w/buffalo)
(5)   1930s   13.5in Glass $450-$800
White globe face with black outline ring. Black and white detailed buf-
falo in center of face. Red "WESTLAND" arched around top, "GASO-
LINE" around bottom.
WESTLAND (no buffalo)
(4)   1930s   13.5in Glass $250-$375
Description not available.
BUFFALO GASOLINE (w/buffalo)
(4)   1930s   13.5in Glass $450-$775
Same as above, with "BUFFALO" replacing "WESTLAND."
ETHYL GASOLINE (w/buffalo)
(5)   1930s   13.5in Glass $400-$750
Same as above, with "ETHYL" replacing "WESTLAND."
BUFFALO GASOLINE
(4)   1946-1960   13.5in Glass $250-$375
Green globe face with red outline ring and red ring around white center circle. White "BUFFALO" arched around top, "GASOLINE"
around bottom, with detailed red and black buffalo in center.
BUFFALO PREMIUM GASOLINE
(4)   1946-1960   13.5in Glass $250-$375
White globe face with green outline ring and green outline around
white center circle. Green band across center. White "PREMIUM" in
band. Red "BUFFALO" arched around top, "GASOLINE" around bottom.

Weston Oil Company, Weston, Ohio
Company history unknown.
WESTON
(5)   1920s   One-piece etched   No Listing
Purple Glass. Description not available.

White Flyer
Company history unknown.
WHITE FLYER (w/bird)
(5)   1940s   13.5in Glass $400-$650
White globe face with black outline ring. Black ring around red circle
on lower globe face. White bird with wings up over circles and lower
globe face. Black "WHITE FLYER" arched around top.

White Lily
Company history unknown.
WHITE LILY
(5)   1920s   15in Metal $650-$900
White globe face with black script "White" over "Lily," with black outline of lily between, in center of face. Red "GASOLINE" arched around
bottom.

Tri-State Oil Supply Corporation
Company history unknown.
WHITE LINE GASOLINE
(5)   1920s   15in Metal   No Listing
White globe face with red bowtie band across center. White line
through center of bowtie. Black "WHITE LINE PRODUCTS" above
line, "CREAM OF THE OIL FIELD" below line, with "TRI-STATE
OIL SUPPLY CORP." arched along top of band, "WHITE LINE
GASOLINE" below.

White Mule
See listing for ANTHONY in this section.

White Plume
Company history unknown.
WHITE PLUME GAS
(5)   1910s   One-piece etched   No Listing
White globe with black outline ring and black ring around white cen-
ter circle. Black and white detailed feather in center circle. Red
"WHITE PLUME" arched around top, "GAS" around bottom.

Cincinnati Oil Works Company, Cincinnati, Ohio
Company history unknown.
WHITE ROSE FILTERED GAS
(5)   1910s   One-piece etched $750-$1,300

White globe with red "WHITE ROSE" arched around top, "GASO-
LINE" around bottom, and black "FILTERED" across center.
WHITE ROSE
(4)   1920s   15in Metal $300-$500
White globe face with red circle around white center circle. Blue
"WHITE ROSE" in bowtie lettering across center.

Whiting Oil Company, Clifton Forge, Virginia
A jobber for Conoco (later Cities Service) and Gulf, and currently
operates a small chain of private-brand Whiting stations in Virginia's
Shenandoah Valley.
WHITING GASOLINE
(5)   1932-1940   15in Metal $275-$400
White globe face with red circle in center. White "W" in red circle.
Black "WHITING" arched around top, "GASOLINE" around bottom.

Whitlock
Company history unknown.
WHITLOCK
(5)   1950s   13.5in Capco $75-$125
White globe face with blue outline ring. Blue-outlined red "WHIT-
LOCK" across center.
WHITLOCK SUPER GASOLINE ETHYL (EC)
(5)   1950s   13.5in Red Capco $175-$325
White globe face with blue outline ring. Blue-outlined red "WHIT-
LOCK" arched around top, with black "SUPER GASOLINE" across
center. Large Ethyl (EC) logo on lower globe face.
WHITLOCK US MOTOR GASOLINE
(5)   1930s   13.5in Capco   No Listing
Description not available.

Wilcox, Tulsa, Oklahoma
Company history unknown.
WILCOX
(4)   1940s   13.5in Capco $100-$150
White globe face with blue outline ring. Large red "X" and blue diamond "WILCOX" logo in center of face.
WILCOX ETHYL
(4)   1940s   13.5in Capco $100-$150
White globe face with blue outline ring. Red "WILCOX" arched around
top, "GASOLINE" around bottom, with large Ethyl (EC) logo in center.

Williams Oil Company
Company history unknown.
WILLIAMS GASOLINE
(5)   1920s   One-piece etched   No Listing
White globe with green circle in center of globe face. Black "W" in center circle, with white band across center. Red "WILLIAMS OIL CO."
in band. Black "WILLIAMS" arched around top, "GASOLINE" around
bottom.

Wings—The Security Oil Company, Wichita, Kansas
Company history unknown.
WINGS "HI IN ANTI KNOCK"
(5)   1920s   15in Metal $700-$1,200
Blue globe face with white shield in center. Detailed blue and white
wings to either side of shield, with red "High/in" in shield. White
"WINGS" arched around top, "ANTI-KNOCK" around bottom.
WINGS (w/birds)
(5)   1930s   Gill $325-$550
Description not available.
WINGS (w/Ethyl logo—EGC and birds)
(5)   1930s   Gill $325-$550
White globe face with black and red outline rings. Black zigzag lines
forming banner across upper face. Red "wings" in banner. Black birds
in flight above banner, large Ethyl (EGC) logo covering lower face.
ALLFIRE
(5)   1930s   Gill   No Listing
Blue globe face with red, white, and red outline rings. Large red an-
chor in center. White banner arched across upper face, with red "ALL-
FIRE" in banner. White "THE/SECURITY/OIL CO." above banner,
"WICHITA/KANSAS" below.

WNAX—The House of Gurney, Yankton, South Dakota
Founded about 1930 by radio promoter D. B. Gurney as a cooperative of gasoline station owners in the northern plains states. Using his
radio station as a promotional source, Gurney expanded the "fair-
price" WNAX chain until the war forced restrictions on gasoline con-
sumption. Gurney turned his interests to securing other "fair-price"

items for plains farmers.
WNAX GAS
(4)   1930s   13.5in Capco $200-$375
White globe face with black and red outline ring. Black "WNAX" over "GAS" in center of face. Red lightning bolt horizontally through "WNAX."
WNAX
(5)   1930s   13.5in Capco $300-$550
White globe face with black outline ring. Detailed green, grey, and black picture of radio station building and tower on lower globe face. Red "WNAX" across upper face.
GURNEY-WNAX
(4)   1930s   13.5in Glass $450-$800
Same as above, with red "GURNEY" replacing "WNAX" across upper globe face.

Wood
Company history unknown.
WOOD OILS GASOLINE (w/lion)
(5)   1920s   15in Metal   No Listing
Blue globe face with white outline ring. Detailed multicolored lion's head in center of face. White "WOOD OILS" arched around top, "GASOLINE" around bottom.
WOOD HI TEST
(5)   1920s   15in Metal   No Listing
Similar to above globe.
WOOD HI TEST
(5)   1930s   13.5in Glass   No Listing
Red globe face with detailed multicolored lion's head in center. White "WOOD" arched around top, "HI-TEST" around bottom.

WOW
Company history unknown.
WOW ANTI-KNOCK GASOLINE
(5)   1920s   15in Metal $300-$500
White globe face with blue and yellow checkerboard design arched around top and bottom. Large yellow "WOW" with blue shading in center of face. Blue "ANTI-KNOCK" above "WOW," "GAS" below.

Zip Rose
Company history unknown.
ZIP ROSE HIGH COMPRESSION
(5)   1930s   15in Metal $350-$600
Red globe face with white outline ring and small white circle in center. Large blue "ZIP/ROSE" diagonally across upper face, over smaller blue "HIGH/COMPRESSION."

Zing
Company history unknown.
ZING
(5)   1930s   13.5in Glass $200-$325
Red globe face with white "ZING" across center.

Zoom
Company history unknown.
ZOOM
(5)   1930s   15in Metal   No Listing
White globe face with red globe ring. Black-outlined red "ZOOM" arched over "GAS" in center of face. Blue "SMOOTH POWER" arched around top, "ANTI-CARBON" around bottom.

Independents From Which No Globes are Known

In the two years of research involved in the creation of this book, numerous gasoline marketers, some affiliated with major oil companies and some independent, were identified from which no globes are known to exist. The list was expanded to include additional companies, and in turn globes from some of the companies surfaced and those companies were deleted. Below is the final listing of independent companies that the authors feel probably used globes at one time or another. Globes from these companies, along with the major oil affiliates listed for which a notation is added "No globes are known to exist," will probably be discovered with the publication of this list.

Company name	Base location
Charge	Tampa, Florida
Cone	Nashville, Tennessee
Early Bird	Jeffersonville, Indiana
East Coast	Richmond, Virginia
El Paso	El Paso, Texas
Etna	Winston-Salem, North Carolina
Gastown	Cleveland, Ohio
Holiday	Minneapolis, Minnesota
Imperial	Greenwood, Virginia
J&L	Vernon Hills, Illinois
Kocolene	Seymour, Indiana
Mustang	Monroe, North Carolina
Perfect Power	Chicago, Illinois
Pilot	Knoxville, Tennessee
Port	Charleston, South Carolina
Red Bird	Evansville, Indiana
Rich	Ironton, Ohio
Sail-Bonus-Peer	Lafollette, Tennessee
Shamrock	Traverse City, Michigan
Sing	Thomasville, Georgia
Smile	Hickory, North Carolina
Swifty	Seymour, Indiana
Tops	Durham, North Carolina
Value	Greenville, South Carolina
Whiting Brothers	Phoenix, Arizona
Wilco	Winston-Salem, North Carolina
Wisco 99	Rockford, Illinois

In addition to listing companies from which no globes are known, a list of globes that *should be* out there was created. In the course of our research, many of those globes were confirmed. Here are a few that were not. Again, there is no firm indication that these globes exist.

Amoco: One-piece Amoco Gas
Ashland: Valvoline Ethyl 15in metal
Atlantic: Atlantic Imperial with 1966 logo
Esso: Golden Esso Extra
Esso: Enco globes
Fina: More Amlico globes
Fina: American Fina globe
Kendall: Kendall Super Deluxe
Kerr McGee: Triangle with red cloverleaf
Kerr McGee: Sparky Regular
Mobil: General Petroleum 13.5in globes other than general Ethyl
Pure: Pure Pep
Richfield: Richfield Benzol
Signal: Early Billups Regular
Sinclair: Chimney-top Sinclair

The First Globes—Generic, Grade, or Gasoline Globes

BLUE COMPETITIVE GAS
(5)   1950s   13.5in Capco $75-$125
White globe face with blue outline ring and blue-outlined white half-circles above and below center. Blue-colored "BLUE" arched around top, "GAS" around bottom, with blue "COMPETITIVE" across center

CLEAR VISION-CRAUSE
(5)   1910s   15in Metal inserts $300-$650
                              on Metal
Green globe face with white "CLEAR" at top, "CRAUSE" across center, and "VISION" at bottom.

CLEAR VISION
(4)   1910s   One-piece etched $400-$650
White globe with red "CLEAR" arched across top, "VISION" across bottom of face.

DIESEL (yellow letters)
(4)   1950s   13.5in Capco $50-$100
White globe face with yellow "DIESEL" across center.

DIESEL FUEL (blue on white)
(5)   1950s   Oval Capco $125-$175
White oval globe face with blue "DIESEL FUEL" across center.

ETHYL (red letters)
(4)   1950s   13.5in Capco $50-$100
White globe face with red "ETHYL" across center.

ETHYL (red on white)
(5)   1950s   Oval Capco $125-$175
White oval globe face with red "ETHYL" across center.

FILTERED GASOLINE (blue perforated lenses)
(5)   1910s   15in Metal $300-$550
Blue globe face with white outline ring. Perforated metal face with white "FILTERED/GASOLINE" across center.

FILTERED GASOLINE
(4)   1910s   15in Metal $225-$400
White globe with red "FILTERED" arched around top, "GASOLINE" around bottom.

FILTERED GASOLINE (reverse bowtie)
(5)   1910s   One-piece etched $350-$600
White globe with red distorted lettering "FILTERED GASOLINE."

FILTERED GASOLINE
(4)   1910s   One-piece etched $300-$550
White globe with red "FILTERED GASOLINE" across face.

FILTERED GASOLINE (chimney cap)
(5)   1910s   One-piece etched $700-$1,100
Same as above, with chimney cap.

FILTERED GASOLENE (small: 4in base, 8in tall)
(4)   1910s   One-piece etched $300-$600
Eight-inch-diameter white globe with 4in base. Red "FILTERED/GASOLINE" across face.

FILTERED GASOLINE (sphere shaped)
(4)   1910s   One-piece etched $300-$500
White sphere-shaped globe with red "FILTERED GASOLINE" across globe.

FILTERED GASOLINE "YOU SEE WHAT YOU GET" (chimney cap, small)
(5)   1910s   One-piece etched   No Listing
Description not available.

FILTERED GASOLINE
(5)   1910s   One-piece etched $450-$650
Red letters "FILTERED" above "GASOLINE," but with small design above and below words.

FILTERED GASOLINE (round with blue letters)
(5)   1910s   One-piece baked $300-$500
White globe with blue "FILTERED GASOLINE" across face.

FULL MEASURE GASOLINE (sphere shaped)
(5)   1910s   One-piece etched $350-$650
White sphere-shaped globe with "FULL MEASURE GASOLINE" across globe.

GASOLENE (4in base, 12in tall)
(4)   1910s   One-piece etched $350-$600
Small white globe with red "GASOLENE" across center. Red lines arched above and below "GASOLENE."

GASOLINE (blue on yellow, reverse bowtie)
(5)   1910s   15in Metal $350-$550
Yellow globe face with blue "GASOLINE" in reverse-bowtie lettering across center.

GASOLINE (orange letters w/lines)
(5)   1910s   15in Metal $350-$550
Silver globe face with orange outlines. Orange "GASOLINE" across center.

GASOLINE (red fancy letters)
(4)   1910s   15in Metal $250-$400
White globe face with red script "Gasoline" across center.

GASOLINE (green background)
(4)   1910s   15in Metal $250-$450
Green globe face with white outlines top and bottom. White "GASO-LINE" (large "G") across center.

GASOLINE (green background, perforated lenses)
(4)   1910s   15in Metal $300-$500
Green globe face with white "GASOLINE" (large "G") across center.

GASOLINE
(5)   1910s   10.25in Metal $350-$600
White globe with red "Gasoline" (large "G") across center.

GASOLINE (black letters)
(5)   1910s   One-piece etched $300-$550
Same as above, with black lettering.

GASOLINE (blue letters)
(5)   1910s   One-piece etched $300-$575
Same as above, with blue lettering.

GASOLINE (fancy, normal size)
(5)   1910s   One-piece etched $350-$625
White globe with red "GASOLINE" in serif lettering, with large "G" across face.

GASOLINE (red letters, 4in base, 12in tall)
(4)   1910s   One-piece etched $300-$575
Small white globe with red "GASOLINE" (large "G") across center. Arched lines above and below "GASOLINE."

GASOLINE (chimney cap 12in)
(5)   1910s   One-piece etched $700-$1,200
Same as above except larger, chimney-cap globe.

GASOLINE (red letters, 4in base, 8in tall)
(4)   1910s   One-piece etched $300-$550
Same as above, except no arched lines.

GASOLINE (green background, 6in base, 12in tall)
(4)   1910s   One-piece etched $325-$650
White globe with green face. White lines arched top and bottom, with white "GASOLINE" (large "G") across center of face.

GASOLINE (normal size)
(3)   1910s   One-piece etched $275-$550
White globe with red "Gasoline" (large "G") across center.

GASOLINE (normal size)
(4)   1920s   One-piece baked $250-$450
Same as above, with baked-on lettering.

GASOLINE (normal size)
(3)   1910s   One-piece etched $250-$525
Same as above, with all lettering same size.

GASOLINE (blue letters)
(5)   1920s   One-piece baked $250-$450
White globe face with blue "GASOLINE" across center.

GUARANTEED MEASURE
(4)   1910s   One-piece etched $350-$625
White globe with red "GUARANTEED" arched across above center, "MEASURE" below, forming reverse bowtie.

GUARANTEE MEASURE (chimney cap)
(5)   1910s   One-piece etched $700-$1,200
Same as above, but with chimney cap.

GUARANTEE VISIBLE PUMP (chimney cap)
(5)   1910s   One-piece etched $700-$1,300
Small white chimney-cap globe with red "GUARANTEE" arched across top of face and "VISIBLE PUMP" across lower face.

GUARANTEED FRY VISIBLE
(5)   1910s   15in Metal   No Listing
White globe face with "GUARANTEED" arched around top, "VISI-BLE" around bottom, with "Fry" logotype in center.

HIGH TEST KEROSENE
(5)   1950s   13.5in Capco $100-$175

White globe face with red outline ring. Blue "HIGH TEST" diagonally across top, red "KEROSENE" below.

INDEPENDENT GAS (black letters arched)
(5)   1930s   15in Metal $225-$325
White globe face with black "INDEPENDENT" arched around top over black "GAS."

KEROSENE (red letters)
(4)   1920s   15in Metal $200-$300
White globe face with red "KEROSENE" across center.

KEROSENE (blue letters)
(4)   1920s   15in Metal $225-$325
White globe face with blue "KEROSENE" across center.

KEROSENE (red letters)
(5)   1910s   One-piece etched $350-$650
White globe with red "KEROSENE" across center of face.

KEROSENE (blue on white)
(4)   1940s   13.5in Glass $175-$275
White globe face with blue "KEROSENE" across center.

KEROSENE SMOKELESS ODORLESS
(4)   1950s 13.5in Capco $100-$175
Description not available.

KEROSENE
(5)   1950s   Oval Capco $125-$175
White oval globe face with red "KEROSENE" across face.

LOW PRICE
(5)   1960s   13.5in Capco $75-$125
White globe face with black "LOW PRICE" across center.

MARINE GAS (w/boat)
(4)   1930s   15in Metal $900-$1,600
White globe face with blue-outlined white "MARINE" across upper face. Red, white, and blue speedboat scene in red-outlined oval in center, with blue and white anchors to either side and white "GASO-LINE" in blue banner across bottom.

MARINE GAS (w/sunset)
(5)   1930s   15in Metal   No Listing
Same as above, with sunset scene replacing speedboat scene in center.

MARINE GASOLINE (red/white, w/waves)
(4)   1950s   13.5in Capco $150-$300
Red upper half and white lower half of globe face, with white wave area across center. White "MARINE" in upper area, red "GASOLINE" across lower white area.

MARINE OIL BLENDED
(5)   1950s   13.5in Capco $150-$325
Same design as above, with dark blue over light blue. White "MA-RINE" in upper area, blue "OIL BLENDED/GASOLINE" in lower area.

MOTOR OIL
(5)   1920s   15in Metal $225-$325
Green globe face with white "MOTOR/OIL" and randomly placed white designs on face.

PENNSYLVANIA 100% PURE OIL
(5)   1920s   One-piece etched   No Listing
Description not available.

PREMIUM (red letters)
(4)   1960s   13.5in Capco $50-$75
White globe face with red "PREMIUM" across center.

RANGE OIL (red letters)
(5)   1960s   13.5in Capco $75-$125

White globe face with "RANGE/OIL" across face.

REGULAR (blue letters)
(4)   1960s   13.5in Capco $50-$75
White globe face with blue "REGULAR" across center.

REGULAR (black letters)
(4)   1960s   13.5in Capco $50-$75
White globe face with black "REGULAR" across center.

TRUCK GASOLENE PUMP
(5)   1940s   13.5in Glass $225-$350
Red globe face with blue-outlined white band across center. White "TRUCK" in upper red area, "PUMP" in lower red area, with blue "GASOLENE" in center band.

UNBRANDED (red letters)
(5)   1930s   15in Metal $200-$300
White globe face with red "UNBRANDED" across face.

U.S. AVIATION
(5)   1920s   One-piece etched $750-$1,300
Large "U.S." over "Aviation." Colors unknown.

U.S. MOTOR
(5)   1930s   One-piece etched $600-$850
White globe with red "U.S." over "MOTOR."

U.S. MOTOR
(5)   1920s   15in Metal $250-$350
White globe face with red "U.S. MOTOR" across face.

U.S. MOTOR GASOLINE
(5)   1920s   15in Metal $250-$375
White globe face with red "U.S.MOTOR/GASOLINE" across face.

U.S. MOTOR GASOLINE (green letters)
(5)   1920s   15in Metal $275-$375
Same as above, green lettering.

U.S. MOTOR
(5)   1940s   13.5in Glass $175-$250
White globe face with red "U.S. MOTOR" across face.

VISIBLE GASOLINE
(4)   1910s   One-piece etched $300-$550
White globe with red "VISIBLE" over "GASOLINE."

VISIBLE GASOLINE (chimney cap)
(5)   1910s   One-piece etched $750-$1,200
Same as above, with chimney-top globe.

VISIBLE GASOLINE (sphere shaped, red letters)
(3)   1910s   One-piece etched $300-$600
White sphere-shaped globe with red "VISIBLE" arched across top, "GASOLINE" across bottom.

VISIBLE GASOLINE (sphere shaped, black letters)
(5)   1910s   One-piece etched $300-$600
Same as above, with black lettering.

VISIBLE GASOLINE (sphere shaped w/design)
(5)   1910s   One-piece etched $300-$675
Same as above, but with red lettering and design in center.

VISIBLE MEASURE
(5)   1910s   One-piece etched $325-$625
White globe with red "VISIBLE/MEASURE" across face.

WHITE
(5)   1950s   13.5in Capco $50-$75
White globe face with black "WHITE" across center.

Globe Body Styles

Prices are for bodies only

The following prices are for mint original globe bodies only. Dates approximate the introduction date for this bodystyle. Globes with copper or steel bases are usually older and originally commanded a higher price. They are more desirable among collectors.

WIDE 13.5in GLASS BODY
(2)   1928 $50-$100
White glass body approximately 8in wide, designed to hold 13.5in glass lenses with two machine screws.

NARROW 13.5in GLASS BODY
(2)   1928 $50-$100

White glass body approximately 5in wide, designed to hold 13.5in glass lenses with two machine screws.

12.5in GLASS BODY
(4)   1935 $75-$125
White glass body approximately 6in wide, designed to hold 12.5in glass lenses with two machine screws.

BANDED BODY
(4)   1930 $125-$200
White glass body designed to hold approximately 13 5/8in diameter lenses, with an internal ring attached to the body by four screws.

BALCRANK THREE-SCREW BODY
(5)   1930 $125-$250
White glass body designed to hold 13.5in glass lenses, with three machine screws positioned at twelve, four, and eight o'clock.
15in GLASS BODY
(5)   1925 $150-$250
Special glass body designed to hold 15in diameter glass lenses.
CLOVER BODY
(4)   1932 $150-$250
White glass body designed to hold Cities Service clover-shaped glass lenses.
CLOVER BODY FOR ROUND INSERTS
(5)   1932 $150-$300
White glass clover-shaped hull body designed to hold a special 14in diameter lens with two machine screws.
GLASS OVAL BODY
(5)   1930 $150-$250
White glass body designed to hold oval-shaped glass lenses with two machine screws.
CAPCOLITE 216 BODY
(1)   1933 $20-$35
Two-piece white plastic body, introduced in 1933, designed to hold notched glass lenses by sandwiching them between the two plastic halves.
CAPCOLITE 218 OVAL BODY
(2)   1946 $35-$75
Same as CAPCOLITE 216 above, designed to hold oval lenses without notches.
RED CAPCO
(3)   1933 $50-$75
Same as CAPCOLITE 216 above, but cast in red plastic.
BLUE CAPCO
(5)   1933 $75-$125
Same as CAPCOLITE 216 above, but cast in blue plastic.
GREEN CAPCO
(4)   1933 $50-$100
Same as CAPCOLITE 216 above, but cast in green plastic.
YELLOW CAPCO
(4)   1933 $50-$100
Same as CAPCOLITE 216 above, but cast in yellow plastic.
ORANGE CAPCO
(4)   1933 $75-$125
Same as CAPCOLITE 216 above, but cast in orange plastic.
Note: There are early plastic bodies dating from 1932 or 1933 that only say "CAPCOLITE" at the bottom. Each plastic halve is different where they come together at the top. Also, some are very wide.
HULL 13.5in GLASS BODY
(3)   1928 $50-$100
White narrow glass body with hollowed-out area behind globe faces.
RED HULL BODY
(5)   1930 $400-$700

Same as HULL above, but cast in red glass.
ORANGE HULL BODY
(5)   1930 $500-$800
Same as HULL above, but cast in orange glass.
METAL BODY LOW PROFILE
(2)   1914 $50-$125
Rolled metal globe body with the band formed in one piece, thereby appearing nearly flat when looking at the lenses.
METAL BODY HIGH PROFILE
(2)   1914 $50-$135
Stamped metal globe body formed as two halves and assembled back-to-back with a high seam in the center, appearing much larger than the lens it holds.
JEWELED METAL BODY
(5)   1928 $600-$1,000
Metal body with holes around the circumference, fitted with 1in glass jewels that light up.
GILL BODY
(3)   1927 $100-$200
White glass hollow body designed to hold a 13 5/8in +/- lens, with an external band that is joined at the bottom by a single machine screw.
14in GILL BODY
(5)   1927 $150-$225
Same as Gill above, for larger diameter lenses. Usually wider than a standard Gill body.
CLEAR RIPPLE GILL
(4)   1930 $300-$500
Gill body, same as above, except cast in clear glass with a textured surface designed to diffuse light.
RED RIPPLE GILL
(3)   1930 $400-$800
Clear ripple Gill body with a baked-on red finish inside.
BLUE RIPPLE GILL
(4)   1930 $750-$1,500
Clear ripple Gill body with a baked-on blue finish inside.
WHITE RIPPLE GILL
(4)   1930 $350-$550
Clear ripple Gill body with a baked-on white finish inside.
GREEN RIPPLE GILL
(5)   1930 $900-$2,000
Clear ripple Gill body with a baked-on green finish inside.
ORANGE RIPPLE GILL
(4)   1930 $500-$1100
Clear ripple Gill body with a baked-on orange finish inside.
YELLOW RIPPLE GILL
(3)   1930 $450-$900
Clear ripple Gill body with a baked-on yellow finish inside.
BROWN RIPPLE GILL
(5)   1930   No Listing
Clear ripple Gill body with a baked-on brown finish inside.

Epilogue

As Bob, Jr., sorts through his late father's belongings preparing for an estate auction, he notices a long-forgotten box. It must have been put away when they moved in 1954. He opens the box. Suddenly he finds himself grinning, remembering the distant past. "I haven't seen this in years!" he exclaims. "I couldn't have been more than four, maybe five when Dad found this Texaco globe. He was so proud, telling the story of Jerry's station and the snowy night he first saw this beautiful globe."

As he carefully removes the globe from the box, he remembers how his father kept the globe in the study. "I didn't realize he'd put it away. This won't be going in any auction!"

Within the hour, Bob, Jr., takes the globe home and proudly displays it on the fireplace mantle. He is already wondering where other globes could be found when his youngest son, never having seen Grandpa's globe, asks what it is. "Sit down, son. It's a long story."

Index